AN AFRICAN IN IMPERIAL LONDON

DANELL JONES

An African in Imperial London

The Indomitable Life of
A. B. C. Merriman-Labor

HURST & COMPANY, LONDON

First published in the United Kingdom in 2018 by
C. Hurst & Co. (Publishers) Ltd.,
41 Great Russell Street, London, WC1B 3PL
This paperback edition first published in 2021 by
C. Hurst & Co. (Publishers) Ltd.,
New Wing, Somerset House, Strand, London, WC2R 1LA
© Danell Jones, 2021
All rights reserved.

Distributed in the United States, Canada and Latin America by
Oxford University Press, 198 Madison Avenue, New York, NY 10016,
United States of America.

A Cataloguing-in-Publication data record for this book
is available from the British Library.

ISBN: 9781787386068

This book is printed using paper from registered sustainable
and managed sources.

www.hurstpublishers.com

To Tim, always

CONTENTS

ACKNOWLEDGMENTS

I am humbled by the help and support I have received from scholars, journalists, librarians, writers, friends, and family during the writing of this book. To each of them, I extend my deepest thanks. If any errors linger, they are all mine.

The undaunted guide for this book has been David Killingray. I reached out to him in the early days of my research, and he responded with amazing generosity and kindness. It is no exaggeration to say that without him, the book would never have been written. He answered innumerable questions, shared critical documents, illuminated key issues, read the manuscript closely, and gave indispensable advice.

For nearly as long, Jeffery Green has also been exceptionally generous with his knowledge of Black Edwardians and their history. His close reading of the manuscript has been invaluable.

Without the preservation work of libraries and archives around the world, Merriman-Labor's story would have been lost completely. The librarians and archivists I have encountered have gone well beyond the call of duty to track down rare books, newspapers, and documents. I have spent many rewarding hours in the British Library and am particularly grateful for online access to its African newspapers collection. Thank you to all the British Library staff, especially Kathryn Mouncey and Andy Simons. I would also like to thank Stephanie Alder at the Archives of the British Museum who helped me track down records related to Merriman-Labor's reading room ticket. The librarians at the remarkable Lincoln's Inn Library were unfailingly generous with their time and information. Thank you to Guy Holborn, Josephine Hutchings,

ACKNOWLEDGMENTS

and especially Mrs. F. Bellis who answered many questions and supplied numerous essential documents. Jon Newman at Lambeth Archives and his staff not only helped with historical documents, but supplied priceless advice, maps, and timetables to help me navigate South London buses. The staff at the National Archives Kew were fantastic both in person and online. Thank you to Sheila Gopaulen, Steven Cable, and Mark Dunton. Professor W. R. Owens at University of Bedfordshire connected me to Jennifer Ayley, the librarian at Bunyan Meeting, who sent me copies of the register containing Merriman-Labor's signature. Ruth Ann Jones and Peter Limb of Michigan State University Libraries were able make microfilm of the *African Telegraph* available to me in Montana. Lucy McCann at the Bodleian Library has been ever helpful and aided me in tracking down several indispensable letters. I would also like to thank Guy at the London Metropolitan Archives for guiding me through their holdings for the Lambeth Infirmary. Others librarians and archivists who were indispensable include Rachel M. Rowe and John Cardwell at University of Cambridge; Michael Mullen, Sonia Gomes, and Sue Donnelly at the London School of Economics and Political Science; Gareth Lloyd at the University of Manchester; Brigette C. Kamsler and Betty Bolden at The Burke Library at Union Theological Seminary; Alyson Rogers and Catherine Poucher at Historic England Archive; Andrew Mussell at Honourable Society of Gray's Inn; Adele Allen at Inner Temple; Theresa Thurston from The Law Society Library; Marie Smith at the Ministry of Defence; Brandon High at King's College, London; Angela M. Wootton at the Imperial War Museum; Lewis Wyman and Gary Johnson at the Library of Congress; Sheila Breeding, Ruby Bell-Gam, and Robert Hill from the UCLA African Studies Center; Gemma at Royal African Society; Christine Herne, from Woking Homes; Mark Butterworth at the Magic Lantern Society; and Todd Gustavson from the George Eastman House.

Several adroit librarians here in Montana were able to find key resources for me. The brilliant Bethany Schatzke at Rocky Mountain College was never daunted by my challenging interlibrary loan requests. Cheryl Hoover and the entire interlibrary loan staff at Montana State University Billings supplied numerous books and articles. Jan Zauha and Mary Guthmiller at Montana State University Bozeman were always ready to track down what I needed.

ACKNOWLEDGMENTS

I met Caroline Bressey early in my research and her work inspired me to continue to try to know more about Merriman-Labor. Patrick Polden provided indispensable expertise regarding the context and meaning of Merriman-Labor's disbarment. Leo Spitzer shared his knowledge, encouragement, and the only surviving image of Merriman-Labor. Christopher Draper provided additional insight about Colwyn Bay African Institute. Marika Sherwood shared her knowledge of Merriman-Labor's Pan-African milieu. Richard Anderson's generous replies guided my understanding of Liberated Africans in Sierra Leone. Heather Heggem and Patti States of the Rocky Mountain College Physician's Assistant Program used Merriman-Labor's medical history as a case study for their students, and the discussion was illuminating. Many individuals shared their knowledge and offered guidance including James Gibbs, Tamba E. M'bayo, Mac Dixon-Fyle, Gabril Cole, Tracey Harding, Assan Sarr, Sean Creighton, Gary Wayne Loew, Sascha Auerbach, Sam South, and Charles Kay.

Victor Labor, Merriman-Labor descendant, graciously answered many questions and as a doctor provided special expertise in my thinking about Merriman-Labor's health. Monty Labor shared fascinating family information that gave me important insight into Merriman-Labor's life.

As with all things in life, friends have been critical beyond measure. Special thanks go to the ever-insightful Celia Maddox whose enthusiasm for the project and wise suggestions improved the book enormously. Ken Egan's sharp eye helped me make connections I would not have otherwise seen. Several members of my community Shakespeare class generously read the manuscript and provided important feedback: Charles Collier, Bev Ross, and Jennifer Lyman.

Three writing friends were part of this project from the very beginning: Cara Chamberlain, Tami Haaland, and Virginia Tranel. It is no exaggeration to say they read and commented on every page. They provided not just criticism, but selfless support.

Peter and Isobel McMillan, friends for three decades now, have been unfailingly generous. They housed, fed, and entertained my husband and me for weeks on end and traveled with us on excursions throughout Britain in search of scraps of information about Merriman-Labor. Their kindness, love, and friendship are truly matchless.

ACKNOWLEDGMENTS

My parents Joan and John Pastrick have been unsparingly generous, always ready to help finance research trips and listen to stories about my findings. Their encouragement never flagged over the many years it took to unearth Merriman-Labor's story.

My agent Jon Curzon has been a writer's dream: intelligent, incredibly hard-working wonderfully supportive. He has believed in this project from the start. I am so deeply grateful for his efforts to bring this story to the world. I also would like to thank the other members of his team at Artellus Ltd.: Darryl Samaraweera for taking care of the details, and Leslie Gardner for her vision and advice. My profound thanks to Michael Dwyer of Hurst Publishing for bringing Merriman-Labor's story to the world and to incredible people at Hurst: Jon de Peyer, Alison Alexanian, Daisy Leitch, and Russell Martin.

Lastly, I thank my husband, Tim Lehman. His enthusiasm for this project has sustained me for close to a decade now. He believed in the story and my ability to tell it even when I doubted. He has logged countless hours in museums, libraries, and archives as an active participant in the research process. At the end of a long day staring at microfilm or combing through colonial registers, when I was too tired to go on, he often stayed at it. More than once, his diligence and determination unearthed a vital document. He is a true partner of the heart, soul, and mind. His love and wisdom inspire my life and make writing possible.

PROLOGUE

FREETOWN, SIERRA LEONE, CIRCA 1881

Augustus Boyle Chamberlayne Merriman-Labor was a naughty little boy.

As the only child of a busy single mother, he took to "bellowing continuously." Only his mother's solemn warning, "The white man is coming, the white man will come and take you away," seemed to quell his noise.[1]

Soon, however, little Augustus no longer cared "a rap about the kidnapping white somebody whose advent she daily predicted, for this sluggish individual always by the way coming—coming—coming— like the final Judgment, never once arrived."

Exasperated, his mother asked her brother to hide behind a door and, when the child began bawling, to reply with deep, menacing growls. For a while the fearsome sounds seemed to work. It "shook all the naughtiness out of me," Merriman-Labor recalled.

Being an irrepressible child, however, it was not long before mere growling no longer intimidated him. How could he take seriously "a big white man in hiding who seemed much afraid to meet a little black boy face to face?"[2]

His audacity forced his mother to even greater lengths.

One day, when his bellowing commenced and the warnings went unheeded, little Augustus was shocked to see the terrible bogeyman his mother had long promised. The drama—starring his uncle wearing a white mask—finally produced the desired effect. "The dreadful sight of this fierce-looking white-faced demon, completely convulsed a bad little black sinner," Merriman-Labor later laughed, "into a good little saint."[3]

As an adult, the story of the white bogeyman not only tickled his fancy, but provided Merriman-Labor with a playful parable of race relations. The source of the white devil, he observed, had been the missionaries themselves. The illustrations in the books they offered Africans to teach them about Christianity inevitably portrayed Satan as white. Consequently, he noted, there was "an idea now current in the minds of millions of black people that white men belong to the supernatural creation of angels, ghosts, and devils."[4] Devout Christian though he was, Merriman-Labor delighted in the irony: those who had brought the Word of God to Sierra Leone had, it seems, inadvertently created an arch-demon in their own image.

For him, such misunderstandings and miscommunication were the sources of racial discord. "Whites have always been a mystery to the Blacks, just as the Blacks have ever been to the Whites," he wrote. "This, a mystery to that: the one, a puzzle to the other."[5] This troubled relationship could change, he believed, if the "members of the great human family" knew one another better.[6] As a bookish boy, he saw only one way to bring about this happy circumstance. He would become a writer.

Merriman-Labor succeeded in establishing a name for himself in British West Africa as a talented author.[7] Witty and enterprising, he worked his way up the civil service ladder in the Colonial Secretary's Office and was thought of as "one of our most able and energetic native West African officials."[8] Yet, the life of a mid-range civil service clerk in Freetown was not his idea of success. His family and friends advised him to go to the Inns of Court in London to pursue the respected profession of barrister, but his dearest dreams did not include briefs, clients, and quarter sessions. He saw the written word as his weapon against the injustices of colonialism, and London as his literary home. There, he had read in the *Sierra Leone Weekly News*, "his colour is no barrier to recognition. He can go anywhere, wherever his merits, either intellectual or social, will take him."[9]

In early 1904, twenty-six-year-old Merriman-Labor left his family and friends to take a journey he hoped would change his life forever. In London he planned to demonstrate his mettle and talent. In the heart of empire, he imagined himself as a West African Mark Twain, using wit and satire to expose hypocrisy, corruption, and injustice.[10]

But things did not work out as planned. In the late winter of 1904 he had yet to learn that African writers who poked fun at Briton's shortcomings could find themselves in conflict with bogeymen far more dangerous than the white devils created to frighten little boys.

INTRODUCTION

LAMBETH WORKHOUSE INFIRMARY, SOUTH LONDON, 1919

On the drizzly days and cool nights of late June 1919, porters in the Lambeth Workhouse Infirmary heaped coal into the ward's open fireplaces to keep patients warm. The flames jumped and quivered as nurses attended the long rows of metal beds, propping men on pillows, giving them sips of water, tablets of Iceland moss, or injections of morphine. Cobalt-blue Dettweiler flasks for the disposal of sputa sat on each bedside table next to vases of cornflowers, popular novels, and crumpled pages of the daily newspapers.

Most of the patients suffered from high temperatures, night sweats, excessive weight loss, extreme fatigue, and the tell-tale coughing of blood. This was a tuberculosis ward treating men in the advanced stages of the disease. The privations of World War I—food rationing, housing shortages, overcrowded workplaces—had intensified the epidemic. Since 1914, the death rate from tuberculosis in Britain had surged by 12 percent. Now some one hundred and fifty thousand people were infected, enduring, as the poet Keats had written a century before "the weariness, the fever, and the fret."[1] Among the seriously ill in the Lambeth ward was a man from Sierra Leone, a British Crown Colony three thousand miles to the south. Admitted on Friday, June 13, 1919, he may well have been the only African in the ward. By the time he arrived, he was desperately ill. The disease was wasting away his slim physique. Clothes hung from bony shoulders. His once lively face was gaunt and frail.

1

The sunken cheeks, the weak limbs, the chronic cough, and the blood-soaked handkerchiefs could not hide the man he was: high-principled, educated, and literary. Though he spent only a month in the tuberculosis ward, he made an impression on the nurses. A gifted storyteller, he must have described for them the silvery beaches of Freetown where he was born, the country's stunning forest-covered mountains soaring upward from the sea, and surf so powerful it sounded like a lion's roar. One can almost see caregivers, orderlies, and fellow patients gathered around his bed listening to him tell of his encounters with a "wild class of men" on the Niger River during his fifteen-thousand-mile journey across Africa. Perhaps they were enchanted by his experiences in Paris, too, and Liverpool, Edinburgh, and Dublin.[2] For the past fifteen years, he had made London his home—giant, unwieldy, unforgiving London, the biggest city on the planet, the heart and brain of the world's largest empire.

The only picture of him that survives is a black-and-white studio portrait taken in Africa around 1904. In it, he wears an evening tailcoat with one elegantly gloved hand on his hip, the other dangling a silk top hat and walking stick. He looks perfectly at ease—at once an Edwardian gentleman and one of Britain's thirty-five million African subjects. For many Britons used to thinking of Africans as wild, naked savages rather than well-dressed, eloquent fellow subjects of the King, this combination would have been unsettling. Africans were not an uncommon sight in Edwardian London: they came to study medicine or law; to perform in music halls; to work as domestics, bus drivers and waiters; and perhaps most important of all, they came as British subjects to protest colonial abuses in their homelands. Yet for many white Britons, Africans were "rudimentary souls," as Conrad put it in *Heart of Darkness*, people marooned on a low rung of the evolutionary ladder, without rational thought, moral integrity, or comprehensible language.[3] In the realm of polite conversation, it was not untoward for a white Briton to say he or she was "working like a nigger" or to describe an earthy color as "nigger brown." For some, including the writer Virginia Woolf, the sight of an African in European clothing triggered instant contempt. Woolf recorded in her diary that she had passed "a nigger gentleman, perfectly fitted out in swallow tail &

bowler & gold headed cane; & what were his thoughts? Of the degradation stamped on him, every time he raised his hand & saw it black as a monkeys outside, tinged with flesh colour within?"[4] For her, blackness was a defect. How could she begin to fathom Merriman-Labor as a proud twenty-year-old confidently asserting that black skin reminded the African of "his individuality and his special mission in the world"?[5]

I stumbled across Merriman-Labor's writing several years ago. Although I had studied modern British literature for two decades and had encountered ugly racist remarks sprinkled throughout the canon, I knew nothing about Africans or people of African descent living in Britain at the time. I had never heard of Merriman-Labor and had no idea that he had come to London—just like T.S. Eliot, Katherine Mansfield, Jean Rhys, Ezra Pound and others—to claim his place among the world's literary elite. But unlike these other literary immigrants, he never found success or recognition in Britain. Why, I wondered. Did he lack talent? Did he want for drive or tenacity? Or did he simply have the misfortune to die young?

The book that made me want to know more about him was *Britons through Negro Spectacles*. In it, Merriman-Labor offers a lively portrait of the age. He invites us to experience the thrill of the early-twentieth-century metropolis with its beggars, scandal sheets, and motor cars; its music halls, department stores, and fashionable diseases. We get glimpses of all manner of Londoners from the "smart set" to street people, evangelical preachers to fake Messiahs, suffragettes to Gaiety girls. Yet, *Britons* also seems ahead of its time. While its form—a day-long journey through London—anticipates the single-day novels of Virginia Woolf and James Joyce, its mixture of high and low culture, its wordplay, blending of genres, and flashes of metafiction gives it a playful feel often associated with postmodernism. As one early reviewer remarked, it "is another of those surprises which Africa has always been springing on enquirers and seekers."[6] Reading *Britons* made me want to know more about the man.

For seven years, I have been painstakingly unearthing his story, not an easy task as he left behind no diary and few letters. While one can fashion a rich portrait of, say, the Bloomsbury group from a bounty of personal documents, far fewer records survive to illuminate the lives of the African men and women who lived in London during the Edwardian period. While it is clear, for example, that Merriman-Labor knew many people, both black and white, the warm, life-giving details about his personal interactions, his loves and hates, his friends and foes, have been mostly lost. This means his story cannot be told in the ordinary way, built on a foundation of memoirs, diaries, letters, and the recollections of those who knew him. Fortunately, copies of his books and pamphlets have been preserved in the British Library. Using these as my reference points, I combed through newspaper articles, court records, business documents, advertisements, passenger lists, and other archival materials and found strands of his life entangled in the social history of his time. Memoirs and histories of the period helped me to understand the historical forces and racial attitudes that made his struggle to achieve literary success so difficult. By pulling together evidence from many sources, I have been able to create a portrait of a man possessed of seemingly boundless resilience, a writer who could never resist a pun.

Achieving recognition as a writer is a struggle for anyone in any age, but in early-twentieth-century Britain, A.B.C. Merriman-Labor had to work harder than many of his white contemporaries seeking literary success, and when he made mistakes, he was punished more severely. Now when I look at those eager eyes in that surviving photograph, I see not just his intelligence and readiness to laugh, but his indomitable spirit. In 1904, when the photograph was taken, he was a young man with big dreams. He had no inkling that in the years to come he would lose everything but his dignity.

In his lifetime, he made his living as an educator, a civil servant, a businessman, a barrister, a journalist, and a munitions worker, but at heart he was always a writer. At eighteen he published a novella (now lost) in a Gambian newspaper, followed by pamphlets on race, the slave trade, the Hut Tax War, and a tribute to his grandfather. Later, he wrote a play, "Court Life in Egypt" (also lost), and edited two editions of a guidebook, *The Handbook of Sierra Leone*, all before the age of twenty-seven.[7] When he arrived in England in 1904, he began to write travel articles, sending a series of "Impressions from a Young African in England" to the *Sierra Leone Weekly News*. After five years in London, he published *Britons through Negro Spectacles*, his only surviving full-length book. Part travelogue, part ethnography, and part treatise, often satirical and sometimes serious, it is a work that is difficult to classify. Merriman-Labor tells—or warns—his readers that it will offer "much sense and nonsense, facts and fiction,—the old, the new and the 'novel' concerning Britons and Blacks."[8] *Britons* is rich with observations of British life, silly puns, verses from hymns, and biblical quotations. Its many allusions reveal not just Merriman-Labor's familiarity with and affection for the British literary tradition, but, I think, his dream of finding his name among the luminaries he cites: William Shakespeare, Rudyard Kipling, Henry Wadsworth Longfellow, Owen Meredith, William Cooper, Geoffrey Chaucer, Herbert Spencer, and Charles Lamb.

Ultimately, what makes *Britons* truly extraordinary is the fact that such a book was written at all. In a world dominated by European empires, at a time when black people were considered inferior to white, an African man claimed his right to describe the world as he found it. In *Britons through Negro Spectacles*, Merriman-Labor looked at the greatest city in the greatest empire the world had ever known and laughed.

His last book never saw print. "A Tour in Negroland," which he described as a "charming, novel-like story of a tour of 15,000 miles through West, South-west and Central Africa," has also been lost. Merriman-Labor died in a workhouse infirmary before he could publish it.[9]

Fifty years ago, the *Encyclopedia Americana* called Merriman-Labor a pioneer of modern African literature.[10] Today, his works are out of print, and he is virtually unknown to the reading public. All that survives are *Britons through Negro Spectacles*, his guidebooks, newspaper articles and pamphlets, but taken together they testify to a grand dream that began in Freetown, Sierra Leone, and ended in the Lambeth Workhouse Infirmary. Until now, the story of the tragic spiral that pulled him down the social ladder from barrister to munitions worker, from witty observer of the social order to patient in a state-run hospital for the poor, has been a mystery.

Although he never realized his dream of transforming the colonial system or writing books that influenced millions, his achievements and failures reveal not just the circumstances of one life, but also the social forces that shaped the lives of millions. His is the story of one African man, and also the saga of a great metropolis writhing its way into a new century awash with unheard-of extravagance, appalling social inequity, world-transforming inventions, unprecedented demands for civil rights, and a monstrous world war. It is part of the epic tale of human foibles and institutional injustice, of individual struggle and global slaughter. Merriman-Labor's story is part of the vast hidden history of individuals fighting the prejudices and caprices of their time as they strive to reach their fullest human potential.

The Province of Freedom

For Augustus Merriman-Labor, the land of his birth was a shining example of African exceptionalism. As European empires devoured African nations in the late nineteenth century, he was proud that Sierra Leone was not, nor ever had been, a conquered country. In compensation for the crime of slavery, he wrote with pride, Britain had "*specially*" created an African settlement, a place of salvation and resurrection.[11] From the beginning, as he saw it, Sierra Leone was different from anything else in Africa.

The plan to establish a colony where formerly enslaved people could enjoy self-determination was conceived at an extraordinary historical moment: an era enthralled by global commerce, inspired by philanthropic initiative, and ablaze with groundbreaking calls for liberty. Yet in the midst of this ferment, four million human beings lived in slavery in the Americas.[12] This mix of revolutionary fervor and massive enslavement gave birth to the Sierra Leone experiment, which in time would bring together four remarkably dissimilar, but highly resilient, groups of displaced people. Together, they would build not only a settlement but a new African identity.

The story of Merriman-Labor's Sierra Leone begins with escaped slaves who had fought with the British during the American Revolution. With Britain's defeat, these black loyalists fled to London where they joined thousands of other black people—servants, slaves, seamen, refugees, and others—in the bustling metropolis.[13] As newcomers without connections, they lacked networks to introduce them to trades or apprenticeships. They may have been war veterans, but they were also foreigners with no parish to offer them Poor Law relief.[14] Unable to find work, they begged on the streets, "distressing the kind-hearted," historian

Christopher Fyfe writes, "and alarming the timorous and propertied."[15] A group of concerned businessmen and philanthropists formed the Committee for the Black Poor in 1786 to provide food and medical care for them, but recession and high unemployment made it unlikely that they would ever find work. Inspired by other programs that transported the poor and criminal to faraway colonies, the committee proposed that the British government relocate these people, now called the Black Poor, to a place where they could be self-sufficient.[16]

Enter dissembling amateur botanist Henry Smeathman—known in Africa as the "Flycatcher"—who had spent three years rummaging around the Sierra Leone estuary gathering plants for the Royal Society.[17] With intimate knowledge of the region, he convinced the committee that Sierra Leone would be an ideal place to relocate these impoverished souls. He heaped praises on its temperate climate, its fertility—"the soil need only be scratched with a hoe to yield grain in abundance"—and its commercial potential. He spun a story of a land where plantation-style agriculture could flourish, providing revenue that would make the colony prosperous. Money-strapped himself, Smeathman offered to guide the settlers and set up a base near the Sierra Leone River for £4 per person. He neglected to mention that the year before he had warned a House of Commons committee against establishing a convict station in Sierra Leone because "convicts would die there at the rate of a hundred a month."[18] With the Committee for the Black Poor, it seems, Smeathman had snagged his biggest fly yet.

The committee embraced the Sierra Leone scheme, its motives a fascinating tangle of utopian vision, commercial aspiration, egalitarian principles, and patronizing, sometimes racist attitudes.[19] It saw Sierra Leone as the site for a grand social experiment proving the capacity of previously enslaved people for self-determination as well as the power of the marketplace to undermine slavery. With guidance from white mentors, the paternalistic thinking went, they could bring prosperity, European civilization, and, most importantly of all, Christianity to an unenlightened continent. Abolitionist Granville Sharp, one of the key players in the new enterprise, christened the settlement the "Province of Freedom." No one realized yet that the kind of freedom the committee was willing to offer was not at all the kind of freedom the former slaves desired.

Many of the Black Poor wanted nothing to do with the Sierra Leone enterprise. Some of them were afraid that the plan was a ruse either to drag them back into slavery or dump them with criminals in Australia. Even if they were guaranteed certificates verifying their status as free people, many did not think it wise to relocate to a colony in the middle of prime slave-trading territory. The organizers tapped the respected former slave Olaudah Equiano for a position overseeing the supplies for the journey, hoping, no doubt, that his presence would convince reluctant settlers to join. Eventually over four hundred people did: black and mixed-race families as well as various white artisans, doctors, and preachers.[20] Together they set sail for a new home in West Africa, a place most of them had never seen.

Adversity struck the expedition at every step. Fever broke out even before the ships left British waters. One of the vessels lost its fore topmast in the Thames. Equiano accused the management of cheating, fraud, and mistreatment, which led to his dismissal and only increased the settlers' anxiety and distrust. After months of setbacks, the convoy finally set out, but the delays landed the settlers in Sierra Leone at the worst possible time: the height of the rainy season. Besieged by torrential rain and ravaged by tropical diseases, they endured a string of disasters, culminating in an attack by indigenous people who burned their settlement to the ground. A year after their arrival, no more than seventy survived.[21] In the face of their devastation, a handful of them deserted their abolitionist ideals and joined forces with local slave-traders. The Committee for the Black Poor could do nothing—it had dissolved months before, believing that once the ships had sailed, its job was done.[22]

But British abolitionists, fervent in their belief that commerce and Christianity could extinguish the slave trade, were not ready to let the experiment die. With the help of well-heeled investors, they formed the Sierra Leone Company to finance and administer the fledgling colony. To thrive, however, it must have more people. The promise of new settlers arrived in the shape of Thomas Peters, a formerly enslaved millwright who had fought with the British in the American Revolution. He travelled to London in 1791 to present a petition describing the unacceptable state of affairs for black loyalists in Nova Scotia. They were paid a fraction of what white laborers earned, and the land they had been promised was either never given or was so poor it could not be cultivated. No longer American slaves, but now faithful subjects of the King, they hoped to have their grievances heard. When Peters's story reached the directors of the Sierra Leone Company, they offered to transport Nova Scotian settlers to their colony in Africa and enlisted the twenty-eight-year-old naval lieutenant John Clarkson—brother of leading abolitionist campaigner Thomas Clarkson—to sail to North America to persuade as many as he could to make the daring leap.

The two zealous men convinced nearly twelve hundred people to make a fresh start in Sierra Leone. As part of his bid, Clarkson promised land and equality under the law, including the right to participate fully in government. The Nova Scotians had risked their lives in the American war to gain their liberty. Now they were being offered their own settlement, a place to shape according to their own principles and needs.[23] But they also perceived a weighty spiritual purpose attached to the voyage. As deeply Christian people, they saw their exodus to Africa as a journey to a promised land where they would convert the heathen masses into God-fearing Christians. In Sierra Leone they would discard the chains of slavery forever and be restored to their rightful place among the free, Christian people of the world, bringing their African brothers and sisters along with them.[24]

The Nova Scotians, like most Europeans, had no doubt that the naked savages of Africa needed spiritual and cultural enlightenment and would welcome their teaching. They didn't consider that the indigenous people of the West African coast had been interacting with explorers, traders, slavers, and missionaries for two hundred years, or that they highly valued their own religions and traditions. The Nova Scotians thought they would be welcomed by the local people who would be eager to hear the Word of God, but for the indigenous Temne and Foulah the settlers hardly differed from the British. "The new imperial interlopers spoke a common European language, worshiped the same god, and dressed in similar clothes," historians Isaac Land and Andrew M. Schocket explain, "all alien to the locals." Ironically, these former slaves were being invited to carve out their liberty in someone else's home.[25]

When they first encountered Naimbana, a powerful Temne leader well acquainted with European culture, the settlers must have begun to realize that Africa was not the blank slate they had imagined.[26] He attended his first diplomatic meeting with John Clarkson wearing a cerulean silk and lace jacket over a ruffled shirt and a tricorn hat, a pendant of a lamb and cross swinging on his chest. His expression of European sartorial authority clearly matched Clarkson's own "full-dress Windsor uniform, with a brilliant star." A sophisticated man, Naimbana saw that the future of his dynasty relied on his descendants' ability to maneuver in a global world and made a point of exposing his sons to diverse cultures and beliefs. One he sent to France to study with the Catholics, another to Muslim clerics, and the third would go to England.[27] The settlers' new home, they must have been beginning to see, was less a promised land than a brave new world.

The Nova Scotians endured bitter challenges as they set to work building Freetown, their new settlement. The inhospitable climate of the tropics battered them with sweltering heat and torrential rain. The humidity rotted their cloth, rusted their metal tools, and covered leather with mold. Swarms of insects stung them and infested their stores of food. Eighteen-foot-long snakes slithered into their tents and makeshift huts.[28] Illness and death were constant shadows. Anna Maria Falconbridge, wife of the colony's drunken commercial agent, observed that "it is quite customary of a morning to ask, 'how many died last night?'"[29] They would make tentative progress, only to be beaten down by another catastrophe. During the British wars with France, for example, seven enemy ships attacked the town. Crews ransacked homes and churches, ruthlessly destroying prayerbooks, smashing the printing press, shattering medicine vials, tearing apart furniture, crushing telescopes, and savagely slaughtering the settlers' animals—livestock, pigs, dogs, and cats—until almost nothing at all was left.[30]

But the settlers were not without victories. One achievement, in particular, would become a hallmark of Sierra Leonean identity. By the mid-1790s, realizing that commerce rather than agriculture was the path to success, many Nova Scotians abandoned their farms and began to ply the trade routes along the coast and local rivers. They were brilliantly successful. Their shrewd trading filled the colony with all manner of provisions, from cattle, goats, rice, and yams to ivory and camwood.[31] This venture not only improved their pocketbooks and bellies, but elevated their social status as well. The men and women who used their wits to grow rich by trading produce and products rather than human beings garnered wide admiration from their fellow settlers.

Yet even as they endured seemingly endless trials, the independence they risked life and limb to possess was not granted. Through mismanagement or miscommunication or both, the directors had not told Clarkson about their intention for the colony's government to be run by a cadre of white officials. On their arrival in Sierra Leone, the settlers found themselves not independent but at the mercy of a debauched band of arrogant, bickering, incompetent white administrators. Although the constitution the Sierra Leone Company directors had drawn up was not without goodwill—it supported law courts, schools, and even wages while the settlers built their plantations—it denied the Nova Scotians the liberty they most wanted.[32] Acutely aware of the rights denied them, they challenged a succession of colonial governments for what they felt was legitimately theirs: ownership of their land and control of their government. The directors and administrators resisted, accusing them alternately of being ignorant children and radical revolutionaries.[33] By 1800, the escalating conflict between government and people threatened to explode into open rebellion. At the last minute, a regiment of British soldiers and a shipload of guerrilla fighters arrived from Jamaica, changing everything.

A century and a half earlier, Oliver Cromwell, the Lord Protector, had ordered his English fleet to oust the Spanish from Jamaica. In the heat of battle, the slaves on the island's sugar plantations fled, establishing settlements in the rugged mountains where they waged a protracted war against the new English invaders. Unable to subdue these sharp guerrilla warriors after years of conflict, the English negotiated a treaty. In return for sovereignty over their lands, the Maroons—as they were called—agreed to assist the English in repelling invasions, putting down insurrections, and hunting runaway plantation slaves. This uneasy alliance survived half a century, until the flogging of two Maroons in 1795 triggered new hostilities. Unable to conquer the Maroons through conventional military means, the British imported attack-trained Mastiffs to subdue them. Fearful of being hunted, the Maroons came to the negotiating table where they were assured they would not be exiled if they surrendered peacefully. But no sooner did the Maroons capitulate than they and their families were deported to Nova Scotia.

They might have happily settled in their new home had it not been for the brutal winter of 1796/97—the coldest on record. They pleaded with the British government to relocate them somewhere, anywhere, so they wouldn't have to endure arctic blasts. Monetary inducements persuaded the apprehensive directors of the Sierra Leone Company to incorporate these 550 independent-minded, militaristic people into their colony in Africa. They were escorted to Freetown by a detachment of British soldiers, but the tightly knit, highly disciplined fighting force required no oversight. They arrived in Sierra Leone just as tensions between Nova Scotian rebels and the government were reaching a crisis. On arrival, the British soldiers volunteered to help put down the rebellion. Not understanding the conflict they were entering—and later regretting their participation—the Maroons, too, offered their services. In a surprise attack, the government forces and their new allies crushed the rebellion. Defeated by colonial administrators, betrayed by black newcomers, the Nova Scotians' demands for full rights were devastated yet again.[34]

Now thrown together as countrymen, the Nova Scotians and Maroons could scarcely have been more different. An abiding memory of slavery, a deep Christian faith, a passion for education, and a talent for commerce pulsed the heart of the Nova Scotians. The Maroons, by contrast, had escaped their chains decades earlier and had held fast to their freedom through the force of arms. Their society was a quasi-martial machine run by men with European-style military titles and ranks: lieutenant, captain, major, colonel, and general. They liked to swagger with their muskets through the Freetown streets intimidating the Nova Scotians. Even though they allowed their children to attend school and church, they had little interest themselves.[35] The Nova Scotians were convinced of their own superiority but were fearful of the Maroons and had little to do with them. It would take another, vastly larger group of strangers to turn them into a community.

In 1807, the Sierra Leone Company realized it could no longer afford to maintain the colony. It had been twenty years since London's Black Poor had first settled, more than fifteen since the Company had taken over, and none of the lucrative agricultural profits the founders envisioned had materialized. On January 1, 1808, Sierra Leone became a Crown Colony in an expanding British empire; its fate now directed by governors responsible to the King. The change invited reflection on the nature of the grand experiment. Had the dream failed? Thomas Ludlam, the last Company governor, didn't think so, observing, "the wonder is that the Colony exists rather than it has not flourished."[36] In the face of serious difficulties—tropical disease, lack of proper supplies, limited funds, conflicts with the French and Temne, and an inhospitable climate—it had prevailed. No one doubted the extraordinary resilience of the settlers. A comparison, wrote the African Institute in 1807, between the Sierra Leoneans and European settlers in other colonial enterprises around the world would be "highly advantageous to the African character."[37]

Another development in Britain would also fundamentally change the character of the colony. After decades of agitation, abolitionists were at last able to pass legislation in the British Parliament outlawing the buying and selling of slaves in the empire. After having transported some three million Africans to the new world since 1650, Britain committed itself to ending the slave trade. Because of its extraordinary harbor and location in prime slaving territory, Sierra Leone provided an ideal spot from which to launch the suppression campaign. During the next six decades, the British Navy would deliver nearly a hundred thousand rescued slaves to Freetown, a tiny two-thousand-person colony in 1807.[38] It is at the beginning of this dramatic influx of people that Merriman-Labor's family story becomes clearly entwined with British history. As he explained to a reporter for the *Manchester Evening Chronicle* in 1907, "His great grandparents were on board ship to be sold as slaves when the British Government intervened."[39] In his family story, these ancestors were delivered from slavery by God and the British Navy.[40]

Perhaps his great-grandparents counted themselves among the lucky few, but by the time they had reached Freetown they had no doubt already endured a harrowing voyage of weeks or months. Wrenched from their homeland and probably enslaved inland for a time, they were then crammed with hundreds of other captives into putrid lower decks of slave ships with insufficient sanitation or ventilation. The space was so cramped they could only crouch or lie down. They watched helplessly as people around them died of fever, smallpox, dysentery, and starvation. Some survivors never shed the psychic and physical imprint of their captivity. "I have seen liberated slaves in every conceivable state of distortion," wrote English observer F. Harrison Rankin. "Many can never resume the upright posture."[41]

In Freetown, they were given rice and clothes and were told that they were free. Their names and descriptions of what they looked like were recorded in a register of Liberated Africans.[42] Although we don't know what his great-grandparents were called, their names almost certainly appear somewhere in the first two registers. These extremely fragile volumes are so badly damaged that many entries are now illegible.[43] Could Merriman-Labor's great-grandfather have been Brima, age twenty, with a diamond-shaped tattoo on his forehead? Or Demba, fifteen, with a yellow face? Was his great-grandmother Simity, Sochra, or Catteyan?[44] They were probably not from any place near Freetown because those people simply returned home after being rescued.[45] His great-grandmother may have been apprenticed to Europeans or settlers in whose employ she would have been expected to learn new skills and rehabilitate a work ethic Europeans believed was destroyed by slavery. The apprentice system in Freetown was notoriously corrupt—one governor considered it tantamount to slavery—but a range of employment conditions was possible. Merriman-Labor's great-grandmother may have found a home in a humane household and formed close bonds with her masters, or she may have been brutally exploited, even tortured, until the terms of her employment came to an end.

His great-grandfather might have been employed in public works, sent for schooling, hospitalized, or resettled in a nearby village.[46] Most likely, he was enlisted in the military as most able-bodied men were.[47] If he was "recruited" into the Royal African Corps—though the rescued Africans had little choice in the matter—he would have been stationed in nearby "Soldier Town," where he would have protected the colony from attack by indigenous people.[48] It is also possible he was sent to Cape Coast, the Gambia, or Gorée, other British possessions in West Africa that needed a military presence. He may even have been enlisted in the West India Regiment and sent all the way to the Caribbean to defend British interests there.

Though we don't know exactly where he served, there is little doubt that Merriman-Labor's great-grandfather was a soldier. In his descriptions of the man, Merriman-Labor recalled that he "fought for His late Majesty King George the Third in the War against Napoleon Bonaparte" and "saw some fighting at Waterloo." Yet, how he might have reached the European battlefield and in what capacity he served is not clear. Individual black soldiers are known to have fought at Waterloo, but none of them have been identified as Liberated Africans. It is possible this much-admired great-grandfather served King George by fighting against French forces in the Caribbean. Yet, we cannot rule out the possibility that he made his way to Europe and joined the British forces there.[49]

By 1830, Merriman-Labor's great-grandfather was back in Sierra Leone, where he and his wife settled in Leicester, a village near Freetown. There they welcomed a son they named John Merriman, suggesting they had given up all or part of their African names by that time. Like other Liberated Africans, the experience of captivity, rescue, and resettlement in an unfamiliar land required them to adapt to the demands of their new circumstances. As indigenous people, they were radically different from the original setters in Freetown, who had long been assimilated to European life. Nor did the Liberated Africans share a common background with one another but came from a wide range of African peoples: Yorubas, Ibos, Congos, Popos, Mocos, Kakandahs, Calabars, and others.[50] Because some 160 languages and numerous dialects were spoken in the colony, English became the lingua franca even between married people who might have had no other language in common. The Merrimans cultivated new relationships to help replace the kinship structures they had lost. They almost certainly participated in benefit societies with other disbanded soldier families to provide aid when one of them was in need. And they undoubtedly connected with people from their own ethnic group with whom they could celebrate and maintain the traditions of their homeland.[51] We can tell by the way they raised their son John—a prominent educator renowned for his Christian piety—that they converted to Christianity and brought up their children in the Anglican Church.

So many children and adults wanted to learn, the colony's schools could not keep up with the demand. By 1840, a fifth of the colony's population was in school. By the middle of the nineteenth century, Sierra Leone had a higher literacy rate than many countries in Europe.

By the 1850s the four disparate groups that had been thrown together in Sierra Leone began to blend into a new kind of African. Krios they called themselves.[52] Intermarrying and adapting to the British values that missionaries, government agents, and anglicized settlers offered or imposed, yet maintaining important rituals and beliefs of their lost homelands, they developed a vibrant hybrid culture, part African, part British. By the middle of the nineteenth century, the well-to-do of the colony proudly followed British current events, read the latest English books, wore fashionable clothes imported from London, and revered their British God and education.

As people who had enthusiastically adapted to British culture and identified themselves as citizens of one of the oldest and most loyal of colonies, upper-class Krios called themselves "Britain's favorite and favored Africans."[53] A Sierra Leone governor once told the members of London's Royal African Society that "a more loyal place you could not find" and described the Krios in glowingly patriotic terms. "You will find highly educated men who keenly discuss the public questions occupying the attention of Englishmen ... [who have] a most fervent belief in the principles of British justice, including trial by jury; and indeed, it may well be said that the Colony of Sierra Leone—this tiny twenty square miles—is really England in Africa."[54] He neglected to mention that a number of colonial administrators and other Britons living in Freetown despised the Krios, considering their British manners and morals shallow imitations of European values which they could not possibly understand.

Family Ties

John Merriman, the son of the Liberated Africans, would become the most important male figure in Merriman-Labor's life. Educated at the elite Church Missionary Society Grammar School in Freetown, he possessed two burning qualities: fierce intelligence and profound piety. He used his British education to become an extraordinary teacher, and his students went on to important careers as leading men in the colony. "The late John Merriman of blessed memory," one student recalled, "spared not the rod to emphasize the great importance and utility of the knowledge of English Grammar to his pupils."[55] Struck blind and barred from teaching in the public schools in midlife, Merriman began his own private academy. His instruction was so ingenious, his abilities so impressive, a former Governor of Sierra Leone Sir Arthur Havelock, tried to hire him as an interpreter for the colony's aborigines.

Because of his religious devotion, he became affectionately known in Freetown as Father Merriman. When he fell into poverty, a letter appeared in the *Sierra Leone Weekly News* asking that a pension be set aside for the man "to whom many of our respected citizens are so much indebted for the pains he bestowed on them to make them what they are."[56] Merriman continued to teach until the day before he died at the age of seventy. This adored grandfather nurtured his grandson's intellect and inspired his spiritual passion. Delivering this great man's funeral oration at his graveside in February 1900, his grandson remembered his "great mental capacity, his uncompromising principles of Christianity, his magnanimity of mind, and unflinching resolution."[57] John Merriman, he said, "made me what I am today."[58] Inspired by this virtuous example, Merriman-Labor took his grandfather's name and made it part of his own.[59]

Merriman-Labor's mother, Gillian Merriman-Wilson, was one of John Merriman's six children and made of the same stern, loving stuff as her father. She named her only son after a Roman emperor and did not hesitate to pour her righteous affection on him. In English Augustus meant "great" and "venerable" and bespoke her aspirations for her only child.[60] Because she left Freetown when he was small to become a school matron in a distant colony, Merriman-Labor's relationship with her was largely epistolary. He knew her love by the curves and lines of her words as they rippled across the pages of her weekly letters. Despite the distance, her missives of affection and admonition inspired him "with a sense of devotion to duty in order that I may one day 'do or die' in the battle of life."[61] Even though she was always far away, she was his foundation. When it came time to write the acknowledgement for the book he believed would earn him literary fame in England, there was only one person to whom it could be dedicated: his "darling mother."

Contemporary accounts portray Merriman-Labor's father, Joshua Labor, as a force to be reckoned with: industrious, enterprising, and strong-willed. He and his son shared a passion for the written word—even if that passion landed both in trouble. According to one contemporary account, while working as a clerk for the police department in the village of Waterloo about eighteen miles from Freetown, Joshua Labor wrote a series of "sensational articles" called "Three Years What I Saw." Apparently, what he saw disturbed the people of Waterloo so much that they "forcibly ejected" him from the village."[62]

Joshua Labor was a man of many trades: printer, shipping clerk, civil servant, newspaperman, and aspiring restaurateur. Those who knew him said he "had a strong will and never allowed himself to be led blindly."[63] Merriman-Labor lauded his father's talents, observing that the man not only had "a smart knowledge of law and a little of medicine," but he could also "dye clothes, trade, manufacture articles for domestic use, print, [and] edit a newspaper."[64] As the proprietor of the Michael Maurice Printing Works, he did commercial printing and published *City Chats*, an occasional paper, under the pseudonym "Junius," the pen name of an eighteenth-century political writer in London.[65] In contrast to his son's weak constitution, Labor was physically strong. He supervised sporting events for the Central Athletic Club, and most Sundays hiked several steep miles into the Mountain District to "render spiritual assistance" at an Anglican church in the village of Lacca. Labor married three times and had several children in addition to Merriman-Labor.[66]

"An Africanised Englishman Twenty Years in British West Africa"

Sierra Leone had been built on the ideals of equality and brotherhood, but when Merriman-Labor was born in 1877, it festered with racial hostility. A pseudo-scientific racism, which set black people at the bottom of a supposed hierarchy of human intelligence, permeated the British colonial psyche. Now Krios never knew when they would have to endure a rude word, paternalistic tone, a shove in the street, or worse.[67] Krios were barred from the upper echelons of the medical, legal, and civil services even if they held more prestigious professional degrees than their white counterparts. At one time, the colonial government had aimed to build an African administration prepared to take on the responsibilities of self-government. By the 1890s, that idea had vanished. In the Sierra Leone of Merriman-Labor's childhood, as

INTRODUCTION

Christopher Fyfe explains, "authority was to be grounded on a simple racial principle—white gives order, black obeys."[68]

In the name of health, segregation had recently come to Freetown. Ostensibly to escape the malaria-ridden town, Europeans established a fenced "white only" community built high on Tower Hill. A few African servants would be allowed to work there during the day, but all non-Europeans were required to leave by nightfall. In 1904, the government celebrated the opening of a railway linking the new white enclave to the city center and offered two inaugural trips: one "especially for Europeans" and the other "exclusively for natives." Hearing of the plan, J.A. Fitz-John, the editor of the *Sierra Leone Times*, cuttingly wrote, "Let us trust that the authorities fumigated the carriages afterwards, in order to run no risks."[69] Was this how loyal subjects were to be regarded?

Krios were horrified by the repulsive stories about educated Africans published by choleric colonial administrators such as Alfred Burdon Ellis, a British officer in command of troops in West Africa. "The Sierra Leone negro is the most insufferably insolent and ostentatiously vain and arrogant of his species," Ellis declared. "Being besottedly ignorant, he imagines that since white men take so much trouble about him he must be a person of immense importance."[70] Ellis charged that Sierra Leoneans deliberately provoked whites in order to sue them for assault. "A white man's oath," he insisted, "possesses no weight, in comparison with a negro's, at Sierra Leone."[71] His portrait of white impotence defied reality. In truth, it was the Krios who had very little power. An elected mayor and city council were nominally in charge of Freetown, but British administrators controlled so many decisions that the council did little more than collect taxes.[72]

Ellis called anglicized Africans "grotesque caricatures" and asked his readers to imagine the ludicrous figure of a "tall, splay-footed negro" in "a white opera-hat, swallow-tail coat, green necktie, lavender continuations, patent-leather boots, and the loudest gloves he can obtain, while he gracefully bears a green-lined umbrella to preserve his complexion from the rays of the sun."[73] He went on to belittle white Britons who believed that Africans should be treated as equals. "They never have to mix with negroes," he wrote disparagingly. "They have not to endure their insufferable insolence, their ostentatious vanity, and their overpowering odour."[74]

In this fraught environment a little pamphlet entitled "The Last Military Expedition in Sierra Leone" exploded onto the West African literary scene and became all the rage. Published in Liverpool and written by "An Africanised Englishman Twenty Years in British West Africa," the forty-page missive provided a first-hand account of a recent African uprising. The author promised a dashing war story that would make "pleasurable reading ... for every loyal English subject anxious for the cultivation of genuine manliness in the boys of the British Empire."[75] But this dashing war story also turned the colonial world on its head.

In the pamphlet, the author described a tone-deaf, out-of-touch colonial administration in Sierra Leone that understood very little of what was happening in the vast land it governed. He went on to suggest that the uprising was caused by a dubious tax collected by unscrupulous Frontier Policemen who not only abused the indigenous people, but stole their property. Insensitive to the local customs, a bumbling British captain named Sharpe had to collect the tax "at the point of a bayonet." Sharpe's folly peaked when he decided to arrest a Temne chief named Bai Bureh. Bai Bureh, the author joked, was "sharper than Sharpe," and managed not only to escape capture, but to rally thousands of warriors to defend his refusal to pay an unfair tax and, more generally, to resist alien rule.[76]

Our troops, the author wrote, were totally unprepared to respond to Bai Bureh's shrewd military tactics. The British were too bogged down with equipment and supplies to be a nimble fighting force in the Sierra Leone hinterland: 400 British troops required 530 native men to carry their supplies. Marching single-file along narrow trails in the bush, carriers and soldiers alike were easy targets for the rebels. When attacked, the carriers rushed into the jungle for safety, abandoning their sixty-pound loads which the indigenous warriors quickly confiscated.

Although the British possessed superior arms and numbers, they completely underestimated Bai Bureh, who cleverly sent spies to take jobs as carriers for the British forces and report on troop movements. He constructed stone stockades in forests so dense that the British were under attack before they knew the enemy was there. Battling with limited arms and ammunition, Bai Bureh collected British spent shell casings and recycled them into new bullets. He even devised homemade guns made from bamboo. Despite our "mortars, cannons, bombs, rockets, cordite, and every other available and imaginable weapon of destruction" as well as a hundred thousand rounds of ammunition, the author lamented, Bai Bureh was able to inflict more casualties on British forces than could be replaced with reinforcements, even when emergency detachments were sent from England.[77] The conflict, which the Governor had anticipated as "an affair of ten days from start to finish," stretched into nine months of combat in which 600 British troops were wounded and 200 killed or missing.[78]

In view of the English disadvantages, the author of the pamphlet told his readers, "one is filled with wonder and admiration for the endurance displayed, and feels that England possesses gallant soldiers."[79] Although Bai Bureh's forces were ultimately defeated and Bai Bureh himself captured, the "Africanised Englishman" characterized him as a leader of wit, cunning, and honor and concluded his pamphlet with the observation that "a notable chief named Bai Bureh, with a number of natives, undisciplined, unintelligent, and indifferently armed, withstood for several months together, an English army of 5,000 souls."[80] The African was not only an excellent fighter, he suggested, but pluckier than the British themselves.

The exposé became a bestseller on the West Coast. A review in the *Lagos Weekly Record* marveled at its novelty: "For once in the history of the wars waged by the civilized nations of Europe against native tribes the world is favoured with a truthful account." It seemed amazing that a story of an African war could be told without racial prejudice.[81]

But who was this "Africanised Englishman Twenty Years in British West Africa," a man willing not only to admire African intelligence, but to criticize colonial policy? A crusty old colonial administrator who had seen enough exploitation? A long-time missionary moved to speak truth to power?

It was neither. The writer was Merriman-Labor, then a junior clerk in the Colonial Secretary's Office, who had earned a West Africa medal for his service in the Sierra Leone Volunteers during the war.[82] As an African-born, English-speaking, missionary-educated Krio, he was at once vexed by and grateful for the British influence in his life. Despite his disapproval of overreaching colonial power, he saw himself as a proud and loyal British subject.[83] In this sense, his pseudonym of an "Africanised Englishman" was only casually ironic. As for the twenty years in Africa, that was not ironic at all. When he wrote his account, Merriman-Labor was just twenty years old.

Pan-African

From his teenage years Merriman-Labor felt called to add his voice to those championing the African cause. Nurtured by politically conscious friends and family as well as the writings of prominent black thinkers, he began giving lectures and publishing pamphlets about the African experience.[84] Since childhood, the violence of the slave trade had been as tangible to him as the searing winds of the harmattan covering the country in Saharan dust from December to February. "Ever since I came to know the story," he wrote, "I labored under a keen sense of the grievous injuries which the white man perpetrated in Africa several centuries together."[85] It infuriated him that European firms extracted hundreds of thousands of pounds' worth of raw materials from African soil, while Africans could barely make a living. In his view, Africans were still enchained—now shackled to a slavery of the mind that identified them as a "backward race," ever subordinate to and requiring the guidance of the "advanced" races.

Merriman-Labor may have questioned elements of his British identity, but he clung to his Christianity and erudition and used them as weapons in his battle for justice.[86] While still a teenager, he lectured on the origins of the "Negro race" in Freetown, drawing his authority and evidence from the pages of the Bible. The pamphlet he published based on the lecture was sold in Africa, Britain, and even the United States. Three years later, he lectured on *The Story of the African Slave Trade in a Nutshell*, arguing that the deliverance of Africans came about as the result of a divine alliance between Christian virtue and British justice. His vision of a divine plan which wove together British and African history won wide approval in Freetown. Sir Samuel Lewis, the first African to be knighted, was so impressed, he declared that the pamphlet "should be in the hand of every young man in Sierra Leone" and ordered forty copies.[87]

Merriman-Labor's concern for Africa and its place in the world was not formed in isolation. He was riding the wave of dissent that had been building in the colonial world and had caught him in its current.

INTRODUCTION

In 1897, Trinidadian law student Henry Sylvester Williams formed the African Association in London to promote awareness about colonial issues and the rights of Afro-British subjects. Its vice president was Merriman-Labor's friend, fellow Sierra Leonean Thomas John Thompson—future editor of Freetown's *Colonial and Provincial Reporter*. Under Williams's leadership, the association convened a groundbreaking international conference in the great metropolis in 1900. During three scorching days in July, some forty people from Africa, America, Britain, and the Caribbean gathered in the Westminster Town Hall in London for the first Pan-African Conference. For the next three days, men and women gathered in the public hall for lectures, discussions, and music. As they listened to each inspiring speaker, a stained-glass window celebrating "Prospero revealing his power over the World of Spirits" shone a rainbow of color over them. As they sat in the sweltering heat, perhaps they remarked that Caliban, Shakespeare's native son stripped of land and enslaved by his European visitor, was conspicuously absent from the tableau of glass.

Henry Sylvester Williams saw the conference as a watershed moment when black people could "speak for themselves on a public platform and tell their own story."[88] The aims of the conference were not extreme. The delegates wanted better race relations and improved conditions for Afro-British subjects around the world as well as greater access to education and business opportunities. There were no calls for revolution or the dismantling of the British empire; quite the contrary. "Everything should be done," Williams said later, "to foster the native's love for the Empire, that he may feel himself part and parcel of it."[89] Williams wasn't even asking for full social equality. That, he believed, would be "of natural growth." But what he did want as a British subject and taxpayer was the right to "fully enjoy the privileges of citizenship."[90]

The papers and discussions during the conference hit on important Pan-Africanist themes, many of which Merriman-Labor explored in his youthful writing, including celebrations of black achievement; accounts of injustices suffered by people of African descent in America and the West Indies; colonial abuses in Africa; denunciations of racist scientific ideas alleging inferiority; and, because many of the members were devout Christians, discussions of God's plan for "the future of black people."[91] In the evening, the musical entertainment was organized by

Samuel Coleridge-Taylor, a celebrated London-born, Afro-British composer whose *Song of Hiawatha* trilogy had recently been performed by
the Royal Choral Society at the princely Albert Hall.

British newspaper articles about the Pan-African Conference
exposed how deeply the idea of black inferiority was embedded in the
British public consciousness. The liberal and widely read *Daily News*
seemed amazed by the sophistication of the participants, reporting
that visitors to the conference "must have been struck" by the delegates' "capacity, intelligence, and moderation, and the remarkable
eloquence with which their claims were advanced."[92] It seems aston-
ishing now that W. T. Stead, the radical editor of the *Review of Reviews*,
who took a keen interest in civil rights and in the conference, could
say that "the notion that even black men have rights is no doubt novel
to most of us." Justice for black people, he went on, did not require
black equality, because "the weaker, the stupider, the more barbarous
he is, the more careful ought the strong, the wise, the civilised to be
to see to it that he is not cheated, pursued, murdered and plundered
by the superior race."[93]

After the conference, the newly named Pan-African Association
planned regular meetings, the creation of global branches, and a
monthly magazine. But lack of money and far-flung membership made
the organization difficult to sustain. Nor was it universally supported
by the African elite. "The agitation for Pan-African Congresses," wrote
Merriman-Labor's friend Cornelius May in the *Sierra Leone Weekly News*,
"is not favored by the real leaders of African thought." May's own newspaper had "always declined to take any part in discussions on this
unnecessary and impolitic subject."[94] By the time Merriman-Labor
arrived in London, the Pan-African Association had ceased to exist.

Yet an address expressing the concerns of the participants read by
American W.E.B. Du Bois on the last day of the conference was to
become a significant document in the history of black rights. "To the
Nations of the World" asked how long race would "be made the basis of
denying to over half the world the right of sharing to their utmost
ability the opportunities and privileges of modern civilization". With
steely insight that would reverberate into the next millennium, Du Bois
articulated the importance of race into the foreseeable future: "The
problem of the twentieth century," he declaimed," is the problem of the

color-line."[95] For Merriman-Labor, it was the issue that would inspire his writing and shape his life.

He longed to see black faces—his face—among his pantheon of literary heroes. He felt he had taken his first step toward this goal when he was accepted into the London-based Society of Authors in 1903, an acknowledgment from the revered metropolis that he had earned a place in the sacred profession of letters. "We trust that this will be an encouragement to the young gentleman," wrote May in the *Sierra Leone Weekly News*.[96] He was not shy about praising his friend's literary abilities. "Everything from Mr. Merriman-Labor's pen is well written and deserves perusal," he lauded, noting that he was "pursuing with diligence and industry the literary road and it is our belief that he will ultimately succeed to make his mark in this special field."[97]

He was indeed pursuing the literary road, but for him it had only one indisputable destination: London. Freetown teachers had long been inspiring pupils to work harder by holding out the possibility of going to Britain to study law or medicine. "It was almost as far as heaven in our imagination," wrote one Krio, "and just as magical."[98] Recently, the *Weekly News* had advised a stay in Britain to advance one's education and personal refinement. "The more we see and know of the patriotism, philanthropy and liberality of Englishmen at home," it counseled, "the better."[99] Sierra Leoneans were so enamored of England that when they spoke of going there, they called it "going home."

London, 1904

The year Merriman-Labor arrived, London was the biggest city in the world, home to six million people, famous for its traffic, its fog, its international port, its powerful financial center, and its pickpockets. A massive 693 square miles, greater London was bigger than Paris, Berlin, or New York. As the center of a global empire, it governed the lives and fortunes of some four hundred million people. Its port was the busiest in the world, the center of a trading network that stretched to every continent. Warehouses, some of them eight stories high, lined the north bank of the Thames and housed international goods: tea, wool, rubber, coffee, meat, cinnamon, wine, animal hides, cotton, produce, timber, feathers, ivory, and more. Because the more delectable freight attracted swarms of rats, the city employed cats by the thousands.

The discrepancies between rich and poor in the great metropolis were mind-boggling. A high court judge might make £15,000 a year or more; a charwoman barely £30. Women of the upper class were expected to wear different attire for every activity—tea dresses, ball gowns, walking clothes, and cycling gear, not to mention costumes for motoring, traveling by sea, getting married, or mourning the death of a loved one. Laborers and their families had to get by with one set of tattered clothes and one ragged pair of shoes. Wealthy families rattled around country houses with a hundred rooms and more than fifty servants at their disposal while families of dockworkers crammed together in tight quarters near river warehouses to avoid transportation costs. Those lucky enough to be born into the upper class could live into their seventies. But those with the misfortune to be members of the working class would be lucky to reach forty.[100]

Britain's colossal empire and financial system created enormous wealth for a privileged few, but left a third of Londoners too poor to afford sufficient food.[101] Millions scrounged from street gutters or rubbish heaps for rotting fruit, cracked eggs, and moldy bread. In this wealthy city, the poorest children were so covered with vermin they were barred from school. Many of them regularly went to bed with empty stomachs. South London doctor Alfred Salter reported that in one neighborhood he found "*one* water-closet for the twenty-five houses ... queues lined up outside that water-closet, men, women and children, every morning before they went to work ... There was no possibility of decency, modesty or health."[102] As the wealthy dumped leftover cream down the sink and threw away platters of half-eaten roasts, untouched chickens, perfectly cooked vegetables, and lavish cake, the poor groveled under fishmongers' wheelbarrows scavenging for enough tails and heads to make soup for their starving children.[103]

Here, in the city idealized by the Krio, there were places where people lived with broken windows, rotting floors, and rain coming through the roof; they slept on beds made of piled coats and fashioned furniture from discarded orange crates; youngsters queued at the back of pubs for half-eaten food; and four-year-olds cared for infants. Here people died of starvation, and their corpses decayed in crowded rooms until there was money to bury them.[104] In such a world, nothing was wasted. When one of London's one hundred and eighty thousand horses died, its skin was made into leather, its bones into buttons, its flesh became cat food, its hooves turned to glue, and its bones boiled for oil or ground into fertilizer.[105]

Probably upwards of ten thousand African people were living in Britain in the early twentieth century, the great majority non-literate seafaring men living in port cities. But, as historian Jeffrey Green has shown, people of African origin could be found in many walks of life. Their roles were not limited to manual laborers and domestic servants; they also served as pastors, doctors, lawyers, businessmen, entertainers, athletes, soldiers, artisans, and nurses.[106]

Even though black people were comfortably integrated into a variety of white communities, the idea of black people as strange exotics still seized the popular imagination. Turn-of-the-century Britons were fascinated by ethnographic shows or "human zoos" where Africans—or other non-European people—appeared on stage, in music halls, or in specially constructed "native villages" ostensibly going about their daily activities as they would in their homelands. From the 1880s, when European colonization of Africa was at its height, until the beginning of World War I, entertainment based on ethnographic display increased tenfold.[107] During that time, some two to three thousand of these performers worked in Britain each year.

One of the most popular of these displays was "Savage South Africa," billed by British impresario Frank Fillis as a "vivid realistic and picturesque representation of LIFE IN THE WILDS OF AFRICA."[108] Opening in May 1899, the Fillis troupe of two hundred African warriors performed twice daily at the Empress Theatre in Earls Court as part of the Greater Britain Exhibition. "A sight never previously presented in Europe," it was, he boasted, "a horde of savages direct from their kraals."[109] Customers lined up to pay sixpence each to view African men, women, and children ostensibly living in their traditional homes. Fillis also gave London audiences the chance to see African royalty in the form of "Prince Lobengula, the redoubtable warrior chieftain who was taken prisoner in the Matabele war."[110] According to *The Sketch*, the show was the "talk of London" and drew thousands of people each day.[111] The Aborigines' Protection Society objected to the exploitation of the Africans. Others feared that such "primitive natives" were a threat to white women and a danger to British society. The discovery that Prince Lobengula—who may or may not have been a prince at all—was engaged to an Englishwoman named Kitty Jewell created an uproar. "It is to be hoped," wrote the *Evening News*, "that steps will be taken to prevent so disgraceful an occurrence as the projected marriage, the mere mention of which must produce a feeling of disgust in all decent minds."[112] The *Daily Mail* fanned anxiety about white women interacting with black men, reporting that while visiting the kraals, "women, apparently of gentle birth, crowd round the nearly-naked blacks, give them money" and even "shake hands with them." Nighttime visits, it implied, were even worse. Women, it claimed, "whose IMPROPRIETY IS PLAIN" were certain to have their actions "INTERPRETED IN THE WORST SENSE."[113] By the end of August, women were no longer admitted to the "Kaffir Kraal." By the time the exchanges between English women and African men were reported in American newspapers, they had transformed from friendly handshakes into what one Texas newspaper called the "vilest orgies."[114]

Edwardians looking for objective information about "the Negro" might turn to reference works like the 1910 *Encyclopedia Britannica* (eleventh edition), where the message of black inferiority found in ethnographic exhibitions received "scientific" confirmation. Basing its information on the Victorian pseudo-disciplines of physical or evolutionary anthropology, which claimed to identify the differences between the races, the entry explains that an analysis of arm, cranium, and nose proportions had demonstrated that "the negro would appear to stand on a lower evolutionary plane than the white man, and to be more closely related to the highest anthropoids." The entry goes on to state that "mentally the negro is inferior to the white" because "the brain is ... arrested by the premature closing of the cranial sutures and lateral pressure of the frontal bone" as the black child grows into adulthood.[115]

By the time Merriman-Labor arrived in London, scientific theories of black inferiority, the prevailing belief that black people ranked lower on an imagined racial hierarchy, and the derogatory representations of blacks in mass culture had created a world unlikely to appreciate an African man of wit and intelligence determined to make his name as a writer.

PART I

BRITONS THROUGH NEGRO SPECTACLES

1

THE VOYAGE OUT

Augustus Merriman-Labor stood on the threshold of his grandfather's shabby house on Bombay Street. It was the dry season, and the parched breeze had already made the morning hot. In just a few hours, he would steam away from Freetown, a municipality of fewer than thirty-five thousand people, toward London, a city of six million souls—the biggest, richest metropolis in the world.

He had lived in this house nearly all his life. He knew the feel of each floor mat, the familiar scent of *fufu* and *jollof* rice rising from the outdoor kitchen through glassless windows, the exact weight of the family Bible. His grandfather had been dead four years, but he could still hear the man's stick tapping up the red dirt road. Blind for as long as Merriman-Labor could remember, Father Merriman had never bowed to the darkness. He met it straight on and taught his grandson to do the same. He educated him in the works of William Shakespeare and Geoffrey Chaucer and affirmed for him each day that black skin was noble in the eyes of God. Despite his lack of material goods, Father Merriman educated his grandson as a man of intelligence and wisdom, giving him the intellectual and spiritual skills to hold his own in the world. At twenty, Merriman-Labor confidently quoted from Lucretius, *Patere honoris scirent ut cuncti viam*: "the way to honor is open to all." And when he wrote soaringly of the potential of the black race, he knitted his own high ambitions into his vision of the future. "Before long," he declared, black people will "be deservingly and universally crowned with such superabundance of honours as will make [them] for ever 'a name, a landmark on the cliff of fame.'"[1]

Wearing a fashionable suit from Curzon Brothers of London and carrying a blue *billet de seconde classe* in his jacket pocket, Merriman-Labor watched the white pennant flag flutter up the pole on Tower Hill. It signaled the arrival of the Belgian steamer S.S. *Anversville*, the ship that would take him three thousand miles north on the longest journey of his life. In twelve or fourteen days, depending on the weather, he would be in London.

London. The sacred source of every book Merriman-Labor had ever read, the maps he studied, the hymns he sang in church, the white baby dolls his nieces rocked, the Christmas tins filled with biscuits and gingerbread, and the humble enameled cups emblazoned with portraits of the King and Queen found in Freetown kitchens. It was the home of romance, culture, and justice. It was the sacred homeland of his Anglican God, and the destination of affluent Africans in search of culture and learning.

He was ready to make his mark on the world, but had only a six-month leave of absence from the Colonial Secretary's Office. He might pursue a professional course of study—law, perhaps, or medicine. One thing was certain: he aimed to make a name for himself in the British literary world. He knew the illustrious American author Mark Twain had begun his career writing travel articles for newspapers, and he meant to do the same. He would be an enthusiastic tourist and travel writer, visiting all the famous sites: Trafalgar Square, Oxford Circus, the British Museum, St. Paul's Cathedral, Piccadilly. The names he had known so long tripped musically through his mind. He meant to see everything picturesque, grand, and beautiful.

He pulled closed the door of his grandfather's house, his excitement tinged with the anxiety of stepping into the great unknown, leaving his home, his family, and his profession. He might be gone six months, or much longer if things went well. True, Freetown suffered from bickering, jealousies, and small-town politics, but it was where he grew up, went to school, and created a life. Here, he was part of the elite: his father a well-known printer and businessman; his uncle Joseph Labor a respected druggist and councilman.[2] He enjoyed personal relationships with distinguished men of the day, including Sir Samuel Lewis and Dr. Edward

Blyden, who possessed international reputations as black intellectuals. His friends included dozens of illustrious Sierra Leoneans: the wealthy, the literary, the philanthropic, and the religious.[3] The Freetown literary scene had been an exuberant incubator for his ambitions with its social and literary clubs, public library, and two weekly newspapers.[4] He was an integral member of the faith community. In London, he would be nobody—a man without reputation and connections.

In West Africa, he had built no small name for himself as an able civil servant, champion of his people, and dependable friend. In January 1901, his fellow clerks asked him to serve as their spokesman in a labor dispute with the colonial government. He took their demands to the Governor and returned with salary increases. He must have impressed the Governor because his own pay doubled. Merriman-Labor had earned the eternal gratitude of his fellow civil servants. "When you count on Labor," his colleagues lauded, "your labour's not lost."[5]

But no one in London would know of his accomplishments. His name and family would mean nothing in the metropolis. Whatever he might achieve would need to be built from scratch, using only his own hard work and ingenuity.

His wool suit already felt too hot for the mile-long walk to the pier, but there were no cabs or omnibuses in Freetown. When the well-to-do wanted to get around, strong men pulled them in rickshaws, carried them in sedan chairs, or hauled them in low-slung hammocks. His ill health over the last months might have given him an excuse to be carried to the wharf, but Father Merriman's admonishments against vanity still lingered in his ears. He sucked in a deep breath and began walking.

At the Colonial Secretary's Office in George Street, his civil service friends stepped out to wish him luck. He had been eighteen when he joined their ranks, the top scorer on the civil service exam. "Remember," someone joked, "you've only got a six-month leave. Don't forget to come back."

On this hot day in early March, there was no way he could have known that Freetown would never be his home again.

Three majestic stories of the Church Missionary Society Grammar School—the most prestigious academy in West Africa—soared above

33

Oxford Street and reminded him of his happy days as a student. How he had loved striding through town in his navy blazer, clutching his cherished slate chalked with the day's lesson. He took special pride in his school cap with its white-and-purple badge, featuring a book, a telescope, and the school motto in Greek, "To pursue." He had excelled at all his subjects—history, literature, theology, shorthand, and bookkeeping—but wondered why his well-meaning teachers taught him to recite Kipling poems and sing "Britannia Rules the Waves," but offered no lessons about his own land. Why did students learn, he quipped later, "all the knotty names in the Bible, more knotty ones in British history and geography, and the thousand and one meaningless rules in English grammar," but nothing about African languages, history, or geography?[6]

At sixteen he learned the bitter lesson that top scores mean nothing without money for tuition, books, and navy blazers. After two short years, his family could no longer scrape together the pound and a half for his quarterly fees, nor the extra eight shillings for instruction in Latin, Greek, and mathematics. He was forced to withdraw; his formal education cut short.

His health deteriorated almost immediately. Plagued by indigestion, insomnia, and headaches, he tried every kind of patent tonic and sought out "every shade and degree of African and English doctors and medicines."[7] Several physicians told him he was fine. Two concluded that his ailment was imaginary. Still, he could not shake off an uneasy feeling that something was wrong. Instead of tracing his ailment to financial worries, blunted aspirations, and the chronic discrimination of colonial life, he blamed it on his poor physique.

Yet he refused to let his ill health limit him. During the 1900 Christmas season, he presented a "grand Magical Entertainment" for the boys of the CMS Grammar School, impressing the crowd with a spectacular watch trick.[8] He asked an unsuspecting volunteer to hand over his timepiece, which he immediately smashed with a hammer. Scraping the pieces of the watch into his hand, he loaded them into a gun and fired. Then he sent a papaya around the room. To their amazement, the audience found the watch inside, fully intact. The response to his performance was so enthusiastic, he began to advertise his services.

THE VOYAGE OUT

MAGIC, MIRTH, AND MYSTERY

Whenever you desire a little merriment in your home after the hours
of labour,
send for Mr. Merriman-Labor, of Bombay Street,
who is ready to entertain you with up-to-date tricks in
Conjuring, Jugglery, and Spiritualistic performances.[9]

Despite his success with magic, his health worsened. He complained
of a ticking in his head and difficulty walking.[10] Convinced he was suffering from some life-threatening disease, he took a three-month leave
of absence to seek out medical help in other West African capitals. But
his search for a cure was fruitless, and he returned home no better than
when he left.

Failed by the medical establishment, he pursued a regimen prescribed
by the latest theories of physical culture: he became a vegetarian, took
cold baths every morning, and exercised daily. He felt briefly better, until
his lungs began to bother him. Desperate for relief, he wrote to the
advice column of *Health and Strength*, a magazine published by the
National Amateur Bodybuilders' Association in London, explaining that
he was born "without constitution" and asking for the guidance of "an
experienced specialist in the study of nervous ailments, who goes in for
the natural remedy treatment." At 5′6′′ and 140 pounds, with a chest 32
inches wide, an arm 18 inches in diameter, and a pulse of 62 beats a
minute, he described himself as not quite sickly, but not strong. He wrote
that he was "thin, and somewhat wiry."[11] The medical officer at *Health and
Strength* attributed his ill health to a poor constitution further weakened
by "too assiduous an application to mental attainments at the expense of
[his] physical welfare."[12] Advising him to stick to his regime of cold baths
and exercise, the doctor counseled deep breathing exercises in the open
air and walking at least four miles each day.

Merriman-Labor could smell the salt air as he approached the harbor.
In every direction, women in bright pink-and-yellow calico wraps balanced baskets of sweet potatoes and mangos on their heads as they
made their way toward the market. Not far from the wharf, he watched
naked boys splash each other under a water spigot, then shower an
enthusiastic dog. When he saw a barrister in black robes striding toward
the courthouse, white wig flung carelessly on his head, Merriman-

Labor wondered if he might be seeing a vision of himself three years from now. Nothing would make his parents prouder.

The dock buzzed with activity. Men heaved bags of palm kernels and groundnuts, heavy crates of fruit, and big drums of palm oil—the raw materials of empire—into flat-bottom sculls to be rowed out to a dozen or more European and American ships anchored in the harbor.

Merriman-Labor's friends and family gathered on the dock to see him off, pressing little gifts of sweets and coins into his hand. His mother, of course, could not be there. She had left years ago. Standing on the sun-bleached boards of the wharf, the gulls shrieking overhead, Merriman-Labor remembered the day she had left Freetown—twenty years ago now—very much like this one. He was only six years old. The handkerchiefs of well-wishers had fluttered over his head like a swarm of white butterflies as he nestled his shoulder against his grandfather's hip. He had watched the rowers splash their oars into the water and pull his mother away. Then the boat was gone, and he did not know when he would see her again. Her steamer had rumbled out of Freetown harbor and sailed north for nearly five hundred miles to Bathurst where she took up her position as the headmistress of St. Mary's School. This, his grandfather had told him, was a great achievement and the will of God. Despite his best effort, tears flooded the boy's eyes. He couldn't understand why she had left him behind. At six years old, Augustus Merriman-Labor discovered that the will of God was a very lonely thing.

Today, at the start of his three-thousand-mile journey, his father, the steely Joshua Labor, was probably there to see him off. Labor had left his mother when Merriman-Labor was very young. Like other first-borns who watch their fathers raise other families, he admired the man who kept him at arm's length. He respected his father's wide-ranging talents, especially what he called his *cacoethes scribendi*, "the insatiable urge to write."[13] Josh Labor had never been shy about composing letters to the editors of the Freetown papers and even published his own occasional magazine.

Most of all, Merriman-Labor loved the Michael Maurice Printing Works, his father's print shop. It was filled with the scent of fresh ink and dozens of wooden trays holding perfectly organized lead type. He knew precisely how his father's hands moved across the rows, swiftly picking out letters. He enjoyed watching him feed the clean white paper into the press with one hand, while turning the large wheel with the other until beautifully printed handbills or posters or holiday cards came spilling out.

As they stood on the breezy wharf, Labor must have warned his son to be mindful of his choices. If he went to London to gain accolades and failed, his relatives—both living and dead—would curse his name. But if he made them proud, if he returned to his people a successful barrister, a man of reputation and importance, he would be praised and his family celebrated for bringing such a person into the world.[14] The message couldn't have been clearer. As a barrister, he would be a son his father could be proud of. And if he were a writer?

Among the friends on the dock that day was the dapper Cornelius May. Twenty years Merriman-Labor's senior, the newspaper editor had taken a liking to the bright, bookish young man and had encouraged his literary ambitions. May had lived in London for seven years and plied his friend with advice about life in the big city—what museums to visit, which shops to frequent, and how to seek out both fellow countrymen and sympathetic Britons. He took pains to ensure that his young protégé was properly attired for his tour. Known for his stylish clothes—the front page of every issue of the *Sierra Leone Weekly News* advertised the latest fashions from London—May knew exactly what was required for a gentleman's life in the imperial capital. He made sure that Merriman-Labor's trunk included a dress suit, dinner coat, two waistcoats, dress shirt and tie, collars, shirts, cuff studs, cane, umbrella, silk hat, white gloves, flannel shirts, suspenders, and hot-water bottle. He instructed Merriman-Labor to keep a small case of calling cards in his breast pocket.

As was the custom at the time, a small entourage escorted the departing passenger to the vessel. From the deck of the *Anversville*, the visitors and passengers alike admired the panoramic view of Freetown's sandy beaches, its picturesque yellow and red houses tucked among banana and palm trees. At the signal to disembark, Merriman-Labor's friends and family enveloped him in hugs. There was no need to say what they must be thinking. Was this long journey to a distant land a good idea? Could someone with his fragile health survive the rough two-week voyage? How would his weak constitution stand up to London's notorious fogs and bone-chilling rain?

As a boatman rowed his companions to shore, Merriman-Labor leaned against the ship's railings and watched until he could no longer make out their faces. In the next instant, the steamer groaned into life and shuddered into motion.

Rough seas violently tossed the *Anversville* during the first half of his journey. The turbulence made some passengers so sick they couldn't leave their cabins. Those who did go on deck found themselves swaying like drunkards as the vessel lurched across the white-capped ocean. Dining, too, was a challenge when a sudden pitch could send wine or potatoes careening into the lap of one's dinner companion.

At first, the Christians on board gathered for daily prayer every morning and evening as Merriman-Labor's family had done at home. For him, life without these sacred punctuations of dawn and dusk was unthinkable. But as the weather improved and the congregation dwindled, he realized that only rough seas had swelled their little flock. As he and the other devout followed the liturgy and sang hymns, the rest of the passengers curled up in deck chairs, pitched quoits, or sent the biscuit along the deck in a game of shuffleboard. Apparently Christian piety was not exactly the spiritual cornerstone of British life that his missionary teachers had led him to believe.

Life aboard a steamer had its rhythms and rituals which Merriman-Labor quickly recognized. To his surprise the overarching pattern of the day was arranged around copious amounts of food. Onboard refrigeration made it possible to offer a vast array of items in the grand marble and wood-paneled dining room, and the breakfast menu alone included codfish in cream, kippered herring, steak, ham, bacon, potatoes, eggs, and fruit. After an enormous lunch, tea was served, including sausages or Welsh rarebit for those who had worked up an appetite napping in their deck chairs. Dinner was a lavish affair of six or seven courses followed by ice cream, cheese and coffee.

Passengers provided the entertainment to while away the tedious hours. When the familiar groove of after-dinner recitations and standard songs in the ship's saloon had grown wearisome, it is easy to imagine Merriman-Labor offering to perform a few of his magic tricks. Creating the right atmosphere would not have been hard. Instead of harsh electric light, he could illuminate the saloon with flickering candles. As his fellow passengers settled into plush velvet armchairs, he might have begun with a simple sleight of hand, pulling a florin from behind the sunburnt ear of a colonial officer. One can see him holding a heavy handkerchief high in the air and inviting the audience to examine it for imperfections. Once the audience admits it is without holes or flaws of any kind, a volunteer blindfolds him. He hands her a florin and asks her to spin it. She sends it whirling. It spins, wobbles, stops.

"Tails," he calls out. Tails it is. His assistant claps her gloved hands.

Three, four, five more times the coin spins. Each time the able magician knows which side is face-up.

Next, he places a large tub and a pitcher of seawater on the table and calls for red silk handkerchiefs. When three good-natured gentlemen offer theirs, he drops them into the tub and, to the astonishment of the audience, dumps the pitcher of seawater over them. He pulls out a dripping mess.

"Oh dear," he says, then taps the tub three times with his magic wand and reaches inside. Voilà! Three perfectly dry red silk handkerchiefs. With a dramatic sweep, he returns them to their owners. He bows as the ladies and gentlemen applaud. Some of the men hoot and whistle.

Suddenly, there is a burst of light and smoke. In the moment it takes to clear, the young man disappears.

The loud groan of the *Anversille*'s horn woke Merriman-Labor early. A thick fog had settled along the English coast, forcing the captain to bring the ship to a complete halt twenty miles from Southampton. So close to his destination, yet unable to reach it, he listened for hours as the horn bellowed out its sorrowful note. After ten idle hours in coastal waters, the *Anversville* finally steamed its way up the tidal estuary toward Southampton and the world of possibility that lay beyond.

In the afternoon light, the Southampton docks unfolded before him as an enormous tangle of wharves and warehouses, grain elevators and cattle jetties, cold-storage rooms and coal yards. Somewhere, he heard the bellowing of cows from the guts of a giant ship. An unfamiliar breeze stung his face as he descended to the shore. Not knowing which way to go, he joined a stream of people and found himself in the custom-house shed where he collected his luggage. The few black faces he saw along the way belonged mostly to sailors and laborers—rough, tired men loading coal or heaving carts.

The London and South Western Railway express stood just across from the pier. Its beautifully upholstered carriages carried passengers the seventy-eight miles to London in just an hour and forty-one minutes— more than four times faster than the speed of the Sierra Leone Government Railway. As they roared through the countryside, Merriman-Labor got his first view of the place he had read so much about. He caught glimpses of bridges, farms, and the grand lines of ancient manor houses attended by long avenues of oaks. He watched solitary homes rally into villages then disperse again into meadows and woods. When they entered suburban London, its gray monotony alarmed him: miles of grim streets lined with miles of grim houses. The train finally crawled into the vast iron-and-glass canopy of Waterloo Station and exhaled to a stop in a cloud of steam and smoke. He was in London.

He couldn't believe the buzz of commotion on a Sunday, which he had always been taught should be observed as the Lord's day of rest. All around him, porters pushed heavy wheelbarrows piled with luggage or struggled under armloads of rugs and handbags. Shrill-voiced newspaper boys shouted out headlines and waved their papers as if clearing smoke. Weaving through a confusing labyrinth of platforms, he made his way to the street where horse-drawn cabs were lined up two and three deep. He approached cautiously as the enormous, glossy horses whinnied, neighed, and tossed their heads. The smell around them was pungent, like rotting wood mixed with fresh grass. Tentatively, he pulled open the folding doors of a hansom cab and settled back onto the damp seat, keenly aware of the disquieting proximity of the horse's backside. He'd scarcely deposited himself, when the cabbie snorted out a quick shout, gave the reins a slap, and trotted the horse out of the station at an alarming clip. After a few incomprehensible turns, they emerged onto the brightly lit Westminster Bridge, the famous Thames flowing beneath. Ahead stood Big Ben, the Houses of Parliament, and all the promise of central London.

He couldn't believe how small the mighty Thames looked compared to African rivers. His school books seemed to have greatly exaggerated its impressiveness. "Nature has provided London with a navigable, but rather dirty-looking brook, the Thames," he joked, "which their geographers class under Rivers."[15]

But the city. The city at dusk was as magnificent as he had imagined. Two-thousand-candle electric lamps danced a chain of lights along the Victoria Embankment. Across the river, hotels and government buildings soared many stories high. To the east, the dome of St. Paul's towered over the skyline, God's faithful sentry. It was a perfect world, he thought, ready for everything he had to offer.

On his first day in the great metropolis, Merriman-Labor stood in the center of the urban bustle as throngs of people rushed by him. He must have contemplated what it would feel like to be in a city of white people, but he had not imagined how profoundly insignificant he would feel. He had never seen so few black faces and—grossly underestimating the actual population—supposed that "Negroes in London do not much exceed one hundred." They "are simply a nonentity," he told those at home, existing in England "the same way as a drop of water does in St. George's Bay in Freetown."[16] Even more disconcerting was the sight of white people sweeping gutters. In Sierra Leone whites held positions of importance—colonial administrators, nurses, businessmen, and missionaries. It was almost unthinkable to imagine them as poor laborers, maids of all work, or homeless beggars with "filthy broken boots," long nails, and clothes so full of holes one could see through them.[17]

Seemingly countless horses hauled vehicles of every description through the congested streets. Hanson cabs and four-wheelers swerved around wagons loaded with coal as omnibus drivers drew to a stop and shouted out their destinations. From time to time, a motor car rumbled past. As they paced along their weary way, the horses lifted their tails and spilled out crumbling wads of dung. The London streets, Merriman-Labor quipped, were not paved "in gold as people in Sierra Leone sometimes think, but with wood, tar, or stone, usually plastered over with mud and something (which for our present purpose must be nameless) left behind by the hundreds of thousands of horses."[18] Despite the best efforts of the scrawny boys in uniform who darted recklessly into the traffic with scoops and brushes to clean them, the much-admired streets of the capital were forever greasy with mud, dirt, and horse manure.

41

He couldn't believe that such an important city seemed to have no planning. Its streets were so narrow in places that he could stretch out his arms and almost touch buildings on both sides. And they were hopelessly zigzag. Not even a student of Euclid, he laughed, could find two that were parallel. It may be a modern urban center, he mocked, but it bore "the finger-prints of a barbarous age ... more suitable for some far-off towns in the Australian wilds."[19] He found the capital's deceptive place names perfect sport for jests. "The stranger is misled to think that there is a sea at the suburb of Chelsea or that of Battersea," he laughed. "He is surprised to find no shore or ditch at Shoreditch or Houndsditch. Nothing like a gate can be met at Ludgate, Bishopsgate, or Highgate. No similarity to a bar appears at Temple Bar or Holborn Bar. No shadow of a field exists at Snowfields or Moorfields, no cross at Charing Cross or King's Cross, and no hill worth the name at Ludgate Hill or Cornhill."[20]

Friends in Sierra Leone would be astonished to learn that no surface in London was safe from advertising. A poster of a Greek goddess proclaimed, "Beecham's Pills are worth a guinea a box." Next to it another displayed a giggling baby joyfully wielding a Gillette Safety Razor. Ads for Bovril meat extract, Pears Soap, and Milkmaid Condensed Milk plastered the sides of omnibuses. He became aware that "every conceivable thing under the sun" in London was for sale and anybody with a product had a poster, handbill, or gimmick. "Amidst the rush and crush and the noise and bustle of business," he thought, "only he who shouts loudest is heard most."[21] He must have wondered how he would ever make his voice audible above the clamor.

Coming from Freetown, which had no electricity, he was impressed by an electric plant that powered trams ten miles away, calling it "something above the comprehension of ordinary mortals."[22] The famous Tube was simply a "most wonderful piece of engineering." He marveled at the thought of people zipping along in electric trains two hundred feet below ground or striding through pedestrian passages under the Thames, while others cruised in steamships on the river above, strolled on bridges arching over the ships, and raced past in trains on elevated tracks. High above it all, workmen dangled from ropes as they installed telephone wires. Merriman-Labor dubbed the varied strata of London's technology: "Overhead and Underfoot,

Overground and Underground, Terrestrial and Celestial."[23] London possessed a geography of motion unlike anything he had ever known.

Perhaps most curious of all, in London his health improved.[24] Perhaps something in the English climate suited him, or British food ameliorated a nutritional deficiency. Maybe he found beneficial medical advice, or the excitement of a metropolis where few people knew him gave him a liberating sense of freedom.[25]

As a devout Anglican, he anticipated attending a service at St. Paul's Cathedral as a highlight of his spiritual life. He called its designer Christopher Wren a "great poet in brick and mortar," and the building a "masterpiece of architectural ingenuity." As he stepped inside during his first Sunday in London, the organ swelled, and warm light filtered through stained glass. He had no doubt this was "the house of God ... the gate of heaven."[26] But even sacred London was not what he had expected. "Such a sorry state of impropriety," he complained. Here, in this holy sanctuary, this magnificent house of the Lord, well-dressed people promenaded through the nave, more eager to see and be seen than to pray. They chatted as though they were in a public house rather than a place of worship. Tourists with their guidebooks and Kodaks shuffled around the monuments, sculptures, and paintings. Hardly anyone participated in the service. Even fewer sang the hymns. Accustomed to missionary preachers threatening "the everlasting fire and pain," he found the pastor's sermon distinctly tepid, especially on such a chilly March day. If any place needed hell-fires, he joked, it was England. The weather was so cold "we could conveniently do with twenty hell-fires together."[27]

Back at his lodgings, he discovered he had been the only one to attend services. In West Africa, he explained to his landlady and her daughters, anyone not attending church would be regarded as a hopeless sinner. They were amused by his piety and explained that "religion was a thing of the heart and not one of forms and ceremonies." They scarcely believed him when he told them that the Anglican church in Freetown kept a list of members who were expected to donate a penny a week to the congregation. When he suggested they hold family prayers together, they simply laughed. He retired to his room and blazed out a letter to his friends: "The Britons," he declared with delight, "are barbarians and heathens."[28]

Merriman-Labor was relishing London, but he had to decide whether this was going to be an extended holiday or the start of a radical new direction in his life. Should he return to the safety of Freetown, to his family and job, or should he risk everything for the chance to embrace all the metropolis had to offer?

There was pressure from home to study law. He had no passion for it, but it offered a respectable career path that could help him in his goal to improve the status of Africans. If the Colonial Secretary's Office would allow him a leave of absence for his whole term of study, he would not even have to give up his job security. Writing was his true calling, he knew, but law seemed the way forward.

But the study of law in London was a daunting enterprise with dubious returns. An advice book, *How to Become a Barrister*, advised aspiring lawyers not to pursue a career at the bar unless they had "a regular income of at least £250 a year, or a small fortune of at least £2000."[29] Merriman-Labor had neither. A business columnist cautioned that "there is probably no calling into which the poor man is at so great a disadvantage" because the financial burden of the legal profession extended well past one's studies and into the indefinite period it took to build a practice.[30] While a legal career delivered tremendous rewards for the few, it was not so generous with the many. According to the *English Illustrated Magazine*, of the seven thousand barristers on the Law List, only twenty-five or so reaped top incomes of £10,000 to £20,000 a year. Nearly three thousand, the writer ventured, were attempting to practice and "desperately clinging on." The rest, he added, made "practically nothing at all."[31]

Entering Lincoln's Inn—one of London's four Inns of Court— Merriman-Labor stepped into an ancient world of privilege and tradition. Cloistered from the busy city, its quiet squares featured a seventeenth-century chapel, celebrated gardens, and the oldest library in London. To enroll, he had to prove his mastery of English, Latin, and English history and provide character references.[32] It could not have been easy to hand over the £200 cost of admission—more than twice his annual clerk's salary. He felt the weight of the investment and hoped it would pay significant dividends.

He looked for lodging in nearby Bloomsbury, known for its cheap hotels and boarding houses, but also famously attractive to those longing to live by their pens. The adulterous Percy Bysshe Shelley and his pregnant girlfriend, Mary Godwin, had lived on Marchmont Street and Dickens had written *Bleak House* in Tavistock Square. In a few months, aspiring writer Virginia Woolf—for now the unpublished and unmarried Virginia Stephen—would move into 46 Gordon Square with her sister and brother. Journalist E.T. Cook envisioned a multitude of optimistic poets and novelists drawn to the promise of fame, only to starve in Bloomsbury garrets: "Bloomsbury to which place, it is said, more MSS. are returned than to any other locality in the British Isles." For her, Bloomsbury epitomized London as, in Thomas De Quincey's words, a stony-hearted stepmother. Indeed, she reminded her readers, the biographies of great writers sometimes recounted early trials, but of those who failed and gave up or who died in the process, "the submerged ones," as she called them, "you do not hear."[33]

On the threshold of his English literary career, Merriman-Labor was determined never to sink to the sorry depths of the "submerged ones." He began writing a series of articles called "Impressions of a Young African in England" for the *Sierra Leone Weekly News*, recording a world his readers might never know first-hand: London's soaring buildings, technological wonders, celebrated landmarks, and, of course, miserable weather.[34]

In 1904, some black men coming to the heart of empire to study and work encountered discrimination from the moment they arrived. Jamaican medical student Harold Moody—who would later found the League of Coloured Peoples—came to London not long after Merriman-Labor. Although he had a list of available lodgings from the YMCA, he wrote that "everyone seemed unable to take me." "England, the mother country whom I had learnt was bubbling forth with love and charity towards … colonials," he wrote, "had given me anything but a warm welcome."[35] But Merriman-Labor was lucky. He found a comfortable home at a Bloomsbury hotel where he received "the most considerate treatment" from the owners and enjoyed "delightful companionship" with the other guests.[36] He liked his situation so well that in the spring of 1904 he became a permanent lodger. Touristy, dingy, international, economical Bloomsbury became his home for six months.

Law school, it turned out, was frustrating, expensive, and tedious. Instilled with a love of rigorous study from his grandfather, he felt adrift in a program with no mandatory attendance or required reading. If one hired a "cram coach," there wasn't even any need for disciplined study before taking the exams. The benchers—the senior barristers who governed the Inn—only seemed to care that a student paid fees and kept terms. Keeping terms meant dining in the Great Hall six days each session—twenty-four dinners a year, for three years. They saw these meals as part of the Honourable Society's ancient founding traditions, a feature of life at the Inns of Court since the fifteenth century. They were not merely a "ritualistic gesture," the barristers believed, but helped introduce students to "the traditions and corporate spirit of the Society which they had joined, and the Profession to which they aspired."[37] Merriman-Labor found them pointless and expensive. It cost him three shillings and sixpence to join students, barristers, and prominent guests gathered at long polished tables in the hall where they consumed what he described as "huge pieces of meat and quarts of wine." Those studying law were not so much students, he mocked, as "*stewdents*." Forget rigorous study, he advised, "you will have to dine long and often, if you must be a barrister."[38]

To create a portrait of London for this readers, he posed as an anthropologist of Englishness, cataloging the denizens of the metropolis, from "the stalwart policeman, fine fellow, six feet high, fifty inches around the chest" to the "newspaper boy on his bicycle" darting in and out of "the mighty traffic of horses and vehicles" like an arrow. With pity he described elderly women tottering along, "bowed with the weight of eighty winters," "ill-clad, miserable looking" street boys, and destitute sandwich men, so desperate they fixed boards to their bodies and marched in the gutter for ninepence a day.[39] With advertisements strapped front, back, and even over their heads, they looked as if they were already in their coffins, buried alive by the demands of Edwardian commerce.

London noise was like nothing in Africa. Here a costermonger shouted *Apples! Brussels sprouts! Leeks!* as a Church Lads' Brigade band played their rousing marches. A "screeching Punch and Judy show" at the edge of a park did its best to overwhelm the tinny notes of the organ-grinder while a Salvation Army trombone groaned over both of them. "These noise-making people," he laughingly lamented, "should learn that though music hath charms, *charms* is only one step removed from *harms*." Only the song of the flower girl—*Who will buy my roses? Nice roses, three a penny*—brought "cheer and gladness" to the busy metropolitan heart.[40]

He soon grasped that London, regarded by well-to-do Sierra Leoneans as the place to attain refinement and sophistication, was all about conspicuous consumption. In May, "High Society" arrived from their giant country homes with four or five tons of luggage in tow. Grand residences in Mayfair and Belgravia heaved into life with scurrying servants, hampers of food, and mountains of bags, chests, and trunks.[41] A family of four could easily engage fourteen servants for their care and handling, although some households required many more. Radical aristocrat Arthur Ponsonby described a sixty-two-bedroom London home employing thirty-six indoor servants.[42] Needless to say, the gentleman who owned it engaged an even larger staff in his several country houses. The true god of this imperial world was money, Merriman-Labor recognized, as much of it as possible.[43]

Those in "the Smart Set, the Upper Tens, and the Golden Circle" lived by different rules from those of ordinary mortals. Walking through Hyde Park during the season, Merriman-Labor watched society people make their morning appearances on horseback on Rotten Row, a fashionable bridle path. One day a gentlewoman daringly rode "her horse astride like a man"—a decidedly bold practice in 1904.[44] In the afternoon, tall footmen—and prominent households only employed tall footmen—handed ladies into carriages to be whisked off to tea or calls or shopping at some exclusive establishment. It was not unheard of for tea parties to include high-stakes bridge games, where, it was said, even schoolgirls were known to lose £70 in an afternoon. Behind the elegant doors of grand houses, liveried footmen served ten-course meals, costing enough to support a charwoman and her family for two years. In a world of such extravagance, Merriman-Labor's encounters with the "smart set" came only in glimpses of black ties and glittering jewels as they sailed across the city pavements into receptions, balls, or theaters.

As much as Cornelius May had tried to make him fashionable for life in the big city, on his limited budget Merriman-Labor could never keep up with the requirements for a London man of fashion. The fashionable gentleman was expected to have twenty suits at the start of the season, enough for three changes of clothes a day.[45] And each activity—motoring, biking, yachting or lunching, for example—would have its own sartorial requirements. Supreme care for detail meant the gentleman's uniform—frock coat, silk top hat, stick and gloves—must reflect the current demands of style.[46] The size and shape of last year's hat could not possibly be smart enough for the new season.[47]

No one had prepared him for the mind-boggling poverty that lived in the shadow of this ostentatious wealth. He nearly buckled at the sight of an emaciated woman on a street corner, an infant in her arms, trying to sell matches to passers-by. A large dirty card pinned to her ragged blouse read: "Kind friend, have pity. I am the mother of eighteen, all starving."[48] She probably spent fourteen hours a day making matches that would earn her just a few pennies.

He sought out the poorest neighborhoods of the notorious East End to understand the suffering there, although he did not write publicly of the misery he observed. Jack London had recently described London's poorest neighborhoods in their full horror. The American writer recorded watching elderly men and women search "in the garbage … for rotten potatoes, beans, and vegetables, while little children clustered like flies around a festering mass of fruit, thrusting their arms to the shoulders into the liquid corruption, and drawing forth morsels, but partially decayed, which they devoured on the spot."[49] Thirty-five thousand dispossessed people—more than the entire population of Freetown—wandered the London streets each night. "The street bench," Merriman-Labor lamented, "is so hard and cold that this homeless wanderer cannot manage to lie outstretched on it." But, he added, "he *must* not lie outstretched on it."[50] As a student of the law he knew that sleeping on park benches was illegal. Notwithstanding his faith in British justice, such laws, he felt, created more suffering for people whose lives were already undone by hardship.

Any day of the week he saw men, women, and children in "the street parade of the battalion of Foodless Marchers." These processions of the poor straggled down dreary wet streets carrying dirty banners declaring "It's Work We Need, Not Charity." They rattled coin boxes in the hopes of a donation. Some called the unemployed men "loafers" who were too lazy to work. "Perhaps the truth is," kind-hearted Merriman-Labor ventured, "that he cannot find work."[51]

Even if the Colonial Secretary's Office granted him extended leave, he would need a job to support himself during law school, so he searched the city for a clerical position. With eight years of experience, he was well qualified, but that meant little in a saturated job market. Even though growing global markets had created a lot of clerical work, competition was fierce. Clerks now had to contend not only with a better-educated working class and, in certain cases, even with women, but with an influx of skilled Europeans. To make matters worse, companies tended to reject experienced clerks when they could hire the inexperienced for less money.[52] The novelist E.M. Forster dramatized the problem in his 1910 novel *Howards End*. When energetic capitalist Henry Wilcox tells do-gooder Margaret Schlegel that "he knew by his own office—seldom a vacant post, and hundreds of applicants for it," he is describing the employment market that Merriman-Labor faced.[53]

To survive, desperate men and woman resorted to anything that might earn them a coin. Some ran after cabs, opening doors for fine ladies or carrying heavy luggage for a tip. Others scavenged stray oats and hay from the street to sell to drivers, oiled garden gates for a halfpenny, or collected cigar butts for florists who used them for fumigation. In the early morning, men acted as human alarm clocks, using long rods to tap on windows to wake sleepers. The most desperate collected discarded newspapers and handbills to sell to the homeless as make-do blankets.[54] Perhaps the most heart-wrenching of all were the elderly crossing sweepers who brushed away manure from pedestrian crossings, so ladies and gentlemen could walk without dirtying their shoes or the hems of their expensive clothes. These old men and women were "too feeble to earn a living in any other way," children's writer Marian George observed, "dependent on pennies or halfpennies dropped into their hands by the people who hurry by."[55]

Job hunting left Merriman-Labor discouraged. "No one, not even a Briton," he complained, "can get a chance here, unless he is able to do an old work in a new way."[56] Being black only made matters worse. Some people were surprised that an African could speak English. "Even the sewage-man whose English is as bad as his job will consider himself better spoken."[57] Others were put off by his West African accent. To fit in, he sought out "refined" people who could help him develop a middle-class pronunciation. "Your best teachers," he advised his fellow Africans hoping to acquire conventional British enunciation, were "intelligent ladies of the middle class."[58]

Despite his qualifications, nothing was available. An African, he concluded, had no chance unless he could work "three times better than the best."[59] The conclusions of a parliamentary Committee of Inquiry into Distressed Colonial and Indian Subjects confirmed his experience. Investigating why colonial subjects had difficulty making a living in Britain, they identified "a prejudice in the labour market against the coloured British subject."[60] Racial discrimination made it impossible for him to get a position, and without the opportunity to support himself, he didn't know how he could continue law school or remain in England.

His exclusion from the workforce took a psychological toll. Unless you possess "tremendous energy," he wrote to friends back home, "which the non-recognition of our race entails on those who would succeed," he recommended they remain in Africa and find work there. "The raging sea of British clerkdom," he told them, was "too cold and rough" for the black man to swim.[61]

2

IMPRESSIONS OF A YOUNG AFRICAN IN ENGLAND

On June 7, 1904, just three months after arriving in London, Merriman-Labor joined four hundred people packed into the Clothworkers' Hall in Mincing Lane for a grand reception honoring the Alake of Abeokuta, a traditional ruler from south-western Nigeria.[1] Merriman-Labor's illustrious companion for the reception was almost certainly the distinguished Sierra Leonean clergyman George James Macauley.[2] As the guests waited for the Alake to arrive—he was having tea with the Mayor of London—they mingled and inspected samples of Abeokuta cotton and native cloth.

Under the glittering chandeliers of the hall, the two men rubbed shoulders with the wide range of people interested in African affairs, from colonial administrators to businessmen, from doctors to society ladies. The elegant oak-paneled room brimmed with luminaries.[3] During the reception, Merriman-Labor very likely sought out Edmund Dene Morel, who had advertised his newly launched *West African Mail* in the second edition of Merriman-Labor's Sierra Leone guidebook. Morel, a former shipping clerk, was engaged in a historic campaign to expose atrocities in the Congo. Through coercion, mutilation, and murder King Leopold of Belgium had enslaved thousands, perhaps millions, of people to create a private fortune in rubber and ivory. This was the horrific world of European exploitation Joseph Conrad had witnessed and dramatized in *Heart of Darkness*. In the loud, crowded hall, the tall, barrel-chested Morel was glowing. The first meeting of his new Congo Reform Association in Liverpool just two weeks earlier had attracted more than a thousand people. In the years to come, Morel's campaign would evolve into the biggest social justice movement of the day.[4]

At a quarter to four, a hush fell over the crowd as the Alake swept in, robed in a ruby tunic and embroidered tasseled cap. The audience applauded enthusiastically. His speech—given in Yoruba then translated by his secretary of state—described the warm reception he had received in Britain. "The best and noblest in England had welcomed him," reported his secretary. "It showed the great interest that England still took in Africa." While the Alake spoke, a large crowd gathered outside, eager to catch a glimpse of the African prince. According to the *African World*, as the Alake departed waving his elaborate goat's hair fly-swatter, the spectators cheered madly, shouting until they were hoarse.[5]

In the coming days, the Alake would be welcomed all over Britain, and the press keenly followed his travels, particularly the *Daily Mail*, which splashed a giant picture of him across the front page at the end of May. Merriman-Labor took the courtesy and attention given to the Alake as a sign of increasing goodwill toward Africans everywhere. But a streak of prejudice lurked below the gossamer of civility. It didn't take long to reveal itself.

In mid-June, the Alake journeyed to Scotland for a luncheon with the Provost of the University of Aberdeen. On campus, a group of students trotted alongside his open carriage, seemingly part of the enthusiastic crowd that had gathered to welcome him. Suddenly, one of the boys leapt into the carriage, knocked off the Alake's cap, and jammed a straw hat on his head, tearing his imperial gown in the process. The perpetrators scattered in all directions, leaving the Alake shaken and furious. At the elaborate banquet given in his honor, the Provost tried to explain the incident as boys having a bit of fun, but the Alake took the prank as an insult to his dignity. Deeply vexed, he refused to touch any of the food prepared for him.

The *Journal of Education* called the stunt a "disgraceful insult," noting that the culprits deserved to be suspended.[6] The *Lagos Standard* characterized it as a racist insult. For Theophilus Scholes, a Jamaican writer living in London, the incident served as example of growing racist attitudes in Britain. "Imagine," he wrote, "such an indignity ... offered to a prince of European blood." It was unthinkable. And these young men, he bemoaned, were "the future moulders of British opinion."[7] As punishment for their actions, the students were fined £10 each. Merriman-Labor rationalized the offence as youthful indiscretion and praised the swift penalty meted out by the university administrators. For him, the episode was an unfortunate consequence of poor upbringing, happily redeemed by a British sense of justice. He preferred to believe that such attitudes were held only by children and those who lacked education.

The following year Aberdeen University Press published the "Alakeia," a 240-line parodic poem in Greek hexameters "on the visit to Aberdeen of the Alake of Abeokuta ... descriptive of the saucy and mischievous humours and turbulence of some misguided learners."[8] The long, mock-scholarly introduction claimed that "of Alakes nothing is known" and his country, "Abiokouta," "is of course a mere fiction."[9] The poem with its faux footnotes, mock-Homeric verse, and parodic introduction was an elaborate farce lampooning not only the Alake himself, but the very idea of African sovereignty. Beneath the honors given to the African monarch seethed a reservoir of contempt. Merriman-Labor didn't yet understand that even educated people could despise others for the color of their skin.

"Now all nature is gay," Merriman-Labor wrote in midsummer as snapdragons spilled color over terraces, plane trees thickened with foliage, and wrens filled the air with birdsong. Never had he experienced such long days. The sky started to lighten as early as two in the morning, he explained to Africans who had never ventured so far north, and lingered "nearly as late as ten o'clock at night." Twilight was as beautiful, he assured them, as the lyric poets claimed. He felt a new energy invigorating the nation.

In a country where more than three-quarters of the people lived in cities, nature was a universal passion.[10] In the summer months, Britons fled their urban homes and poured into the countryside. The young poet Rupert Brooke relished "dancing and leaping through the New Forest ... singing to the birds, tumbling about in the flowers, bathing in the rivers, and in general, behaving naturally."[11] After each performance at the Lyceum, the famous actress Ellen Terry bolted to her farmhouse in Winchelsea. The writer Ford Madox Ford wore gaiters and loose-fitting clothes and grew vegetables at a cooperative farm in Surrey. When fellow writer H.G. Wells came calling, Ford served him homemade mead brewed according to a medieval recipe.[12] Even Toad in Kenneth Grahame's *The Wind in the Willows* escaped to his gypsy caravan to seek "the simplicity of the primitive life."[13]

Britons knew their ancient pastoral life only through books, but Africans, Merriman-Labor contended, could see the power of their ancestral ways in the lives of their aboriginal cousins. In an article he penned for *West Africa* comparing the lives of educated Krios in Sierra Leone with the indigenous people from the Protectorate, he argued that the indigenous were "strong, hardy, and robust," while the Krio were "sickly, weak, puny, and short-lived." "The educated Sierra Leonean," he bemoaned, "has no language of his own to-day ... he is neither English nor African."[14] One need only turn to the latest census, he argued, to see that Krios were dying out, and he blamed European influence for the decline. "Sudden deaths, and deaths by childbirth are prevalent," he wrote. "This is the result of white man's civilisation in West Africa."[15]

He could not blame his religion for African misfortune. For him, Christianity was "the greatest and most heroic and praiseworthy achievement of the past century in the interests of down-trodden humanity." But he could and did impugn the requirements for so-called civilization: a British education requiring Greek and Latin but no botany or agriculture; British clothes which were hot and binding; the habits of eating meat, smoking cigarettes, and drinking alcoholic beverages, as well as the expectation of living in airless stone buildings decorated with heavy furnishings. Krios were told that these things were evidence of civilization, he explained. They were led to believe "it is the proper thing to be English, and English they are." He called for Krios to be like those Britons seeking revitalization in the fields of Kent or Sussex, inviting them to "seek out the old paths and walk therein."[16] Joining his voice with the Romantic poets, with Brooke and Terry, with Ford, and even with Toad, Merriman-Labor advised his fellow Sierra Leoneans to "go back to Nature." He quoted Shakespeare as he counseled both Africans and Britons to find "tongues in trees, books in the running brooks, sermons in stones, and good in everything."[17]

Merriman-Labor was never more British, it would seem, than when he was encouraging his fellow Sierra Leoneans to abandon the trappings of British life and embrace an authentic existence in nature.

He found relief from his worries about his future in the intoxicating world of London's great music halls. One warm summer evening, he and John Roberts, a friend from Sierra Leone who had come to London to study pharmaceutical chemistry, joined the queue gathered in front of the London Pavilion in Piccadilly Circus.[18] When the doors opened, he and Roberts snaked along with the crowd across the red-carpeted lobby and up the marble staircase. As they inched forward, Merriman-Labor caught the scent of patchouli and jasmine as the ladies' perfume mingled with the lingering aroma of cigar smoke on men's jackets. In the grand auditorium an enormous dome swelled upward, garnished on every side with Corinthian columns and rippling tides of arches. The roof opened to the evening sky. Merriman-Labor and Roberts took their velvet-covered seats. All around them, flowers spilled out of hanging baskets, crimson tapestry draped private boxes, gilded mirrors shimmered, and a garden of floral paintings bloomed over the cream-and-gold walls. It felt like a palace.

In the expensive private boxes and the dress circle below, women encrusted with diamonds and sapphires arranged themselves in their seats while their gentleman stood waiting. Merriman-Labor couldn't have been more thrilled. "Everything and everybody being so brilliant and attractive," he whispered to his friend, my "heart seems to be striking with delight."[19] Then suddenly the curtain rose and the show began with an unexpectedly risqué ditty.

> "Girls, girls, how we love to please you,
> Girls, girls, how we love to tease you,
> Girls, girls, how we love to squeeze you,
> Spooning in the park.
> Girls, you may be plain or pretty,
> Girls, you may be dull or witty,
> But, girls, there's one thing I'm glad of
> You all look alike in the dark.[20]

When it ended, the crowd went crazy—clapping, cheering, and bellowing out, "Again! Once more!'"[21]

He loved everything about it: the music, the dancing, and the irreverent humor of the comic sketches. One dazzling act followed another—singers and then cyclists, skaters then acrobats. He saw trained animals, illusionists, burlesque actors, female impersonators, Japanese jiu-jitsu wrestlers, Chinese jugglers, Indian magicians, even black boxers.[22]

When ballet dancers pirouetted on stage, "the pick and the prime of England's youth and beauty," he felt dumbstruck. "Could these be human beings?" he asked. Dropping a sixpence into little boxes next to their seats, he and Roberts pulled out opera glasses to see more closely these women who look like cherry blossoms. Their beauty, it turned out, was a triumph of artifice. "God and the dressmaker, the hairdresser, the perfumer, and the milliner together," he quipped, had "made them half divine."[23]

He explained to Roberts that meeting a music hall artiste required both money and status. It was said that the London *jeunesse dorée*—young people of wealth and fashion—as well as military officers, men of standing, and men of cash, "bought the three or four front rows of the dress circle every evening in order to applaud" the lovely music hall performers. So-called Gaiety girls—named after the famous theater where they performed—dined with rich men and married peers of the realm.

"If you were sitting in a five-guinea box, and had name and money, you could send word to ask your fancy to come with a friend and take supper with you," he told Roberts. "But sitting as you are, in a five-shilling seat and without name or position in this country, if you send to ask one of them to meet you after the performance, you will no doubt be treated as a madman."[24] In London, having money mattered and showing you had money mattered even more.

After the performance, he and John Roberts strolled through Piccadilly Circus taking in the nightlife. Everywhere, laughing young people loped along the pavement. Wealthy men sipped coffee and puffed on cheroots in cigar divans. Ladies of the night lingered under the street lamps, casting seductive invitations in their direction. At coffee stalls, cabmen, policemen, and other thin-pocketed wanderers huddled together downing mugs of tea and fried eggs. Wandering as far as Fleet Street, they caught the smell of ink and heard the thump of newspaper presses as they pumped out the next morning's edition. In the wee hours, they watched men hose and scour the quiet streets, their voices rising together in the chorus of the latest music hall hit.

At a corner near Chancery Lane, not far from Lincoln's Inn, they stopped. Perhaps it was here that Merriman-Labor shared his bad news with Roberts. The Colonial Secretary's Office had denied his request for a three-year leave of absence.[25] If he wanted to stay in London, he would be forced to resign his civil service post. Now he must decide. Did he want to hold on to his job security even if it meant dropping out of law school and returning to Freetown? Was he willing to surrender his dream of literary success in England?

As they talked, "a poor sickly-looking man" approached and asked for alms. "This beggar's condition was so apparently pitiable," Merriman-Labor remembered, "that we raised about sixpence ... and gave it to the poor fellow." Taking the coins, the old man shuffled off. "No sooner had he gone ten yards from us," Merriman-Labor wrote, "than he shouted, at the same time, taking to his heels, 'Nigger, nigger, show me your tail, your coal-black tail!'"[26] In return for the coins they could ill-afford to give, this disgusting epithet had been hurled at them. In the workings of race and class in Edwardian England, even a beggar felt himself superior to respectable gentlemen if their skin happened to be black.

At the same time, London offered liberties Merriman-Labor might never have in his colonial home. He was free to pursue his career as a barrister, marry a white woman if he wished (even though it would have been frowned upon), buy property, live where he wanted, and, if he met the income, property, and residency requirements, vote in local and parliamentary elections.[27] The opportunities for learning were unsurpassed, and Merriman-Labor wanted to partake in the feast of knowledge available through "evening classes, public libraries, museums, exhibitions, botanic and zoological gardens."[28] During his many walks in Hyde Park, he surely stopped at Speakers' Corner and heard, like George Ponderevo in H. G. Wells's *Tono-Bungay*, "men discussing the very existence of God, denying the rights of property, debating a hundred things that one dared not think about" at home.[29] He could scarcely imagine another place so full of exciting possibilities. He must have felt much as Charlotte Brontë did when she confessed, "I like the spirit of this great London which I feel around me. Who but a coward would pass his whole life in hamlets; and for ever abandon his faculties to the eating rust of obscurity?"[30]

In July, a heat wave sizzled through Britain, bringing temperatures in London to a sweltering 90° Fahrenheit. "It has been so exceedingly hot this month," Merriman-Labor laughingly complained to his Sierra Leone readers, "one wonders whether he is in tropical Africa or in England."[31]

Friendly Britons reached out to Merriman-Labor and delighted in showing him around their country. A "kind gentleman and his amiable lady living in the neighborhood," he wrote, treated him to outings every Wednesday. In their company, Merriman-Labor explored all manner of tourist sights including the Naval Museum in Greenwich, Hampton Court Palace, Leith Hill, the Botanic Gardens, the Zoological Gardens, Windsor Castle, and the seaside town of Whitstable—famous for its oysters.[32]

In September, as their train rumbled eastward toward the popular seaside resort of Herne Bay, Merriman-Labor's host pointed out the abandoned hundred-and-twenty-foot Tower of Jezreel sitting atop Chatham Hill in Kent. This incredible structure had been built in the 1880s by the followers of James White, a former private in the British Army who took the name Jezreel and believed himself a prophet. The tower was meant to house the elect until the Day of Judgement. Merriman-Labor was amused by the "fanaticism of a sect of Christians who imagined that the Master at his second coming would descend on the spot where the Tower now stands."[33] Despite the unusual practice of wearing long hair tucked under purple caps, White's fourteen hundred followers managed to raise £100,000 to construct their settlement. Yet, even with such considerable efforts, the tower was never finished.[34] When White died in 1885, the sect collapsed, and the money to complete it dried up. Only its fireproof stone walls—built to withstand the expected inferno on Judgement Day—survived. Tickled by the remains of this modern Tower of Babel, Merriman-Labor joked that God "dispersed the workmen, not this time by an increase of tongues, but by a decrease of funds."[35]

Another bizarre sect in the news at the time was the Agapemonites, led by defrocked Anglican clergyman J.H. Smyth-Pigott, who believed he was the Messiah.[36] When Smyth-Pigott announced his divinity to the public in 1902, police had to protect him from a violent mob. Recently, a Plymouth man had made headlines by claiming that the group had "robbed him of his wife."[37] The *Daily Mirror* proclaimed that "Wealthy but Foolish Women Flock to the 'Abode of Love,'" the sect's retreat in Somerset, and that a "large number of wealthy people" had joined.[38] The *Daily Express* titillated its audience by reporting that their temple looked "more like a ladies' boudoir than a place of worship." Supposedly the congregation consisted mostly of "women ... dressed in the height of fashion, endowed with wealth, health, and beauty—with everything in this world that is prized" along with a few "old, decrepit specimens of humanity" and some innocuous youths. The decor of the Abode of Love, the newspaper claimed, flowed with the "richest red silk plush," including a pulpit "emblazoned with gold and precious stones."[39]

The missionaries in Sierra Leone who had instructed Merriman-Labor had neglected to mention that Britons in this period "floated new sects as optimistically as they floated new railway companies," as historian John Kent explains, and with equally bewildering results.[40] In his articles for the *Sierra Leone Weekly News*, Merriman-Labor didn't need to sensationalize the stories of Jezreel or the Agapemonites; his readers would have been appalled to learn that a former Anglican clergyman was declaring himself the Messiah and had amassed a band of devoted followers. Africans had long endured articles by European travel writers fixated on weird religious sects on their continent. Now Merriman-Labor gleefully revealed that the home country had its share of bizarre spiritual encampments as well.

In Herne Bay, Merriman-Labor took his first ride in a motor car. He had seen them in London, of course, where they dashed "with headlong haste at the rate of some seventy miles an hour through the congested streets," terrorizing "peaceful citizens on foot." But one turn in a car won him over. "Our men of wealth should import them," he suggested, even though the cost could run as high as £2,000.[41] Later, he would befriend A.W. Leslie, an African American rubber dealer who was probably the first black man in Britain to own one of the fast, new machines, and in the days to come, Merriman-Labor surely enjoyed roaring through the streets of Islington in Leslie's sleek automobile.

On August 10, 1904, Merriman-Labor took a dramatic leap of faith. He composed a letter to the Under-Secretary of State for the Colonies thanking the government for nine years of respectable employment in the civil service and tendered his resignation.[42] London, he had decided, would be the place where he would risk everything to become the writer who proved Africa's importance to the world.

Changing British minds about Africa was daunting, especially when something as seemingly innocuous as a children's play underscored black inferiority. On November 23, 1904, snowflakes were just starting to come down as a matinee of *Little Black Sambo and Little White Barbara* was beginning at the Garrick Theatre. The *Daily Mirror* had given the play a rave review the day before, describing it as a story about a little girl who lives in "the country of coons" and a black boy who must teach her to laugh. "The gem of the performance," the review noted, was the enactment of the poem "Ten Little Nigger Boys"—a children's learn-to-count verse.

TEN LITTLE NIGGER BOYS

Ten little nigger boys went out to dine;
One choked his little self, and then there were nine.

Nine little nigger boys sat up very late;
One overslept himself, and then there were eight.

Eight little nigger boys traveling in Devon;
One said he'd stay there, and then there were seven.

Seven little nigger boys chopping up sticks;
One chopped himself in half, and then there were six.

Six little nigger boys playing with a hive;
A bumble-bee stung one, and then there were five.

Five little nigger boys going in for law;
One got in chancery, and then there were four.

Four little nigger boys going out to sea;
A red herring swallowed one, and then there were three.

Three little nigger boys walking in the zoo;
A big bear hugged one, and then there were two.

Two little nigger boys sitting in the sun;
One got frizzled up, and then there was one.

One little nigger boy living all alone;
He got married, and then there were none.[43]

"A huge white bear had hardly hugged one little nigger boy to death," the reviewer gushed, "before another was shriveled up by the sun and disappeared." Delighted by the production and impervious to its genocidal theme, the reviewer declared that "every child in London ought to see the piece."[44] No one seemed to notice the glaring message that black children were disposable.

By the time the audience emerged from the theater, snow was falling heavily. This was Merriman-Labor's first experience of an English winter. "Just fancy," he wrote to those in tropical Sierra Leone, "all the roads, roofs of buildings, trees, and everything else, under the broad canopy of heaven, being covered over in all directions with a thick blanket or sea of white."[45] The icy temperatures froze lakes, ponds, and small rivers. Imagine, Merriman-Labor told his African readers, thousands of people skating and jumping and dancing on a river that was full of ships just two days earlier. With this first blast of real cold, he discovered that he hated wearing an overcoat. Two undershirts "of the best wool each with a double front" were all he needed to stay warm. He reported to worried friends back home that the winter didn't bother him at all. "Personally," he assured them, "I do not suffer from the rough handling of dreary winter."[46]

On December 16, he undertook a literary rite of passage: he wrote to the British Museum Library requesting a reader's ticket.[47]

Demand for access to the famous library's two-and-a-half-million volumes was high and admission strictly limited. As *A Guide to the Reading Room* explained, the library was "a literary workshop and not a place for recreation, self-improvement or reference to books obtainable elsewhere."[48] One applied for a reading ticket by giving details about profession, qualifications, and scope of studies. A letter of recommendation from a "person of recognised position" with personal knowledge of the applicant was essential.[49] In his request, Merriman-Labor explained that he was a law student seeking admission "for the purpose of research in preparing a special work in the interest of my country—Sierra Leone" and mentioned that he was a fellow of the Society of Authors. He included a letter of recommendation from British friend William Curtis Edmonds, an eighty-year-old bookseller. They had met six months earlier, and Edmonds had taken an immediate liking to Merriman-Labor. In his letter, Edmonds assured the library of their close acquaintance.

To fully understand Merriman-Labor's relationship with Edmonds we would have to wring more of the past than it offers, but we do know this: Edmonds went out of his way to make his young friend feel at home. After Edmonds's death, Merriman-Labor's mother sent a wreath and marble tablet to be placed on his grave in Norwood Cemetery. The inscription read, "a human tribute from beyond the seas, in testimony of a West African mother's appreciation of the incessant efforts of our departed brother, William Curtis Edmonds, during his lifetime, to make her son feel himself less a stranger in the White man's country."[50] Thinking perhaps that an intellectual black man might be an anomaly for the library, Edmonds made sure to identify Merriman-Labor's race—"coloured"—then lauded his young friend with a Victorian trinity of virtues, saying he was "high principled, educated, and gentlemanly."[51]

The acceptance letter Merriman-Labor received from the library a few days later encouraged his sense of destiny. It was further proof that he was a professional in the world of letters. He readied to take his place in the sacred institution of learning, confident that his literary career was unfolding as it should.

A paralyzing London fog descended on December 21, 1904, delaying Merriman-Labor's first trip to the library. London was notorious for its fog—a combination of natural mists, soot, and sulphur dioxide that tended to collect on still, cold days—but Merriman-Labor had never experienced anything like it. Daytime grew dark as night and every lamp in the house had to be lit. The mist was so "thick and black that if you stretch your hand it will be impossible for you to see it," he wrote.[52] The *Daily Express* reported that street lamps were invisible even when one stood next to them.[53] Throughout the city, omnibus horses scrambled "in the impenetrable darkness" until "conductors took the lamps from the doorways and walked ahead of the horses as pilots."[54] Vehicles were backed up for hours in Piccadilly and Charing Cross. Christmas shopping came to a standstill. "The nervous dare not venture out," wrote Merriman-Labor, "unless guides with thick blazon lights known as devil fires, lead them for a penny each across places where two streets meet."[55] Pedestrians joined into small groups for protection as they groped their way along the damp sidewalks. Although policemen with lanterns and flaming torches were dispatched to help, several people stumbled into the Thames and drowned.[56]

When the fog finally lifted, Merriman-Labor pushed through the swinging doors into the Great Hall of the British Museum. At the entrance to the library a clerk exchanged his acceptance letter for the coveted reader's ticket, and he entered the inner sanctum.

A giant dome soared a hundred and six feet over the round hall, its gold-gilded ribs and azure panels browned with age. Sunlight poured in from a round window at the top.[57] In the middle of the hall, two concentric rings of catalogs encircled the raised Superintendent's desk like rays of light emanating from the sun. Thirty-five glossy tables flared outward, seating for 458 readers including Merriman-Labor. Writers whose names would soon be famous might have been there with him. Rupert Brooke, T.S. Eliot, Ezra Pound, and Virginia Woolf all held reader's tickets at this time and may have been thumbing through the catalog or sitting at a desk nearby.[58]

Tucking his reader's ticket into his breast pocket, Merriman-Labor selected a seat at one of the tables. Each place came with a number, glow lamp, mahogany chair, folding shelf, pen rack, penwiper, and inkstand. From the catalog, he copied titles and pressmarks on tickets and placed them in a basket at the central desk. Receiving books was time-consuming, but he waited happily as attendants navigated the forty-four miles of shelving to locate his chosen volumes and deliver them to his seat.[59] Merriman-Labor examined the stack of books before him. He reached for the one at the top and opened it. If later developments are any indication, it could have been Beatrice Webb's *Cooperative Movement in Great Britain* or C.F. Bastable's *Theory of International Trade*. But then again, it might have been something entirely different. Maybe it was *The Princess Passes: A Romance of a Motor-car*, the current runaway bestseller by the scribbling couple Charles and Alice Williamson.

As he entered the dining room of his Bloomsbury hotel that evening, the proprietor pulled him aside and asked if he would mind changing his mealtime. Fluttering one hand toward a party already seated, the man explained that they were Americans who did not want to dine in the company of a black man.

"I am not prepared to change my meal time one second to please them or the likes of their kidney," Merriman-Labor told him. He approached the table and informed the Americans that he was not only a permanent lodger at the hotel, but a British subject.

"I have a better right to this hotel and better right in this country than any of you," he announced. With enormous dignity, he took his customary place.

His waiter handed him a menu as the Americans retreated.

"Looks like they have decided to change *their* mealtime," the waiter noted dryly.

"Which," Merriman-Labor observed with hard-won composure, "they have a perfect right to do."[60]

London's religious fascinations never ceased to amaze him. On February 4, Torrey and Alexander, American revivalists who intended to take "London by storm for Christ," opened to an audience of twelve thousand people at the Albert Hall.[61] Merriman-Labor reported that both the "curious and the earnest thronged the sitting and standing capacity of the great Hall" to hear Dr. Torrey's message and listen to Mr. Alexander's thousand-member choir. It was odd, he thought, that they would pitch their battle for souls in the "rich and aristocratic West" of London "as if it is an easy thing to get the rich to enter the Kingdom of Heaven."[62]

As the Americans saved souls through their West End revival palooza, Merriman-Labor had more practical religious matters in mind when he joined some two hundred people at St. Barnabas Church in the poverty-riddled borough of South Lambeth to discuss how to teach Sunday School. He captured the audience's attention with his bold remarks about the narrowness of the Anglican catechism, and his recommendation to use Christian teachings beyond the church's own traditions. According to the *Church Times*, "the best speech was made undoubtedly by an African gentleman."[63] He made a particularly strong impression on the "Railwaymen's Parson," Canon Allen Edwards, who had established the London and South Western Railway Servants' Orphanage in Clapham two decades earlier. Railroad work was extremely dangerous—nearly five hundred workers had been killed in 1903 alone—and the orphanage took children of deceased railwaymen whose mothers could not afford to support them. Impressed by the young African's ideas and knowledge of Scripture, Edwards recruited him into service. By summer, Merriman-Labor reported to his readers that he was "conducting a Sunday School of about eighty English boys" at the orphanage.[64] The work couldn't have added much, if anything, to his pocketbook, but it felt like a wonderfully ironic twist of fate: a son of Africa bringing Christianity to British schoolchildren.

The common wisdom in Freetown said the study of law was the most effective way to create social change. But after living in Britain for more than a year, Merriman-Labor made the telling realization that "the lawyer per se did not count."[65] Only one thing conferred power in London and that was money—and lots of it. Men of wealth controlled finance, directed newspapers, influenced government, raced their loud, expensive cars through the streets, and married Gaiety girls. Those with large bank accounts rather than impressive pedigrees penetrated the bastions of high society. As society hostess Lady Dorothy Nevill commented, "birth today is of small account, whilst wealth wields an unquestioned sway."[66] He saw, too, that the power of money applied not just to individuals, but to countries. "The wealthiest nations," he concluded, "have the last word in the affairs of the universe." No one, he asserted, "not even a lawyer, could be an effective champion without wealth behind him."[67]

He now dismissed Sierra Leonean Bishop James Johnson's idea that Christianity was the key to racial harmony; he questioned American Booker T. Washington's faith in education; he "begged to differ" with Liberian Edward Blyden, who contended that black individuality was the source of racial strength; he disputed Gambian Chief Justice Renner Maxwell's philosophy of miscegenation; and he rejected Jamaican Theophilus Scholes's claim that "the force of arms will make us powerful." His own observations convinced him that the "Negro race is powerless and despised chiefly because as a whole it is poor" and that wealth was the way to "solve the Negro problems."[68]

"If Africa is to be powerful," he decided, "she must be wealthy." The continent abounded in natural resources, and Europeans were making fortunes from them. Some of London's wealthiest men were called "Randlords," after the location of the mines in South Africa where they had made millions in diamonds and gold. West Africa, too, possessed gold (to the tune of £345,000 from the Gold Coast alone in 1904), and also cotton, rubber, and highly prized palm kernels that could be converted into margarine and soap or used as oil for explosives and machine lubrication. Moreover, eighty million people of African descent bought £125,000 worth of British goods annually, a sizable consumer market. Merriman-Labor calculated West African trade was worth £50 million a year.[69]

In early 1905, as he prepared for his constitutional law and legal history exams, he also threw himself into a self-directed study of commerce. As part of his education, he toured the Bank of England where he stood in gold-weighing rooms filled with thousands of sovereigns and saw vaults holding "about fifty million pounds of solid cash." Each year, this Old Lady of Threadneedle Street, as the enormous, three-acre building was nicknamed, handled business which ran into the billions of pounds sterling. Nearby commercial houses, he discovered, could boast "a turnover of a hundred thousand pounds in one day." This was, he observed, truly "the richest spot on earth."[70]

He also became keenly interested in the British rail system. Standing within the mighty walls of St. Pancras station, which loomed fifty times bigger than the station at Freetown, he noted that eight hundred trains moved in and out daily. He calculated that the 50,624 miles of track covering the country meant that "the Railway lines of the United Kingdom, if laid in a straight course round the world would encircle this mighty globe over two times." The sheer numbers staggered him: 580,000 employees, 23,000 locomotive engines, and 1 million carriages which, he learned, conveyed "no fewer than 1,195,265,000 passengers" in 1903 and brought in £48 million. Considering these facts, he concluded, "we are brought face to face with the stupendous magnitude of the achievement."[71]

But the revenue wasn't the real source of Merriman-Labor's admiration. What excited him was the idea of human cooperation in a great enterprise. "Just think," he remarked "that all these great developments are brought about by the combination of a few individuals who know how to collect a pound here from this man and a pound there from that."[72] The key was cooperation. He saw the same principle at work with the London and South Western Railway Servants' Orphanage where the railway workers owned the orphanage themselves, famously using collection dogs mounted with brass boxes on padded saddles to solicit donations. Through their own initiative—and the use of dogs willing to shake hands, bark, or perform tricks for a contribution—they were able to help the children of fellow workers killed in the line of duty.[73]

He was inching toward an idea he believed had the power to transform Africa's future. He researched British cooperative organizations, which taught poor people how to organize, pool their resources, and increase their buying power. In 1904, Britain boasted nearly fifteen hundred such societies with nearly two million members nationwide.[74] Merriman-Labor became convinced that success came from people joining together. "Truly," he concluded, "unity is strength."[75]

During his time in London Merriman-Labor sometimes felt like a target for beggars, confidence men, and those who wanted "to know how well or badly" he could speak English. Taking him for a wealthy man, some rapscallion would "send a polite note for a five-pound loan" or ask for an invitation "to spend an evening at the theatre or a week end at the sea-side" after making his acquaintance. He was amused to discover how many Britons believed "that every Negro with a decent overcoat and a clean collar is an African prince."[76]

He met white Britons who were welcoming, but whose ideas about black people were, as he generously put it, "very limited."[77] One eccentric British matron—no doubt combining the superstition "touch a nigger for luck" with the ancient practice of "first footing"—insisted that he visit her at the stroke of midnight on New Year's Eve to give her good fortune in the coming year. Merriman-Labor kindly obliged her and later observed that she had indeed been lucky in the New Year. All her earthly pains, he joked, had been relieved when she shuffled off her mortal coil. During a visit to a family in Stockwell, South London, a little girl asked if his hands and face were the only black parts of his body. "Little Mary," he continued, "being a child who had been properly trained, did not bother to use her tongue and spittle on my hand to see if the blackness will come off."[78]

Through his developing contacts, he became acquainted with men in high places. An introduction to Sir William Baillie Hamilton, a senior member of the Colonial Office, brought an invitation to join the Corona Club, a social organization founded in 1900 for current and former civil servants of Britain's Crown colonies.[79] Earlier in the year, he had met William Court Gully, the Speaker of the House. On March 20, he reported, "the Speaker graciously granted me a permit to enter the House of Commons." There the boisterous debate surprised him. "One member rose and made a long speech, amidst vociferous cheers of his party," he recalled, "and the noisome laughter and display of indifference on the part of the opposition." How the House was able to do business "in the midst of confusion" confounded him. In time, he would become discouragingly familiar with the workings of Parliament especially when it dealt with questions relating to Africa.[80]

He left his comfortable Bloomsbury hotel in early 1905 and took cheaper accommodation in South London. William Edmonds, who had owned a bookstore at 420 Brixton Road for fifty years, probably persuaded him to relocate to "London across the water" in order to stretch his savings.[81] The move meant traveling five miles to the Inns of Court, but inexpensive electric trams made commuting quick and affordable. After living in central London, he found the monotony of the suburbs comically dull. A stranger "has to keep in mind the number of his residence," he laughed, "otherwise, he may have to enjoy the unenviable experience ... of being turned out from the bedroom of a neighbor."[82]

South London was home to artisans, teachers, clerks, prosperous shopkeepers and other professional people with incomes that allowed them to live in comfort. But it also contained great swathes of poverty. Charles Booth's London survey had surprised Britons by revealing that the number of poor in South London exceeded that of the East End. While living in Brixton and Stockwell, Merriman-Labor learned the hard way that certain neighborhoods were dangerous for him. "In the low class suburbs a black man stands the chance of being laughed at to scorn until he takes to his heels," he wrote. There, "bad boys will not hesitate to shower stones or rotten eggs on any passing black man." Even schoolchildren in these areas could be hateful. "They will call you all kinds of names, sing you all sorts of songs," he recalled, "whilst following you about until a passing vehicle flies you out of their sight."The so-called fairer sex was no less venomous. White factory girls, he reported, "will make fun of you by throwing kisses to you when not making hisses at you, whilst others shout 'Go wash your face guv'nor' or sometimes call out 'nigger! nigger! nigger!'"[83]

Although afraid for his safety at times, he took a philosophical attitude toward those who felt entitled to sling stones or shout insults. "Such words or actions, to my mind," he wrote, "are but the result of an early defective training, of a misdirected education which tends to make them ... appear as Negro-haters." Possessing a faith in the basic goodness of people, he believed that with better education and mature deliberations, such people would soon show themselves "as friends of the Negro." He still firmly believed that all people were "members of the great human family."[84] In the coming years, this readiness to see the best in people would be sorely tested.

3

THE AFRICAN GENERAL AGENCY

If Merriman-Labor had been a different man, 1905 could have destroyed him. His savings dwindling, he might have abandoned law school, packed his bags, and returned home defeated. But to realize his dream of literary success, he knew he had to stay in London and that meant finding a way to make money. He needed to discover something new, something bold and original.

Since the previous summer, he was very likely augmenting his savings by working as the London agent for his father's auction business. About the time he resigned his civil service job, his father had begun to advertise "Labor Labor and Co., Licensed Auctioneers," which held weekly auctions in Freetown promoting "consignments of Merchandise from England ... received and disposed of to advantage."[1] Lincoln's Inn was not far from the commercial district where Merriman-Labor could buy bargain goods from salvage warehouses, bankruptcies, and clearance auctions to send to his father. Navigating London commerce for nearly a year may have inspired him to do on a large scale what he was doing for his father on a small one.

His idea was big. Preaching a gospel of commerce, cooperation, and self-sufficiency, Merriman-Labor argued that wealth would come to Africa "when we understand that it will pay us a million times better ... if ... we can convert our cotton to cloth, our palm-oil to butter and soap, the rubber into tires, instead of allowing the foreigner to enrich himself by taking these products away."[2] Africans were not yet in a position to manufacture, but he would help them with the first step. By setting up a company that would buy and sell on behalf of native traders, he would get the best value on their investments as well as the best prices for their products. By cutting out the European middleman, he and his customers would bring about a fundamental shift in imperial relations. If he could persuade Africans to join into cooperative groups, they would at last be able to compete with the large European firms that dominated West African trade. In time, they would generate capital and develop their own manufacturing and agricultural industries. He would be the mercantile agent not motivated merely by profit, but by a sense of duty toward his fellow Africans. He called his new business the West African Agency and Information Bureau.

The most inventive part of the enterprise was the Information Bureau, an international Afrocentric network connecting customers with reliable sources of information, goods, and services. Something like an Edwardian LinkedIn, it would provide information "on any subject whatsoever." The possibilities listed in one of his advertising circulars ranged from the practical to the occult. "You can consult us," he wrote, concerning:

> African Affairs, Agriculture, Amusements, Arts, Astrology, Banks and Finance, Commerce, Current Topics, Education, Engineering, Fortune-telling, Freemasonry, Friendly Societies, Governments, Health Resorts, Hotels and Apartments, Insurance, Industries, Investments, Journalism, Law, Literature, Manufactures, Medicine, Mining, Money Markets, Music, Palmistry, Patents and Inventions, Philanthropy, Phrenology, Politics, Polytechnic, Printing and Lithography, Professions, Railways, Religion, Science, Shipping, Spiritualism, Stocks and Shares, Trades, etc.[3]

He envisioned the West African Information Bureau as an essential contact point bringing together investors, suppliers, buyers, producers, clients, and advisors. The information, services, and products that could be offered were limitless. Working as a commercial agent had not been in his original plan. But it just might allow him to stay in London, finish his law degree, fulfill his duty to his people, and write the books he dreamed would change the world.

As he planned his new business, the promise of open spaces lured Merriman-Labor farther south to the suburb of Dulwich, "a select neighborhood," he wrote, "so quiet, so country-like." He loved this "garden of the South" for its beauty and safety.[4] Because it possessed no electric trams connecting it to central London, he noticed that "working men and labourers and men of that class avoid Dulwich." Thinking of the harassment he endured in other neighborhoods, he added, "and it is well for the student that they do."[5]

He enjoyed outings with John Roberts and other African friends who lived in the area. "Many a bright Saturday afternoon," he recalled, "we have cycled thirty miles, thither and back," often to Richmond, which he called one of his "favourite haunts." Cycling had been wildly popular in Britain for a decade, and except for the frightening traffic which contained an ever-growing number of motor cars and motor omnibuses, Merriman-Labor found it "an ideal pastime." Other days during that temperate summer, he and Roberts took to the water, boating at Dulwich Park.[6] Rowing to the middle of the shimmering three-acre lake, they drifted under the blue afternoon sky, talking about England, home, and the life unfolding before them.

But these idyllic summer afternoons were bittersweet. Eight West Africans would be called to the bar in the coming weeks. Eight friends would collect laurels from their respective Inns of Court, pack their bags, and make the long journey home. Few black barristers made their careers in Britain. Their place, everyone seemed to agree, was in the colonial system. With a few exceptions, black lawyers lived in Britain as sojourners; no one—not even their families and friends— expected them to stay.

"This month has been pre-eminently one for Negroes," Merriman-Labor announced in July 1905. "We are in evidence everywhere in England." He reported "naked Somalis," "pigmies", and "about 40 Negro Messengers from America" all in the capital that summer.[7] Eager to publicize the popularity of Africans in Britain, Merriman-Labor did not delve too deeply into the nature of their celebrity. If he had, he might have been better prepared for later events.

The Colonial and Indian Exhibition—one of the biggest draws of the summer, packing crowds into the Crystal Palace—brought Merriman-Labor's friend James Jonathan Thomas to town. Thomas, a prosperous Freetown businessman and legislator, arrived in London with a display of native-made gold ornaments for the exhibition. For Sierra Leoneans, Thomas embodied a true success story. He had made a fortune in Lagos, then returned to Freetown, where he served on the city council, supported numerous charities, and even endowed the public library. He was presented to King Edward at St. James's Palace and was celebrated in the London press as a "West African Diplomatist." Several national magazines featured his portrait in full court dress—white gloves, black waistcoat, velvet knee breeches, silk hose, steel buckled shoes, and a sword—although it is unclear if the pictures were honoring him as an ambassador or mocking him as a freakish curiosity.[8]

Merriman-Labor's conversation with one of the African American delegates of the Baptist World Congress inspired his patriotism. Thousands of Baptists from all over the globe were gathering in Exeter Hall to discuss issues related to "their mission … to save and uplift humanity everywhere." The Reverend J.H. Shakespeare, the British secretary of the congress, explained that the "picturesque element was supplied by the negro brethren, of whom about fifty were present." American representatives were astonished by the friendliness of the British toward the black delegates. "Indeed," Shakespeare wrote, "the cordiality of their reception was so marked that one American was heard to say, 'Would you rather be the governor of your State or a negro delegate in London?'"[9] Merriman-Labor met Dr. Frank of Louisville, who confessed that "he was not prepared to find Negro Barristers and Doctors practising and Negro Clergymen under employment in England." Frank declared at the end of his visit that Britain was "far in advance of America in international and inter-racial relations." The thought of black British subjects at the vanguard of racial advancement pleased Merriman-Labor, who proudly reported Frank's praise to the readers of the *Sierra Leone Weekly News*.[10]

It would have been hard for Merriman-Labor to miss the *Daily Mirror*'s media blitz promoting the visit to London of several Mbuti people. Earlier that spring, the *Daily Mirror* had splashed a giant picture across its front page of big-game hunter Colonel James Harrison standing with four Mbuti and the headline "PIGMIES COMING FROM THE FORESTS OF CENTRAL AFRICA TO ENGLAND."[11] Despite concerns of the Foreign Office and the House of Commons—who feared the Africans had been coerced into coming—the Mbuti arrived in London on June 1.[12] By the 5th, they were performing to packed houses at the Hippodrome. The *Daily Mirror* proclaimed that "never before have such strange human beings as these .... been brought into a civilised country."[13] One of the women, *The Sphere* disparagingly reported, was "perhaps the nearest thing to a human monkey Europe has ever seen."[14] The Yorkshire *Beverley Guardian* called them "ape-like in the extreme, with copper-coloured faces, woolly hair, spreading noses, and great gashes for mouths."[15] The unconscionable practice of promoting these visitors as curiosities rather than people created an instant theatrical success: the Mbuti performances became the hottest ticket in town.

Sandwiched between acrobats, jugglers, trapeze artists, a Rob Roy sketch, musical comedians, and an instrumental quartet, the Mbuti danced, drummed, and sang for two shows daily at 2:00 and 8:00 p.m.[16] During their time in London, they were inspected by anthropologists, taken to the Foreign Office, evaluated by a celebrated phrenologist, driven in motor cars, and widely discussed in the press. They performed at Buckingham Palace for Princess Victoria's birthday. On August 25, they visited the Gramophone Company, where, for the first time, the sound of Africans singing, talking, and drumming was commercially recorded onto phonographic disks. They would spend three more years in Britain and Europe performing for nearly a million people before they finally made their way home.[17]

While the Mbuti played to eager audiences at the Hippodrome, thousands more flocked to South London to see other Africans on display at the Crystal Palace. For just sixpence, advertisements promised audiences "the greatest programme ever offered: the GREAT SOMALI ANIMAL CAMP." The spectacle, it proclaimed, included "Native (Men, Women, and Children), with their Huts and Household Utensils, etc., together with WILD ANIMALS including Giraffes, Zebras, Elephants, Lions, Leopards, etc of the Somaliland." Promoters guaranteed it was the "most complete settlement ever brought to England," featuring displays of Somali "hunting and travelling across the desert and other ingredients of their every-day life."[18] It became one of the most popular shows in London that summer, attracting more than a hundred and seventy-five thousand people including Merriman-Labor.

On August 9, Merriman-Labor stood in the center of the Great Nave of the Crystal Palace. On either side of him, two long rows of orange and pomegranate trees stretched the length of the hall, infusing the air with fragrance.[19] Above him, three hundred vases in the upper galleries cascaded wisteria, lobelia, and other trailing plants. Everywhere azaleas and camellias packed circular beds, and palm trees of every variety soared upward, some arching a dramatic thirty-five feet. Here and there milk-white statues posed elegantly, while thrushes, wrens and robins flitted through the air. Bubbling fountains graced the room with artful notes. All round him, five stories of sparkling glass and iron created a cathedral of air and light, giving the impression that nothing separated the covered garden from the summer skies outside.

A self-conscious blending of education and entertainment, the Crystal Palace was part art history, botany, geology, commerce, and ethnology lesson and part amusement park. It was both "the Palace of the People's Instruction" and "the Palace of the People's Pleasure."[20] In places, the foliage in the Great Nave gave way to walkways into large courts filled with reproductions of famous architecture and sculpture. But Merriman-Labor didn't have time to inspect the eight enormous figures of Rameses the Great or a frieze from the Parthenon. The Venus of Arles, a recumbent effigy of Richard Coeur de Lion, a portrait of Lorenzo de' Medici, a bust of Shakespeare, and Bernini's St. Sebastian would all have to wait. So, too, would the restaurants, the reading room, the shoeblack, the barber, the aquarium, gymnasium, skating rink, and billiard room. The wide stone terrace outside opened to a panoramic view of the two-hundred-acre park. In addition to ornamental gardens, water features, and forests, it offered amusements of every variety: archery grounds, boating lake, cricket pitch, dancing platform, switchback railway, maze, and water carnival pond. There was even a large geological display and islands featuring "antediluvian animals"—life-size concrete replicas of dinosaurs.[21] A brisk walk took him to the eight-acre sports area that German impresario Carl Hagenbeck had transformed into the "Somali Village."

Dropping his silver sixpence into the attendant's hand, he entered the arena.[22] Huge backdrops, some thirty feet high, painted with palms and savannahs to represent Somaliland, encircled the stadium. Giant lath-and-plaster mountains and strategically placed shrubbery strained to give an air of similitude. In the center of the grounds, just in front of the grandstand, stood a dozen or so thatched huts. At one of them, a blacksmith hammered out implements over a small fire, at another a potter shaped clay. When Merriman-Labor arrived, a group of women were bent over large metal tubs laundering clothes, their children practicing their numbers with a teacher nearby. At the edges of the camp, ponies, camels, zebras, elephants, sheep, goats, and rabbits quietly grazed.

Several warriors in flowing white cotton robes assembled in front of the grandstand where they performed war dances and engaged in mock battles with spears and swords. Afterward, horsemen wheeled their ponies in dramatic displays of dexterity. Hunters came next, crouching low to the ground and firing arrows into the sides of grazing rabbits. The women and children of the village were settled in the grass, eating oranges and apples given to them by the crowd. At the end of the performance, the warriors led a procession of people, camels, zebras, and elephants through the village and then disappeared into the imaginary Somaliland behind the fabricated mountains.

"I went to see the Somalis from East Africa," Merriman-Labor announced in the *Sierra Leone Weekly News*. "I find them a handsome race of people with a build and features similar to those of the Fulas of Sierra Leone or the Polos of the Gambia."[23] As the words of a man deeply committed to elevating the position of black people in the world, the comment is hard to explain. He clearly identifies with the Mbuti and Somalis as fellow Africans, yet he doesn't appear to object to seeing them on display. Why didn't he express outrage as Trinidadian attorney Henry Sylvester Williams had over the Savage South African exhibition two years earlier? "There can be no doubt," Williams had argued, "about the delusion upon which these poor unfortunates were induced to leave their primitive homes to be made a spectacle of constant ridicule and caricature."[24] Another Sierra Leonean visiting a Somali village exhibition in London several years later also expressed no indignation at seeing black families on display for British audiences.[25] Did Merriman-Labor see the Somalis and Mbuti as self-aware agents who had chosen to come to Britain to perform, make money, and see a strange land before returning home? Because he was strongly influenced by Edward Blyden, did he believe the exhibits celebrated the unspoiled African, so much stronger, healthier, and happier than his poor anglicized cousins? Perhaps he simply felt that in a world where Africans seemed largely insignificant, any interest in their talents, customs, and lives was positive. Or did he mean his remarks to be taken ironically?

To get the African General Agency ready for business, Merriman-Labor used friends, family, and church connections to establish "enquiry agents" up and down the west coast of Africa.[26] An Englishman he met in Dulwich agreed to put him "in touch with firms in Brussels, Antwerp, France and Germany."[27] He also contacted the London business firm of Curtis, Gardner, and Boxwell, who assured him they would find investors "to give it a strong financial basis," if he could prove the agency was succeeding.[28] At the end of August, he placed advertisements in two key journals, the *African World and Cape-Cairo Express* and *West African Mail*. They generated more than a hundred requests.

Not everyone, however, was enthusiastic about his enterprise. When British trade protection societies got wind of it, they questioned his credibility, but he easily attributed their objections to the fact that his scheme was in "direct opposition to the interest of the financial lords of West Africa."[29] Attacks closer to home, however, caught him off guard. He was disappointed when the editor of a South African black newspaper wrote disparagingly of his new venture and was blind-sided when his own father refused to have anything to do with it. After seeing the notice in the *West African Mail*, Joshua Labor contacted his son to demand the already printed prospectus be revised. Merriman-Labor attempted to smooth over the rift by adding an addendum explaining Joshua Labor would be unable to assist the agency owing to his many duties. Apparently, Labor considered the private reprimand insufficient and a few days later sent a letter to the *Sierra Leone Weekly News* informing readers that his name had been "set down without my knowledge." Hoping, perhaps, to save his young friend further embarrassment, Cornelius May, the editor, also published Merriman-Labor's conciliatory note.[30] Shaken perhaps, but not daunted, Merriman-Labor stayed the course.

The next step was a two-week, two-thousand-mile tour of England, Scotland, and Ireland where he arranged to visit more than a hundred manufacturers to make the case for dealing directly with Africans.[31] Although the focus of the trip was the African General Agency, his writing career was never far from his mind, and he hoped to publish a series of articles or possibly even a pamphlet about his travels. An African's view of Britain would be a novelty sure to capture the interest of the general public.[32] He also wanted to illustrate his articles with photographs. A Kodak Brownie camera package cost just twenty-two shillings and included everything he needed to take and develop his own pictures. Before leaving, he made sure he had pen, paper, and camera—everything the modern travel writer needed to attract the world's attention.

He woke early on September 11, 1905, to cloudy skies and intermittent rain. At 7:30, he bid his friends farewell and walked twenty minutes to Camberwell Green where he boarded an electric tram towards Blackfriars Bridge. He loved the trams. They were so bright and airy, and they glided along so smoothly—a far cry from the plodding horse-drawn omnibuses with their crowded, uncomfortable seats and dim, foul-smelling oil lamps. Travelling at the exhilarating speed of ten miles an hour, he was at Blackfriars Bridge in just eighteen minutes.

Electric trams did not cross any of the city's bridges, so Merriman-Labor had to walk into central London on Blackfriars' wet, muddy pavement. Could anyone in Freetown imagine him now, surrounded by hundreds of clerks and laborers, shop girls and office boys, a giant wave of people flowing over the river? Some hundred and ten thousand pedestrians—three times the population of Freetown—crossed London Bridge daily. Add the people on the other bridges, and the numbers were staggering. "Thousands upon thousands," he declared, "congregating in the centre of the great metropolis."[33] And there, beneath the daily mass migration, the Thames flowed anciently along, dull and gray in the morning light.

A tram at Farringdon Station took him to King's Cross where he walked to the Gothic wonder of St. Pancras and boarded his train. With a gush of steam and smoke, it jerked forward and rattled out of the station at 8:40 a.m. There was only one other person in the compartment, as the train rumbled northward. The man introduced himself as Mr. Arthur Simpson and asked Merriman-Labor if he was from Africa. When he replied that he was from Sierra Leone, Simpson slapped his knee, and told him his brother-in-law Mr. Sidney Harvey worked for the railroad there. Simpson said that he had heard many wonderful things about his country, especially for the man of commerce, so Merriman-Labor naturally "tried to interest him with particulars respecting the African General Agency."[34] When Simpson reached his stop, he gave his new acquaintance a firm handshake and a friendly goodbye, then disembarked.

At a quarter past nine, he reached St. Albans. With copies of the African General Agency prospectus in his bag and a well-rehearsed speech on his lips, he made his way toward his first meeting with a manager of a straw-hat factory. The showroom overflowed with rows of beautiful hats: tricorns spiked with daffodils and twists of satin ribbon; purple ovals with pansies and tulle; and rose-colored oblongs dotted with pink roses and green foliage. Given that it was the slow season for hat-making, the manager may have shown him around. Perhaps they looked into the machinists' room where women in white aprons hunched over whirring machines sewing the straw into shapes, or the blocking halls where men stiffened the hats with gelatin then molded them onto pieces of wood. Perhaps in the finishing room, awash with linings, feathers, ribbons, and silk flowers of every description, the manager told Merriman-Labor he was not interested in the African General Agency because he didn't want to alienate his regular buyers in Liverpool and wasn't sure that Africans could be trusted to pay their bills.

Indignation rose up in Merriman-Labor's throat. He "took the opportunity there and then to disabuse his mind of the impression that the African merchants were greater sinners as debtors than merchants elsewhere."[35] Although he admitted there were some unscrupulous Africans, he insisted that they did not have a monopoly on dubious business practices.

"It is true," he told the manager, "we have our inveterate and hardened sinners ... men without a sense of honour ... or commercial competence." But, he added, it is a "wellknown fact that the number of bankrupt cases in this country ... is increasing year by year, amounting to the appalling figure of 9,829 in 1903."[36] Merriman-Labor was shocked to think that nearly ten thousand Britons had gone bankrupt the year before, and he hoped the manager would be, too.

Swayed by his impassioned defense, the manager took Merriman-Labor's comments "in good parts, and expressed the belief that our merchants might not be after all as bad as all that." The two men parted on good terms, and Merriman-Labor, ever the networker, asked him for referrals to other manufacturers. As it turned out, most of them did not share the hat-maker's concerns—they simply wanted more trade "and it mattered little to them," he noted, "where the trade came from."[37]

During the afternoon, he explored St. Albans. He stopped at its famous cathedral just as a service was beginning. "Besides myself and the man in white," he wrote, "there were only four women, we six filling the places of the thousands the Cathedral could accommodate." Afterward, he made a brief pilgrimage to Bedford to visit the chapel of John Bunyan, whose *Pilgrim's Progress*, he believed, was "treasured perhaps next to the Bible by Christians the world over." At the end of his visit, the "kind and generous" chapel keeper asked Merriman-Labor to sign the guest register. He noted with pleasure that the book included the signature of a "distinguished African, the young son of the Sultan of Zanzibar" who had recently been in England. He felt gratified to sign his own name on the same page as another African travelling abroad.[38]

He went on to Leicester that afternoon where "the Heads of these manufacturing establishments opened my eyes to the ridiculously low prices," he wrote, "at which they are compelled to sell their goods especially when the season is over and winter is coming." Buying merchandise that would soon be out of season in Britain, but perfectly suitable for the tropics, would be a boon for African importers. When he arrived in Birmingham that evening, he presented his "humble self and a letter of introduction to the gracious Miss S," then spent the night with a 'Mr. and Mrs. H' of Gladys Road, who, he wrote, made him feel "extremely comfortable, homely, happy, and well."[39]

Arriving in Lancashire the next day, he observed the "lofty columns of chimneys ... belching out, like an active Vesuvius in miniature, volumes of smoke and fire" and hailed his arrival in "the very bee-hive of industrial England."[40] In Manchester, he carved out a whole day with John Heywood, the man who had published the works that created his literary reputation in West Africa, and spent the evening with an old friend from the Freetown Colonial Secretary's Office, Christian Everett Athanasius Macauley, who would later go on to Oxford

University.[41] Joining two other fellow Sierra Leoneans—Mr. Clay and Mr. Ashwood—they ate dinner in the college dining hall, where students ask them "to speechify—a thing I so much dread," Merriman-Labor said, feigning shyness. Clay and Ashwood, he remembered, "made nice little speeches sparkling with wit and humor," which so delighted everyone present that they "cheered lustily and loud."[42]

His travels brought him into contact with other old friends whose hopes for Africa's future resonated strongly with his own. Samuel Forster, from the Gambia, was studying business at the University of Manchester. Merriman-Labor thought him "very sensibly advised." It was time, Merriman-Labor believed, for Africans to start pursuing commerce, agriculture, and industry rather than law and medicine if they were to "arrest that stream of wealth which is leaving Africa." Forster's experience underscored his own disappointment with the law. If he could start over again, he admitted, he would "abandon Law for good."[43]

His travels to Liverpool brought him in contact with Isaac Augustus Johnson, a Sierra Leonean friend who had just become president of the newly created Ethiopian Progressive Association. This student organization dedicated itself to raising "the social status of the Ethiopian race at home and abroad." Like Merriman-Labor, the young men in the Ethiopian Progressive Association felt "assured of the good will of the educated class of the British nation" and believed they would win respect regardless "of colour or nationality" by possessing exemplary "character, intelligence, and efficiency."[44] He must have been gratified to learn that they were not only committed to teaching people "how to gain recognition constitutionally," but were actively working "to prepare the minds of the African students in England to receive the gospel of united effort on which the salvation of the African race depends."[45]

As they talked of their experiences in Britain, Johnson likely told Merriman-Labor about the cruel treatment of black people in Liverpool. An impoverished man had recently been turned away from a workhouse because of his color and others were routinely "refused a night's lodgings for the same reason."[46] Despite these brutalities, Johnson and the Ethiopian Progressive Association chose to walk a moral high road in accordance with their Christian faith. They vowed in their constitution to instill in their members "the necessity for cultivating manly principles, thereby impressing in the hearts of all those with whom it is their opportunity to associate the true efficiency and worth of their misunderstood race." They were claiming, Johnson said, recognition not merely as men, but as honorable men.[47]

Merriman-Labor was drawn to this circle and surely brought them into his growing network. Within eighteen months, the African General Agency and Information Bureau boasted a registry of "2,000 names and addresses of Africans and Asiatics in the United Kingdom."[48] His vision of cooperation was unfolding and, with it, the promise of African prosperity.

After several days in the major cities of northern England, Merriman-Labor boarded the 4:00 a.m. express train from Carlisle to Edinburgh. In the dim light of one hissing gas lamp, he stashed his bag in the luggage rack above and settled into a spot near the window. At such an early hour, he was not surprised to find only one other person in the compartment—a well-dressed, intelligent-looking man comfortably arranged opposite him who introduced himself as Mr. Johnson and chatted about the ungodly hour and the sorry state of the lighting in British trains. As they rolled out of the station into the early morning darkness, Johnson remarked that they would be travelling through the "Land of Scott"—the region where novelist Sir Walter Scott set his novels—on their way to Edinburgh, which sparked a literary conversation. Merriman-Labor felt fortunate that his companion was turning out to be an excellent conversationalist, cultured and interesting.[49]

The compartment began to fill gradually as the train made its regular stops. When several men had accumulated in their car, someone suggested a game of cards with a bit of friendly betting to pass the time.

"Will you join us?" Mr. Johnson asked Merriman-Labor as he fanned out a deck of Goodall's.

He politely declined, thankful he had not taken up this method of passing the time which seemed to have pervaded every level of English society.

Later, one of his fellow travelers began thumbing through his expensive leather wallet.

"I say," he said looking to his fellow travelers, "might anyone change a five-pound note? I am headed to a rather small village where it will be hell to get the thing cashed."

The other men jumbled around their wallets and waistcoats. Mr. Jones had a pound, and Johnson had two, but no one could change five pounds.

"Sir," he said looking at Merriman-Labor, "you look every inch a gentleman. If I take three pounds from these men, would you be willing to take this five-pound note as security? You can change it in Edinburgh and fix a time to meet Mr. Johnson and Mr. Jones to give them their money?"

"Perhaps we can meet at one o'clock at Waverley Station," Johnson added, "if that suits you."

For someone living on his savings, handing over two pounds was not an easy thing to do. But the men were amiable and friendly, so he confidently handed over his two pounds and folded the crisp five-pound note into his wallet. Even if something went wrong, he thought, the whole proposal was in his favor. One man left the train a short while later. Johnson and Jones left a little farther on, showering Merriman-Labor with au revoirs and warm wishes as they stepped onto the platform.

After morning meetings in Edinburgh, Merriman-Labor stopped at a bank to change the note before meeting his new friends at Waverley. The teller gingerly accepted the bill and was about to give change, when he paused, wrinkled his brow, and excused himself. Two minutes later, Merriman-Labor was being interrogated by the bank manager.

"I was nearly arrested for passing a bogus bank-note," he told friends later.[50] The experience didn't make him angry, but philosophical. Britain was not the only place with bad men, he reflected. Africa, too, had its share. But there was a pronounced difference between the two.

"In West Africa," he joked, "the scoundrel who would help himself to a few of your coppers, or the worthless old overcoat bequeathed to you by your mother-in-law's deceased god-uncle, approaches your house at dead of night when you are fast asleep." In Britain, the confidence tricksters, cardsharpers, luggage thieves, and scoundrels used an entirely different means.

"In West Europe," Merriman-Labor went on, "the artful dodger who would live like a lord at the expense of your diamond pin or purse of notes, has only to give you a friendly hand-shake or a gentle tap on the shoulder while saying, 'Kind friend, beware, motor-car coming.' A moment later, and with you none the wiser, your belongings are in his pocket."[51]

With his usual good humor, Merriman-Labor did not let this misadventure ruin his trip. He left Edinburgh two pounds poorer but, he confessed whenever he told the story, considerably wiser.[52]

Night after night in January and early February 1906 crowds gathered in Trafalgar Square and Aldwych, on the Embankment, Westminster Bridge, and Waterloo Bridge, turning up their collars and stamping their feet against the cold. People huddled in the entrance of the Savoy Hotel and in corners of the Criterion and New Gaiety restaurants. They collected round the biograph screen at the Coliseum and lingered after midnight at the Hippodrome, the Lyceum, and a dozen other music halls. Swept up in the excitement of a general election and disinclined to wait for a morning paper, Londoners congregated wherever they could see the day's results. A keen observer of contemporary events, Merriman-Labor was no doubt caught in the fervor and probably found himself standing on the Embankment on a rainy evening in January scrutinizing a magic lantern slide projected onto a wind-blown sheet. All around him, well-to-do men in frock coats and pearl-gray top hats stood next to women typists in dark overcoats, or working men in caps. As the names of candidates and their tallies appeared on the blustering sheet, applause rang out at each Liberal victory. The *Daily Express* was creating a sensation by using a searchlight to project returns onto the 163-foot Shot Tower on the south bank of the Thames, each political party color-coded: Unionist/red, Liberal/green, Labour/white, Nationalist/orange and white. With each blaze of green, the roar of what seemed like a thousand voices echoed over the river, undercut here and there with a groan or hiss.

"It ain't no use, Sir," an old man said to the brow-furrowed businessman next to him. "It's just a walk-over for us this time, that's what it is."[53]

As Liberals swept overwhelmingly into power with their heady agenda of social reform, including old-age pensions, labour exchanges for the unemployed, workers' compensation, health insurance, eight-hour working days, and school meals for poor children, Merriman-Labor felt confident about his own unfolding projects. The *Sierra Leone Weekly News* had published five of his travel articles and was ready for more. He had made a few rookie mistakes with the African General

Agency—his initial advertisements, for example, had given some readers the impression that services were rendered at no charge—but the business was starting to make money. Although he still characterized it as an "experimental enterprise," he was hoping to turn it into a company that could offer shares and distribute profits among the investors. He wanted to use the tools of European commerce to build an African presence in the global economy.

As the election wound up, Merriman-Labor followed closely as violence exploded in the British colony of Natal, South Africa. There Africans outnumbered whites ten to one, but possessed almost no rights. Although they were ostensibly entitled to vote, the rules for qualification were so stringent that by 1903 only two Africans were registered and both were thought dead.[54] Lord Milner, the High Commissioner for Southern Africa, expressed the colonial view this way: "A political equality of white and black is impossible. The white man must rule because he is elevated by many, many steps above the black man; steps which it will take the latter centuries to climb."[55] Merriman-Labor almost certainly knew that segregation in South Africa was the order of the day. Prohibited from owning land in white-designated areas, Africans worked as tenant farmers, or leased land from whites at high rents, or resigned themselves to overcrowded reserves. By early 1906, lack of arable land combined with drought and other natural disasters had led to widespread poverty. The final straw arrived in early 1906 when the colonial government of Natal began collecting a newly levied poll tax among the financially strapped people.[56] Merriman-Labor could well understand their anger at taxation without, as one South African black paper put it, "a scrap of adequate representation in Parliament." Many in Sierra Leone had made the same argument. When twenty-seven peasant farmers refused to pay, policemen were sent to arrest them, but an altercation broke out, leaving two officers dead.[57] The colonial government declared martial law and sent in the militia. The commander, Colonel Duncan McKenzie, welcomed martial law because it allowed him to use, as he put it, "the most drastic punishment on all leading natives found guilty of treason" in order to teach them "a proper respect for the white man."[58] A large field force was sent to find any "tribes who have defied the Government" with the promise that "an example" would be made of them.[59] On March 6, a field force shelled a village which, according to one officer, may have been "somewhat theatrical" but achieved the "splendid effect" of terrifying the people. "The result has been far-reaching," Sir Henry McCallum, the Governor of Natal, reported to Lord Elgin, the Colonial Secretary, and "recent reports show that natives have changed from their attitude of studied insolence to one of thorough submission."[60]

Twelve men connected to the policemen's deaths were captured, tried in a court martial by five colonial officers, found guilty, and sentenced to death.[61] On learning of the verdicts, Lord Elgin telegraphed Governor McCallum on March 28 explaining that the executions under martial law would "excite strong criticism" in London and instructing him to suspend the executions until he had considered the situation further. The directive infuriated the Premier of Natal, who tendered his resignation, arguing that "it is all important that the gravity of the offense should be brought home to the natives."[62] Distressed by the resignation, Elgin ultimately withdrew his suspension order, and the executions were set for April 2.

Alfred Mangena, a South African who was studying law at Lincoln's Inn with Merriman-Labor, flew into action on behalf of the condemned men. He urgently telegraphed Governor McCallum requesting a stay of execution and hired barrister E.G. Jellicoe to appear before the Judicial Committee of the Privy Council—the highest colonial appeals court in the land—for permission to appeal the sentences of the twelve.[63] Jellicoe argued that the entire trial was illegal because the military court had no jurisdiction over the natives. The petition was dismissed.

On April 1, the condemned men, all Christians, spent the day praying with a local clergyman. A newspaper reported that they "confessed their guilt and expressed regret to their spiritual advisor."[64] That night, they sang hymns and prayed.

In London the next day, Labour M.P. J. Ramsay MacDonald introduced a motion that the House of Commons adjourn in protest at the introduction of martial law in Natal which, he argued, had created "grave and imminent danger to the natives."[65] The military court was biased, he contended, and the natives were entitled to a civil trial. Major John Seely, another Liberal member who had served in the

Anglo-Boer War, reminded the House that "the great principle on which the Empire was founded was a common respect for the law, which gave the right to every man, black, white, or yellow, to have a fair trial before a properly-constituted Court."[66] Mr. H. Myer, a Liberal member from North Lambeth, characterized the planned executions as "bloodthirsty murders."[67]

At noon in Natal the condemned men were read the sentence of death in the courthouse, then escorted by a firing squad of two hundred policemen to a nearby valley. The prisoners, it was widely reported, went "unflinchingly to their doom, showing no fear whatever." Six were selected, lined up, turned with their backs to the rifles, handcuffed, and blindfolded. As the policemen cocked their rifles, the clergyman probably bestowed one final prayer, then stepped aside. At that point, the officer-in-command raised his hand or perhaps a sword. When he brought it toward the earth, the policemen fired. After the deaths of the first six, the *Mafeking Mail* reported, a British officer "addressed the large gathering of natives present pointing out the lesson of the proceedings." The remaining men were shot and "all buried together in a trench previously dug near the scene."[68]

When the news of the executions reached the House of Commons that afternoon, outraged Liberal and Labour M.P.s interrupted the debate and filled the great chamber with cries of "SHAME!"

Resentment of the poll tax compounded by the brutal punishments of the protestors ignited more violence in Natal. In the coming weeks, twenty-four whites were killed in the uprising. Three thousand Africans were slain, seven thousand imprisoned, and seven hundred flogged until their backs were "lashed to ribbons."[69] Villages were burned and crops destroyed. As one observer wrote, although the colonists vehemently feared the "Black Peril," whites had always proved a more "deadly peril to the Blacks."[70] The Natal Police Commissioner blamed educated Africans for inciting the hostilities by promoting the idea of a universal franchise which, he said, was "a dangerous doctrine in Natal, and must result in discontent in the subject race."[71]

In the face of these atrocities, Alfred Mangena invited "coloured students" and African businessmen to the Saracen's Head Hotel in London to establish the United African Association, whose goals were to "render mutual help, discuss social and political subjects connected with the race" and work for the progress and advancement of Africans.[72] Merriman-Labor—who possibly knew Mangena—did not attend. His absence from the small meeting of nine men with whom he shared a number of goals seems strange. He may simply have had another obligation, or his absence may hint at fissures in the Pan-African fellowship. If Mangena believed, as black South African newspaper editor Allan Kirkland Soga did, that Africans would soon realize "their economic salvation rests with socialism," he may well have disapproved of Merriman-Labor's conviction that capitalism was the answer for African prosperity.[73] The *Sierra Leone Weekly News* carried little coverage of the events in Natal, printing just a few brief government telegrams. Colonial subjects like Merriman-Labor or even a young Mohandas Gandhi, the future Mahatma, suffered from painfully conflicting loyalties. Gandhi was living in South Africa at the time of the Natal uprising and, despite his own experience with racism, supported the British, even leading an Indian Ambulance Corps during the conflict. Reflecting on it later, Gandhi wrote, "I believed then that the British Empire existed for the welfare of the world. A genuine sense of loyalty prevented me from ever wishing ill to the empire."[74]

Mangena, who would become one of the first African barristers in South Africa and a leader of the African National Congress when it was founded in 1912, argued that the issue at the heart of the Natal uprising had been the British demand for cheap labor at the all-important gold mines. "The English have shelled our villages," he wrote, "looted our cattle, destroyed our crops, burned our churches. Their end is attained … the native can do nothing but go and work in the mines."[75]

As colonial forces unleashed their imperial power in South Africa, killing, imprisoning, and flogging people and razing villages, a swarm of men in German military uniforms invaded central London on a bright, cold March morning. Caught off guard by their spiked helmets glinting in the morning light, passers-by in Piccadilly reacted with alarm, until they registered the sandwich boards fastened to the men's backs and chests. This was not the long-dreaded invasion by the German army, but a dramatic advertising ploy on the part of Lord Northcliffe, the owner of the *Daily Mail*, who was promoting "THE INVASION OF 1910, WITH A FULL ACCOUNT OF THE SIEGE OF LONDON," a novel that was to be serialized in the paper the following day. Hoping to capitalize on popular fears of Germany, Northcliffe had commissioned writer William Le Queux to produce an invasion story that would alert the country to what he saw as the sorry state of its military preparedness. Assisted by naval historian H.W. Wilson and Field Marshal Lord Roberts, former Commander-in-Chief in South Africa during the Boer War, Le Queux fashioned a thriller that made invasion all the rage. Local papers published maps showing where the German army was expected to invade, and music hall artists performed invasion sketches on stage.[76]

Eager readers in Britain devoured each installment of Le Queux's deliciously terrifying novel of a powerful imperial army invading their homeland, declaring martial law, executing people in front of firing squads, and burning English villages to the ground. Few of the readers seemed to realize that Le Queux's fiction uncannily mirrored the tragic events in South Africa, where the military brutality was carried out not by ruthless German troops on Britons, but by British soldiers on fellow subjects of the King.

Merriman-Labor stood in front of the sculpture of the black soldier holding a drum. It was early June 1906, and he had been in Paris for three days taking in its famous sights. Now he was standing in the Hôtel des Invalides thinking about black soldiers in Napoleon's army. He remembered being at William Edmonds's home in Tooting, South London, where he had seen a painting of Wellington with a black attendant.[77] His own great-grandfather had fought with Wellington. The sculpture, the painting, and the stories of his great-grandfather were further proof that Africans had played a significant role in world events.

He was thoroughly enjoying his holiday. He found art and beauty all over Paris: in museums and churches, in the Seine as it curved through the heart of the city, and in the narrow cobblestone streets and the broad tree-lined boulevards. He had arrived on Sunday afternoon in time to watch the fashionable crowd parade to and from the Bois de Boulogne. From the comfort of a sidewalk café, he spent four hours watching cabs and motor cars rumble along, carrying ladies clutching toy terriers and gentlemen sporting fine silk hats.

The next day he stood at the base of the Eiffel Tower, dazzled by the massive structure soaring nearly a quarter mile high. "The height," he wrote, "is bewildering." He joined one hundred fellow sightseers in an enormous elevator which creaked upward for ten minutes before opening to an upper platform where he saw the whole of Paris before him. The sight took his breath away. Given the unparalleled view, the café, the post office, and the restaurant, he could not bring himself to leave. He spent the entire afternoon there.[78]

Staying at the Grand Hotel de Lausanne in the arty district of Montmartre, he quickly made the acquaintance of some "merry friends" who suggested an evening at the Olympia, one of Paris's largest music halls. After the show, nearly the whole audience descended to the restaurant in the basement where they dallied and drank as an orchestra played. When Merriman-Labor emerged at two in the morning, he was amazed to find the boulevards still crowded with people. "There was an appreciable show under the many electric lights," he noticed, "of fine clothing, and sumptuous living, and plenty of chats of 'sweet nothings.'" He fell into bed around three, just as the sun was beginning to rise.[79]

On Wednesday, as he dined alone at the Café Riche, famous for its literary connections—Flaubert, Maupassant, Baudelaire and Dumas père and fils had all famously frequented it—Merriman-Labor no doubt contemplated his own literary future. Sipping his Perrier—the naturally sparkling water that had come on the market just two years before—he probably contemplated how he would describe for his readers the flower-filled Tuileries, the graves at Père Lachaise, and the heaving baskets of snails and frogs at Les Halles, Paris's great open market. He was relishing this holiday and was grateful that the African General Agency was profitable enough to make it possible.

An intelligent-looking Englishman interrupted his reveries, introducing himself as Mr. Chapman. Their exchange was so delightful, Chapman invited him for breakfast and a stroll on Friday, Merriman-Labor's last day in Paris.[80] Thinking of the good time he had had with his new hotel friends, Merriman-Labor cheerfully agreed. Paris, he found, was full of friendly, charming people.

Tired of the "tramp life" of the tourist, as he called it, he spent Thursday enjoying himself more leisurely at concerts and cafés where he could drink coffee, listen to music, and relish the pulse of Paris. Intrigued by his guidebook's warnings that some cafés were not suitable for ladies, he decided to find out why. He set off for the "heart of Paris" to track down some of these notorious haunts. What he discovered was not so very wicked, he thought. Young men and women smoking, gambling, swilling cheap wine, and dancing suggestively. It all seemed harmless enough, until he stumbled on a club whose spectacles repulsed him. "One had better leave unsaid," he wrote, "what I saw there. It was a veritable unholy of unholies." As he slipped out of the door and into the narrow Parisian street, he thanked "God that Africa is not Europe."

Taking breakfast the next morning in an open-air café on Boulevard Saint-Germain with Mr. Chapman, Merriman-Labor found his new acquaintance "a delightful conversationalist, widely travelled, and evidently a man of no ordinary culture and intelligence." As they were eating, a gentleman approached their table.

"Pardon me," he said, "but could you direct me to the Church of the Madeleine?" Merriman-Labor detected an Irish lilt in his voice. As they pulled out their guidebooks and inspected maps, the man introduced himself as Mr. Riley.

"I have just come from Ireland on my way to Rome," he told them, "you see, I must ask the Pope to pray for the soul of my uncle who has just died in South Africa." Merriman-Labor extended his condolences.

"I am the prime beneficiary," Riley went on as he pulled a roll of banknotes from his coat, "of a fortune worth nearly seven figures." Merriman-Labor found himself exhilarated to be thrown by chance into the company of a millionaire, but a little amazed that the man was carrying what looked to be about £10,000 in his pocket.

"My uncle's will requires," Riley went on, "that I distribute £20,000 to the poor of the earth, irrespective of colour, race, or locality." He had just given away £1,000 while in Ireland, he told them.

"I say," Chapman asked, "do you intend to do something for the poor of Africa?" Merriman-Labor liked his new friend all the more for asking a question dear to his own heart.

"I do not think there are poor people in Africa," Riley told him.

"Oh," Merriman-Labor interrupted, "there are thousands of poor people there, and in view of the fact that your uncle made his money in Africa, he must have meant by his will to benefit the poor of that part of the world." Chapman agreed. Convinced by their remarks,

Riley promised to send some of the money to the poor in Africa, perhaps one or two thousand pounds.

"But, I need a responsible person to whom I could entrust the distribution," he said.

"I would gladly do that for you," Merriman-Labor offered.

"Well," Riley said, "if you could show me you are a man of means, I would be pleased to trust you with the donation." He looked at his feet. "But I cannot be foolish with this money. I must have some evidence that you are not a man of straw." If Merriman-Labor could prove he had a few hundred, Riley said he would be well satisfied he had chosen a respectable person.

"Look here," said Chapman, "I would like to add £800 to the sum to be distributed. That is, if you can show you are a man of resources," he said smiling warmly, "which no doubt you can."

"I can wire London and have a Banker's certificate for you in just a few hours," Merriman-Labor told them.

"Now I'm not sure about that," Riley said. "I am just a simple country Irishman, and we don't have doings with banker's certificates and such. Show me gold and silver I can feel in my hand. That's how I weigh a man's worth." Chapman agreed that seemed the best idea, but Merriman-Labor resisted.

"On your way back from Rome," he suggested, "meet me in London, and I promise to prove to you I am a man of means." Riley looked a little crestfallen, but agreed.

"That I will," Riley told him, "that I will." He shook their hands and wandered off in search of the Madeleine.

When he was gone, Merriman-Labor and Chapman laughed that such a vast sum of money should have been entrusted into the hands of such a simpleton. Chapman shook his head in disbelief as he wiped his mouth with the fine linen napkin.

"Please excuse me," he said rising, "I must find the lavatory."

Merriman-Labor sat at the table sipping his coffee and watching Parisians and tourists strolling past. It was a beautiful afternoon and the world seemed full of strange and interesting possibilities. After a time, he began to wonder what was keeping Chapman.

An hour passed, and Chapman had not yet returned. Merriman-Labor figured that Chapman had been tempted by the bundle of banknotes and must have gone after Riley. Through an interpreter, he explained the situation to the restaurant manager, who simply shrugged his shoulders and told him that he was responsible for the bill. By chance, a policeman overheard the conservation and told Merriman-Labor that Chapman and Riley were very likely confidence men working together to swindle tourists. The banknotes, he said, were probably just "flash" paper—ordinary writing paper made to look like money.

There was nothing to be done but pay for the two breakfasts. Upset that he had been swindled once again, but grateful he had been taken for only several francs, Merriman-Labor jokingly wrote later that he swore "vengeance and curses on Chapman and Riley and the likes of them."

He spent the remainder of the day wandering the city. On his return to his hotel, he crossed paths with his merry hotel friends who insisted on seeing him off. At the station, he felt buoyed by the warm goodbyes of his new friends. By the time he reached London the following morning, he had nothing but "pleasant reminiscences of the gay Parisians and their charming City, and a longing desire to spend another holiday in the land of the French."

The competing demands of law school and business forced him to leave bucolic Dulwich and relocate closer to central London for better access to commercial salerooms, dealers, auctions, packers, and shippers. Until now, he had been running the African General Agency from his lodgings, but, if all went well in the coming months, he intended to lease space in the new Birkbeck Bank Building, one of London's largest commercial structures with some eight hundred offices and modern conveniences. For the time being, he paid a small fee to a shopkeeper at 31 Chancery Lane for the use of a central postal address which would lend his business credibility.[81]

To increase business, he also punched up his publicity. His new advertisements in the *Sierra Leone Weekly News* encouraged potential clients "wishing to buy direct from manufacturers or to sell direct to consumers" to "combine and send orders or consignments amounting to several hundreds of pounds." He had to make people understand that larger shipments meant better profits for everyone. His study of commerce may also have prompted him to include testimonials from Mr. Louis Shaal of Dulwich, who thanked him for his "very interesting particulars respecting colonial appointments," and Mr. Eben

J. Greywoode of Sierra Leone, who affirmed that "the goods arrived in good condition" and promised that "you shall hear from me again."[82]

After Paris, the most delightful experience that summer was the arrival of Cornelius May from Freetown. Every inch the cultured gentleman in his tasteful British suit with his carefully trimmed mustache, May felt quite at home in London, where he had once lived. Merriman-Labor had not seen his friend in two years, and one imagines the warm greeting he gave to the man who was helping him fulfill his literary ambitions by publishing his travel writing. Both men were avid readers as well as writers, who appreciated art, literature, architecture, and intellectual conversation. They no doubt visited favorite haunts and landmarks, eagerly sharing the latest news from Britain and Africa. As the highly respected publisher of the *Sierra Leone Weekly News*, May was familiar to many in London's African community, and his visit must have included numerous social calls. Doing the rounds together, perhaps the two men even crossed paths with Henry Sylvester Williams, who was working hard to launch a political career. In the coming local elections, Marylebone voters would elect him to their borough council, making him one of the first men of African descent to serve in public office in London.

Gloomy skies settled over London the week before Christmas 1906, forcing proprietors to burn lights all day in hopes of attracting shoppers. According to one observer, the West End was a virtual "fairyland of electric lamps."[83] Slogging through the cold, damp streets on December 18, Merriman-Labor made his way toward Middle Temple—another of London's Inns of Court—where he would take his law finals, a grueling four-day affair. He passed through the red brick gateway into the Middle Temple grounds. The gray, leafless trees yearned upward as he wound his way through Brick Court, an Elizabethan relic; Essex Court with its two-hundred-year-old fountain; and finally across Garden Court to the Middle Temple Hall, another Renaissance construction. Elizabeth I had only been on the throne five years when it was begun and seventeen years into her reign when it was finally finished.

More than a hundred law students from the various Inns of Court assembled for the final exam.[84] They shuffled into the hall and took their seats beneath the spectacular hammerbeam roof, its elaborate oak truss echoing a ship's hull. Three hundred years before, Shakespeare had gathered his players here for a performance of *Twelfth Night*. As Merriman-Labor dipped his pen into his inkwell and began answering the first question on Roman law—"Describe the character of the Digest, or Pandects"—he must have been filled with wonder that Shakespeare himself had been in this room.

From 2:00 p.m. to 5:00 p.m., Merriman-Labor provided "an account of the nature of the right of personal freedom accorded in British law, and of the remedies by which it is secured" and other questions about Constitutional Law and Legal History. On Wednesday morning he did Evidence, Procedure, and Criminal Law followed by an afternoon of Real and Personal Property and Conveyancing. All day Thursday was given up to Law and Equity. On Friday morning, he took the last part of the exam, the General Paper, which consisted of ten questions drawn from all areas of legal knowledge. The very last question asked him to explain what was meant by the expression "Act of God."[85] As his tired hand scrawled thoughts about natural catastrophes and legal responsibility, he could not have known that soon he would come face to face with a catastrophe not produced by God, but by a conflict with the Honourable Masters of the Bench of Lincoln's Inn that would change the course of his life forever.

4

BE RIGHT AND PERSIST

Icy rain came down all morning as women gathered in Hyde Park on February 9 1907, some coming from as far away as Edinburgh, Newcastle, and Manchester. By two o'clock, the assembled procession stretched half a mile.[1] With white-and-scarlet badges proudly fastened to their cloaks, the women strode through the muddy London streets, their bright but soggy suffragist banners held high.

The history of British women and black people, Merriman-Labor believed, shared a similar trajectory. Women had endured a "domestic slavery," he wrote, and, like black people, were considered "intellectually, physically, morally, and socially inferior" to white men. Education had inspired some British women to "clamour for equal political and social rights," so now well-educated women, just like educated people of African descent, were "demanding the necessary representation."[2] It is easy to imagine him among the onlookers on that cold afternoon in February, when three thousand women asking for voting rights paraded through the wet London streets to convince men that "women's suffrage is a live question in politics."[3] Despite the awful weather, this giant suffrage march was the largest assembled to date.

If Merriman-Labor was, indeed, standing with onlookers at Piccadilly, he would have first heard the snare drums, cornets, and trombones of the brass bands thumping out the measures of a marching tune before seeing a squad of policemen heading the procession. The police presence was thought necessary to discourage violence from hostile spectators. Next came Mrs. Fawcett, Lady Frances Balfour, Lady Strachey, and Dr. Edith Pechey-Phipson, the hems of their long dresses already caked with mud.[4] The suffragists' red-and-white colors blazed in every direction on that cold, gray day: on badges, rosettes, ribbons, favours, and programs sold by street vendors.[5] Every few yards, broad banners proclaimed mottos such as "Gentle but Resolute," "Be Right and Persist," "Representation Is our Goal." Such words spoke to Merriman-Labor, who admired the tenacity to march at a time when a woman protesting on a public street was considered the height of impropriety.[6] As the procession passed the conservative clubs in Piccadilly, men peered out of windows and porticoes, their faces showing, as one participant recalled, "every shade of contempt and disgust from mild amusement to furious hate."[7] From the curb, someone overhead a man grumble, "There's not a single good-looking woman among the lot."[8] But at the Lyceum, a ladies' social club established just three years earlier, beaming women leaned from every window waving handkerchiefs and cheering. Behind the marchers came supporters in a long line of carriages and motor cars, including one electric cab crammed with "Manchester lads who had accompanied their suffragist sweethearts."[9]

The procession—which came to be known as the "Mud March"—was an inspiring feat of cooperation. It included, as one newspaper put it, a remarkable collection of women from every social class, "from a peeress to the humblest working woman."[10] Thousands of women had successfully organized, and Merriman-Labor admired their methods. "The agitative women," he wrote, "will effect much … before long, if they know that money and unity are the two greatest factors of strength at the present time, if they get the sympathy … of the general body of electors in Britain." Black people, he felt, could learn from them. "Negroes will not effect much for a long time," he lamented, "unless Negroes have money, unless they are united, unless they are less jealous of themselves, unless they study ways … to arrest the sympathy of the general electors of this country."[11]

Merriman-Labor respected the courage of the suffragists and enjoyed friendships with British women, but we don't know if he had any relationships. The intimate part of his life remains frustratingly opaque.

After living in the capital for five years, he confessed that he had never been in love, but given his kind and affable nature, it is hard to believe love never found him. If he wrote letters or kept journals recording his happiness, they have not survived. The story of his heart is a mystery.

The month before the Mud March, Merriman-Labor had transformed the African General Agency from an experimental undertaking run from a London lodging house to a formal business with offices in the newly built Birkbeck Bank Building. His modern workplace included telephone and telegraph service—giving him the ability to determine London market prices within minutes—a clerical assistant, new furniture, and a library of manufacturers' catalogs. With the Holborn Institute of Typewriting, Stewart's Shorthand and Business Academy, and other services nearby, he could hire, as he put it, "over one hundred white lady clerks ... at least once a week ... to assist my permanent staff."[12] The sheer exuberance of his letterhead indicates the joy he took in this new phase of his enterprise: an elaborately scrolled banner rainbows over a map of Africa announcing THE AFRICAN GENERAL AGENCY. In the left margin, "Manager: A.B.C. Merriman-Labor" appears in a modish font.

After eighteen months, his business was truly global. "Clients in South, West, and East Africa, in Black America, the West Indies, and British India," he wrote, "are now appointing us their General Agents."[13] Traders contacted him about selling consignments of hides, kola nuts, palm oil and other products. Individuals asked for help with a wide range of matters, from buying spectacles to settling disputes.[14] By the end of 1907, he was receiving hundreds of letters each week.[15]

Taking his cues from the hyperbolic contemporary advertising scene where the Jewel fountain pen was "praised by all who use it," and Thomas Crompton made the "best, the cheapest and the most durable hinges and locks," his advertisements offered to "conduct any kind of financial business whatsoever from one farthing to a million pounds."[16] He guaranteed traders they could "buy 50 per cent. cheaper and sell to better advantage than any other firm can." If hyperbole and guarantees didn't work, he used propinquity. "Appoint us your Agents now," the adverts instructed, "we are on the spot. We should know better of Business here than you thousands of miles away."[17] Blind to his own tendency toward paternalism, Merriman-Labor explained in a circular that "in all cases, we would obey every word of instruction from a client unless we are certain it is not well for him that we should."[18] In the years to come, this inclination to assume he could make better decisions for others than they could for themselves would prove a fatal flaw.

By 1907, the African General Agency was a successful concern with a bright future. And despite the overblown language of some of his advertising, Merriman-Labor provided real advantages to African traders. In 1910, a man calling himself Malumba wrote to the *Sierra Leone Weekly News* from the Congo describing how he had shipped palm kernels to a "well-known house in England," but after his expenses—purchasing bags, sewing, weighing, marking, transporting to the steamer, and paying export duty—he ended up losing 15 percent, even though the European broker lost nothing. We still need the African General Agency, he wrote, to look out for our interests.[19] But by the time Malumba wrote his letter, Merriman-Labor's dream of an African cooperative movement had been completely shattered.

As he was settling into his new offices, Merriman-Labor learned that he had passed his final law exams and was eligible to be called to the bar. As with almost everything related to legal study, the call was expensive with fees amounting to nearly a hundred pounds. Newly minted lawyers typically entered the chambers of an established barrister for at least a year where they practiced writing claims and looking up points of law. For the privilege of performing the firm's drudge work, they could expect to pay an additional hundred pounds. Colonial students almost never followed this course, but returned to their home countries. Having little interest in practicing law and now pouring money into building the African General Agency, Merriman-Labor decided to postpone his legal career indefinitely.

He did, however, visit Lincoln's Inn in mid-February 1907. William Edmonds, the Brixton bookseller, had died eighteen months earlier, and now Merriman-Labor was asking that his widow and her nephew serve as his new guarantors to free up a £50 bond. During his conversation with the steward, he was made aware of a new regulation that no person engaged in trade would be admitted without permission of the Inn. As he had already been admitted, he did not feel the regulation applied to him. Nonetheless, he made a formal request to the Masters of the Bench—the barristers who made up the governing body of the Inn—seeking permission to "be allowed to continue my connection with Lincoln's Inn and to carry on business as a Mercantile Agent."[20] He explained that he had entered the Inn before the regulation was established and, although he had passed his examinations and was eligible to be called to the bar, "it is not my intention to seek Call at the present time." "I trust," he signed confidently, "I shall have the privilege hereby asked for."[21] The benchers approved the change of sureties, but regarding the other request they were less accommodating. "It is inconsistent with the practice of the Inn," they told him, "to give their sanction to a Student carrying on Trade."[22] Merriman-Labor did not interpret this remark as an order to close the agency, and carried on with business as usual. It was a decision that would have devastating consequences.

Under leafless trees, among listing headstones and tilted crosses, not far from marble-winged angels kneeling in prayer, a solemn congregation of mourners huddled over an open grave. A sharp February wind cut into Merriman-Labor's face as they lowered the body into the cold earth. "We have entrusted our brother John Roberts to God's mercy," the minister intoned over the raspy chant of the graveyard crows, "and we now commit his body to the ground." Earth to earth.

Merriman-Labor stumbled to the head of the grave to speak about his friend. Promising student of pharmaceutical chemistry in London, reliable dispenser of medicine to the ill in Sierra Leone, honorable warrior of the Hut Tax campaign, dear friend hardly thirty-three years old. He had arrived in London not long after Merriman-Labor. Death had come unexpectedly. A young Krio man of promise and ability struck down in his prime. Grabbing a scoop of earth, Merriman-Labor trickled it slowly into the grave. Returning home, he scrawled out a letter to the *Sierra Leone Weekly News*. "Kindly favour us," he wrote, "by reporting the sudden death of Mr. John Roberts, a Sierra Leonean …"[23]

Except for two ghostly traces, nothing survives about John Roberts or his friendship with Merriman-Labor. The little we have comes from a few lines in the *Sierra Leone Weekly News* and a brief 1909 notice of the publication of "A Funeral Oration Delivered at Norwood Cemetery, London."[24] The fact that Merriman-Labor intended to publish the oration and took it upon himself to notify the Freetown public of his friend's death suggests the two men had a close bond. We know they served together in the Hut Tax War.[25] But the jokes and books, ideas and passions that fused their friendship, like the oration itself, have been lost. It is here, as in so many parts of Merriman-Labor's story, where we rub together two ghostly remnants in the hopes of sparking a little imaginative light into the obscured corners of a life.

In February, Dr. William Renner published a letter in the newly launched *Sierra Leone Guardian and Foreign Mails*, begun by Merriman-Labor's uncle, reminding Freetown readers that March 25, 1907, would mark the one-hundredth anniversary of the abolition of the slave trade. Merriman-Labor quickly contacted Renner and the Mayor of Freetown, proposing that they help finance a prominent celebration of the anniversary in London. Envisioning an event worthy of the occasion, he suggested they collect funds to pay for "wreaths-laying, dinner for a hundred, [and] a book as memento." He sent letters to a hundred Africans living in the U.K. announcing the anniversary and assembled a number of others in London to serve as a planning committee.[26]

Merriman-Labor corresponded with Travers Buxton, the secretary of the Anti-Slavery Society, for help with logistics, and Buxton put him in touch with Dean Joseph Robinson of Westminster, who granted permission for a wreath-laying ceremony in the Abbey. With the location in place, Merriman-Labor sent letters to "all known Africans in the United Kingdom" as well as West African and West Indian governors asking for subscriptions.[27] More announcements went to African newspapers, London morning papers, and a range of societies and individuals who might have an interest in participating. "We would welcome names and addresses of persons whose ancestors were connected with Wilberforce and Buxton," he wrote to *The Times* of London, and "English friends who are interested in Africa from an evangelical standpoint, and Africans, Afro-Americans, and black West Indians now in the United Kingdom."[28] Responses poured in.

At two o'clock on a bright Monday afternoon, March 25, the Very Reverend Joseph Robinson welcomed Merriman-Labor and three hundred other guests to the Jerusalem Chamber of Westminster Abbey.[29] Among those gathered were members of London's African community as well as dozens of prominent Britons: two M.P.'s—Sir Charles Dilke and Sir Brampton Gurdon—Bishop Ingham, the former Bishop of Sierra Leone, as well as representatives of the Anti-Slavery Society, the Society of Friends, the Church Missionary and Wesleyan Missionary Societies, the Congo Reform Association, the African Society, and the League of Universal Brotherhood. Robinson introduced the Archdeacon of Westminster, the Venerable Albert Basil Orme Wilberforce, grandson of the famous abolitionist, then spoke briefly of the philanthropists whose memories they had gathered to commemorate. He extended his appreciation to Sir Thomas Fowell Buxton, grandson of another great abolitionist, and other direct descendants of the anti-slavery leaders who had joined them for the celebration, then led the group into the Abbey.

In contrast to the human dimensions of the Jerusalem Chamber, the nave of Westminster Abbey with its hundred-foot ceilings and giant columns felt vast and hallowed. It was so "quiet and serene," Merriman-Labor recalled, that it seemed to echo "peace, perfect peace."[30] Light shimmered through stained glass as the large group drifted past gilt screens, marble figures, and flickering candles toward the north aisle, where they gathered around the Wilberforce monument. The white marble statue portrayed the great man in a wry mood, sitting in his eternal chair, legs crossed, slightly twisted at the hips, his penetrating eyes scrutinizing the world.

Dean Robinson invited the assembled group to recall the words of Harriet Beecher Stowe, author of *Uncle Tom's Cabin*: "Remember what God has done, remember that this great curse of slavery has gone forever."[31] It was a noble thought for a noble occasion, even if, as many of those present knew, at this very moment Europeans continued to enslave Africans in the Congo and elsewhere.

Merriman-Labor stepped forward bearing a wreath of lilies and daffodils.

"In the name of Sierra Leone, Lagos, and other countries," he said, "I place this wreath bearing the inscription, 'From Grateful Africans.'"[32]

His friend Chris Macauley from Manchester approached next. He laid a wreath on behalf of Africans in America and the West Indies. After him, Barrister Wilfred Maxwell laid a third from Africans in the United Kingdom. Then J.L. Franklin of the Great Ormond Street Homeopathic Hospital, J.E. Barnes, a civil engineer from Jamaica, as well as African students Samuel Lewis, Jr., J. Otonba Payne, G.D. Montsioa, and E.A. Ejesa-Osora placed additional wreaths on monuments to three other abolitionists: Buxton, Macaulay, and Granville Sharp.[33] Dean Robinson concluded with a few brief words. Remembering the celebration later, Merriman-Labor wrote, "in our own little way, we tried, on that occasion, to do honour to the memory of those able men who had done so much for Africa and the Africans."[34]

The following day, the London Standard, the Daily News, and the Morning Leader all contained short articles on the event.[35] The Daily Mail printed an interview with one of the wreath-bearers, G.D. Montsioa, identified as "Prince Montsioa of Bechuanaland." Despite the recent events in South Africa, Montsioa's remarks emphasized his people's patriotism and carried only a hint of reproof. "We in Bechuanaland," he told the reporter,

> are very grateful to the English nation for what they have done for our education and civilization. We are ... glad of the privilege of living under British rule, and as long as we are treated as fairly as we have been we will always be loyal and willing subjects.[36]

The writer for the Manchester Evening Chronicle seemed more interested in Merriman-Labor, whom he described as a "gentle, pleasant, and highly-educated negro," than in the centenary celebration. Merriman-Labor told him he was not convinced that European civilization had been good for Africans. "I am proud to be called a black Englishman," he acknowledged. "I have never spoken any language but English; I have never known any other influence but English influence, English training." He went on to wonder if Africans "might have been happier left to our own civilisation, to hunt in the wilds, and to live with nature!" He laughingly suggested that if he had lived in nature, he would never have had to suffer indigestion or go bald. His humor obviously charmed the reporter. Calling him a "polished and most courteous gentleman," the writer admitted he "could not see the slightest sign of a diminishing crop of black, frizzy hair at the summit of his remarkably well-developed brow."[37] Merriman-Labor enjoyed the interview and called special attention to the article when he reported the centenary events to the Sierra Leone Weekly News.[38]

He was honored to receive a congratulatory note from Sir Thomas Fowell Buxton, the grandson of the revered abolitionist. "Let me take the opportunity," Buxton wrote, "of saying how well I think all passed off yesterday. It was excellently arranged and it was a most interesting ceremony."[39]

Merriman-Labor understood that a global business required global promotion, so throughout 1907 he circulated a biographical article to black newspapers in Nigeria, Jamaica, and America called "The African General Agency and Its Founder" in which he offered a brief description of his life and the motivation for his Afrocentric business.[40] Feeling "called upon to champion the African cause," he explained his belief that Africans must work cooperatively to prevent the vast wealth of the continent from being "carried away to enrich the impoverishers of Africa."[41] Readers could help the continent's people achieve financial independence by doing business through the agency and spreading the word about its work.

Merriman-Labor also made use of a variety of contemporary marketing techniques to grow his business. He built his mailing list—a hot property even in 1907—by sending out an information booklet free of charge to enquirers.[42] Cheap postage rates made advertising by mail wildly popular, and companies frequently offered samples, catalogs, pricelists, and booklets at no cost simply to collect names and addresses of potential clients.[43] He also put into place a referral campaign, a strategy considered a powerful marketing tool even today. If clients persuaded their friends to use the agency, they were rewarded with "handsome presents and fees." The more referrals they generated, the more money they could earn. Merriman-Labor even set up a special Christmas and Easter promotion: "If through your recommendation we get no less than ten new clients before any Christmas or Easter, you will receive from us Christmas or Easter presents in the shape of cash, gold or silver ornaments, jewellery, fancy goods or novelties, books or such like."[44] The techniques were effective: the African General Agency continued to grow.

The sweeping range of services offered in his salmon-colored booklet suggests that he was using his large African network to provide information on, as he put it, "any financial, commercial, mining, agricultural, political, municipal, legal, religious, educational, industrial or other business in which Africans or persons of African descent may be concerned." Some of this information related to serious matters including African affairs, investments, stocks, market reports, shipping, and trade. The agency worked with mining and timber properties and concessions. It sold produce in Liverpool, London, and Hamburg. It was an authorized agent of several insurance companies. If necessary, it engaged private detectives for confidential inquiries. It also offered guidance on questions of art and literature, education, journalism, politics, and religion. The company's investment advice, the booklet explained, came from a "financial expert of a well-known London bank"; its solicitors enjoyed "a large City practice"; and its barrister was "a Senior Reader to the Four Inns of Court."[45]

It also provided information concerning occult matters: astrology, fortune-telling, freemasonry, palmistry, phrenology, and spiritualism. At the time, many respectable people—including psychologists William James and Sigmund Freud, prime minister Arthur James Balfour and physicist Sir Oliver Lodge—took seriously the work of the Society of Psychical Research, which investigated extrasensory perception, poltergeists, spiritualism, dowsing rods, automatic writing, and other "obscure phenomena which lie … on the outskirts of our organised knowledge."[46] Discoveries and inventions such as X-rays, radioactivity, the electron, and wireless telegraphy suggested previously unimagined forces at work in the world. At the turn of the century, as professor Samuel Hynes puts it, "English intellectual life was in a state of open uncertainty." What we see as quackery, he explains, Edwardians were willing to view as merely "unproven."[47]

The African General Agency also asked clients to make the firm aware of "weapons, carvings, idols, and curiosities" as well as "freaks of nature" and "native magicians" because curios and "wonder working people of exceptional merit are always wanted here."[48] Merriman-Labor may have discovered the English appetite for "curiosities" at Stevens's famous auction in Covent Garden, where collectors, dealers, and wealthy ladies feverishly bid for silk jackets from China, mummies from Egypt, figures of Burmese dragons, ancient British constable staves, and even an embroidered collar supposedly worn by Sir Francis Drake.[49] As for the market in human oddities, one could find that on any busy London street. For just a penny, sideshow barkers invited the curious into a world of never-before-seen grotesques. After mounting a dark staircase, as writer A. St. John Adcock describes it, one could "admire a bearded lady" or "three reputed Africans" licking "red-hot pokers that sizzle on their tongues."[50] The following week the show might feature "an elegant 'electric lady' who communicates electric shocks to those who touch her" or a "noble savage" who "exerts himself in a war dance when enough penny spectators are present."[51] No records survive explaining what Merriman-Labor thought about African curiosities or freak shows, or how he might have been involved with them. Perhaps he saw them as an extension of his interest in magic. But one thing is certain: he collected enough photographs of "African curiosities" to sell a book on the subject a few years later.[52]

By Christmas Eve 1907, the success of the African General Agency put Merriman-Labor in a thankful frame of mind. Sending out his information booklet for the new year, he included a letter of gratitude to supporters. "I have learnt a great deal more of business," he wrote, "than I knew twelve months ago." He thanked his "clients, patrons, and correspondents throughout West and South Africa, Afro-America, and the West Indies," especially friends in Niger, Lagos, São Tomé, Fernando Po, and the Congo "through whose kind recommendations we have received an appreciable amount of patronage."[53] He acknowledged the support of the *Jamaica Times*, the *South African Spectator*, *Detroit Informer*, *Alexander's Magazine*, and the *St. Lucia Guardian*, and expressed his appreciation to a West African bishop who "encouraged us not a little."[54]

He admitted that the editor of a South African black paper had accused him of being a "self-praiser and sensation monger," to which he said, "the charge may be true. But what business man does not advertise nowadays?" He explained the modern business world as he saw it. "Amidst the rush and crush and the noise and bustle of business, only he who shouts loudest is heard most. All keen students of business and of human nature will, I respectfully maintain, see nothing wrong in the methods I have adopted to enlist for this venture the sympathy and patronage of Africans the world over."[55]

He was proud of his success. "I have conducted this business ... without a hitch," he boasted, which was "the best evidence that I am able to bear, not only to bear, to carry the agreeable burden I have placed on my shoulders." It had been a notable achievement. "With capital of less than £5 expended on printing," he would remember later, "I brought in, handled, and solely controlled cash of £2000 in a few months."[56] He had accomplished this work not only competently, but honorably. "I can look the whole world in the face," he told his clients, "and say I owe no man anything."[57]

He stressed his philosophy of cooperation as he had done ceaselessly for more than two years. "Simply let us pull together," he enjoined. "It will be good for you. It will be good for ourselves. It will be good for those coming behind us."[58] He signed the letter with his customarily flamboyant signature, tilted upward and underscored with a series of artistic loops. Buoyed by a deep sense of achievement, Merriman-Labor felt certain that his dream of African cooperation and economic independence would soon become a reality.

On March 19, 1908, Merriman-Labor received a vexed letter from the Masters of the Bench of Lincoln's Inn demanding to know if he was "the gentleman whose name appeared at the foot of the Circular dated 24 December 1907." Had he "authorized such a use of his name or the name of the Society?"[59] In late January, someone had brought his booklet and Christmas Eve letter to the benchers' attention. They had since organized a Special Committee to investigate him and his business. On reviewing Merriman-Labor's materials, the committee members were outraged. "The business carried on by Mr. Merriman-Labor is of a very objectionable character," they determined, and his use of the name of the Inn in his promotional materials discredited it.[60] The benchers advised him once more that his enterprise was "wholly inconsistent with the character of a member of this Society" and threatened to strike him from the books unless he could "satisfactorily explain his conduct" or "give an unconditional undertaking to discontinue the business."[61]

The idea of discontinuing the agency was inconceivable: it provided his only income. Moreover, he had hardly been concealing his business from the benchers: his offices were directly across the street from Lincoln's Inn. He could not help thinking that there had been a misunderstanding that would soon be resolved.

He replied immediately, fully admitting he was the person whose name appeared on the circular and asking "pardon of the Society if by the use of their name in such connection he was guilty of an offence."[62]

He assured them that he did not understand that identifying himself as a member of the Inn was a breach of professional etiquette and "promised never in the future to use the name of the Society in any literature relating to any trading business." He "earnestly prayed not to be struck off the books of the Society for a breach of etiquette which was not accompanied with an intention to offend." Hoping to find a way to keep his business going without angering the benchers, he asked if he might have "permission to continue in trade until such time as [he] intended to seek Call." And if that were not agreeable, he was willing to give up his personal connection with parts of the business that had to do with buying and selling or with legal advice. He even devised a plan to sell the business and asked permission to suspend his membership in Lincoln's Inn "to the end of the present year by which time he should have transferred his business to a Company."[63] He firmly believed if he could just explain things to the committee, they would see reason. He failed to grasp that he was caught in a collision of two profoundly different worlds.

Krio businessmen were among the most prominent members of society in colonial Sierra Leone. Wealth accumulated through successful commerce allowed them to acquire British clothing, British houses, and British education, and the other status symbols which demonstrated their position as cultured gentlemen. In Britain, the place of businessmen couldn't have been more different. Although immensely wealthy men of business had begun to infiltrate high society, in general those in high positions disdained the idea of soiling their character by associating with those in commerce. Lady Warwick's instructions to novelist Elinor Glyn offer a glimpse of the strict social hierarchy of the time.

> Army or naval officers, diplomats or clergymen, it was explained, might be invited to lunch or dinner. The vicar might be invited regularly to Sunday lunch or supper, if he was a gentleman. Doctors and solicitors might be invited to garden parties, though never, of course, to lunch or dinner. Anyone engaged in the arts, the stage, trade or commerce, no matter how well-connected, could not be asked to the house at all.[64]

The barristers' code of professional conduct was based on qualities designed to affirm their status as gentlemen. To ensure their commitment to justice before self-interest, for example, they were forbidden to confer with clients directly (they had to hire a solicitor who communicated with the barrister), nor could they discuss fees (a duty handled either by the solicitor or a clerk).[65] The very thought of a barrister directly connected with monetary transactions horrified the benchers' sense of propriety and impartiality. They found it debasing for the name of the Inn to be mingled with trade transactions. While Merriman-Labor saw advertising as a normal part of business, to the benchers it was disgraceful, even unscrupulous. They marked the copy of his booklet which had come into their hands with large, angry red X's and underlined passages that included the words "seller and buyer," asked for money to be sent, or offered legal advice. One can only imagine their horror at the request for curiosities and freaks of nature, or the "handsome presents and fees" for successful canvassers.[66]

On March 27, Merriman-Labor met with the Special Committee assigned to assess his activities and told them, "although he described himself as the Manager ... he was solely concerned in the business." "His own description of his position," the committee reported, "was 'I am the Agency.'"[67] Because he had said previously that he had a "staff of Africans" (including employees in uniform meeting people at trains) it seems almost certain that he was shielding law students from censure. He must have feared that the many Africans providing services through the agency might somehow now be compromised by their association with it.

Merriman-Labor apologized for having used the name of the society and explained that he had included it because it was "his only distinction," and he had thought of it as one thinks of one's connection to a university. When the benchers called his attention to the letter they had sent him the previous summer regarding his business, he explained that he had misunderstood their meaning and "that he did not take it as amounting to a prohibition against trading." Cecil Henry Russell, the treasurer of the Inn and the chair of the committee, clarified their position in no uncertain terms, warning him that "he could hold out no hope that [his] connection with the Society would be allowed to continue unless he absolutely and bona fide ceased to be connected to the business." Merriman-Labor explained he had "thought over it very carefully" and was willing to abandon the agency entirely, "but if he should do so his idea was to have an Association which would not be a business in any way, but an Association to which people would subscribe." Clearly not persuaded, the committee advised him to take time "to consider his position and the course he would be willing to take as regards severing his connection with the business" and adjourned the meeting.[68]

Resigned to the fact that he had to give up his position as manager, but hoping to keep the agency afloat and salvage some of his investment, Merriman-Labor pursued the idea of transforming it into a limited company owned by others in which his only role would be as a shareholder. By early April, he had an indenture prepared laying out the plan to sell the agency for £200 worth of stock in the company.[69] Who the buyer or buyers were is unknown, but the fact that he indicated the manager would be "a native of this country" suggests that he thought a British-born administrator would give the plan more credibility.[70] To underscore his intention to separate himself from the daily work of the company he updated his letterhead, informing clients that "Merriman-Labor ceases to be manager from April 1st 1908."[71]

When he met again with the Special Committee on Tuesday, April 7, he explained he was abandoning his business and a "limited Company was being formed to take over the ownership and control of the Agency."[72] He had already convinced "several influential Africans and Englishmen" to subscribe to the "necessary foundation shares."[73] He spoke frankly about his fiscal realities. He had "put £200 into the business," he told them, and the agency was "his sole means of support." Without it, he would have no funds to get called to the bar. He promised his role would merely be that of shareholder, and he "had no intention to retain any control of the business." Anticipating that the owning of shares could hardly be objectionable, he must have entered the meeting with every confidence he had hit on a workable solution, but the plan inspired no support from the Special Committee. He was stunned when they asked if he was prepared not to take shares in the company. The question, he wrote, "suggests the possibility of my not being allowed to remain on the books of the Inn because I mean to hold shares in a trading company."[74] The idea was nonsensical. Surely the men sitting in front of him were shareholders in various companies themselves. Thinking the problem must be that he wasn't making himself understood, he asked permission to be represented when he

111

appeared before the larger Special Council convened to decide his case. The committee agreed. Merriman-Labor engaged Cambridge-educated Alfred Frank Topham, an expert in company law, the author of *Principles of Company Law*, and a reader at Lincoln's Inn.[75] If anyone could clearly explain his plan to the benchers, he must have felt, Topham could.

On the verge of being forced to give up the agency, Merriman-Labor realized he had to arrange his call to the bar as soon as possible. As he was waiting for the Special Council to meet, he asked to participate in the next call night: May 13. Three days later, he wrote again, asking to know soon if he would be allowed to be called, so he could write to friends in Sierra Leone "by this week's mail respecting my Call fee."[76] The African General Agency might have been bringing in enough income to keep him afloat in the metropolis, but it didn't have enough cash on hand for big ticket items like call fees.

By that time, however, the committee had reported to the benchers that they were "fully satisfied" Merriman-Labor had no intention of severing his connection with a business of an "objectionable character" and recommended that his "name be struck off the Books of the Society."[77]

Not even Alfred Topham was able to convince the twenty-two-member Special Council convened on May 6 of the validity of Merriman-Labor's shareholder plan, and they ordered his name be struck from the books. The council did, however, allow the steward to "intimate" to him that they would consider restoring him to the Society in future if he could prove that he had "completely severed his connection" with his business.[78]

Being forced to close down the agency meant losing not only all the money he had invested—probably his life savings—but also his only source of income. It meant abandoning his dream of African cooperation and economic independence. Without a way to pay the bills, it also meant abandoning London and his aspirations of a European literary career. Yet, to have his name permanently struck from the books of the Society of Lincoln's Inn was unthinkable. He had already invested a great deal of money in fees and dinners, completed his course work, kept his terms, and passed all the exams. To walk away from a law career now meant losing the status of barrister. He could not bear the thought of returning to Africa without having gained the laurels which his family expected.

Once he made up his mind, he acted swiftly to shut down his firm. He gave up the lease of his offices, referred existing clients to other firms, publicized the closure of his business, sent letters to his suppliers, packers, and shippers, and requested certificates from his solicitors and accountant testifying that the agency had been terminated.[79] He found his assistant clerk a new position with the London Glove Company. Without enough cash on hand to pay off outstanding orders and bills, he borrowed £150 from his mother to bring his business affairs to a speedy close. Only sixteen days after his name had been struck from the books, Merriman-Labor wrote again to the benchers, this time requesting to have his name restored.[80] He had done everything in his power to demonstrate that he had dissolved the business. By the end of May 1908, the African General Agency had been completely dispatched.

The cost of closing the agency had been high. He had lost over one hundred pounds outright. Worse, he had given up a thriving business, which, he wrote, "last year had a turnover of two thousand pounds."[81] But still the benchers were unsatisfied. At the end of June, they met with Merriman-Labor, his solicitor, and accountant to scrutinize his company ledgers. They identified four people in Africa to whom he owed money and refused to close his case until these debts had been paid.[82]

He was in a terrible bind. He couldn't be called to the bar until he had paid off the company debts, yet the benchers had cut off his only source of income. The worse possible solution would be to return home penniless, unable to take up a legal career. If he was going to stay in London, he had to come up with a way to make money. The quicker he could figure out how, the better.

Merriman-Labor stood on a busy London street corner watching cabs, lorries, and motor cars rushing by. All at once, one of the new double-decker motor omnibuses roared past with ten enormous letters blazoned on its side: TRAVELOGUE.

The world-renowned lecturer Burton Holmes had recently coined the word. Although travel lectures accompanied by magic lantern slides had been popular for decades, Holmes in his elegant suit and trim goatee had recently created a sensation by interspersing short moving pictures between slides. Now Londoners flocked to see the films and

113

hear his captivating stories. For the small price of admission, the audience could enjoy intimate views of distant lands and exotic peoples without the inconvenience or expense of actual travel.[83]

In a flash, Merriman-Labor saw lecturing as a lucrative occupation that would play to his strengths: a well-educated mind, a passion for writing, and a talent for performance. It also had the merit, he believed, of being a suitable occupation for a gentleman, and would not, he hoped, be offensive to the benchers. He did not intend to compete with Holmes or others on the British lecture circuit, but would take his lectures to Africa, where people had fewer opportunities for high-quality educational entertainment. He considered giving two informative lectures called "The Commercial and Political Outlook of West Africa" and "The Place of Religion and Education in Modern Existence," but it was the travelogue based on his life in London—"Five Years with the White Man: What I Saw"—that excited him most.[84] If he could attract audiences of at least a hundred people at every stop, he could make ten pounds a lecture—equal to his monthly earnings at the African General Agency.

Anxious not to offend the benchers further, he wrote to Cecil Russell to ask if there was any harm in his plan to give lectures abroad. After outlining the subjects of his lectures, Merriman-Labor also explained that he had asked newspapers not to "describe me as of 'Lincoln's Inn.'"[85] In his reply, Russell only said that he could not "express any opinion as to the propriety or otherwise ... [of] delivering lectures abroad on the subjects mentioned." In a subsequent note to the steward, Russell observed that "the matter ought to be dealt with officially," but apparently there was no further action and it was dropped.[86]

Merriman-Labor scraped together the money to engage an optical company to construct a magic lantern suitable for the kind of demanding tour he had in mind. Powerful lanterns fueled by electricity were widely available in England, but electric power would be scarce in Africa, so the practical fuel choice would be kerosene. It might be considered old school in Britain, but he could be sure to find it throughout most of the continent. The optical company built a custom-made machine capable of projecting the life-size images Merriman-Labor wanted and sturdy enough to endure the West African climate. They christened it the Telescopigraph.[87]

On July 18, 1908, Merriman-Labor boarded the African steamer *Karina* with his Telescopigraph and his slides, ready to travel some ten thousand miles across the African continent.[88] If all went according to plan, those ten letters—travelogue—would not only provide the money to get called to the bar, but would pave the way toward the literary career at the heart of his aspirations.

PART II

STONEY-HEARTED STEP-MOTHER

FIVE YEARS WITH THE WHITE MAN

WHAT I SAW

As the *Karina* entered the tropics, the ship's crew unfurled heavy awnings over the decks to protect against the hot sun, and the officers slipped into their white uniforms. In the desolate stretch of ocean between the Cape Verde Islands and Sierra Leone, steamy air lulled khaki-clad men to sleep in damp deckchairs and seeped into the pages of the women's novels, making them soggy and hard to turn. Merriman-Labor leaned against the railing of the ship, gazing at a sea barren of any guiding markers. The vast blank ocean resembled his own uncertain future. Returning to Freetown neither a barrister nor a successful businessman, he feared he would be thought a failure.

He was counting on his upcoming lectures to fill his pocketbook and shore up his reputation. The strategy, he knew, had risks: his first attempt at a magic lantern show—a dozen years before, when he was just eighteen—had been a disaster. With grand ambitions, he had ordered slides from Reliance Magic Lantern Company in England, but the box had been dropped into the sea as it was being unloaded from the steamer. Miraculously not one was broken. Relieved, the young Merriman-Labor placarded the entire town with advertisements for the Monday night lecture, which would feature four men with university degrees talking on a variety of subjects.[1]

But when he opened the box of slides two days before the event, he discovered that the contact with salt water had faded them to near invisibility. The hall had been booked, tickets sold, and now the slides were useless. In a panic, he flew to his uncle's photographic studio in Garrison Street. There J.C. Merriman dowsed them in an alchemy of chemicals until they were sufficiently restored to allow the show to go on.[2] The worst, Merriman-Labor thought, was over.

At seven o'clock on Monday a large crowd had gathered. At half past, he was still struggling to trim the wick of his new-fangled lantern. Irritated by the delay, a group of young men beat the floor and demanded their money back. When he was finally able to illuminate the slides, the ghostly images infuriated the young men further, and they rushed the exhibition table, toppling the lantern, which burst into flames. The fire was quickly extinguished, but the evening ended in mayhem, smoke, and disappointment.

An anonymous writer sent a letter to the *Sierra Leone Times* about the failed lecture a few days later, laying the entire blame for the fracas at Merriman-Labor's teenaged feet. "It was he," the critic charged, "who undertook the ambitious task of elevating and amusing the audience, and he failed in doing so."[3] In his reply, Merriman-Labor openly admitted his mistakes, apologized to all who attended, and hoped "when more years shall have added themselves to his eighteen, he will be in a position to show the world that his aim is to elevate and amuse." The "Reliance" slides proved unreliable, he joked, and the whole attempt to elevate proved a "rather collapsible undertaking."[4]

Now, he was returning to the Freetown lecture stage with a custom-made Telescopigraph, a carefully composed lecture, and a dozen years' worth of experience. This time his future depended on his success.

Fortunately, he had loyal friends in Sierra Leone rooting for him. One of them, Okagoo, wrote a letter to the *Sierra Leone Guardian* shortly before Merriman-Labor's arrival, praising his friend's strength in the face of obstacles. He compared him to Achilles, writing that "difficulties make him courageous" and the "unpatriotism on the part of his own kith and kin makes him all the more resolute." Merriman-Labor's larger purpose, Okagoo argued, was unimpeachable: "all he has in his mind's eye," he said, "is a way to ameliorate our depression."[5]

But circumstances were working against Merriman-Labor. He arrived in Sierra Leone during the rainy season when torrential storms regularly unleashed thirty inches of rain a month. Even worse, the Reverend J.R. King, a well-known missionary, had given two magic lantern lectures on England just four weeks before.[6] But there was too much at stake not to go on as planned. If the tour succeeded, he would get his life back on track. If it failed, his future felt as empty as the great sea beyond the ship's deck.

As the *Karina* approached Freetown two days later, Sierra Leone welcomed him with its sheer natural beauty: spectacular golden beaches, tall, graceful palms, swirling mists enclosing the foothills, and thick white clouds hugging the mountains. A familiar sultry air hung on his body like a second skin, sending rivulets of sweat along his temples and down the back of his neck.

After five years away, Merriman-Labor was almost certainly welcomed at the landing by a throng of friends and family. As they headed up the hill toward his father's house, the beauty and squalor of the Freetown streets blossomed around him. Barefoot women in bright dresses and artfully folded head scarves carried sweet-smelling cassava bread in baskets. Old ladies squatted on the dirt floors of open-air shops next to giant bowls overflowing with roasted peanuts and ripe cherries. The streets were muddy, and untamed grasses grew along the sidewalks. The air was a steamy bath of scents: sweat, fried fish, smoke, pepper-mint, animal excrement, spicy rice, sea salt, tangerines, coconut, gua-vas, and coffee. It made him hungry for something smooth and spicy, something African. He paid a silent homage to the tattered landmarks of Freetown: St. George's Cathedral, the customs house, the vegetable market, and the law courts. As he ambled up the hill with his family, he noticed that some of the stately stone buildings had begun to list and seemed to be sinking into the ground, as if the continent were swal-lowing up these European impositions. Dust to dust. Or in this case, as he stepped through the messy Freetown streets, mud to mud.

The following day, he ducked into the offices of the *Sierra Leone Weekly News* in Oxford Street just as heavy clouds swelled over Freetown, drumming out powerful rolls of thunder. Bowed over his desk as he attacked a sheet of paper with a red pencil, Cornelius May looked much the same as when Merriman-Labor had seen him in London: stout and elegant in his European suit. "Mr. Merriman-Labor,"

May's paper announced on his arrival, "belongs to that class of men who are never daunted by difficulties. He is still full of resources and is determined to make his way in life."[7]

"My enterprising young countryman!" May said, raising his head and reaching out his hand. He was full of questions. What did Merriman-Labor know of the new dreadnought battleships which would give the British the edge over the Germans? And his trouble with the benchers?

"The African General Agency would have been of great advantage both to Africans and to me," Merriman-Labor acknowledged. A wild wind whipping trees and bushes into a frenzy drew the two friends to the window.

"And now what course will you take?"

"I mean to devote my life to either Literature or to Law," Merriman-Labor told his friend. If he did pursue the law, they could expect him to be back in West Africa in the new year. May was pleased to know his young friend would be back home soon.

"And your lectures?" May asked, wondering if he would still be preaching his pet doctrine of cooperation. Merriman-Labor laughed.

"It will be all wit and humor," he said. He planned to leave out race, politics, religion, or anything else that might be controversial. For years he had fought hard to persuade traders to buy collectively, but he had come to the conclusion that they lacked confidence in one another and no amount of urging on his part could change that.

A violent crack of lightning seemed to split apart the huge dark belly of clouds, releasing a gush of water that beat so heavily on the corrugated iron roof that they had to raise their voices to hear each other. Merriman-Labor recognized that May didn't quite approve of his endless plea for cooperation, and he admitted his urgings had not inspired change. "After five years, I am getting to think that it will be very difficult for the present generation to see things the way I see things," he confessed.

They watched Oxford Street turn into a river of water. A drenched pedestrian waded through the ankle-deep current, holding a mangled umbrella uselessly over his head. Merriman-Labor told May that his lectures would present "manners and customs of Europeans likely to surprise Africans." He would give them comedy, but he also hoped the jokes, puns, and lampoons would communicate a powerful message about Africans and Britons. May wished him every success.

But his tour got off to a rocky start. After the first night, a reviewer for the *Sierra Leone Weekly News*—perhaps May himself—suggested the lecture needed to be shortened and the slides brought in earlier. A week later, the second lecture was dramatically improved. Although nearly two hours long, it was so "full of wit and humour," reported the *Weekly News*, that it "evoked a continuous expression of applause from those present," including many of the town's most eminent citizens. Merriman-Labor was now in demand and gave the lecture twice more—once in the schoolroom of the Holy Trinity Church and once in the Buxton Church basement. To celebrate, Cornelius May gave a dinner for him with a "small but distinguished company," and the Freetown Negro Progressive Association held a tea party in his honor.[8]

After his resounding success in Sierra Leone, Merriman-Labor set out, ready to present his travelogue to audiences in halls, courthouses, church basements, and schoolrooms in Liberia, Senegal, the Gambia, the Gold Coast, the Congo, Northern and Southern Nigeria as well as Fernando Po and São Tomé.[9] His first stop was Bathurst, the Gambia, where he stayed nearly two weeks, giving three successful lectures. "The patrons," he wrote, "included all the leading people on the island, white and black, Christian and Mohammedan." This auspicious beginning to his tour, he said, "encouraged me not a little."[10] By early November he was in the Gold Coast, then Lagos by the end of the month.[11] The enthusiastic reception he received from African audiences, he acknowledged, "flattered me beyond measure."[12]

The journey to Lokoja, Nigeria, was notoriously arduous, requiring passage up the Niger River on a government-run stern-wheeler with first- and second-class cabins for whites on the open upper deck. "Natives" were relegated to the lower deck, which they shared with the cargo, fuel, machinery, and luggage.[13] Leaving Burutu in the evening, the steamer chugged up narrow waterways that British traveler Constance Larymore described as "a liquid silver path, walled on each side with straight lines of mangroves, dense black shadows, and weird, bare white roots and stems."[14] As the small steamer splashed past riverside villages, Merriman-Labor anticipated his reception at Lokoja, more than three hundred miles upriver. He expected a sizable audience drawn from the community of educated Africans who had relocated from other West African colonies for high-paying jobs.

Unwelcomed at entertainments for African locals or British officers, these visiting clerks and artisans often found themselves with little to do in the evenings. They did not socialize with the "natives"—the word they used for non-anglicized Africans—who worked as poorly paid porters carrying sixty-pound loads fifteen miles a day for ninepence. Scottish geologist John Downie Falconer called these educated Africans "a class entirely by themselves."[15] In order to keep them entertained, colonial administrators routinely arranged lectures and other amusements. Merriman-Labor could expect that nearly everyone in Lokoja's official world would attend his program.[16]

A bevy of little canoes surrounded the paddleboat.[17] Boys and girls waved their oars and shouted enthusiastic greetings as European travelers on the upper deck tossed empty tin cans and glass bottles down to them. Merriman-Labor watched as the children scrambled after them, knocking each other's canoes aside in eager anticipation of gaining a treasure. While cheering and laughter came from both above and below, Merriman-Labor had to wonder how long Africans would compete against one another for such meager prizes.

When British barrister George Hazzledine arrived in Lokoja at the turn of the century to take up a position in the colonial court, he found it bedraggled and lacking in "material comfort." The roofs of the little wooden houses leaked, and violent storms rushed inside through "window-frames innocent of glass for months," he wrote, and "doors have no latches, tables no legs, washstands no tops, chairs no bottoms."[18] Constance Larymore, arriving just a few years later, also found her accommodation in a "ruinous condition," but described Lokoja as a picturesque town of bungalows and gardens on the banks of the Niger, surrounded by delightful, lush mountains. In every direction, she said, one found flowering trees and hedges, acacias, oleanders, and fragrant fruit trees: limes and oranges, mangos and guavas.[19] They both admired its extensive recreation grounds where British officers and civilians played polo, tennis, and cricket.

Merriman-Labor posted placards and distributed handbills throughout Lokoja during the days leading up to the lecture. His signs promised a witty yet educational lecture combined with life-size images from his Telescopigraph. As it happened, John Downie Falconer was in Lokoja at the time and found Merriman-Labor's advertisement so amusing, he transcribed it:

TWO-SHILLING TRIP FROM WEST AFRICA TO EUROPE.

GRAND TELESCOPIGRAPH DISPLAY

Straight and striking talks respecting scenes and life in the United Kingdom and France.

Mr. MERRIMAN-LABOR,

who is now touring 10,000 miles from London around Africa and back, will lecture on "Five Years with the White Man: or Scenes and Life in England, Scotland, Ireland, and France." The lecture will be found to be witty, chatty, humorous, instructive, and entertaining. It will be accompanied by

LIFE-SIZE PICTURES FROM A POWERFUL

TELESCOPIGRAPH

specially constructed for this lecture and superior to anything you have seen for a long time.

DON'T MISS THIS TREAT.

You have never heard the like before. It will take you some time to see the like again. We shall have such a fine time, hours together, to-night, commencing 9 p.m., at the Courthouse, under the chairmanship of the Cantonment Magistrate. Tickets 2s. each.

COME AND BRING A FRIEND.[20]

On the night of the performance a crowd gathered at the courthouse, a plain wooden building elevated on piles, its corrugated iron roof tinted red with rust. Croaking frogs and twittering crickets in the thick grass created rhythmic music as sunburned British officers loitered on the front steps smoking cigarettes, Muslim men chatted with their neighbors, and clerks from Sierra Leone and the Gambia filed in eager for a seat. As a group of British nurses arrived from the hospital, African mothers twisted in their seats talking with friends as their children dashed up and down aisles of mismatched chairs, unsteady stools, and overturned buckets. A cooling breeze drifted inside through glass-less windows.

In the center of the room, Merriman-Labor set up his Tele-scopigraph. As the crowd grew, he pulled back the hood of the lantern and polished the lenses and condenser with a clean cotton cloth.[21] He had probably learned through experience that any soot would distort the image and sometimes create an unpleasant burning smell. He pushed clean wicks into their slots and trimmed them. They needed to be perfectly dry to soak up the rich kerosene and produce a hot flame which was essential to a bright picture. Next, he filled the reservoir with fuel. The kerosene seemed of good quality: perfectly clear and odorless—a sign that he would get a clean, bright light. Poor fuel pro-duced an annoying yellow and smoky flame, which a teaspoon of table salt might improve but not cure.

Many minutes before the lecture was to begin he dragged a match across the tabletop. Keeping the flame very low, he slipped it into the lantern. The process could not be rushed. He had learned to let the light build up slowly. Only gradually would he turn up the wicks to their full height. Although the audience had already begun to murmur with antici-pation, it would be a full ten minutes before he could begin. He pulled the lantern's chimney to its full length and tightened the thumbscrews, then inspected the screen to ensure it was flat and clean. Many in the audience had seen their first magic lantern slides projected onto bed sheets hung from a mangrove tree by an enthusiastic missionary, but Merriman-Labor was probably using a high-quality linen screen to guar-antee a superior image. As he stood at the lectern, a small paraffin read-ing lamp threw just enough light for him to see his notes.

Some in the audience must have thought it strange that a young African should call his lecture "Five Years with the White Man," but others instantly realized that it was a send-up of popular European books about Africa like Herbert Ward's *Five Years with the Congo Cannibals*; Lionel Decle's *Three Years in Savage Africa*; or Agnes McAllister's *A Lone Woman in Africa: Six Years on the Kroo Coast*.[22] Merriman-Labor satirized so-called African experts, people who had merely viewed the country from the deck of a steamer, taken a quick trip to the interior, or served one term of a colonial appointment, and then returned "to Britain to write vol-umes about Africans and Negroes the world over." "Dr. Liarous," he called one such traveler who claimed to be writing a "most interesting book on the customs and manners of the black niggers."[23] Britons seemed perfectly comfortable with European travelers making grand pronouncements about African life, however little experience they had of it. Merriman-Labor upturned the usual order of things by claiming the right to be the observer rather than the observed. He would show how Britain looked through African eyes.

He nodded to the chairman of the evening, indicating it was time for his opening remarks. Looking into a small blue-tinted window at the back of the Telescopigraph, he saw a high, forked flame—the perfect intensity to project his images. When the chairman concluded, the audience whispered with excitement. Merriman-Labor surrendered his machine to a lantern operator and walked confidently to the front of the room. With a nod of his head a huge image of a bustling London street appeared on the screen.

"Away we go!" he cried, "From West Africa we are flying thither with the wings of thought." The audience gazed at the lively scene in front of them. "See how 'multitudes upon multitudes' rush hither and thither, helter-skelter-like, with so much motion and commotion, verging and converging in all directions ..."[24]

He asked them to envision themselves in London, a city of skyscraping buildings—some an exhilarating fourteen stories tall—so full of people that if you placed them "one behind the other, one foot apart, they would extend three thousand miles."[25] If they were willing, he would transport them to this magical place with its mysterious inhabitants. "If you will walk about the first City in the British Empire arm in arm with Merriman-Labor," he promised, "you are sure to see Britons in *merriment* and at *labour*."[26]

The next slide blazed a breathtaking bird's-eye view of London showing the star-shaped convergence of Poultry, Princes, Threadneedle, Cornhill, King William, and Queen Victoria streets.[27] "All roads," he said, pointing to the massive Old Lady of Threadneedle Street, "lead to the Bank!" Noting the curvy nature of the streets, he added that some were very zigzag—like the road to wealth.[28]

Projecting slides of Westminster Abbey, he described its sublime beauty: its marble columns, mosaic pavements, stained glass, and glorious monuments to kings and poets. What pleasure I had, he told his audience, to stand upon the bones of Shakespeare, Wordsworth, Tennyson, and all the kings of England![29]

John Downie Falconer, who attended the lecture, remembered that Merriman-Labor described Cleopatra's Needle on the Embankment "with a thrill of pride" and the beauty of "snow on the Embankment steps on a winter's morning." He recalled Merriman-Labor's surprise "at seeing ladies on horseback, dressed in hats and coats like men, at the public love-making in the parks, and at the rows and rows of suburban homes, whose sameness made it difficult to recollect one's house unless one remembered the number."[30]

After sharing dozens of slides and anecdotes, Merriman-Labor told his audience that five years in Britain had confirmed his belief that no matter his or her color, the respectable person "will, as a rule, receive amongst a liberal-minded people, any position that his ability merits."[31] "Take it from me," he continued, "in Britain, we have already justice for the Blacks and equality for Blacks and Whites. We shall have equality and justice elsewhere some day."[32] It was a statement of faith and hope shared by many in the audience.

Merriman-Labor's final images displayed "a series of photographs of military and naval reviews, with pictures of the King and Queen." The moment the monarchs appeared, Falconer remembered, "the whole audience rose and sang 'God Save the King.'" It was only after the audience had given a second resounding rendition of the British national anthem that Merriman-Labor shut off the magic lantern and brought the evening to a close.[33]

After his successful performance in Lokoja, Merriman-Labor traveled north to Zungeru, probably going by boat or canoe to Barijuko, then the last twenty-four miles by a government-run tram.[34] Constance Larymore recalled the tram as a noisy, dirty, and smoky affair, which "rattled, bumped and swayed along the tiny line, with much shouting and vociferation."[35] Merriman-Labor was drawn to Zungeru not only because it was the capital of the British Protectorate of Northern Nigeria, but also because it was now home to the most important person in his life: his mother.

Gillian Merriman-Wilson had not seen her only child for six years.[36] Since October 1903, she had been employed at the government-run

Freed Slaves Home in Zungeru providing health care, elementary education, and practical training for formerly enslaved women and children.[37] When she wrote to her son each week, she must have described her life educating dozens of children, many of whom had been sold into slavery for a few shillings' worth of corn or salt by their poverty-stricken parents.[38] She had witnessed heartbreaking scenes. Children arrived at the home suffering "from guinea worm and other diseases and usually reach Zungeru in a terribly emaciated condition."[39] How filled with joy she must have been to see her son enjoying good health and success.

By the time Merriman-Labor arrived in 1908, she must have realized that she would not be in Nigeria much longer. The previous year a government committee found that the home did not help the inmates (as the children were called) become self-supporting or useful to their society.[40] It is easy to imagine her frustration to learn that the government men considered the training they provided in hygiene "premature" and "unnecessary." The committee accused the home of providing the children with too many essentials. "Neither food, nor clothing, nor housing entirely depended on the activities of the inmates themselves," they observed, and so did not "inculcate in them self-reliance." They concluded that the children were not prepared for what their lives would be outside the institution.[41]

Gillian Wilson and the other teachers no doubt argued that the training they provided prepared the children for a better life. Many former residents from the home went on to train at missionary schools to become teachers, clerks, clergymen, maids, and skilled workers.[42] In fact, as historian G.O. Olusanya argues, "the inmates of the Freed Slaves Home were … amongst the first group of indigenous pioneers of western education and influence in Northern Nigeria."[43]

In Zungeru, the Deputy Governor and Chief Justice barred Merriman-Labor from lecturing. On humanitarian grounds, they explained to him, the government had pledged not to allow the local people to adopt European customs and manners because they found they "had a deteriorating effect." Merriman-Labor left no comment other than to remark that the government officials had "received him very courteously."[44] He had long felt European influence had enervated Sierra Leoneans, but he could not have been happy about being prevented from lecturing, especially when it meant he would not be able to perform his witty lectures for his mother.

Here one longs again for a surviving diary, note, letter, or photograph, some tangible message from the past to suggest the tenderness or tensions between mother and child. Only two things we know for certain. First, Gillian's example inspired her son "with a sense of devotion to duty."[45] And second, as she watched her only child board the steamer or canoe that carried him to his next stop, she had no idea when she would see him again.

Merriman-Labor travelled some ten thousand miles and lectured to "hundreds of Europeans and thousands of Africans."[46] Leaving Zungeru, he returned to Lokoja, but his subsequent route is unknown. He hoped to be in South Africa by the middle of February.[47] From there, he planned to return to London through Central and East Africa, then into Palestine, and finally Europe.[48] He was keen to visit Greece and Rome. Eager, perhaps, to see the ruins of great empires that had each conquered, commanded, and then, in their turn, collapsed.

6

HOME TRUTHS

By early 1909, Merriman-Labor was back in wintery London and ready
to settle things with the benchers. As snow flurries dusted the city in
late February, his accountant and solicitor reported to Lincoln's Inn
that the outstanding liabilities of the African General Agency had been
fully discharged. Not until they had all gathered on a cold April 1 were
the benchers at last satisfied and informed the Society of Lincoln's Inn
that Merriman-Labor had entirely "discontinued his objectionable business." After nearly a year, he was finally given permission to be called
to the bar.[1]

On Call Night at Lincoln's Inn, May 5, 1909, the benchers sat at a
large table in the Great Hall, their "august state" separated, as one lawyer described it, "from the vulgar crowd of barristers and students by
an array of sideboards."[2] Distinguished guests in white tie and tails
floated among the venerable silk-robed King's Counsel as roasts were
served and taken away; glasses raised and lowered; congratulations
given and received. The evening thrilled with ancient privilege. No one
mentioned that only one or two of the new barristers would actually
earn a living practicing law.[3]

Merriman-Labor thought the event a silly ritual. After the men had
eaten a "grand dinner" and drunk "champagne *ad libitum*," he wrote, a
distinguished bencher "takes the student by the hand and repeats these
magic words, 'By the authority and permission of the Masters of the

131

Bench, I hereby call you to the Bar of this honourable Society.'" The words "instantly change the student into a full bloom barrister," making him "a legalised and licensed liar." "Pardon me," he added teasingly, "I mean a lawyer."[4]

Writing to Cornelius May in Sierra Leone, he reported that "I was called (to the Bar) yesterday by shaking hands with and hearing some formal words from the Right Honourable the Master of the Rolls. This morning I was enrolled a Barrister at the Lord Chief Justice's Court."[5] Seeing Merriman-Labor's name among the newly called barristers in the clipping from the London *Times*, his family and friends must have been simultaneously delighted at his achievement and gratified that he would soon return home.[6] He considered moving to South Africa to practice and requested a Certificate of Admission from Lincoln's Inn, a document given to colonial barristers intending to practice law abroad. But then he changed his mind. He decided to remain in England to work, he told the *Sierra Leone Weekly News*, as an advisor on colonial and international law.[7]

His decision to remain in Britain did not sit well with his supporters in Africa. "Whilst congratulating Mr. Labor, and wishing him every success," Cornelius May wrote in the *Weekly News*, "we trust that circumstances will soon point out to him that his true sphere of labour is at home among his own race and people."[8] The editor of the *Gold Coast Leader* expressed the same sentiment, noting that his "wide separation" from home would make it difficult for him to achieve his life-long goal of benefiting Africa and Africans.[9] What they didn't know was that his motive for staying in London had little to do with colonial law and everything to do with his writing career. In a private meeting in April, he had told the benchers that he intended "to devote myself to writing and not go into trade." He might have told the *Sierra Leone Weekly News* that he would pursue literature in his "spare time," but in private he was already planning the book he felt sure would win him accolades in Europe.[10]

He was determined to turn the "Five Years with the White Man" lecture into a wickedly funny book, one which would "reveal such truths as may best be spoken in jests."[11] Wit and humor, he was convinced, would be essential for the black man writing about a white world. "Considering my racial connection," he wrote, "the world will be better prepared to hear me if I come in the guise of a jester."[12]

Throughout 1909, he expanded his articles and lectures about living in Britain. Embracing the idea that "the sublime always has a ridiculous counterpart," he combined "sense and nonsense, facts and fiction,—the old, the new and the 'novel' concerning Britons and Blacks."[13] He confined the action to one day. In the book, the famous bells of London—Big Ben and St. Mary-le-Bow—would keep time as Merriman-Labor guided a fellow African through the streets of the metropolis, making witty observations on British life. He called it *Britons through Negro Spectacles*.

He drew not only from his personal experiences, but from current events to craft his portrait of modern Britain. For the last month, the country had been gripped in a "naval scare." Since 1906, in response to an escalating arms race with Germany, the British Navy had been building powerful dreadnought battleships, but they were expensive and the Liberal government wanted to spend less on armaments and more on social programs. The front page of the *Daily Express* on February 8, 1909, declared "Today is fraught with the gravest possible consequences to the future of British Empire."[14] Conservatives lamented what they saw as their country's dwindling lead in the arms race, predicting the country's naval supremacy was at an end. "Is Britain going to surrender her maritime supremacy to provide old age pensions?" the *Daily Mail* asked.[15] Conservative M.P. George Wyndham demanded eight new dreadnoughts: "We want eight and we won't wait," he famously declared.[16] The phrase caught on like wildfire. Navy supporters chalked the slogan on sidewalks and the walls of buildings. They chanted it in the streets. The press flashed it across their pages. Music hall singers took it up and spun it into martial ditties.

Merriman-Labor had enormous respect for the navy—a hundred years before, it had delivered his great-grandparents from the bowels of a slave ship and given them a new life in Freetown. But he found the current naval scare preposterous and lampooned the current hysteria without mentioning a single warship. Taking up his pen, he wrote: "In the House of Commons the member for Nervousburgh is responsible for the announcement last night that a powerful State in the planet Mars is about to wage war against Britain." Instead of dreadnoughts, he substituted a novel invention that few people associated with war. According to the member from Nervousburgh, he joked, the Martians own "ten thousand areoplanes to Britain's one thousand. If war is declared, it means we are done for. We shall be mere strangers in our own land."[17]

Growing up in a British colony, he knew better than any M.P. what it was to be treated as a stranger in one's own land. "Is not the Saxon-Briton a stranger in Britain?" he wrote, suggesting that Britons had been conquering other peoples for so long, they had forgotten this island was not their ancestral home. The Briton is also a stranger in Africa, he added. "I wonder where his home is?" he asked sardonically.[18]

Merriman-Labor watched with apprehension as the movement for South African independence steamrolled the rights of black subjects. A national convention had met from October 1908 to May 1909 to determine how to combine four British colonies into a unified South African dominion. Of the thirty delegates involved in the negotiations, not one was black.[19] During the conference, the question of political rights for black Africans proved contentious: the Cape Colony fought to maintain its policy of allowing any man who met literacy and property qualifications to vote, but the Transvaal and Orange River Colony rejected black representation entirely. Ultimately, the framers of the proposed constitution agreed to allow each colony to dictate its own franchise laws, but ruled that "only persons of European descent" could serve in the new nation's parliament.[20]

Black South Africans vigorously protested against the prospective constitution, urging the British government to assert its power to protect their rights. William Schreiner, a former Prime Minister of the Cape Colony and brother of the novelist Olive Schreiner, joined their cause and led an African deputation to London in July 1909 to appeal to the government directly. Schreiner felt the subjugation of black subjects violated the British sense of justice and honor. "The coloured inhabitants of South Africa," he argued, "are barred from the opportunity to rise and evolve naturally, which is the right of every man in a free country." To be clear, he was not arguing, he explained, for "equality of all men," but rather making his case "upon the doctrine of the right to freedom of opportunity."[21] South African officials took every opportunity to undermine Schreiner and the African deputation by calling them "extreme negrophilists" who would do irreparable harm to native people. John X. Merriman, the current Prime Minister of the

Cape Colony, insisted that "Mr. Schreiner's present mission is one of the most unkind things ever done to the natives." The "spirit of justice and fair play," the official delegates maintained, would guarantee fair treatment of native Africans. [22]

After years of following British politics, it was easy for Merriman-Labor to imagine how arguments about Africa would unfold, and he caricatured them in a chapter of *Britons* called "The Spirit of Imperialism." The House, he joked, was currently considering "the proposed new Constitution for Disunited West Africa." [23] The first question would come from a friend of Africa, very likely the radical politician Sir Charles Dilke, whom he would camouflage as "Sir Charles Goodman." "How is it that notwithstanding one hundred and twenty years of British rule and civilisation in parts of West Africa," Sir Goodman asks in *Britons*, "the natives are not considered fit to have a representative government?" [24] The Irish could be counted on for a home rule speech, so he created "Mr. Harry Hardbone, representing an Irish constituency," who "is anxious to know why the natives cannot be allowed to rule themselves." Finally, Mr. Carr Harding, a Labour member" (almost certainly James Keir Hardie), takes the floor, skewering the government's position, which supports the "octopus hands of the grabbing financier squeezing the life-blood of the poor and sweated Africans." [25]

When the House debated the proposed South African constitution in August, his characterization was not far off the mark: Sir Charles Dilke strenuously objected. "We have set before the world," he argued, "the doctrine of 'no bar of race or colour.' Our going back is to turn our backs on our great past." [26] Liberal M.P. Harold Cox maintained that the language of the color bar violated the very foundation of liberalism and was an "insult to the whole British Empire." Despite their protests, a new constitution for South Africa depriving black subjects (except those in the Cape) of voting rights won an easy approval from the British government.

"SOUTH AFRICA BILL PASSED" read the front page of the *Daily Express* on August 20. [27] Merriman-Labor tossed the newspaper on the table and gazed into the rainy afternoon. The heart of the problem, he was convinced, lay in the fact that neither the British Parliament nor the British people were particularly interested in Africa. He had known for some time that, as he put it, "the mind of the average elector in

Britain as regards West Africa is a perfect blank." The British voter didn't even know where Africa was, he laughed dispiritedly, and was "too busy with his own troubles to think about those of the Negro." When it came down to it, the average Briton knew little about Africa and cared even less. Of the rights and fortunes of black colonial subjects, he concluded, "he is not concerned."[28]

Standing in the post office, Merriman-Labor ran an affectionate hand over his parcel. Where others saw a package neatly secured with string, he saw a world he had built, a product of years of observation, thought, and struggle. Who would know that his very essence wound through the inky letters? He passed his sturdy bundle to the mail clerk the way a mother hands her baby to a sitter—gently, nervously, with every hope for its safe and generous handling. Now all he could do was wait for a publisher to accept it.

It might have taken weeks, or it might have taken months, but the result of Merriman-Labor's wait was clear. Even though London was the biggest market in the world for books, nobody wanted *Britons through Negro Spectacles*. It must have come as a shock. He had never doubted the book's appeal. Perhaps Adam Lorimer, author of *The Author's Progress: Or the Literary Book of the Road*, had it right. British publishing, he maintained, was a fundamentally conservative business. While editors "are always on the alert for something fresh and original," he contended, "it must not be too fresh or too original."[29] They had never seen anything like *Britons through Negro Spectacles*.

Or perhaps Merriman-Labor's playful lampooning of British courtship—from his descriptions of couples "spooning" in city parks to his mocking report of advertisements in newspapers for husbands and wives—spooked publishers afraid of censorship. James Joyce's *Dubliners* had been suppressed since 1905 for his use of the word "bloody" as well as his light-handed description of sexual attraction. It would be held back for another five years, not published till 1914. Circulating libraries—which controlled most of the bookstores selling new books in London—were secretly agreeing to censor any book which "by reason of the personally scandalous, libelous, immoral, or otherwise disagreeable nature of its contents, is in our opinion likely to prove offensive to any considerable section of our subscribers."[30] Merriman-Labor's playful satire of British institutions, they may have reasoned, was sure to offend at least some of their subscribers.

If his family had been in a position to support him, if connections in law or business had landed him lucrative legal cases, or if he'd simply had the income from the African General Agency, he might have been able to wait for a perceptive editor to see the merits of his work. But he had no regular income and, as a new barrister, he might spend years trying to build a practice. Before lack of money forced him back to Africa, he had to get *Britons through Negro Spectacles* into print.

To self-publish a book in Edwardian England was an enormous gamble that conventional wisdom warned against. "The young Author," Lorimer cautioned, "must be strongly dissuaded from risking his own money in a venture which does not recommend itself to publishers."[31] But Merriman-Labor believed he had advantages over other young authors. First, he came from a printing family and knew something of the business and, second, the success of his lectures proved the appeal of his story. Surely the thousands who had heard him speak could be counted on to buy the book.

He threw himself into the production and promotion of the work that he hoped would be a sensation in Europe and Africa. The cost to produce, distribute, and promote *Britons* would be high: printing, shipping, and advertising on the scale he had in mind would run to at least £200. He ordered two thousand copies—double the size of most first printings—from W. Cave & Co, a Brixton stationer, and planned to pay the £80 of outstanding charges once sales receipts rolled in. Willing to support Merriman-Labor in his venture, Cave also allowed the "Imperial and Foreign Company"—Merriman-Labor's self-publishing entity—to use his office for its business address. A.W. Leslie, his prosperous African American rubber merchant friend, lent him £30 toward publication costs. Merriman-Labor may have received smaller contributions from others to begin production.[32]

Expecting lively sales in Africa, Merriman-Labor shipped hundreds of books to Sierra Leone, the Gold Coast, Nigeria, and South Africa. Copies went to newspaper editors on consignment with an offer of a discount if they would "keep a continuous advertisement" in their papers. He also included an extra copy in the shipment, explaining he would be "glad to receive a copy of any review for insertion in a possible second edition of the book."³³ Having yet to sell a single copy, he was so certain of success, he was already planning another printing.

But *Britons* was only the tip of his publishing ambition. Even as he launched that book, he had another one in the works. *A Tour in Negroland* would also be completely original: a ripping tale of African adventure told not by a great white hunter, explorer, or missionary, but by an African.³⁴ This book, "which is under preparation," he wrote, "will tell a charming, novel-like story of a tour of 15,000 miles through West, South-west and Central Africa, recently undertaken by the author." *A Tour in Negroland*, he promised, "will hold you spellbound from start to finish."³⁵ Not only would it provide historical information about African life and descriptions of its stunning landscapes, it would chronicle the life and death exploits so essential to the exotic adventure genre. He tantalized readers by promising to "give details of exciting adventures with 'a class of wild men' against whom he had to fight his way along the River Niger."³⁶ It would feature "speaking pictures"— probably photographs or drawings—which he promised would "greatly enhance the attractiveness of this powerful book." For those willing to order a copy, "life, spirit, and fire are in every line of over three hundred pages."³⁷

In August 1909 crisp, bright copies of *Britons through Negro Spectacles* arrived in the offices of some of the best British newspapers and journals of the day, including the London *Times*, *The Athenaeum*, *The Spectator*, *The Academy*, *The Outlook*, *The Observer*, the *Saturday Review*, and the satirical magazine *Punch*. On August 22, Merriman-Labor read the much-anticipated first review. A long paragraph appeared in the "First Glance" column of the respectable, middle-class *Observer*, Britain's oldest Sunday newspaper with a circulation of forty thousand. Wedged between remarks on *The Decay of the Church of Rome* and a biography of naturalist Gilbert White, the review described *Britons* as "a quaint and candid description of life in London from the negro point of view." The reviewer was amused by Merriman-Labor's description of the British climate as "a veritable ten-plague-of-Egypt concern" and his idea that "the negro lady approaches the contour of the Venus de Milo more nearly than the London actress." The brief evaluation concluded by indicating that "suffragettes may be interested in his parallel between the progressive emancipation of women and of the negro."[38] Though it didn't lavish all the praise he might have wished, Merriman-Labor must have felt it was a promising start to the kudos that would inevitably follow.

In the coming days, other short reviews appeared in a variety of regional and national newspapers and magazines. The conservative *Outlook* said, "to see ourselves as others see us is sometimes a profitable if a disagreeable experience, and some home-truths are told in plain English by Mr. A.B.C. Merriman-Labor."[39] The *Manchester Courier* offered an unusually perceptive appreciation which characterized Merriman-Labor as "sharply pertinent and outspoken in his observations" and noted that the "book is a reversal of our ordinary approach to the racial question." If, the reviewer observed, Britons are "not entirely bad as some would paint us, we are not wholly entitled to laud ourselves on our superiority either intellectual or moral."[40] For the *Dundee Courier*, the book offered a "genial" literary style with humor that was a "trifle elementary," but nevertheless would "give a not too critical reader an hour or two's quiet amusement."[41] Merriman-Labor must have been elated when the venerable London *Times* complimented his astute observations about British life. "Although there is much in this book that will amuse," the reviewer related, "it consists in the main of shrewd comments on English manners and customs from the point of view of an educated African."[42]

The first decidedly negative review came from the *Law Journal*, which found little to praise, calling the book unpleasant to read, lacking in genuine humor, and insulting to the legal profession. "It is not funny to call a student a '*stewdent*,'" the reviewer complained, "nor to say that 'as a practicing barrister he becomes a legalized and licensed liar.'"[43] He grudgingly acknowledged that it presented "the outlook of certain sojourners in our country," but concluded that "as a criticism of English institutions it is valueless." To him, Merriman-Labor's jokes were impertinences, and his presence in Britain temporary. Merriman-Labor couldn't know if other benchers shared the reviewer's animosity toward *Britons*. Future events would suggest they did.

In mid-September, the *Sierra Leone Weekly News* published the first African review written by Isaac Augustus Johnson, Merriman-Labor's friend and fellow activist in Liverpool who had introduced him to the work of the Ethiopian Progressive Association. Johnson, who had

recently returned to Freetown to take up a position as the vice principal of the African Methodist Episcopal Seminary, had shed his British
name. He was now known as Algerine Kelfallah Sankoh.[44] The two men
may have shared similar ideas about Africa and race, but Sankoh disapproved of *Britons*. For him, sobriety, solemnity, and seriousness assured
respect for the black man, not puns, satire, and lampoon. He found the
book's humor so distasteful, he accused Merriman-Labor of pandering
to a frivolous reading public. "To the intelligent and serious-minded
reader," he asserted, the book left the impression that its author had "a
predilection to the vulgar and common." But, he wrote, "we know the
author, we respect and admire him" and "we would not like to think of
him as a jester, but as the man of iron-will, of serene disposition, of
calculating judgment."[45]

Sankoh gave the book's serious arguments his full approval, calling
Merriman-Labor's handling of race "masterly and statesman-like." After
a largely negative review, he concluded with an unexpected positive
turn by recommending *Britons* to readers as a "concise and well written
guide to London, in story-form," a "work of exceptional merit," and "a
much needed addition to African and general literature."[46] Would this
tail-end endorsement convince African readers to buy a copy?

Cornelius May must have realized how crucial a good review would
be to his young friend's success and published a second appraisal a
month later. The *Sierra Leone Weekly News* "London Correspondent" gave
Britons generous praise and gentle criticism, admiring its "jesting spirit"
and "wonderfully accurate description of English life and institutions."
While this reviewer also found Merriman-Labor's treatment of the
"delicate matters of sex" vulgar, he celebrated the "rollicking pleasure"
he took with language and noted that "Mr. Labor seldom digs far below
the surface," but "he seldom puts his spade to the ground without
extracting something of value."[47]

As reviews appeared and sales refused to surge, Merriman-Labor felt
dispirited. Snapping his umbrella shut and stepping onto one of the
motor omnibuses that now roared through the London streets belching
their black smoke, he was relieved to squeeze into a dry seat. With the
rain coming down, the upper deck would be a forest of jostling umbrel-
las. The whole of the interior was a jumble of ads: Nestlé's Milk, Grape
Nuts, Pears Soap, Cadbury Cocoa, the latest West End musical. The

conductor shouted at every stop urging more passengers to board the already crowded bus. Despite being sardined next to one another, no one spoke, their eyes glued to their newspapers or books. Even in such a small space, everyone seemed quite alone.[48] On days like this, for both Britons and strangers, Merriman-Labor felt, "this Metropolis of multitudes is as lonely as, and it may be lonelier than, an African desert."[49]

The streets of the city blurred as he looked through the rain-streaked window. He hated thinking of the reviews in the *Sierra Leone Weekly News* and wondered why his friends had called his work vulgar. Did the two men find it uncouth that he had referred to sensational stories published in the London penny papers? A ninety-nine-year-old man marrying a sixteen-year-old girl; the "lightning bigamist" with seventy-two wives; the curate who impregnated his housekeeper; or the woman who—after being arrested for burglary—was revealed to be a man.[50] Were his friends perhaps reacting to his irreverent allusions to the "the trial of Oscar Sodomorrah … for highly objectionable behavior not only towards his groom, Jack John, but also toward his mare"?[51]

Or perhaps the problem was his remark about scandalous London fashion like the "dress which opens on the right and the left of the skirt, the openings being quite above the knee."[52] The Vigilance Society of New York hadn't liked it either and had tried "taking criminal proceedings against the wearers," but, Merriman-Labor wryly noted, the "Chief of Police not seeing things in the same light … the attempt did not succeed."[53] It was possible Sankoh and "London Correspondent" didn't approve of his description of young women sitting on their young men's laps in city parks cuddling and kissing.[54] The London correspondent, who must have seen such things himself, may have been offended by the mention of a dozen periodicals in London "containing nothing but advertisements of women who want men, and of men who want women." Was Merriman-Labor's remark that "the white man or woman advertises for a wife or husband when he or she requires one, just as you will advertise for an article you desire to buy" objectionable?[55] Or did his friends think he had gone too far when he said such advertisers should report all their deformities, especially because, as he'd playfully suggested, "several mutilations, disfigurements, and deformities, are decidedly subpantaloonal"?[56] He smiled as he watched the raindrops splash against the omnibus window.

He freely admitted that "love, women, and marriage" were "somewhat questionable subjects" and had tried to explain that because he was writing about customs and manners, he was thus bound "to refer to these subjects, interwoven as they are with every aspect of human nature."[57] He had felt then—and still believed—that it was his "duty to mention them, notwithstanding their questionableness." He had hoped to make these delicate subjects laughable even to "Puritans and purists."[58]

As a group of young women boarded the bus, he remembered how daring it felt to assert his right as a son of Adam to love any daughter of Eve. "I ... like black girls," he had openly written in *Britons*. "And I like white girls. I like both, because it is right that I should like White and Black."[59] What felt bold to put into print had not aroused any wrath. None of the reviewers in either Africa or Britain had even mentioned what many would have considered an explosive remark. Even his dig at British sexual hypocrisy seemed to have been overlooked. Not one reviewer had responded to his reference to an English gentleman who had told him, "when I am at home in England I love English girls better, and when in Africa, black ones better."[60] Such casual miscegenation often raised hackles, but in the case of *Britons*, it was never mentioned. The simplest answer may be that no one read it. British reviewers were notorious book-skimmers, absorbing just enough to produce a hasty appraisal. Could it be that his provocative comments simply went unnoticed?

Or perhaps there was something about Merriman-Labor's artless innocence that protected him. He had openly confessed that he had no intimate knowledge of sexual matters because, as he told his readers, "I have never loved, nor have I ever been loved."[61]

Between the fall of 1909 and spring of 1910—just as Merriman-Labor was promoting *Britons*—the demand for rubber shares hit a fever pitch, creating what one scholar calls "some of the wildest mania scenes ever witnessed" on the London Stock Exchange."[62] During this boom, the *Financial Outlook*—one of nearly a hundred financial papers in the metropolis—hired Merriman-Labor to write articles on rubber and other West African concessions.[63] The timing couldn't have been better. He could use his knowledge of West African commerce to earn enough money to tide him over until book sales started taking off.

In the fall, he had shipped forty-five copies of *Britons* plus cuttings of favorable reviews to Francis Zaccheus Santiago Peregrino, founder of Cape Town's first black newspaper, the *South African Spectator*. A man well known among West African students in Britain, he was often sent materials and asked to promote them on commission. Although a staunch advocate of Pan-African interests, he saw *Britons through Negro Spectacles* as a dangerous book and refused to endorse it. "It may be regarded in London as the harmless product of a humorously disposed black man aiming at literary fame," Peregrino wrote to William Windham, the Secretary for Native Affairs in the Transvaal, but sensing the volatility of the remarks reviewers had overlooked, he was afraid the book might "create a feeling in the heart of black men akin to that of contempt toward those by whom he must be ruled" and disturb the "equilibrium so indispensable" to both races. He forwarded copies only to a handful of men in "official and political circles," including John X. Merriman, the Prime Minister of the Cape Colony.[64] When Peregrino informed Merriman-Labor in the fall of 1909 that he would not circulate *Britons*, the rejection may have felt like a minor setback, but in the coming months Merriman-Labor would come to see it as a lethal blow.

When now forgotten books such as W. J. Locke's *The Beloved Vagabond* and Guy Thorne's *When It Was Dark* flew off the bookshelves and Florence Barclay's *The Rosary* was becoming a runaway bestseller on both sides of the Atlantic, *Britons through Negro Spectacles* floundered. Although he had sold a thousand copies in England, the book was not doing well in the all-important African markets.[65] When the *Sierra Leone Weekly News* reported that the Cape Prime Minster, John Merriman, had suppressed *Britons* "on the grounds that it was calculated to arouse sedition," Merriman-Labor quickly refuted the statement. Desperate to quell any remarks that might damage both book sales and his reputation, he explained in a letter to the editor that the Prime Minister "did not well understand the tone and spirit of the book" and had made suggestions in his "private capacity" which kept it from circulating in South Africa.[66] Potential readers had to understand that *Britons*, though satirical, was not seditious. He could not afford for it to fail.

On Friday morning, May 6, 1910, Merriman-Labor and millions of other Londoners woke to the news that King Edward was gravely ill. "THE

KING," the headline of the *Daily Express* broadcast, "ANXIETY CAUSED BY AN ATTACK OF BRONCHITIS. TWO DAYS' ILLNESS."[67] The state of the King's health became the crucial subject of the day. Crowds of people gathered at the gates of Buckingham Palace to read the bulletins that royal servants fixed to the railings.[68] "The matter was discussed, the *Sierra Leone Weekly News* reported, "in streets, shops, homes and everywhere."[69] Newspapers printed innumerable special editions that people "eagerly scanned for the latest information."[70]

At midnight, as Merriman-Labor sat writing at his desk, the bells of St. Paul's began tolling. The sound, he thought, cast a "deep and real sorrow into the hearts of the people of London."[71] The King was dead.

The following day as he walked in the cold rain, Merriman-Labor saw signs of mourning everywhere. Shop windows decorated with cheerful pinks and blues the day before were now draped with somber purple and black. Everyone was dressed in mourning clothes. Those who could not afford a black suit of clothes wore black ties. Exhibitions, museums, concert halls, and restaurants were closed. "In every conceivable way," Merriman-Labor observed, "the people are striving to express their grief at the death of the king who was far and away the most popular monarch of his time."[72]

When the news reached Sierra Leone, the *Weekly News* declared, "King EDWARD the VII was our King—ours *de jure*, ours *de facto:* for bastards we are not." It maintained that "we too are a part of the British Empire; a people for whom the British Nation suffered travail and in whose interest and for whose welfare they will shed their blood again if necessary. So, *with the British Nation and as part of the British Empire we sincerely mourn the King's death*."[73] As thousands of people filed through Westminster Hall in London to view the royal body, in Freetown more than a thousand people gathered at St. George's Cathedral for a memorial service in his honor. Colonial administrators, "Chiefs of the Protectorate," civil servants, and seven hundred people of all denominations crowded into the African cathedral to remember the British king.[74] "The great assembly of black and white together," wrote the *Weekly News*, "was deeply moved, and it was apparent that the loss was one that came home to all as a personal calamity." It was a testament, the paper declared, "not only to loyalty but even to love on the part of all."[75]

On the day of the King's funeral Merriman-Labor may have been among the millions of people hoping to get a glimpse of the procession. Arriving at the three-mile route from Buckingham Palace to Westminster Hall at six in the morning, he would have found the sidewalks already densely packed with people of every description. Thousands had spent the night outside to ensure a spot to view the King's final journey. Squeezing through the crowd, he found himself "cheek with jowl with people who were I am sure pleasant enough in their own way, but rather better acquainted with beer than soap and water." It was so tightly packed he "began to envy the insensibility of a tinned sardine."[76] The sun grew blazing hot. Those with fans fluttered them, those without waved the air with whatever they had to hand— hats, newspapers, handkerchiefs. For more than four hours, Merriman-Labor endured the heat and jostling. "Some tried to shove in front of you with a brazen impudence," he recalled wryly, "some used guile, and some shoved because they could not help themselves—but all shoved, and all the time."[77] He watched as people overtaken by the heat sank to the ground. Miraculously, the St. John Ambulance Brigade—"kind-faced nurses, stretchers, sturdy black-uniformed men"—always managed to sail through the throng to revive the fallen spectators.[78] The *Daily Express* reported that some fifteen thousand people collapsed that day, overcome by the sun.[79]

In the distance, mournful horns intoned Beethoven's Funeral March in B-flat minor. As the procession approached, every man in the crowd removed his hat and stood at attention. "With slow and measured step," Merriman-Labor remembered, a detachment of generals and admirals marched past.[80] The crowd fell silent as the gun carriage bearing the King's body appeared: servants in livery led six caparisoned horses; over the coffin, a Union Jack, crown, scepter, and orb; Kildare, the king's favorite horse followed. The beautiful thoroughbred was saddled, a wreath of laurel draped over the pommel, his master's boots reversed in the stirrups, symbolizing the lost leader looking back on his troops for the last time.

And then came the dog.

The sad little white terrier trotted past, pitifully looking for the King, his master, pain in his soulful eyes, sorrow in his small reliable steps. "Not the harrowing music, the shining soldiery, nor yet the coffin itself," Merriman-Labor recalled, "moved one so much as the pathetic and lonely figure of that little dog." Perhaps it was that the terrier seemed so small or so perfectly helpless in his grief, but "the sight of it overwhelmed women who had hitherto struggled successfully with their tears, and set men gulping down lumps which rose strangely in the throat."[81]

When it was all over, Merriman-Labor struggled out of the crowd and walked home. Restaurants and shops were closed. The sun shone hot. During what should have been a joyful summer day, the city was subdued. The greatest metropolis in the world, it seemed, was as shattered by its loss as a little white dog.

By the summer of 1910, Merriman-Labor began to suspect something was terribly wrong with the *Financial Outlook*'s rubber reports. Everywhere unscrupulous promotors were developing companies that, as historian J. Forbes Munro explains, were "fraudulent or near-fraudulent concerns," only "floated to feed speculation in rubber."[82] Some were "vehicles for financial manipulation" of the stock market, others were "fringe companies, ranging from the wildly optimistic to the outright bogus" whose targets were the "gullible small investors."[83] What the *Financial Outlook*'s relationship was to fraudulent firms, Merriman-Labor probably didn't know. But it was clear to him that the *Financial Outlook* was asking him to sign "bogus reports about concessions." When he refused to put his name to them, he was fired.[84]

Counting on this job to pay his bills until he could publish *A Tour in Negroland*, he decided to try to recoup the money he had been promised in the only way open to him: he sued the *Financial Outlook* for breach of contract.

By June, it was clear that *Britons* was not selling in Africa. In London, just as a silk hat confirmed the decency of a gentleman, so a six-shilling price tag affirmed the legitimacy of a book.[85] But six shillings equaled a day's wages for many middle-class workers in Africa, which put his volume out of reach for most readers. Of the three hundred copies he had shipped to Lagos, Nigeria, only eleven had been sold by June 1910.[86] In a desperate attempt to jumpstart sales, he cut the price in half, but it was too late. By the summer of 1910, a year after its publication, he had to accept that *Britons through Negro Spectacles* was a commercial failure.

Unwilling to give up his dream of literary success, and desperate for income, he turned to teaching to sustain himself. He advertised as an experienced instructor and barrister in the *Sierra Leone Weekly News* ready to prepare "students wishing to qualify for Call to the Bar and those undertaking the study of Medicine, Theology, or a University career."[87] A tutor or exam coach in London could make a good living, but it took time to build up a clientele. With creditors pressing on him, Merriman-Labor must have been looking for a regular teaching income when he hit on the idea of going to the African Institute, a Christian training school for Africans and other people of African descent. There he could perhaps teach, escape London's high prices, and even save a little money, while he waited for a judgment in his legal case. Sometime late in 1910, he packed his bags and headed for Colwyn Bay, an unlikely little resort town on the north Welsh coast.

7

ON CAREY STREET

Nestled between five miles of sandy beach and the wooded slopes of the Caernarfonshire Mountains in Wales, the sleepy hamlet of Colwyn Bay was a small resort lauded for its mild weather and fine views. When Merriman-Labor arrived in the winter of 1910, he found a picturesque town with charming avenues, a handful of large beachside hotels, and an elegant seafront promenade bejeweled with cast iron railings and electric lights. At its center, the Victoria Pier featured a three-hundred-foot wooden boardwalk, shops, and a spacious "Moorish" pavilion offering daily concerts in season.

As Merriman-Labor walked up Nant-Y-Glyn Road, he took in the expansive view. The little town snuggled against a vast ocean looked like a colder, grayer version of Freetown. At the top of the street, he arrived at Myrtle Villa, a large Victorian house, home to the African Institute. Surrounded by two acres of grounds, the stately home devoted to spreading the Word of God in Africa seemed the perfect refuge.

The institute was well known in Sierra Leone. When it was newly opened, a feature article in the *Sierra Leone Weekly News* called it "noble work."[1] It was the brainchild of the Reverend William Hughes, a native Welsh-speaker who did not learn English until his teens and thought Christ's message was most powerful when heard in one's native language. "Africa for the Africans," he urged, "and Africa for Christ." From his experience as a missionary in the Congo, Hughes believed that

Africans educated in Britain could become a "powerful civilising medium" in their home countries where they would understand the culture and be suited to the climate.[2] In addition to a typical British education, the young men and women who came to him were also given practical training in printing, tailoring, carpentry, ironwork, and wheel repair. The school even operated its own press, which trained students and produced its promotional materials.

Hughes had been acquainted with Merriman-Labor's writing since at least 1900 when he wrote that he had read his lectures on the Negro race "with deep interest."[3] Meeting him in person, Merriman-Labor saw Hughes as a deeply religious man who had not only dedicated his life to missionary work, but was outspoken about injustices against native Africans. After Parliament's recent approval of the South African constitution, he had written a sharp letter to the *Manchester Guardian* warning that "there is a day coming when the British people will look back upon this colour bar with shame, as we are now looking back upon slavery."[4] There were two Sierra Leonean students enrolled in the institute who, though a few years younger, might have known Merriman-Labor: Arthur Ernest Ajibode Nicholls and Carter Ajagbe Konibagbe.[5]

If Merriman-Labor had planned on teaching, finding only six other full-time students enrolled at the missionary academy must have disheartened him. Hughes may have let him lead a lesson or two, but probably enlisted him to speak at one of the many "deputation visits" he and the students made all over Britain to raise money. With his easy laugh, polite manner, and polished speaking style, Merriman-Labor would have been a natural.

After London, the Welsh resort felt tranquil, and he no doubt spent time exploring the long miles of beach or rambling up the many trails in the foothills. Nearby paths took him to the Clwydian hills, the ridge of Moel Siabod, and the Vale of Conway. High above the ocean, he took in glorious views of the coast.

Former students pursuing advanced studies at prestigious British universities returned to the institute for the Christmas holidays. Among these were the brilliant Ishmael Charles Pratt, born in Freetown, who had qualified as a medical doctor in Edinburgh and was just finishing a diploma course at the Liverpool Tropical Diseases Hospital. Pratt's beautiful singing voice—which Hughes often enlisted for his fundraising efforts—filled the institute with carols and hymns. There was also Nigerian medical student Ladipo Oluwole, who had not only received honors in both medicine and surgery at Liverpool University, but had also proved himself the institute's most talented cricketer during matches with local teams.[6] These well-educated, ambitious men must have spent hours around the table in lively conservation as garlands sparkled on the Christmas tree.

Despite Hughes's efforts to keep it a secret, Merriman-Labor soon realized the school's desperate financial situation. At thirty-three, a barrister, experienced teacher, and published writer, he must have been dumbfounded to discover his name listed on the school roster as a student. In early 1911, he was in dire need of a lifeline, but he could see the circumstances of the African Institute were more precarious than his own. Heartbreakingly aware that the school would not stay afloat much longer, he said his goodbyes and returned to London. How he would survive in the great metropolis he did not know.

The story of aspiring Africans moving to London to pursue their dreams and failing in the attempt was so familiar to Merriman-Labor that he had recounted it as a cautionary tale in *Britons through Negro Spectacles*. There he told the story of "Arthur Adventurer," a former schoolmaster much like himself who uses his savings to go to England to pursue a professional degree. Unable to find employment as a clerk, Arthur drifts until he becomes "a financial wreck," his money having "vanished with the wind." Penniless, he lives in a slum and makes a few pennies by "open-air preaching" in Hyde Park before sending "begging letters" to a rich old man promising "all the happiness of heaven if he only took pity on him, as … he belonged to a distressed and downtrodden race." The rich old man, wrote Merriman-Labor dryly, "evidently preferred the earthly happiness which his wealth made certain to the uncertain happiness hereafter" because he informed Arthur that begging letters were illegal in Britain and he would not hesitate to have him arrested.[7]

Arthur, Merriman-Labor informed his readers, was too ashamed to return to Africa "worse than he left," because people at home would laugh at him and say "this man began to build and was not able to finish." Growing desperate, Arthur becomes a gambler, then a swindler, and finally a fraud. "On the strength of the whiteness of the wrong side of his unwashed collars and on the appearance of a full-buttoned old overcoat pressed to look like new," Merriman-Labor explained, "he managed to impose on credulous landladies everywhere." Arthur dons an array of disguises from "Tom Swell," the son of a Sierra Leonean council member, to "Jack Wealth" a law student. At one point he poses as "James Newrich," a medical student, then as "Dick Merchant," an agent for a trading house in South Africa. Just before the law catches up with him, he takes on the most promising disguise of all. He becomes the wealthy "Prince Omohoba, a possessor of gold fields in West Central Africa." Because of his antics, Merriman-Labor humorously complained, some people assumed a respectable-looking black man must be royalty. As a result, landladies and tradesmen everywhere produce princely bills to Africans "for beggarly supplies." Finally, an astute landlady places "Prince Omohoba and his diamond mines within the iron grip of the police."[8]

"I was in court during the trial," Merriman-Labor recalled, when Arthur was found guilty of procuring lodgings under false pretenses. Because he did not understand the law of the land, the court was merciful. "One week imprisonment was all he got," Merriman-Labor wrote. "Such is British mercy."[9]

This familiar tale of struggle hit closer to home in the spring of 1911: Merriman-Labor found himself in desperate straits.

On a cold April morning, he stood in front of 41 Conduit Street, just a few blocks from Piccadilly, clutching a circular he had probably been handed on a busy street corner. It may have advertised "Money Lent at Five Per Cent," or perhaps "Money Lent on Note of Hand from £10 to £5000" or just "MONEY" in bold capital letters, then promises of "loans granted to responsible persons residing in any part of England" or "the whole to be repaid by EASY PAYMENTS, for any length of time, as will best suit the convenience of the Borrower."[10] Unable to find a permanent position as a clerk or eke out a living as a barrister, he was forced to take a step that would have been unimaginable just a few months before. The very act of borrowing from a moneylender violated his sense of integrity, self-worth, and financial judgement. But his suit against the *Financial Outlook* had not been settled, and he had nowhere to turn. He walked into the offices of A.S. Block.

They glittered with West End opulence. Merriman-Labor took in the elegant reception room, the handsomely decorated oak and mahogany furniture, a case on one side glowing with expensive jewelry.[11] He probably thought he was doing business with someone called "Henry Harris," the pseudonym Block and his two partners used in offices all over England.[12] *Truth* magazine called the trio "bloodsuckers" and cautioned against taking loans from them. It "means ruin for a man," it warned, to fall into their "clutches."[13] Perhaps Merriman-Labor had not been warned of such men or had no alternative. Whatever his reasons, he borrowed £50 from Block on the expectation of a £600 judgment against the *Financial Outlook*. The exchange was humiliating; the terms devastating. Block charged him interest of £25 every three months—an astronomical annual interest rate of 200 percent.[14]

He made a second dramatic decision: he sheared his hyphenated name at this time, becoming simply Augustus Merriman.[15] In a letter to the *African World and Cape-Cairo Express* he explained "that he has abstracted the affix, 'Labor,' from his name, and desires to be known in the future by the name of 'Augustus Boyle Chamberlayne Merriman' only."[16] One has to wonder if the arrival in England of his younger half-brother, Michael Maurice Labor, created a rupture between him and his father.[17] Did Joshua Labor somehow slight his elder son, who shaved off his father's name in anger? Or did he rebrand himself in the spirit of optimism, making himself the "merry man" in the face of financial calamity?

Over four hot days in late July 1911, the Universal Races Congress swept into London. Two thousand delegates from around the globe met to discuss racial matters. They included W.E.B. Du Bois and Mohandas Gandhi, as well as an illustrious assembly of reverends, lawyers, aristocrats, philanthropists, linguists, captains of industry, politicians, explorers, pacifists, professors, soldiers, colonial governors, anti-imperialists, and feminists.[18] It was called "the most important conference ever held upon the mutual relations and duties of various races and peoples."[19] According to journalist Saint Nihal Singh, "among the official delegates were representatives from 160 professional societies, 12 British proconsuls and 8 former prime ministers, over 40 colonial bishops, 130 professors of international law, and the past or current presidents of more than 30 parliaments."[20] The London correspondent for the *Sierra Leone Weekly News* sensed apathy towards the Congress from Africans living in London, but encouraged them to attend because of the "unprecedented opportunities for 'racial' information." What a chance, he explained, to "show the world that we are fit and worthy to join in the Congress with the representatives from the other quarters of the world." He also believed Africans should go in order to demonstrate their appreciation of the "large-hearted white men who give so much of their energy on behalf of the subject races."[21]

In the end, only a handful of Africans attended. W.E.B. Du Bois ventured that only twenty-five black people were there. The *Sierra Leone News* deplored that "of the fifty or sixty West Africans in London exactly five took the trouble to attend."[22] Merriman-Labor is not listed as one of the attendees, but the dramatic shift in his interests away from humor and toward social science suggests he was influenced by the Congress and its publication.[23]

Had he been sitting in the audience, he would have found that several speakers were very much in sympathy with his own views. Franz Boas, a professor at Columbia University, argued that ideas of innate racial superiority and fixed "racial hierarchies"—so influential in the late nineteenth century and still widely held in the early twentieth— were obsolete. Nearly all the anthropologists at the Congress agreed. Contemporary research had convinced Boas that "the supposed mental and material inferiority of the negro race is a mere delusion, that inequality of achievement is due to nothing else but inequality of opportunity, and that the strong development of racial consciousness during the last century is the gravest obstacle to the progress of the negro."[24] Dr. Frances Hoggan's opening question in "The Negro Problem in Relation to White Women" reverberated with Merriman-Labor's own observations in *Britons through Negro Spectacles*. Hoggan observed that "in Africa of late ... the cry has arisen of danger to white women from black men ... one only wonders that so little feeling comparatively is shown when the white man is the aggressor and the victim has coloured skin."[25] For the *Sierra Leone Weekly News* correspondent, W.E.B. Du Bois's paper on the "World Position of the Negro" established him as "the greatest intellect in the Negro world."[26]

It would be hard to overestimate the significance of scholars refuting the scientific basis of race prejudice. Science was at last giving credibility to the notion of racial equality. Among white audiences, however, the Congress failed, as one historian puts it, to create "very much of a stir."[27] The *Morning Post* mocked it as a meeting of "soppy sentimentalists," while the London *Times* ridiculed the participants as a collection of freakish "men with long hair and women with short hair."[28] Although the delegates had ambitious goals for the future, forthcoming global events would destroy their aspirations for world peace and their plans for a second meeting. The Congress never convened again.[29]

Merriman-Labor could not yet pursue the ideas the Congress inspired—his deteriorating financial situation made it difficult to focus on anything other than survival. Cave & Co., the printers of *Britons through Negro Spectacles*, filed a lawsuit against him in July 1911 for nonpayment. With a legal complaint added to his looming debts, it must have seemed that only British justice could rescue him. An award in the full amount against the *Financial Outlook* would provide him with money to pay his outstanding bills and extricate him from poverty. In the meantime, he would live leanly, stripping himself of all but the most elementary requirements. Like other struggling clerks, he probably pursued temporary office work to make ends meet. He had to turn to whatever was available: addressing envelopes, correcting papers for an exam coach, or doing the books for firms that found themselves short-handed.[30] Despite his frugality, his borrowed money ran out before the wheels of British justice turned in his favor. Sometime near the end of 1911, he had no choice but to approach the *Financial Outlook* and ask for a settlement. He had sued for £600 of lost income. They offered to settle at £120. He took it.[31] Though substantially less than he had been hoping for, the settlement from the *Financial Outlook* bought him time and stability.[32]

He inaugurated a new direction for his writing. The failure of *Britons through Negro Spectacles* made him doubt the usefulness of comedy as social critique, and the Universal Races Congress had ignited his enthusiasm for science. Perhaps inspired by the power of Du Bois's empirical research on black lives, he now saw anthropology, sociology, linguistics, and political science as tools for solving Africa's problems. He knew only one place could open up the new world of scientific inquiry he was eager to enter. At the end of September 1911, he renewed his reader's card for the British Museum Library.

A letter in the summer of 1912 from the Reverend John Harris, the secretary of the Anti-Slavery and Aborigines' Protection Society, asked Merriman to send him names of Africans in London who would be interested in attending a forthcoming conference.[33] The names Merriman provided offer a telling glimpse into his London community. He listed forty-one names and addresses of men he called "well-known African natives" working, visiting, or studying in or near the metropolis.[34] Seventeen were businessmen, and twenty-four students at the various Inns of Court. Although he had been called to the bar two years earlier, he had maintained close connections with Africans coming for law training and may very well have guided some of them through their legal careers, perhaps helping with admission, finding accommodation, and coaching for exams. The chauvinism of the period—both British and African—may explain why no women appear on his list. Although many African women participated in trade, it seems few engaged in international business at the time, and, despite attempts by British feminists to enroll in law school, women were excluded from the Inns of Court and the legal profession.

On Tuesday, April 17, 1912, a most remarkable thing happened. London, the largest city in the world, came to a standstill.

Judges adjourned their courts. Brokers abandoned the Stock Exchange. People climbed on roofs, assembled in parks, and gathered on street corners. For nearly two hours, they held little squares of smoked or colored glass toward the cloudless sky to watch an almost total eclipse of the sun—something that hadn't been seen in Britain for more than half a century.

By noon, when the eclipse was nearly complete and the sun transformed into a thin crescent, Merriman would have felt the temperature drop noticeably. "The sky became an ashy blue," one observer reported.[35] The spectacle inspired not only awe, but industry. Wherever people gathered, hawkers loaned pieces of colored glass for a penny. When E. W. Maunder of Greenwich Observatory recommended getting as high as possible for the best view because of "the smokiness of London," Selfridge's department store invited Londoners to see the eclipse from its rooftop garden. Turning the celestial event into a marketing opportunity, Selfridge's promised that "every visitor will be provided with a piece of prepared glass, which he will be asked to keep as a souvenir."[36] It is easy to imagine Merriman standing among the crowds on the rooftop, holding his little rectangle of glass toward the sky.

Some said the eclipse was a sign of impending disaster, but, in truth, the unspeakable had occurred just three days before.

The first Merriman and the world heard about the fate of the *Titanic* came on April 16 in newspaper reports celebrating disaster averted. In a world made global by steamships, a story of the newest and largest luxury liner hitting an iceberg on its maiden voyage across the Atlantic created headline news. "EVERYONE SAFE," the *Daily Mirror* broadcast. "Morning of Suspense Ends in Message of Relief: PASSENGERS TAKEN OFF."[37] It was not until the next day that the world learned that more than 1,490 had drowned.[38] The London correspondent for the *Sierra Leone Weekly News* adopted a philosophical view of the tragedy. Although "this is by far the greatest wreck in history," he wrote, the great misfortune also made possible profound acts of courage. "Worthy of undying fame is the conduct of the ship's band," he wrote, who played lively dance music as people boarded lifeboats, then "Nearer My God to Thee" as the mighty ship went down.[39] Joseph Labor, Merriman's uncle, chastised the local clergy for failing to remind parishioners that the loss of the *Titanic* brought "forcibly to our notice the wonderful power of God against the mighty ingenuity of man."[40] Labor's concerns were surely assuaged by Philip Mauro's twenty-eight-page pamphlet *The Titanic Catastrophe and Its Lessons*, which was "selling like hot loaves" in Freetown by the end of the year.[41] Mauro, who had been on the steamer *Carpathia* that rescued survivors, transformed life and death on the *Titanic* into a religious metaphor: those who died had put their trust in the works of man; those who lived had trusted Christ and were rescued by "God's lifeboat."[42] Although the tract was wildly popular in Freetown and sold out in a matter of weeks, Mauro's interpretation of the *Titanic* overlooked the striking demographics of death on board a liner where a first-class ticket in a luxury suite cost £870 and a third-class ticket in steerage £8. Ninety-seven percent of women in first class survived, while less than fifty percent of women in third class lived. Only a small fraction of the men on board were rescued,

but those travelling first class were almost three times more likely to make it on board a lifeboat.[43]

In Southampton, the White Star Line constructed an enormous blackboard near the dock. "The words which may be written on that board of life and death," a *Daily Express* correspondent reported, "will decide what wives should be widows, what babes shall be orphans, what mothers shall be childless, what lovers forlorn."[44] In the coming hours, officials posted the names of the survivors as they could be verified. Only the names of survivors could be posted, because, as the correspondent noted, "large as the board is, it would never hold the names of all the dead."[45]

By the time Cornelius May, old friend and editor of the *Sierra Leone Weekly News*, arrived in June for an extended stay in London, Merriman's finances were desperately thin. To his delight, May had come to London not only to enjoy the metropolis and speak to "prominent individuals interested in African matters," but also to launch a new commercial enterprise, Gemel Limited. Like the now defunct African General Agency, Gemel's London-based office would provide commercial guidance for Africans doing international trade.[46] May intended to ship £100 worth of produce from Africa every month and offered Merriman a position as the company's legal advisor.[47] The financial lifeline Merriman so urgently needed was within his grasp.

During the unusually cold and wet summer, Merriman watched the sad disintegration of the African Institute, although few could have anticipated that its failure would be marred by scandal. The previous fall, an unmarried twenty-six-year-old seamstress in Colwyn Bay had given birth to an infant with dark skin. Some residents blamed the illegitimate birth on a student at the institute. When William Hughes threatened to sue those spreading the rumor, someone quietly informed scandal-mongering journalist Horatio Bottomley. Deep in debt himself and eager to create money-generating headlines for his sensationalist magazine, *John Bull*, Bottomley sent an undercover reporter to the institute to find or invent something sordid. Just days before Christmas, Bottomley blanketed the seaside resort with posters advertising the Colwyn Bay scandal featured in the current issue of *John Bull*: BLACK BAPTIST'S BROWN BABY.[48]

Two articles about the African Institute appeared in *John Bull* that December, accusing institute students of improper behavior with local women, and Hughes of improper religious instruction. The magazine reported with disapproval that lady visitors could be seen seated with black male students "on the sea front, in earnest, if not affectionate, conversation." Sometimes, in the evening after tea parties, the reporter went on, "'black and white' may frequently be seen strolling together down the road behind the Institute."[49] For *John Bull* and its audience, friendships between British women and African men were seen as immoral, indecent, and dangerous.

The seamstress Edith Dale did have an affair and a child with Grenadian John Lionel Franklin, who had been a student at the institute, but he was quite unlike any of the other men and women there. Franklin was a brilliant con artist with a rare—and for many—irresistible charm. Amiable, handsome, and talented, he had first come to Wales in 1903 as an actor in a production of *Uncle Tom's Cabin*. After attending a service at the institute, he told William Hughes that he had "given his heart to Jesus Christ."[50] In 1906, he enrolled at the institute, and eventually was sent to Nigeria to do missionary work. But instead of saving souls in Africa, he began stealing from and blackmailing the local people until he was finally arrested and jailed.[51] Even though the Church Missionary Society in Nigeria warned Hughes about Franklin's bad character, he welcomed the smooth operator back to Colwyn Bay in early 1911 and employed him on deputation trips, even agreeing to give him a portion of the donations as a commission. The power of Franklin's personal charm is probably best expressed in a remark Edith Dale made to her son. Although she never revealed his father's name, she assured him that she had never married because "she had never found anyone to match" his father.[52]

The accusations in *John Bull* decimated the finances of the already struggling African Institute. Claiming that his subscriptions had plummeted from £1,400 to £600 after the articles were published, Hughes had to close the school. Shortly after, he declared bankruptcy himself with a personal debt of £4,932.[53] In a last-ditch effort to save his reputation, his finances, and the institute, he sued Bottomley and *John Bull* for libel. Bottomley had also gone bankrupt that year—to the tune of £200,000—which suggests he welcomed the case as a chance to garner some much-needed publicity.

News of the scandalous trial hit the pages of northern newspapers and the London *Times* in mid-June 1912. Bottomley, serving as his own defense, destroyed Hughes during the cross-examination, bringing to light a troubling litany of poor business practices bordering on (and sometimes crossing over to) the criminal. Hughes admitted he had written bad checks and doctored the institute's enrollment records to make it look as though he had more students than he did. Bottomley also forced him to reveal that he had hidden the terrible financial state of the institute from his own solicitor and had essentially embezzled funds from a student. After the end of his testimony, the judge mercifully brought the case to a close. "John Bull and the African Institute: Verdict for Mr. Bottomley," reported the *Derby Daily Telegraph* on June 14, 1912.[54] Hughes never recovered from the public humiliation and died a dozen years later in a Welsh workhouse. Although Bottomley rode high for a few years, he ultimately ended up in prison for fraud, scarcely better off than Hughes. According his biographer, in his last years Bottomley "cut a pathetic figure and, a broken old man, he stumbled into obscurity."[55]

Just a few weeks later, a desperate situation closer to home overshadowed concerns about Colwyn Bay. In July, Michael Maurice Labor, Merriman's younger half-brother who had come to England eighteen months earlier to study medicine, had become dangerously ill, probably with pneumonia. The pneumonia itself was extremely dangerous, but Labor's attending doctor realized the case was far worse. He diagnosed the young man with a "gangrenous disease of the lungs"—perhaps necrotizing pneumonia, a rare complication of a bacterial infection—and ordered him home immediately.[56] There was no need to be concerned about the quality of medical attention he would receive in Sierra Leone. The young man was returning home to die.

Michael Maurice Labor arrived in Freetown on August 9 and passed away peacefully in his father's home fourteen days later. He was twenty-six years old.[57]

Just days after the death of his half-brother, Merriman was almost certainly standing with May and "twenty or thirty West Africans" in the soaring nave of St. Michael and All Angels Church in Croydon, just south of London. One of Britain's most celebrated composers, Samuel

Coleridge-Taylor, had been carried off suddenly at the age of thirty-seven. "His death removes from the ranks of British composers one possessed of a sense of beauty, and of undoubted originality," wrote the *Musical News*.[58] Born in Britain, Coleridge-Taylor was well known to the Africans living in London not just as a famous composer, but as the son of a Sierra Leonean and a shining example of African talent reaching its fullest amplitude.[59]

Elaborate floral arrangements filled the church. Here was an arrangement from the Royal Choral Society, there "a substantial floral tribute in white in the shape of Africa with Sierra Leone picked out in red flowers" given, according to the card, "from the sons and daughters of West Africa residents in London."[60] The organist from the Royal Choral Society played a funeral march and selections from Coleridge-Taylor's famous *Hiawatha's Wedding Feast*. Mourners lined the streets for two miles from the church to the cemetery.[61] For Merriman, Coleridge-Taylor's life would live on as evidence that black people were capable of extraordinary things, but his early death provided yet another example of a man of African blood dying in his prime. Crushed by these premature deaths, he returned to the British Museum Library searching for answers.

For Merriman perhaps the best thing to happen that summer was the publication of the first issue of the *African Times and Orient Review*. In July, two men in Merriman's circle, Sierra Leonean businessman John Eldred Taylor and Sudanese-Egyptian actor Dusé Mohamed Ali, launched the first London newspaper which would, as they put it, "lay the aims, desires, and intentions of the Black, Brown, and Yellow Races … at the throne of Caesar."[62] The paper spoke directly to Merriman's long-held concerns. Taylor and Ali proposed to give voice to the "millions of Britain's enlightened dark races" by covering African and Asian politics, people, and commerce, issues they believed were not reported accurately in the British press. If a man wished to be "well-informed as to native aims, capacity and development," they advised, he should "study the pages of *The African Times and Orient Review*."[63]

Dusé Mohamed Ali took over control of the publication when his partnership with Taylor blew up after the first issue. With the financial support of a group of West African businessmen—many of whom were well known to Merriman—Ali built the journal into an international forum read from Memphis to Tokyo. The *Sierra Leone Weekly News* called Ali "one of the most interesting personalities among the little band of coloured men resident in England."[64] Ali used the *African Times and Orient Review*, as historian Ian Duffield puts it, "to preach economic virtues which would … raise the world's coloured peoples."[65] Looking through the first issues, Merriman must have felt the principles and goals of the African General Agency had been resurrected in a new form. As the months went on, many of the services Merriman had extended to his clients also appeared in Ali's journal: offers to find "suitable Schools in England" for African and Asian children, to supply magic lantern lectures (including one on Sierra Leone and its people), and to make arrangements for "suitable hotels and apartments … for strangers in London."[66] Merriman was not listed on the newspaper staff, but if he were sharing his successful practices with Ali to earn a little money, it is tempting to imagine him as the unidentified "Lecture Editor." It is clear the two men knew each other, but impossible to know how much their relationship was based on cooperation or competition.[67]

In November, Cornelius May returned to Freetown, leaving Merriman with plans for the new company, Gemel Limited, to begin shipping produce in January. May also decided to send his son to London for professional training, and asked Merriman to tutor the young man, agreeing to more than £20 worth of coaching fees.[68] It was looking as though 1913 would be the year Merriman's financial troubles would turn around.

A few weeks later, a young African law student named C. J. Williams approached Merriman for help when his father—a ship captain in Nigeria—failed to send money. Convinced he needed to start promoting Gemel Limited immediately, and sure he would soon be able to pay off his loans once the produce began arriving, Merriman contacted David Swyers, a moneylender in the Strand, about securing another loan. For the privilege of borrowing £48 for himself and £20 for Williams, Merriman agreed to pay more than £60 in fees. The total loan amounted to £120: more than his annual salary as the manager of the African General Agency.[69]

He poured the cash into the new business. To make ends meet until Gemel became profitable, he promoted his coaching and educational consulting business in the *Sierra Leone Weekly News*, rebranding himself the principal of the "University and Law Academy." To attract clients, he advertised "an original method of Mnemonics to read for the Examinations of the University of London or the Inns of Court," a technique which would give "the minimum amount of work to the student and a maximum of knowledge."[70] Advertisements for Gemel Limited had also begun to appear in the *Weekly News*. With promises to sell produce in London and "get you the best price for any shipment," offers to provide samples from factories in "Manchester, Birmingham, Liverpool, Paris, and Hamburg," and a willingness to provide "any service we can render to make your business a paying concern," Gemel sounded very much like an incarnation of the African General Agency.[71]

But Gemel was unable to reproduce the agency's success. By the end of March, it was finished, and the advertisements abruptly stopped. To make matters worse, the University and Law Academy was not faring much better. For the first time in his life, Merriman was unable to pay the rent and left his room at 11 Princeton Mansions owing over £3.[72] To survive, he sold his possessions. His office furniture went to a dealer in Stoke Newington for £4. He sold his law books to Sweet and Maxwell of Chancery Lane for £5. Still without sufficient money to live, Merriman took another unthinkable step: he pawned 29 books worth over £15 for a paltry £1 10s. What troubled him was not only the loss of his books or the pittance he received for them. His greater sin was this: the pawned books had not yet been paid for—he still owed the bookseller nearly £16.[73] By March, he had given up his business chambers in High Holborn and was forced to take the cheapest accommodation he could find. With the demise of Gemel Limited, another lifeline had frayed and snapped.

On the afternoon of Friday, April 18, 1913, Merriman stepped into the lobby of the Westminster Palace Hotel, a luxurious establishment situated just across the street from Westminster Abbey and frequented by well-to-do tourists and M.P.'s. As he passed the large glass window of the dining room, he was reminded of a night late in November 1911, when suffragettes—the radical sisters of the suffrage movement—heaved stones tied up in handkerchiefs through windows all over London, including the Home Office, the Treasury, the National Liberal

Club, and the elegant dining room of the Westminster Palace Hotel.[74] Their protests were growing increasingly violent, but in two years they seemed no closer to getting the vote than Africans were to achieving civil rights in their own countries.

Beneath the graceful coved ceilings of the conference room, people clustered in groups greeting friends and engaging in lively conversation. The African Society and the Anti-Slavery and Aborigines' Protection Society had drawn a considerable audience: some forty Africans and dozens of prominent Britons.[75]

Sir Charles P. Lucas, a former Colonial Office administrator, called the meeting to order. When the room settled, he announced the object of the conference: "How best to hold out a helping hand to Africans in London." Given his desperate circumstances, Merriman must have felt a surge of optimism on hearing his words. It was the duty of the British, Lucas went on, "to welcome them as fellow citizens of the Empire, as fellow subjects of His Majesty the King."[76] Great Britain owed a twofold debt to Africans, he explained, first for the suffering caused by the slave trade, and, second, for the wealth Britons were currently extracting from the continent. What was needed was a wider sympathy and a greater effort to extend assistance and friendship.

Sir Harry Johnston, author, artist, explorer, and colonial administrator, made the first resolution, calling for Britons to give African students in Britain "friendly recognition." He lamented that those who objected to African students coming to London to study "wish to keep all negroes on a lower plane," only wanting to educate them "up to a certain limit." He had it on good authority, he said, that black students studying at Cambridge were often treated disrespectfully, some of them even shoved off the pavement by white students. He advocated making London a center for black education and called on his fellow countrymen to help make the Africans' "residence in London attractive and profitable to them."[77]

Wearing his signature fez, Dusé Mohamed Ali stood and explained that he would prefer Africans to be educated at an African university, but was pleased to see "so many friends and well-wishers who were hoping for the material and educational advancement of the black man."[78] Merriman spoke after Ali, expressing his wish that those at "the meeting would not go away with the idea that the generality of Africans held the opinion that London was not the proper place for the education of Africans."[79] Because London was rich with evening classes, public libraries, museums, and exhibitions, he found it the ideal place for the education-minded African.

After his brief comment, he sat back and listened to a chorus of Africans describing how difficult it could be living in the great city. Gold Coast journalist W.F. Hutchison, the new co-editor of the *African Times and Orient Review*, observed that Britons possessed many admirable qualities, but sympathy was not among them. "The African arriving in London felt himself in a great desert," he explained, "and, as a great many of his countrymen knew, they were often treated in a manner which went to their hearts, as coming from subjects of the same Crown, to which they themselves belonged."[80] Law student Padeyemo Assumpçai said he did not understand "why the black man was not popular" in Britain.[81] Another law student, A.E. Richards, observed that "setting race against race was a dangerous thing" which "every man should deplore," then described life at the Inns of Court where Africans, Indians, West Indians, and white Britons didn't mingle. "Each somehow felt that the other was inferior, and each felt himself superior, and out of all that arose bad blood, stupidity, and strife." "Sympathy amongst English and coloured students," he declared, "should be encouraged."[82] C.E.M. Abbensetts brought up the treatment of Africans on board steamers, observing that "it was very painful to many men of colour when they took a voyage to be placed in one part of the vessel while white men occupied another part."[83]

Throughout the afternoon, Merriman listened to his fellow Africans describe so frankly the poor treatment they had received at the heart of the empire. The concern of prominent Britons encouraged him. He was pleased by their praise of Africans, their appreciation of their "wise civilization" and loyalty to the Crown. To hear such men desire "closer communication," even friendship, inspired confidence. Departing from the lavish rooms of the Westminster Palace Hotel, he felt proud to have been in the company of such people—both black and white. A warm flame of optimism lighted his spirits even as he returned to a rented room with greasy walls and dirty carpets, cracked windows and chipped crockery.[84] He could sit in this cramped, squalid world of poverty and hope that, with such people in the world, his suffering would be temporary.

His buoyancy did not last. Shortly after the conference, he received a court summons. The moneylender David Swyers had filed a petition for a receiving order to be taken out against him. Merriman was required to appear at the High Court of Justice within seven days. He was being forced into bankruptcy.

Eight years earlier, he had written of the "appalling" number of bank-ruptcies in Britain, believing such men must lack honor, financial com-petence, or both. Now he found himself, as the saying went, "on Carey Street."[85] He had taken risks, he knew, but he had taken them honestly. He had worked himself to exhaustion to bring his ventures to success. When they failed, he paid back what he could. But his efforts had not been enough.[86] The law had summoned him to its terrible temple of ruin, where he would be forced to face a receiver, a judge, and his creditors. He would be required to reckon his assets and his debts—four hundred and seven pounds, two shillings and ninepence—in pub-lic. He ached with shame and dread.

The next weeks were a blur of humiliation. He completed a lengthy form answering questions about his creditors, sources of his income, and personal expenditures. In the public hearing, he was forced to stand in the dock and answer endless queries. What was his marital status? His assets? What property did he own? Did he possess jewelry, deeds, bonds, life assurance, promissory notes, bank accounts, furni-ture, farming stock, rental property? To the disappointment of his creditors, Merriman's answer to each question about assets and prop-erty was tediously identical: nil, nil, nil.

When he was asked to give the causes of his insolvency, he offered the list of fatal enterprises that had sunk him to such depths: the failure of Gemel Limited; losses caused by a breach of contract by the *Financial Outlook*; the sudden closing of the African General Agency; and the failure of his book, *Britons through Negro Spectacles*. No doubt those to whom he owed money—loan sharks Block and Swyers, printer Cave & Co., an estate agent, bookseller, and even the telephone company—had hoped to discover assets that would recoup their losses. But there was nothing—his books had been pawned, his life assurance policy canceled, his furniture sold, his bank account emptied. Over the next year, the official receiver managed to coax just over £13 from West African firms that had sold copies of *Britons* and had never forwarded the proceeds—just enough to cover court costs. In his final report on the case filed February 25, 1914, official receiver and trustee W.P. Bowyer wrote that "a further amount might be recovered from a book debtor in West Africa, but the sum, if recovered, will be insufficient to pay the costs of petition."[87] The grand struggle to make his name had left Merriman a financial failure.

That summer was marred by the death of another African friend. Ernest James Hayford, well known as a gifted medical doctor, trained in London, who had practiced both in the Gold Coast (present-day Ghana) and Sierra Leone, died unexpectedly in London. A few years earlier, at the height of his medical career, he had abandoned medicine and taken up the study of law at Lincoln's Inn. In the summer of 1913, he had returned to London to be called to the bar, even though his health was failing.[88] He died in the early hours of August 6 of "Congestion of the Lungs caused by a Chill coupled with Weakness of the heart." "Another National Loss," the *Gold Coast Nation* declared, "In the Land of Strangers."[89] The paper praised Hayford for his "ambition, his enterprising spirit, his energy, perseverance, independence, self-reliance and invincible courage." His many accomplishments "vindicated the intellectual capabilities of member of his race."[90] As the funeral cortège made its sad journey from Bloomsbury to Highgate Cemetery, Merriman again grieved with his friends at yet another loss of one of their own.[91]

A visit in the fall of 1913 from Theo Jones, a prominent businessman in the Gambia, lifted his spirits and eased the strain of the bankruptcy proceedings. Jones was making a business trip to London and swept Merriman into a whirlwind of socializing. Writing about the visit in the *Sierra Leone Guardian*, Merriman's uncle reported that Jones "in his London social rounds" had been "accompanied by his fellow-countryman, Mr. A.B. Merriman, the well-known author and barrister, who is at the English Bar."[92] A faithful protector of his nephew's reputation, his uncle didn't breathe a word of his financial troubles.

On November 4, the *Daily Mirror* featured an enormous photograph of a black man with a headline declaring "BURMESE WHO HAS BEEN NOMINATED FOR ELECTION AS MAYOR OF A LONDON BOROUGH."[93] The man was John Richard Archer, aged fifty, who was not Burmese at all, but born, as he put it, "in a little obscure village probably never heard of until now—the city of Liverpool." He was, he boasted, a Lancastrian "bred and born," and on November 10, 1913, Battersea elected this son of a Barbadian father and Irish mother as its mayor.[94] On learning of his win, Archer told the *Daily Express*, "It is a victory such as has never been gained before … I am the proud victor. I am a man of colour."[95] Archer saw his position as the logical result of "all that England has done to free and raise and educate the coloured peoples," and the message his election would send to the world, he declared, would be profound.[96] All the "coloured nations of the world," he said, would look to Battersea and say, "You have shown you have no racial prejudice, but recognize a man for what you think he has done."[97] In his acceptance speech, Archer contended that his election "means a new era in history."[98]

But Archer's success triggered profound racial anxiety for some in Britain. In a letter to the *South Western Star and Battersea and Wandsworth Advertiser* and quoted in the *Daily Express*, a person signed "True Progressive" wrote, "It is not meet that the white man should be governed and controlled by a man of colour. It has always been that the white man ruled and it must always be so. If not, good-bye to the prestige of Great Britain."[99]

For Merriman, John Archer's election must have brought on a hailstorm of emotions. Delighted that a man of color had succeeded in a white world, yet somehow feeling that Archer's success underscored his own failure, he had to ask himself what had gone wrong in his own life. He was a man of intelligence, education, talent, ambition, and drive. Why had he failed?

Standing in court giving an account of his insolvency had forced him to make sense of his decline. If he had been able to rely on the African General Agency while building a law practice, he would never have had to stand before the bankruptcy court. Lincoln's Inn's archaic stipulation that a man in business could not be called to the bar seemed much more about excluding those who lacked family fortune than maintaining the integrity of the profession. As for the *Financial Outlook*, hadn't he been penalized for refusing to help perpetuate sham investments, punished for being a man of honor? Moreover, the lackluster sale of *Britons through Negro Spectacles* in Africa was a result of damning remarks by the Cape Prime Minister and F.Z.S. Peregrino's decision to suppress the book's circulation. It came as a painful realization that it was not only Britons, but also some Africans who had not been ready for the truths he had to tell.

He became convinced that the only way to confront the weighty problems troubling Africans—disease and early death, the decline of small businesses, lack of political power—was to pursue a social science research agenda. Merriman's use of comedy as social critique had failed to inspire self-awareness or bring about social change. Science, he was now convinced, was the only thing with the power to change the world as he knew it.

Merriman's research interests ranged so widely among sociology, commerce, medicine, and politics that only a lengthy course of study could help him identify the powerful forces shaping the destinies of anglicized Africans. But he needed financial backing to pursue his research, and in the spring of 1914 he found three prominent black men to support his newest project: the Merriman Research Fund. With the backing of black philanthropists, he hoped to devote three years to full-time study, then he projected "three to ten years after" he could "earn enough money to start a fund for solving" African problems.[100] His backers were John Richard Archer, the recently elected Mayor of Battersea; long-time friend Cornelius May, Liberian Consul and editor of the *Sierra Leone Weekly News*; and Maximilian "Max" Thompson, a wealthy African businessman, who was so commercially successful that he and his brothers were the first Sierra Leoneans to establish offices in Britain.[101]

With such distinguished trustees, Merriman was ready to put the shame of bankruptcy behind him. He planned a visit to Sierra Leone where he would collect students who wanted to study law or medicine, lecture on the problems of anglicized Africans, and garner support for his research fund. He felt confident that his preliminary research would impress his fellow Sierra Leoneans and help him solicit those all-important contributions for his work. He saw this visit as an important beginning for the next phase of his career as a science-minded intellectual. What he could not have known was that it would be the last time he would be in Africa. He would never go home again.

PART III

DISGRACE

8

DULCE ET DECORUM EST

Difficulties thwarted Merriman's journey to Sierra Leone from the start. He expected to arrive on May 7 and stay for a fortnight, but, unable to book a passage, he was forced to sail on a later steamer, ruining his plan to escort aspiring students back to Britain. Making a virtue of necessity, he decided to extend his trip and embark on a lecture tour of British West Africa. Travelling up and down the coast would give him the chance to bring his ideas to a wider audience, gain even more support for the research fund, and return to London at the end of the year.

He arrived in Freetown early on the morning of May 17, 1914, the beginning of the rainy season, a period of violent thunderstorms and torrential rains. Undaunted by the hot, humid days, he chose the evening of June 4 for his first public lecture. Enlisting the mayor to chair the event and other prominent men to make introductions and speeches, he said in an interview with his uncle's paper that his lecture would discuss "problems of the Anglicised natives," including the "decline of the selling trades, the insecurity of property, ill health, early deaths, legislational impotence, and injustice to natives." Joseph Labor called his nephew's intentions "grand and laudable."[1]

A week later, Merriman addressed a large meeting of Freetown's Central Ratepayers' Association, and the *Sierra Leone Guardian* ran a piece on his forthcoming lecture. In the article, he explained his topic would be "a few socio-anthropological thoughts recently expressed in

Teuton Europe, and which, it seems will in time gain Supremacy in the minds of humanity as a whole."[2] He may have been planning to talk about the ideas of Franz Boas and others who had so authoritatively dispatched the idea of racial inequality at the Universal Races Congress.

His plans appeared to be on track until an article providing a detailed description of his lecture appeared in the *Sierra Leone Weekly News*. Eager to overcome the tarnish of bankruptcy and to make a compelling argument for his research fund, he published an outline of his lecture, but it was such a confusing miasma of scientific and pseudo-scientific jargon of the day, it alienated rather than cultivated supporters. Some of his topics would have been familiar to his readers, but others were not only painfully abstruse but misspelled either by Merriman or by the typesetter: *gnosology*, *phong-logology*, and *nostogy*. While many of these terms consisted of unconventional spellings of philosophical and medical words—gnoseology, the study of learning; phonology, the study of speech sounds; nosology, the classification of disease—the term "didactology" was probably of his own invention, meaning something like the study of education. In his effort to recreate himself as social scientist, he seriously miscalculated, baffling his audience with cryptic concepts and bombastic language.[3]

Yet, beneath the affectation were genuine insights about issues that would shape some of the most important questions of the twentieth century, including the nature of power inherent in language itself and the injustice of the colonial system. A forbearing reading of his outline reveals Merriman's deepening anti-colonial bent: his sense that the governing and the governed possessed starkly different interests; his dissatisfaction with an unfair legislative system and impotent means of governmental change; and his call for a reform of the Sierra Leonean constitution. Perhaps most importantly, he desired a correction of the injustices suffered by Africans through an "unconscious bias" in the British system of justice and at the very core of British moral thought. If he wasn't yet radical, he soon would be.[4]

Another serious misstep might have been the highly polished version of his career which appeared in his uncle's *Sierra Leone Guardian*. In order to establish his credibility, he boasted that "1,000 Copies of my 'Britons' sold in one month in England," never mentioning that eight hundred copies were moldering in storerooms all over West Africa. He stated that he had earned £80 "in one month as educator," but not that he had lacked funds to pay his rent. He also reported that the *Financial Outlook* paid him "about £200 [for] journalism and business advice" without noting that it had done so largely as the result of a lawsuit.[5] His strategy appears to have backfired badly. Ticket sales were miserable. The day before he was to speak, the *Colonial and Provincial Reporter* announced that Merriman had canceled the Freetown lecture, abandoned the West African lecture tour, and would soon depart for England. The cause of this drastic change of plans must have been obvious to everyone in Freetown because the newspaper offered no explanation. Needless to say, the coffers for the Merriman Research Fund remained barren.

No doubt the people of Freetown had various reasons for snubbing Merriman's plan. Some probably did not approve of research to be undertaken in London rather than Africa; others must have wondered why, if his services were so much in demand and so well compensated, he should be asking them for money. Whatever their reasoning, Merriman found himself and his fund icily rejected.

He was not without defenders. A week after the cancellation of his lecture, T.J. Thompson, editor of the *Colonial and Provincial Reporter*, penned a scolding editorial chastising his fellow Sierra Leoneans for their treatment of this "young patriot."[6] What had caused the sudden cancellation of the lecture and the despair of the promising lecturer? "The same old story," Thompson declared, "the same old life-killing foible of ours—*discouragement*." Merriman, he argued, was not asking for charity, but for support. His goals were not selfish, but altruistic. He intended to work for the benefit of the African people. Thompson emphasized Merriman's determination, reminding readers that "alone and unaided" he had "fought every inch of his way up almost to the goal of his ambition." And who should let him down? Those very people on whose behalf he intended to dedicate his labors. Thompson saw the demise of the Merriman Research Fund as the failure of Sierra Leoneans themselves. In his view, they rejected Merriman's ambitious ideas because he was a local man. "A prophet in need," Thompson wrote, quoting the gospel of St. Mark, "is not without honour save in his own country." Merriman's other "crime," he declared, was a determination for "whole-truthfulness." Such frankness, he observed, was not appreciated in a place where more often than not half-truths lined the path of success. The "whole incident," Thompson concluded with disgust, is "a sad commentary on our boasted advancement."[7]

In the end, Merriman did not bolt from his unappreciative country, but stayed for more than a month after his abandoned lecture. It is possible that the strain of repudiation had triggered his nervous ailment, plaguing him with anxiety, dizziness, and headaches, forcing him to postpone his return trip until he was well enough to travel. Amazingly, in this dark hour, Merriman enjoyed a bit of financial luck. Five years earlier, he had encouraged clients to send stories and pictures of "freaks of nature, amusing scenes, native magicians and wonder-working people of exceptional merit." In July 1914, a London publisher advanced him £30 for a book on just such "African curiosities."[8] Although the book was never published and no manuscript survives, several other books about "curiosities" came on the market that year, and it seems likely that his publisher hoped to cash in on British fascination with "artifacts" collected from the empire. At a time when Merriman had no obvious source of income, the timing could not have been better.

As Merriman wrestled with his personal demons in Freetown, terrible events were unfolding three thousand miles away in Europe. On June 28, 1914, in Sarajevo, a nineteen-year-old Serbian nationalist assassinated the heir apparent of the Austro-Hungarian Empire: Archduke Franz Ferdinand. The story was splashed across the headlines of major newspapers around the world, then evaporated. In Sierra Leone, the murder of an Austro-Hungarian archduke seemed so removed from local concerns, it went unreported.[9] As summer storms pounded Sierra Leone, Austro-Hungarian and German plans for vengeance on Serbia would soon unhinge the European world.

In the middle of July, Merriman booked a third-class passage from Freetown to Southampton on the *Lucie Woermann*, a German mail steamer. He had never traveled to Britain in third class, and the plunge into the cramped cabin he would have to share with seven strangers was dispiriting. The narrow-tiered berths in the nine-by-nine room, the dim electric light, the coarse straw mattress, the smell of eight men's tropical sweat, and the prehistoric glint of cockroaches as they scurried into dark corners felt like a descent into the underworld. Escaping to the deck, he settled on a long-slatted bench, reading or watching the sea and contemplating how he could bring himself back to life.

As the *Lucie Woermann* steamed along the west coast of Africa, Germany validated Austria-Hungary's determination to take a hard line with Serbia and assured its support. After delivering an ultimatum Serbia could never fulfill, Austria-Hungary declared war on July 28. Concerned that increased German influence might jeopardize their ethnic and commercial concerns in the Balkan region, Russia began a partial mobilization. The seriousness of the situation was now frighteningly obvious. That evening as the *Lucie Woermann* steamed toward the English Channel, Austrian artillery assaulted Belgrade, the Serbian capital, in a show of strength. By the time Merriman landed in Southampton, Belgium, France, Germany, and Russia were engaged in war preparations. Even Britain—though a nation still very divided about its involvement—put its armed forces on alert and authorized the preliminary mobilization of its navy.

The mood in London was gloomy and foreboding when Merriman arrived. Newspapers everywhere proclaimed the country "Under the Shadow of War."[10] Wondering whether or not Britain would be able to stand aloof from the Continental war and embrace its famous "splendid isolation," Londoners and tourists in town for the August bank holiday swamped newspaper offices in Fleet Street for the latest information. The demand for multiple extra editions overwhelmed the ordinary delivery services, forcing editors to hire taxicabs to get the papers out to an anxious public. War anxieties also triggered financial uncertainty. Overnight, the bank rate doubled, the Stock Exchange closed until further notice, and people converged on the Bank of England, insisting on gold for their paper money.[11]

On August 2, Germany demanded passage through neutral Belgium, an act that unified the divided British Cabinet. For nearly a hundred years, Britain had guaranteed Belgium's autonomy. It saw the German demand as a threat not only to an independent nation, but also to the essential security of the English Channel and British ports, the lifeblood of the island nation.

On the morning of August 4, a cloudless summer day, the British Cabinet delivered an ultimatum to Germany demanding respect for

Belgium's neutrality. In Parliament Square and Whitehall crowds of animated young men and women gathered, waving flags and singing "Rule, Britannia." War supporters and anti-war protestors faced off in Trafalgar Square, one group shouting "We must keep out of it!" while the other cried "Down with Germany!"[12] In front of Buckingham Place crowds sang "God Save the King."[13] When the Cabinet learned at noon that a large German force had invaded Belgium, it sent a second message to Berlin requiring an answer by 11:00 p.m., London time. Fully aware that Germany would never comply, the Cabinet ordered clerks to prepare telegrams for the nation's embassies and consuls informing them of the declaration of war. Margot Asquith, the Prime Minister's wife, remembered the day in her autobiography as one of resignation. "So it is all up?" she asked her husband that afternoon. "Yes, it's all up," he replied.[14]

As evening advanced, Merriman must have been among the thousands of people standing shoulder to shoulder under the summer night sky in Trafalgar Square, the Mall, Whitehall, or Downing Street. When Big Ben boomed eleven times, the country and its empire would be at war. The clock, like an unstoppable bomb of destiny, slowly ticked away. As Big Ben began to chime, a profound silence swept over the crowd. As it struck its eleventh note, people ricocheted in every direction crying out, "War! War! War!"[15]

The next morning the shrill voices of news boys bombarded Merriman with the headline "Britain at War!" Soon bright red-and-blue posters sprang up everywhere declaring "Your King and Country Need You." In the coming weeks, he watched as eager young men in their fashionable straw boaters and cream trousers scrambled to join the long lines assembled in front of recruiting offices. Within two weeks, a hundred thousand men had volunteered. One day in September some thirty thousand men signed on to accept the King's shilling.[16] Some volunteers, like the poet Rupert Brooke, cherished the opportunity to participate in a noble action and celebrate it in poetry. "Now, God be thanked," he famously wrote, "Who has matched us with His hour." For many men in Britain, war served as the expression of a widely held set of beliefs about duty, fortitude, and manliness.[17] The idea of the "Pals Battalions" appealed to those who wanted to serve with their friends, colleagues, and neighbors. Yet, men's motivations to join the war were as varied as their backgrounds. Men joined from feelings of patriotism, a sense of duty, or a deep longing for adventure; they joined to avoid being thought shirkers, out of fear of invasion, or because of a romantic vision of "mounting a horse and wielding a sword and winning all kinds of medals."[18] A number of businesses provided powerful financial incentives to their employees by promising to continue to pay enlisted men some portion of their salaries while they served.[19] Wealthy lords and ladies were known to fill their cars with butlers, footmen, and gardeners and haul them to the recruiting stations.[20] Some destitute men were forced to volunteer when Poor Law guardians refused relief to any "able-bodied" men.[21] Many recruits simply desired escape from crushing poverty and a bleak future.[22] At thirty-seven, Merriman missed the initial recruitment age: nineteen to thirty in the first days of the war and then thirty-five just three weeks later.

Many Africans believed that the war would provide an opportunity for colonial people to prove loyalty, and the right to request post-war reforms. In London, Merriman's friend John Eldred Taylor founded a new Afrocentric newspaper, the *African Telegraph and Gold Coast Mirror*, which was outspoken in its loyalty to Britain and its empire during the war, although it would be critical of British policies later. Like most other British subjects, Taylor embraced the military cause with its heightened demands for individual sacrifice in the name of honor and duty. The first edition of his newspaper featured horrific stories of German atrocities in Africa and lauded France's use of African soldiers on the Western Front. Writing of the Algerian and Senegalese soldiers fighting for France, he said, "we have been able to catch glimpses ... of the daring courage and splendid valour of these men, who are cheerfully willing to lay down their lives for the maintenance of that Empire which has conferred benefits on them."[23]

Many African elites thought a willingness to make such sacrifices was certain to win them a place of equality within the community of British subjects. As Jamaican activist W.G. Hinchcliffe put it, on soldiers "the laurels will fall, which must eventually lift the standard of the African race, and cause oppression into oblivion to fall."[24] An editorial in the *Lagos Weekly Record* also recognized the importance of Africans fighting on behalf of France and asserted that "what France has done on such an appreciable scale, Great Britain could do on a more extensive scale."[25] If African men could demonstrate their equality on the battle-field, they could demand fairness at home.

Voices in Sierra Leone also hoped the war would provide an opportunity to prove allegiance. T. J. Thompson wrote in the *Colonial and Provincial Reporter*, "Our loyalty to the British Throne is proverbial and universal; we appreciate and are grateful for the protection of our lives and property under the Union Jack. England's joys and sorrows are ours." He went on to say that Freetown men had discussed and approved the creation of a "Native Volunteer Corps," but "the Authorities seemed to have relegated it to the limbo of obscurity." Despite his disappointment that Sierra Leoneans would not soon be joining the fight, he concluded his column with the universal declaration of patriotism: "God Save the King."[26]

Merriman may have been reluctant to join up because there was no opportunity for educated Africans to serve as officers. As the *African Telegraph* reported, "the African of decent education is rarely secured as a recruit, and this, we think, is owing to the fact that no commissioned rank is held up to his vision as something to be aimed at and worked for."[27] According to the *King's Regulations*, commissioned ranks—that is, positions as officers—explicitly required "pure European parent-age."[28] Even black men who had gone to British universities and received officer training could be excluded.

Some African men did enlist. One writer for the *Birmingham Daily Post* claimed that the official policy may have limited black British troops to the African theaters, but, he wrote, "a man with a sharp eye … would be able to pick out men of African origin in the new armies." He said he knew "for a fact" that men from both the West Indies and West Africa had joined up.[29] As historian David Killingray explains, some recruiters accepted black recruits without any problems, while others rejected them because of their race. Specialist forces such as the Machine Gun Corps and the Royal Flying Corps, he points out, were especially receptive to qualified black recruits.[30]

As the war dragged on and bloody battles wiped out men by the tens of thousands, including many junior officers, the military color bar sometimes cracked and broke. Under the weight of heavy casualties and the need for good men, some senior officers tapped black men for commissions. As a result, a handful of black Britons rose to the ranks of officers, including George Bemand, J.S Risien Russell, John Albert Gordon Smyth, and former professional soccer player Walter Tull.[31]

The use of black troops in Europe remained controversial throughout the war. The *African Telegraph* may have reported that black troops fighting under British command in Africa had made "excellent fighting material, and compared very favorably with the black troops offered by other nations, for discipline and efficiency," but for the British it was one thing to use African troops in Africa, and another to use them in Europe.[32] The British Army strongly objected to using colonial soldiers on the Western Front, except as military laborers behind the lines. According to radical politician and active-duty soldier Josiah Wedgwood—a proponent of bringing British colonial troops to the European theatre—the British War Office "thought it undesirable to put coloured people on par with white men. It might put ideas into their heads."[33] In 1916, in a speech to the House of Commons, Winston Churchill asked what the future would say of Britain if it knew that during the Great War the country was "forced to make an inconclusive peace because she forgot Africa." He went on to say that "at a time when every man counted," it would be a terrible shame if "Britain was unable to make use of a mighty continent."[34] But some in power feared that allowing black men to witness the daily slaughter of white by white could undermine imperial authority. As former Prime Minister Andrew Bonar Law observed, the government of South Africa objected to black men trained in arms because they might threaten white supremacy should they become discontented when they returned home.[35] The Colonial Office ultimately dismissed the idea of using black troops in Europe, believing them to be unreliable, unsuitably trained, and unlikely to thrive in the unfamiliar climate.[36] They caustically dubbed the idea the "Million Black Army Movement."[37]

The French had no qualms about using African troops on the Western Front and began including them almost immediately. African soldiers from French colonies saw action in every major battle of the war: Ypres, Marne, Verdun, and the Somme. French newspapers claimed Africans wished to "prove by their disciplined heroism their gratitude towards the glorious 'country that civilised them,'" although African motives for fighting were as varied as those of their European counterparts.[38] European war propaganda celebrated the policy of giving African troops some of the most dangerous assignments on the field of battle as a "privilege" which "permitted them to enrich their book of traditions and past glory."[39]

Merriman probably realized that some of the Europeans who supported the use of African troops on the Western Front considered them inferior to white soldiers, believing they possessed less discipline, bravery, and valor. Charles Mangin, a French lieutenant colonel who had urged a "*force noire*," speciously argued that Africans made good soldiers because they were a martial people whose physical constitutions and cultural inheritances—their "underdeveloped nervous system and their hereditary fatalism"—would allow them to "sleep in the trenches in the midst of a battle, if they were ordered to do so."[40] The French regularly used their African units as "shock troops"—that is, those who led an attack—so that when French soldiers saw the arrival of African forces, they recognized them as "an unmistakable sign that an attack was imminent."[41] Records of individual battles show that African death and injury rates, for example, were frequently higher than European—in some cases, more than twice those of the French infantrymen—often because they were given the most dangerous posts.[42] In 1918, a French colonel in charge of training African troops wrote that his men were simply "cannon fodder, who should, in order to save whites' lives, be made use of much more intensely."[43] The Prime Minster of France held much the same view. "We are going to offer civilisation to the Blacks. They will have to pay for that," he asserted. "I would prefer that ten Blacks are killed rather than one Frenchman—although I immensely respect those brave Blacks—, I think that enough Frenchmen are killed anyway and that we should sacrifice as few as possible!"[44]

As Merriman took his reader's seat at one of the long wooden tables in the British Museum Reading Room to continue his research on race, disease, and power, a couple of miles away at Wellington House two dozen prominent authors sat together at their own table in a secret meeting with C. F. G. Masterman, the new head of the War Propaganda Bureau. In the weeks and months to come, celebrated writers including Arthur Conan Doyle, H. G. Wells, Rudyard Kipling, Thomas Hardy, Hall Caine, and James M. Barrie would create millions of pamphlets, posters, films, and lectures supporting the war effort.[45] Fashioning a reassuring myth for the British public, they conjured a world where all the fault lay with Germany, all the honor with Britain. They portrayed soldiers as plucky warriors happily enduring the discomforts of trench warfare and referred to death in battle as a Christ-like sacrament known as the supreme sacrifice.[46] The materials they produced bore no indication that they had been made by a government agency, creating the impression they had been written by private citizens.[47] In fact, well-known firms secretly agreed to let their names appear on materials the government not only generated, but also bought and distributed. As the British government harnessed some of the country's best minds in the service of war, Merriman struggled alone under the grand dome of the British Museum Reading Room trying to understand the social and political dynamics of colonial Africa.

During the first days of war, panic and patriotism unfurled side by side. Merriman could not have missed Londoners queuing for hours at provisions shops, then staggering out later with armfuls of tinned meats, sardines, and ham. Thousands of miles away in Freetown, Sierra Leoneans suffered the same fear of food shortages. In both places, the rush on food drove prices drastically higher for a few days. In Britain, the government quickly fixed prices and restored order, while in Freetown prominent citizens called for cooperative price controls and calmer heads.[48]

By the following week, Merriman and everyone else in Britain began adjusting to increasing state control. The government had already commandeered the railroads and soon would censor war reporting, restrict the illumination of streets and buildings, even limit personal liberties like whistling on the street—which might be taken for an air raid warning—and the hours a public house could serve liquor. At the end of November, it extended its monitoring to anyone—foreign or British—living in hotels or boarding houses. If Merriman merely changed from one rented room to another, he was required to register at the local police station.

From the first days of war, he must have heard rumors burning through London that German grocers were selling food filled with slow-acting poison and other accounts of infiltration and sabotage. During the first six weeks of fighting, Londoners made more than nine thousand reports of suspicious behavior by people purported to be German spies. Not a single one was credible.[49] Anything or anyone of German origin became objects of derision—and sometimes violence—from waiters and watchmakers to Prince Louis of Battenberg, a senior officer in the British Navy who had the misfortune to be the son of a German prince. At moments of heightened anxiety throughout the war, German shops were looted; windows broken; property destroyed. In response, people of German ancestry scrambled to protect themselves by changing their family names and rebranding their businesses. A cartoon in *Punch* satirized what it christened the "Quick Change of Front": a rotund, aproned grocer "Johann Schmidt" becomes "John Smith," his faithful dachshund now a British terrier, his "Frankfurt Sausages" transformed into "Cambridge Sausages."[50] Not long after the start of hostilities, people of German origin living in Britain began filing legal deed polls in which they "formally and absolutely renounced and abandoned" their former names. People like Felix Rosenheim became Percy Rose, Ernest Schwabacher converted to Ernest Shaw, Alfred Schacht into Alfred Dent.[51] After three more years of war, even the monarch of Great Britain, George V, would cast off Saxe-Coburg-Gotha in favor of the more English-sounding Windsor. A name, it seems, could disguise an undesirable history, serve as a sign of respectability, or indicate one's loyalties. Before the war was over, circumstances Merriman could never have imagined would compel him to renounce his own name.

At Waterloo Station—the giant South London rail terminal where he had arrived ten years earlier—boat-trains pulled into the station loaded with wounded soldiers. On his journeys to and from South London, Merriman saw people flocking around the station, giving tribute or gawking at the dazed, bloody, bandaged, mud-covered men tumbling out of railway carriages. When wounded officers filled all available ambulance space, the War Office commandeered blue-and-white Lyons tea shop vans to transport soldiers to the London Hospital. Seeing them helplessly laid out on mattresses, carried on stretchers by young medical students, and stowed away in the back of tea vans, Merriman and other Londoners began to understand the reality beyond the wartime rhetoric. They would grow used to watching men rake straw over the cobbled streets in front of hospitals to quiet the jangle of traffic and accustomed to seeing banners billowing across the hospital brick requesting "Quiet for the Wounded." Journalist Michael MacDonagh described it as the "first shock of the war." There would be many more.[52]

Merriman had long relished the beautiful electric illumination of the capital city, its glittering evening streets and the steady pulse of its clock and church bells. But the face of the London he loved changed in the middle of September 1914. Fearing that the enemy could use street lights, lighted buildings, or clocks to navigate along the Thames and hit vital targets, the government silenced the clocks and established strict limits on lighting. No longer would Big Ben bang out the hours in what Merriman had called its "deep bass tone."[53] Street lamps were either no longer lit or were dimmed with heavy shades or painted dark blue. Lighting in shops was lowered, and the windows of private residences draped with heavy blinds. Driving and even walking in the metropolis at night became difficult. The electric lights of trams and buses grew so shadowy that one could not even read a book on the tedious commute home. In the coming months, the only unfailing illumination would be the giant flashing knives of searchlights slicing through the sky pursuing an unseen aerial enemy.[54]

In November, as soldiers on the Western Front dug deep trenches to wait out the cold winter months, Merriman at last hit on a project he believed could support him while he researched what he felt would be his groundbreaking work. A dozen years earlier, he had done very well financially with the *Handbook of Sierra Leone*; he now planned another guidebook along the same lines but more expansive. Not just a handbook about one small colony, but an essential reference for all of British West Africa; he called it *Merriman's West African Annual*. Through his family connections, his travels, his time in London, and the work of the African General Agency, he had built a wide range of contacts and saw himself in a unique position to provide valuable information to Africans and Europeans doing business in West Africa. Thrilled that he had hit on a lucrative idea, he penciled out a "sheet of figures," calculating large projected profits.[55] He even discovered an innovative way to leverage the book into a regular income. If people would not donate to a scholarship fund, perhaps they would invest in a profitable company. He would create Literature Limited to invest in his publications.[56] As its legal advisor, he would draw a modest £8 monthly income. Once the books began selling, those who had invested could share in the financial rewards. He immediately drew up the legal papers and convinced James Hillier, his landlord, and George Clay, a fellow lodger whom he had originally met in Manchester in 1905, to sign the registration documents and buy one share each.[57] By the end of November, he officially filed Literature Limited with the Registrar of Companies at Somerset House. A few months later, he convinced Ernest Sydney Ashurst, a tobacconist and bookseller, and Tom Davison, a retired printer, to each buy a share and serve as company directors.[58] With the paperwork in place, he could start collecting advertising revenue.

As Christmas approached, new recruitment posters dominated shop windows and the sides of buildings as well as buses and trams. One of the most commanding featured a portrait of a uniformed Lord Kitchener, the Secretary of State for War, pointing a stern finger and exclaiming "I Want You." The giant wings of his mustache, like a condor in flight, implied the magnitude of his undertaking. By the end of 1914, more than one million men had joined up.[59]

The widely held conviction at the start of the war that it would be a short affair, over by Christmas, proved tragically misguided. Ninety thousand British casualties in only four months and 137 civilian deaths in attacks on seaside towns earlier in December destroyed the expectation that the engagement would be brief and relatively painless. Britons who raised their glasses over their roasted goose or joint of beef that Yuletide now only hoped for one thing: that the war would be over by next Christmas.

Had Merriman and his friends ventured into the dark London streets on the first New Year's Eve of the war to join the revelers with their bells and cheers and shouts of best wishes, he might have looked on the coming year as a time of hope, a chance to leave behind old failures and gather up new successes. Perhaps in the darkness, he looked up. Above his head, past the tallest building, even beyond the bright diagonals of the searchlights, he saw something he had never seen before. It had always been there, but had been hidden by the dazzle of the world's greatest city: the night sky over London full of stars.[60]

During the short days of early January, Merriman pulled his worn overcoat over his old suit and began seeking advertisers for the *African Annual*. Traversing London, he couldn't help noticing the differences. No longer did homeless men with holes in their shoes loiter on street corners for handouts; now battalions of soldiers in khaki paraded through the streets instead of armies of the destitute.

The military had not just ended unemployment, but had called so many men to war that women had begun to step into their vacated jobs. As he made his way along the Embankment, Merriman saw women drivers negotiating the busy avenue in their motor cars and vans. In the City, young women worked as clerks; in the cafés around Victoria Station women served customers; and in the department stores along Oxford Street they operated the electric lifts. Soon they would be taking tickets on buses, hauling heavy boxes as railway porters, keeping order as policewomen, making bombs in munitions factories, working the land, and driving ambulances. Women's faces had changed, too. Before the war, only ladies of the stage used make-up. Now one saw ordinary women on the street with darkened eyes, rouged cheeks, and powdered noses. Some even carried little metal tubes of carmine to redden their lips.

In Hyde Park, where Merriman used to see lovers spooning on benches, he now saw officers drilling recruits in the arts of war. As he watched, officers plunged the blades of their bayonets into huge straw-stuffed burlap sacks strung between poles. As the officers stabbed and stabbed again, the timid bags rocked back and forth in obedient surrender. The recruits followed with their own awkward dance of killing, shuffling forward to stab and then withdrawing, stab and withdraw.

Mothers, wives, and children were also drawn into the war effort. One early recruitment poster portrayed an anxious wife hugging her young children as their father marches away. The caption proclaimed, "Women of Britain say GO!" The call to arms was even put into the mouths of babes in another poster of a respectable-looking man seated in his comfortable armchair with his son playing with toy soldiers at his feet and his young daughter in his lap. "Daddy," the child asks, "what did

YOU do in the Great War?"[61] Everywhere in the streets of London, in cafés and restaurants, on trams and buses, young women shoved white feathers—a symbol of cowardice—into the hands of any man out of uniform in the hopes of shaming him to enlist.

On his travels throughout London promoting the *African Annual*, Merriman probably made a point of visiting firms that had advertised his Sierra Leone handbook ten years earlier: Wheeler and Wilson Sewing Machines in Finsbury; Merryweather's hosiery-makers in Covent Garden; and the pharmaceutical company Howards and Sons as well as Curzon Brothers tailors in Islington. Sales were not lively, even though David Lloyd George, the Chancellor of the Exchequer, had pronounced "business as usual," and assured the nation the fighting would not greatly affect ordinary commercial activity. The Associated Chambers of Commerce of the United Kingdom even hoped to corner markets previously dominated by Germany.[62] Buying into this fiscal optimism, Merriman had projected a weekly advertising income of £10 to £100. Through friends in high places, he had secured support for the book from "a high Government official," which he was certain would help him sell advertising.[63] It didn't. He was lucky most weeks to bring in just £2. Unsure of his next move, he continued to promote the *Annual*, not knowing that an unremarkable letter from a stranger would soon trigger a series of events that threatened to ruin everything he had worked so hard to achieve.

The missive was from J.C. Cole in Freetown, a fellow countryman and relative of one of Merriman's oldest friends. Cole had mail-ordered suits from Curzon Brothers tailors in London nine months earlier. At first Cole believed he had been overcharged. Then he had been con-vinced to accept the suits, but never received them. He asked Merriman to demand the £4 he believed Curzon Brothers owed him and to "deduct your professional fee and other charges and post me the balance."[64] He did not understand that British legal practices prohibited barristers from having such contact with clients, a role reserved for solicitors. That Cole should approach Merriman with the details of his case and, even worse, mention fees was a complete breach of profes-sional etiquette.

Merriman had long patronized the Curzon firm. They did a large international mail-order business and had been his personal tailor for some twenty years. He regularly referred clients to them and in return received a discount on his orders. Curzon had a thriving mail-order business with Sierra Leone, and Merriman was hoping to persuade them to advertise in the *West African Annual*. While in Islington to discuss advertising, Merriman broached Cole's complaint. Although he could not represent Cole as a barrister, he felt he could bring up the problem of a fellow countryman to his tailor, and he quickly brought about a happy arrangement. Emphasizing that he had not visited Curzon Brothers as a lawyer, he wrote to Cole that he only needed to resubmit his order and the firm would send him two suits at no further charge. "I trust your difference with C.B. will now be settled," he wrote cheerfully.[65] He asked for no compensation for the solution he had arranged, but added that if Cole was not satisfied with this arrangement, he should send all the original documents and a guinea to pay for a solicitor who would take his case.

Cole was not satisfied. Fearing that Curzon was somehow going to cheat him, he promised to track down the original documents and send them along with the money.[66] In Merriman's view, the decision made no sense for a man who, in the first instance, had believed himself overcharged. The fees to pursue a legal case would far exceed the money Cole was trying to recoup. To Merriman, Cole was throwing good money after bad.

On March 24, the *African Annual* got a much-needed boost: Clements Press, owned by the reputable *Financial Times*, agreed to produce dummy volumes.[67] Merriman could now prove to potential advertisers that the *Annual* had serious backing. On a wet, blustery afternoon two days after Easter, he returned to Curzon Brothers with his red volume in hand and showed them exactly where their advertisements would appear. Then something curious happened. As Merriman stood among the rolls of tweed and cashmere, as he peered over work tables piled with cutting shears, sponges, and hot irons, perhaps he sensed that the manager was upset to learn that the Cole business had not been settled. Or maybe he saw his reflection in one of the long mirrors and realized how shabby his own clothes had grown. In an era when the quality of a man's suit announced him a gentleman worthy of one's trust, Merriman might have begun to wonder if his threadbare attire was undermining his ability to solicit advertising. Perhaps a new set of clothes would make the impression he needed to get the *Annual* off the ground. Or perhaps he was simply trying to come to some kind of peaceful agreement between Cole and his tailor.

As strong winds pounded rain against the arched windows, it occurred to Merriman that Cole wanted cash, he wanted clothes, and Curzon wanted the whole affair finished. As he later explained, he believed that Curzon was about to hand over somewhere between £5 and £40 for advertising, and that Cole would not be "wise to spend the money necessary to contest his claim."[68] In order to "save Cole an ultimate loss of not less than £20 over a £3 odd claim," to help Curzon conclude a tiresome customer complaint, and to secure some much-needed clothes for himself, he asked Curzon to make him an overcoat, a suit, and trousers using Cole's credit, promising to repay the cash to Cole personally.[69] He never doubted that he would be able to pay the money back, very likely within the month. Curzon Brothers was delighted. Merriman was delighted. It would be just a matter of time before Cole would be delighted, too. All of them were going to get exactly what they wanted.

Slogging through the rain-sodden streets of London during an unusually wet May 1915, Merriman worried that the weak stream of advertising revenue was drying up. With all eyes focused on battles and casualties, businessmen were not interested in his ideas for African commerce, and he was getting very little coaching work despite ongoing ads in the *Sierra Leone Weekly News*. Enrollment at educational institutions had plummeted as students abandoned their lectures for the trenches. Lincoln's Inn attendance dropped from 418 to 82.[70] Oxford University's enrollment declined from 3,181 to 491.[71] As German submarines ruthlessly torpedoed passenger vessels as well as merchant ships, fewer foreign students were coming to Britain. In early May 1915, a torpedo had pierced the hull of the Cunard line *Lusitania* traveling from New York to Britain. The world exploded with outrage when it learned that 1,198 civilians, many of them children, had drowned in the attack. For days afterward, bodies of the dead washed ashore on the rock-strewn Irish coast. Before that, a U-boat had attacked an Elder Dempster steamer bound for West Africa. Nearly half of the 242 people on board the *Falaba*—crew and passengers, black and white—had drowned in the rough waters.[72]

In a world of such uncertainty, where travel could suddenly turn deadly, few people were inclined to invest money in a West African guidebook. Life on the home front was hard enough as costs soared: butter, pork sausages, bacon, and cheese all increased by three- or fourpence a pound. The price of sugar sky rocketed.[73] Taking advantage of war-induced housing shortages, London landlords charged ever more exorbitant prices for cramped, rundown rooms.[74]

As the money dwindled, Merriman could no longer afford to search for advertisers. It was not only for himself that he was concerned. He had several young Africans, some of them probably law students, who looked to him for help. He had hoped to employ them as clerks for Literature Limited, but now it was clear that would be impossible. Although he had not wholly abandoned the idea of the *African Annual*, he set out to find a more reliable source of income to take care of himself and the friends who depended on him.

9

MERCY DWELLS NOT HERE

The search for employment took Merriman down the steps of a crowded tram into the mass of people, lorries, and buses known as Beresford Square in Greenwich.[1] Along the pavement, canvas-covered stalls offered goods of every description: piles of turbot, sole, and haddock; crooked lines of spinach, cucumbers, and cauliflower; wicker baskets loaded with whelks and winkles; crude stick cages bustling with ducks and chickens. A sharp breeze jostled shirts and dresses on lengths of rope overhead. In one stall, a large man held up a pair of pliers and promised painless tooth extraction. Merriman stopped at the edge of a small crowd to watch a man in evening dress drape a silk handkerchief over a dove. Three taps with his magic wand, and the bird disappeared. Three more taps, and it fluttered out of his upturned top hat. The crowd sighed with delight, and a nearby cockatoo squawked at the top of its lungs. The sight reminded Merriman of his younger self, conjuring for audiences in Freetown. How far away those days seemed now.

He joined a long queue at the Labour Exchange across the street from the rail station. After a lengthy wait, he emerged with a coveted green admission ticket to the Royal Arsenal. For weeks, the country had been in a munitions crisis. In a rush to produce more armaments, factories were hiring anyone they could get, including women and black people.[2] As the demand for wartime workers increased, black subjects from British colonies immigrated to Britain looking for employment. By the end of the war, the black population would be some twenty thousand.[3]

Two policemen and two sentries controlled the flood rushing through the red brick arch of Arsenal's main gate. Looking at Merriman's admission ticket, a sentry directed him to the drafty interviewing shed where he became another body grinding through the Arsenal personnel machine. First, men were separated from women, then placed into groups of sixteen. Merriman sat on a hard, wooden bench in the interview room waiting to be called to a desk where he would be asked his age and previous occupation. At thirty-eight, with experience in law, trade, and clerking, he was selected for a plum job—the Royal Engineers Stores Inspection Division.[4] The inspectors assessed army supplies, anything from pick-axes to barbed wire, compasses to lamps, telegraph poles to batteries. He might test high-grade wireless instruments or evaluate the loft of paper balloons used to shower leaflets of propaganda over German troops.[5]

Before doing any of that, Merriman was taken to the medical shed where he was directed to a small cubicle and told to remove all clothing except his coat and shoes. Then in groups of three, he and his fellow applicants were led to the examination room where they lined up, as one candidate recalled, "each in a kind of niche, like saints in a row" and were told to remove their coats.[6] He stood naked as doctors listened to his chest, checked his pulse, and inspected his scalp for lice. If he was still suffering from his chronic nervous ailment, the physicians did not detect anything to alarm them. Afterward, he received his identification number and a book of rules. Work went on at the Arsenal twenty-four hours a day. Wanting to leave his days open for researching and writing, Merriman requested the night shift.

The Royal Arsenal at Woolwich was a complex and dangerous island of munitions research, testing, and construction some three and a half miles long and one mile wide. It was so massive that it ran its own rail system with 120 miles of track, 180 locomotives, and 2,000 cars. Its "scores of buildings, sheds, chimneys ... all sooty black," as one worker described them, held more than 10,000 tons of explosives.[7] At its peak during the war, it employed nearly eighty thousand people, all of whom worked at least a twelve-hour shift.[8] Walking to his post through the evening twilight, Merriman passed buildings where foundry furnaces blazed and giant hammers pounded. He passed a large filling shop and heard women singing, their harmonies floating through the dark. In the days to come, more and more women would take on munitions work. In time, he learned the difference between the khaki-and-blue overalls worn by women doing ordinary jobs and the high-collared beige-and-brown gowns worn by those who handled hazardous materials. He recognized the "canaries" in their fireproof robes, their hands and faces tinted lemon yellow by the TNT they handled. He admired the sporty women who drove lorries and heaved heavy boxes as expertly as men. Soon he recognized the Overlookers, important people with blue bands on their upper arms whose careworn faces marked them as men and women responsible for supervising thousands of workers who handled machines and materials that could cut a hand, pierce an eye, sever a limb, poison the organs, or blow a body or a building to kingdom come.[9]

And then there were the children. Boys in brown trousers and caps. Girls in white dresses. They were supposed to be at least fourteen years old, but thin arms and joyless faces suggested some were much younger. At the Arsenal even children worked sixty-hour weeks. Those on the night shifts looked the saddest. In the annual report for 1915, the Chief Inspector of Factories wrote: "Very young girls show almost immediately … symptoms of lassitude, exhaustion, and impaired vitality under the influence of employment at night." Of the boys, he observed, "for the most part … they are 'so spiritless, so dull, so dead in look, so woebegone and attacked with weariness' as to compel attention."[10]

At the end of May, London was attacked from the air. About 11:00 p.m., on May 31, 1915, a silvery leviathan the size of a football field floated thousands of feet above the metropolis. Within a few minutes it unleashed more than a hundred bombs throughout the East End. Dozens of incendiary bombs—meant to cause widespread fires—fell on Hoxton, Shoreditch, and Whitechapel just across the river from Woolwich.[11] Seven civilians died and thirty-five were injured as searchlights crisscrossed the night sky, unable to find the enemy.[12] Had its bombs struck the Arsenal's huge supplies of TNT, fatalities and damage could have been disastrous. Nevertheless, the raid made clear that there would be no bystanders in this war. On any cloudless, moonlit night, Britons at home in their beds might be attacked by Germany's seemingly invincible floating monsters.

In Sierra Leone, J.C. Cole was launching his own attack on the Curzon Brothers tailors. He wrote a letter threatening to engage barrister Merriman to take legal action if they did not immediately refund his money for the never-delivered suits. Curzon responded with a conciliatory letter noting that Mr. Merriman had visited them several times and "at his own request" had used Cole's credit to have clothes made for himself. "No doubt Mr. Merriman has acquainted you with what has been done in this matter," they noted. On receiving the letter, Cole was "astonished and dumbfounded." He showed it to the other clerks in his office, who "were almost paralyzed with wonderment." In the letter he fired off to Merriman, Cole wrote, "I cannot for my life believe a word of it. I believe you to be a gentleman of the truest and most upright nature sure and certain."[13] Nevertheless, he immediately showed the letter, he told Merriman, to "our leading men" and threatened to publish everything in the Freetown newspapers.

Despite fatigue from his grueling night shifts at the Arsenal and his days researching, Merriman prepared a calm reply to Cole's missive. He explained that Curzon was refusing to refund his money. He outlined the expensive fees which would quickly add up if he pursued a legal case: several shillings for each solicitor's letter and more than a pound for each piece of advice from a barrister. "Whether you win or lose," he explained, "you will lose at least a part." He thought it foolish to start a legal battle over a £4 dispute and intended, he told Cole, to "save you undue delay and legal expense." His solution benefited everyone. "You wanted cash and not clothes. Curzon would part with clothes and not cash. I wanted clothes but had no cash then." He assured Cole that he expected income from the sales of the *African Annual*, but admitted it would take him a "few more weeks" to get the money. As soon as he had it, he would take five shillings for expenses and forward the rest. "I did what I did largely in your interest," he concluded, promising to write again by the end of the month.[14]

Despite the equilibrium of the letter, Merriman was furious that Cole had defamed him "to not a few persons in Freetown." Even if he didn't have the cash at hand, he knew he could come up with the money—his mother had returned to Sierra Leone, lived only a few blocks from Cole, and could reimburse him at any time. But Merriman was angry that the man had disparaged him to important people and convinced himself that as Cole "had thus bothered me" he would not "bother my mother on his account."[15] Although he could have settled the matter quickly, he didn't. Certain the foolish man had been slandering him all over his home town, he would make him wait for his money.

Cole wasted no time in contacting the benchers of Lincoln's Inn to complain of Merriman's conduct. "I crave your worships' most gracious forbearance and impartiality," he wrote in the middle of July. "Even if I cannot hope for justice at your hands, Your Worships please extend to me your mercy." He told them he had heard "that there is justice in England even for a Slave." Claiming he had "exhausted all the means at my disposal to right my wrong," he contended "that nothing but the most extreme necessity can compel me to lay my case before you." Despite Cole's charges, there is no evidence that he had used, let alone exhausted, the means at his disposal: he had not demanded immediate payment from Merriman, nor had he asked their mutual friend to serve as intermediary. He had not even approached Merriman's well-known family to intercede. Cole, however, bemoaned the fact that "the very man whom I asked to defend my cause has himself defrauded me" and stated that he had not "the slightest hope of seeing my money again." He requested the benchers "be merciful to me and get Mr. Merriman to send my money without delay," claiming that Merriman "got the suits made for him since February, but he never owned up till I got Curzon's letter." In fact, Merriman had negotiated a resolution to Cole's problem in February and did not order the suits until April. With melodramatic flair, Cole closed his letter by calling Merriman's behavior a "dastardly trick" and vowing that "to my dying day I shall never forget the baseness and treachery of August Merriman— Barrister-at-law."[16] Though histrionic, the letter was effective. Cole's talk around Freetown had wounded Merriman's pride, but his letter to the benchers would draw him into a fight for his professional life.

Merriman would later be convinced that someone put Cole up to it—a lawyer perhaps or someone envious of his achievements.[17] Whatever forces might have been at play, Cole clearly wanted his money and believed the benchers would be able to force Merriman to pay him. Curiously, Cole wrote to Curzon Brothers two weeks after filing his complaint, asking them to "open up business connections" with him. It is unclear why Cole would so swiftly ask to re-establish relations with the company he believed had cheated him, especially when he could not yet have received a reply from Lincoln's Inn. Perhaps Merriman was not far off the mark in his theory that Cole's hand had been guided by someone in Freetown bent on humiliating him. As for Curzon Brothers, they were happy to send Cole their catalog with "a range of patterns for the current season."[18]

On Sunday, August 15, 1915, everyone in Britain between the ages of fifteen and sixty-five queued at local councils for National Registration Day, a nation-wide program to support the war effort by identifying "shirkers" avoiding enlistment as well as skilled workers who were more useful on the job than in the trenches. Each person completed a form identifying his or her name, age, nationality, marital status, occupation, and skills applicable to war work.[19] Because he was a man between eighteen and forty-one, Merriman recorded his information on a pink form indicating a man of military age. Because he was doing essential work, the pink form got a black star. If he had been proved unfit for duty, the clerk would have filled out a blue sheet. In the coming weeks, recruiting officers would comb through neighborhoods with bouquets of pink forms blossoming in their grips, pressuring eligible men to volunteer. In the following year, when there would no longer be enough volunteers to feed the insatiable war machine, the National Register would be used to provide names for compulsory military service.[20] Conscription would be a profound and deeply controversial development that would, as historian Arthur Marwick explains, bring "first-hand experience of the horrors of war, not just to a couple of million volunteers and horny-handed professionals, but willy-nilly to twice as many ordinary unadventurous civilians—one in three of the adult male population."[21] It is hard to say which circumstances made Merriman a less desirable candidate for British military service in 1915: his age (thirty-nine years old), his munitions work, his history of nervous ailments, or the color of his skin.

His night shift at the Woolwich Arsenal typically ran from 7:00 in the evening until 7:00 in the morning, six days a week. But when a "big push" was on, many factories worked twelve- or even fourteen-hour shifts seven days a week.[22] It was also common practice for men to work a punishing thirty-six-hour weekend shift—all day Friday, Friday night, and Saturday—for which they would earn double pay. Despite the demanding hours inspecting vacuum tubes, condensers, or galvanometers, Merriman continued his research and, in early September 1915, renewed his reader's ticket at the British Museum Reading Room again. After a night at the Arsenal perhaps testing Marconi wireless sets for short circuits and closed spark gaps, he would travel to Bloomsbury, the scent of newly manufactured instruments still on his skin, to wait for the library to open at nine. There he would put in another three or four hours of reading. Under the giant dome, he must have lamented the tragic divide between his nights dedicated to wireless sets, fuses, voltmeters, compasses, hammers, and cables, and his days amid the million and a half books housed in the famous library.

Only five years before, Merriman had hoped that the economic cost of war would ultimately make it prohibitive for rational people. "The financial burden necessitated by the up-keep of soldiers and sailors, ships and guns, besides other arms and ammunition, will, in time," he had predicted, "become so unbearable that some international arrangement for the curtailment or abandonment of armament is likely to result."[23] He was wrong. The cost of keeping the British fighting machine in motion now amounted to over three million pounds daily.[24] Despite mounting costs and the profound toll in human suffering, there was no indication that men would soon be beating their swords into plowshares.

He had also believed that science and art would "someday render infernal machines of war so destructive" that no sane person would be willing to fight. But just weeks earlier, an appalling new weapon had inflicted horrible suffering and death on African troops fighting in Belgium. On April 22, 1915, North African colonial soldiers and French troops were resting after a day of battle when the German artillery unexpectedly renewed its assault. As they peered over their parapets, the Africans and Frenchmen observed a strange greenish-yellow cloud billowing up from the German line. It sunk "to the ground like a swamp mist" and then drifted toward them on the early evening breeze.[25] They assumed it was a ruse designed to hide advancing troops, but as the cloud drifted nearer, its iridescent fumes began to sting their eyes, scorch their lungs, and trigger violent nausea. As the heavy toxic wave settled into the trenches, some men collapsed unconscious.[26] Gasping men, blinded men, men vomiting uncontrollably—"guttering, choking, drowning" as the poet Wilfred Owen would later write in "Dulce et Decorum Est"—staggered and stumbled and ran. "Over the fields streamed mobs of infantry, the dusky warriors of French Africa," one observer remembered, "away went their rifles, equipment, even their tunics that they might run the faster."[27] At 5:00 p.m. the Germans had unleashed 150 tons of lethal chlorine gas. By the end of the day, five thousand French Territorials and North Africans had died. Nearly six thousand cylinders hissed their lethal vapor into the Belgian evening, wrapping the very sun in a sickening-green vapor. Death by a fog of poison was a terrifying blow, portending more undreamed-of horrors that soldiers—and perhaps even civilians—would have to endure.

Continual Zeppelin raids throughout Britain that summer and fall extended the danger of war beyond the trenches.[28] On news of an imminent attack policemen pedaled bicycles through dark city streets ringing bells and wearing "Take Cover" signs hooked around their necks. People stumbled out of their beds and rushed down to their cellars where they huddled with other household members—sometimes for hours—until they heard Boy Scouts bugle the "All Clear." No London neighborhood was safe. On September 7, 1915, on an apparent course for the Woolwich Arsenal, Zeppelins attacked docks and neighborhoods south of the Thames—Bermondsey, Deptford, and Greenwich. The raiders returned the following night, hitting targets throughout the West End including Russell Square, Gray's Inn, an enormous warehouse in Wood Street, train tracks, and a city bus.

In mid-September, Cole informed Merriman that the benchers of Lincoln's Inn would be hearing his grievance. He clearly hoped the threat of the benchers' involvement would scare Merriman and force him to repay the money he owed.[29] Having clashed with the benchers seven years earlier over the African General Agency, Merriman believed he had a good idea of what to expect. Confident the issue was a matter of personal debt and that his actions were in no way blameworthy, he anticipated that the accusation would be summarily dismissed. What bothered him was the thought that Cole was continuing to defame him in Freetown. He had probably bragged to everyone he knew that the benchers of Lincoln's Inn were hearing his complaint. It was time, Merriman felt, to make a public statement. Because of "the general monetic disturbance occasioned by the War," he explained in a brief letter to the Freetown newspapers, the books he had hoped to publish were on hold. He promised that "at the very first change for the better," he would "do all in my power to see them through the press."[30] Merriman wrote to the Freetown papers because he wanted people to know that as soon as possible his new publications would put him in a position to make good on his obligations. Controlling the public's perception of him was so important that he published this letter twice: first in his uncle's *Sierra Leone Guardian* and then two weeks later in the *Colonial and Provincial Reporter*.

But there would be no change for the better in the foreseeable future. Contrary to Merriman's hopes, British readers were not interested in African adventure stories or guidebooks. They wanted books about the war, and those that flew off the shelves included Brooke's *Poems*, Buchan's *History of the War*, Jane's *The World's War Ships*, Seaman's *War-Time Verses*, Oliver's *Ordeal by Battle*, and Belloc's *General Sketch of the European War: First Phase*.[31]

As was their usual practice for complaints against barristers, the benchers assigned a committee of three to investigate Cole's grievance: in this instance, the committee consisted of Frank Russell, Edward Beaumont, and William Robert Sheldon.[32] Russell—whose father was formerly the Lord Chief Justice of England—had attended Oxford and advanced to the high-status position of King's Counsel. Edward Beaumont was Cambridge-educated, possessed an extensive and well-regarded practice, and was celebrated for his "learning, integrity, and geniality."[33] William Robert Sheldon, another Oxford graduate, was an expert on real estate and lived in the affluent London district of Kensington with his wife, his cook, and two maids.[34]

On October 13, 1915, after having just received his official summons to meet with the committee of benchers and respond to the charges against him, Merriman was at work at the Arsenal. Not long after 9:00 p.m. three Zeppelins stole into London and began unleashing bombs. One of the raiders hit the theater district, Law Courts, and Inns of Court. Three bombs exploded on the grounds of Lincoln's Inn, blowing out chamber windows, shattering the seventeenth-century stained glass of the chapel, pitting the thick stone walls of ancient buildings, and blasting a gaping hole into the middle of the pavement of New Square.[35]

Another Zeppelin targeted the Arsenal at Woolwich. When the fierce pounding of the anti-aircraft guns began cannonading at about half past nine, Merriman and his fellow munitions workers scrambled to air raid shelters. Through the roar, they could make out the bells of fire trucks. Alerted that Zeppelins were heading for the Arsenal, the firefighters rushed toward the grounds to extinguish any incendiary bombs that could touch off the massive stores of explosives. A number of bombs hit the Arsenal grounds but were snuffed out before they could cause extensive damage and loss of life.[36]

Like the rest of London, Merriman was still jittery from the Zeppelin attacks when he made his way on Friday, October 22, to Lincoln's Inn for his 5:00 p.m. meeting with the committee.[37] If they dismissed the allegation against him quickly, he would have enough time to make it back to the Arsenal for his 7:00 p.m. shift. As the sun set, he followed his familiar route along Chancery Lane. The African General Agency had been housed there, and, now unable to afford an office, Merriman paid a shopkeeper on this street to provide him with a postal address for professional matters. He must have been distressed to see his familiar haunt torn up by the recent Zeppelin raids. A bomb had ripped up the road, blown out shop windows, and gashed a hole six feet wide and three feet deep through the street. Thick blocks of pine mixed with tar and asphalt twisted upward from the road, and jagged shards of glass missed by a shopkeeper's broom glimmered in the fading light.

Facing the committee of barristers selected to hear the grievance against him, Merriman tried to explain the situation plainly.[38] He did not deny what he had done: he had asked for Cole's credit to be passed to him, and he had no money at the time to repay him. He admitted that Curzon, not he, had informed Cole of the arrangement. He respectfully made his argument that "Mr. Cole's claim was for debt" and was "not a concern of the Inn."[39] When he was asked how he had expected to repay the money, he explained that a company had been formed to publish his upcoming *West African Annual* and the proceeds were to supply the money.[40] When one member pressed him about the nature of this company and his role in it, he resisted. "Apart from answers to their questions," he later wrote, "I would not explain to them the inner affairs of the Company, as I hold the internals are not concerned with Mr. Cole's debt."[41]

But this was not the way things worked with the benchers. If Merriman was claiming he had a reasonable expectation to pay the money back shortly, then they were within their powers to assess the validity of this claim. One member of the committee in particular interrogated him about Literature Limited.[42] The line of questioning rattled Merriman. Flustered, he agreed to meet with them again and produce copies of the company's Articles of Association, directors' minutes, check book, and other documents for their inspection.

Merriman emerged from the chambers into the dark night, his hopes dashed for a quick dismissal of the complaint. He didn't understand why he had been put on the defensive, made to feel as if he had done something wrong. He admitted he owed Cole money. He had intended to pay, but the war had disappointed his hopes for an income from book publishing. The shaded lamps and shadowy shop windows offered scant light for him to make his way through the streets. In the dim tram, he replayed the meeting again and again, wishing he had said this or that. By the time he reached the Arsenal the old familiar symptoms of distress must have pulsed through his frame: headache, light-headedness, nausea.

The committee pursued its investigation by writing to Curzon Brothers. "The story seems to the committee so extraordinary," they explained, and they would be "glad to receive any explanation which you can give."[43] They discovered that the tailors had recently declared bankruptcy and the newly organized company was not liable for any of the former debts. Curzon had been willing to make Cole a suit of clothes as a show of good faith, but they refused to reimburse money because they did not legally owe it. To preserve its good name in Sierra Leone, Curzon had not mentioned the bankruptcy to Cole. Evaluating this remarkably relevant information, the committee somehow concluded that it did "not throw new light on the matter."

If Merriman's first meeting with the committee had gone badly, the second was worse. When he tried to make the argument that he had had a "valid and reasonable hope" of paying Cole from the proceeds of his forthcoming book, one of the benchers spent the rest of the meeting grilling him about Literature Limited's directors, resolutions, and finances. At one point, a member suggested that the ink used to indicate Merriman's appointment as business and legal advisor was "different from the rest of the minutes." "The atmosphere," Merriman recalled, "was impregnated with groundless suspicion."[44] Every time he tried to explain why he could reasonably expect money from Literature Limited, he was cut off. One member seemed to be accusing him of so many transgressions, he didn't know if there was a specific charge against him. He suspected two members of the committee possessed what he called an "unconscious prejudice" against him. Why, he wondered, had this simple matter of owing Cole £3 15s turned into an occasion to disparage his character?

There are several reasons that help explain why the committee responded so negatively to Merriman. First, his involvement with Literature Limited violated the "starkly anti-commercial ideology of legal practice" at the time.[45] Legal historian Patrick Polden observes that the idea of a barrister canvassing for advertisements would have been highly objectionable to the committee members. The Inns of Court were intimate societies and, Polden speculates, the benchers might have seen him as an embarrassment.[46] Moreover, the decision doubtlessly included a racial component as Merriman suspected. Most colonial subjects who studied law in Britain returned to their home countries not because there were legal restrictions preventing them from practicing in Britain, but because there were very strong social constraints. Two years earlier, a black barrister was excluded from a circuit court mess. According to one well-known barrister, "the fact of the matter is that although the whites have to mingle with the coloured gentleman at mess when they are students, that association is never a voluntary one." He went on to suggest that if a poll of the members of the bar were taken, it would find "an overwhelming majority throughout the country against the gentleman of colour."[47] While colonials were not officially barred from practicing in Britain, the barristers disliked it and, as Polden explains, "the gatekeepers—chamber clerks and solicitors—would have been hostile."[48] As a well-known barrister at the time remarked, it did the black barristers "no kindness to encourage them to remain here for their scope must inevitably be much less. They have not merely to meet the prejudice of members of their own profession, but the general prejudice of the lay clients."[49] Merriman had broken the unspoken agreement that black men were permitted to become barristers as long as they did not stay in Britain but returned home to carry on the legal work of empire.

A short story by Henry Hesketh Bell, the former Governor of Northern Nigeria, illustrates the contempt some Britons had for Africans who came to London to study law. "His Highness Prince Kwakoo" tells the story of James Jones, an African educated by British missionaries. Jones's veneer of civilization conceals the savage beneath, the narrator asserts, and sooner or later he would "steal sugar or a stray copper, or tell an artistic lie with the best of them."[50] In Bell's story, Jones travels to London with a friend to study law at an Inn of Court. "Our two young darkies," Bell writes, "found there a considerable number of their dusky brothers on legal distinction bent." Possessing a childlike obsession with fancy clothes, they visit a West End tailor who fits "them out in the height of fashion; and James Jones' collars were the tallest, and his boots the shiniest that could be seen within a mile of the Law Courts." In Bell's view, the young Africans' proper timorousness in the face of British culture was all too short-lived. "They dined in the hall like the others," the narrator continues, "and rapidly lost all trace of the awe with which the dignified old buildings at first inspired them." Bell imagines the disbelief of ancient benchers had they learned that Africans were now accepted at the Inns of Court. "The prototypes of the venerable portraits of bygone benchers, which hung on the walls, would probably have waxed very incredulous had it been foretold to them that the woolly Ethiopian … would one day sit cheek by jowl at the tables whereat they themselves had sat and supped according to ancient customs."[51]

An identical view pervades Paul Trent's *A Wife by Purchase*.[52] The central villain in this 1909 novel is Mr. Caesar Reindorf, described as "one of those very weird modern productions, a native who has been sent to England, where he has gone through the ordeal of passing the examinations and eating the dinners for a call to the English bar." While in

England, the narrator continues, "he had been rather spoilt, in the way that the Bayswater boarding-house keepers and their guests generally spoil one of black blood." But to the "white man who has lived on the West Coast of Africa," the narrator adds, the Africans may "wear frock-coats and patent leather boots, while their silk hats are shiny, and they affect much gold jewellery, but they are none the less savages, in mind and thought."[53]

Could it be that some of the "unconscious prejudice" Merriman felt from two of the benchers was a deeply held prejudice that Africans were by their very nature dishonest, cunning, and disreputable? A bigoted conviction that they would do almost anything for a new suit of clothes?

The events that followed his meetings with the committee came as a complete shock. In their report to the benchers, the committee decided that Literature Limited was not a viable source of income. For men who might have been making £15,000 a year, the sums involved were paltry: the company's shares amounted to only £5—scarcely enough to repay Cole, let alone publish a book. The committee concluded that there did not appear "to be any prospect, immediate or remote," of Merriman ever being in a position to repay Cole. In their interpretation of events, he had abused Cole's trust and "acted dishonestly for his own personal benefit." Whether because of his poverty or his race or his forays into trade, or his gentle mocking of lawyers in *Britons through Negro Spectacles*, they wanted nothing more to do with him. They recommended a punishing consequence: "We are of the opinion," they wrote in their report to the benchers, "that he is not a fit person to remain a member of the Bar."[54]

Merriman wrote to the benchers urging them to let him explain his case to them directly before they made the final decision. They ignored his letter. Six days later, twenty-seven Masters of the Bench at a council meeting on November 25 made the following order: "That Mr. Augustus Merriman be and he is hereby disbarred and expelled from this Honourable Society." They went on to stipulate that notice of his disbarment was to be given to the other Inns of Court, to the Judges of the Supreme Court, as well as to the Registrar of the High Court in Freetown, Sierra Leone, where it should be "screened in the Hall."[55] He was not only to be punished, but to be made an example.

Disbarments were exceedingly rare in Britain. Writing about the British legal system at the time, American attorney Thomas Leaming described disbarment as "an extreme penalty ... inflicted only for moral turpitude amounting usually to a crime."[56] As Patrick Polden explains, disbarments were usually reserved for severe offenses which included "a strong element of public importance." What Merriman did, Polden continues, "was foolish and irresponsible and deserving rebuke—but disbarment, even if technically warranted, was excessive."[57] Compared with other disbarments of the era, he adds, Merriman's offense was trivial.

It is no surprise then that the order blind-sided Merriman. It never occurred to him that his actions were worthy of such harsh punishment. How could three men—two of whom seemed prejudiced against him—so swiftly rescind a professional qualification that had taken many years and enormous sacrifice to achieve?

But his faith in the British legal system to defend the rights of individuals against arbitrary power was so strong that not even the benchers' order could destroy it. The judgment of individual men was corruptible, he believed, but the system itself was steadfast. He saw examples of British justice working on behalf of Africans not only in the great triumph against slavery in 1772, when Lord Mansfield ruled that no slave could be removed from Britain to be sold, but also in the legal successes of individual Africans in his own time. When soldier-aristocrat Viscount Wolseley wrote in his 1903 memoir that an African vicar, "the very blackest of Negroes," had "sent for the chief 'fetish man'" on his deathbed, the Reverend Thomas Maxwell—the chaplain in question—happened to be very much alive and sued Wolseley for libel. "When the case reached the highest court in England," Merriman recalled, "the Negro plaintiff was awarded substantial damages. That was British justice."[58] Or perhaps he found hope in the very recent case of Phillip Coker, a Deputy Registrar in Nigeria, who had been arrested in 1909 for allegedly stealing £55 from his office. Coker had been tried by the Chief Justice with three assessors. Although all three assessors found him not guilty, the judge overruled their verdict and sentenced Coker to nine months of hard labor. Released from prison a "physically broken man, financially ruined and socially outcast," he sold his possessions and borrowed money—to the tune of some £500—to appeal his case. Recently, the Nigerian Supreme Court had reviewed Coker's case, found a "miscarriage of justice," and overturned the ruling.[59]

"Take it from me," Merriman had written six years earlier, "here, in Britain, we have already justice for Blacks."[60] This conviction gave him the confidence to write an appeal to the benchers to reopen his case. "I still honestly believe," he explained in a letter, "there is error somewhere and that when the pertinent facts of the case are brought to their Lordships' notice they will take another view of it."[61] He was certain that if he were able to tell his story to a group of impartial, reasonable men, he would be reinstated.

On December 7, Merriman wrote a short letter to the *Sierra Leone Weekly News* advising his friends "not to be anxious about the recent order" from the benchers. He assured them that the complaint against him was "worthless" and the situation would soon be remedied. "You can take it from me," he wrote, "that whatever the result, the friction will make me brighter and better. I am not in the least perturbed."[62] This public expression of confidence downplaying the disaster would, he hoped, help preserve his reputation in Freetown until he could get the order reversed.

He drafted a lengthy petition in time for the next benchers' meeting a week later. In it, he reiterated his actions on Cole's behalf and provided evidence of his previous publishing successes to demonstrate that his expectation of money from the *African Annual* was reasonable. He explained that a reputable publisher as well as an important person in government supported this new project. As for his integrity, people throughout Britain and Africa, he asserted, people from the church, the government, and the community would testify that he was reliable and honest. He had to make the benchers understand that their decision was not just. "I do not deserve," he protested, "being held out to the world as a man of questionable character." In a surprising move, he offered a heartfelt profession of faith in his true calling: "All my time, night and day, has been devoted to study for substantive Literature as my main aim in life, and profession paramount over law, economics, and education. The love of Literature which has detained me in England, is the cause of penury now, and should be the cause of property to be."[63] It was only a matter of time, he felt, before his literary skill would come into full view, and he would garner the economic rewards of his talent. They had to understand that this was a temporary setback—he was aspiring to a higher purpose in life. To such lofty aspiration and such years of dedicated work, they must surely show some compassion.

The benchers responded with a one-sentence letter declining to reopen his case.[64]

It would be hard to overstate the injury of the disbarment. Although Merriman was not currently practicing law, the order cut him off from any future legal career. If his literary aspirations should fail, he could no longer return to Freetown to take his place among the distinguished legal men of his home town. A potentially lucrative career path was permanently cut off. Far worse than any loss of money or opportunity was the public disgrace. For a Krio son to become a barrister was a badge of honor to his family. In a world where many Britons believed that inherent racial differences made Anglo-Saxons fundamentally superior and Africans fundamentally inferior, a black man being called to the bar provided seemingly unassailable proof that he possessed the same intellectual abilities as a Briton. The black barrister had followed the same course of study and taken the same exams as the white. To be expelled from the profession seemed to give credence to the belief that Africans did not have the moral or intellectual nature suitable for lofty pursuits.

Merriman had spent his life trying to prove that he was a man deserving respect. Disbarment meant dishonor and social ruin. What parents would trust him to guide the education of their children? Who would want to listen to his ideas or invest in his books? Twenty years of work, twenty years of dedication and sacrifice undone in twenty minutes by men who knew almost nothing about him.

Merriman could not accept the benchers' judgment. Throughout January 1916, after his long night shifts at the Arsenal, he buried himself in law books. He desperately searched for a way to overturn the decision, but few avenues were open to him. The benchers' decisions regarding the conduct of members of the Inn were outside the jurisdiction of the courts, so he could not sue them. With no clear recourse, he grasped at straws. When the *Sierra Leone Gazette*—the official public record of the colony—printed the disbar order twice, he unearthed a precedent in which a censured barrister won a judgment against a law journal for commenting on a case. He considered action against the newspaper. "If we cannot take the Benchers to court," he reasoned, "we can take those who help them."[65] Later, he discovered a suit in which a disbarred barrister was able to convene a parliamentary committee to overturn the benchers' decision, but that was only accomplished, he had to admit, because the man had been a person of rank and influence. In calmer moments, Merriman considered the possibility that the disbarment might be temporary. He even wrote to the benchers asking when they might be "prepared to consider favourably an application from me for re-instatement to the degree of barrister."[66] They did not respond.

Writing about the disbarment to the *Sierra Leone Weekly News*, he positioned himself as David against an army of Goliaths, claiming "that Mr. Cole, the lawyer or other who advised him at Freetown, the Benchers Committee, and the Benchers Council are all wrong." In his view, the problem arose from what he called the "injustice of ignorance." "Nearly everyone has the notion that the benchers cannot err," he explained, but they could and in his case did.[67] He was not far off the mark. "The normal qualifications for benchers" at the time, Patrick Polden writes, were "age, wealth, and personal convenience rather than professional competence or success." Polden explains that "benchers became a byword for elderly men, remote from the concerns of their juniors and students and more interested in their dinners than anything else."[68]

In his letter, Merriman argued that his course of action had been reasonable, and men with a better understanding of the law would have come to a more just decision. He even expressed some compassion for Cole and said he did not blame him for contacting the benchers. "I might have done the same," he conceded, but pointed out that he would have given him a warning first. Merriman concluded his letter by promising "one or two of my books" would be published within the year, and counseled his supporters not to worry. "All will come out right in the end," he declared.[69] Yet the disjointed logic of the letter and the strange tone—an awkward mix of swagger and muddle—suggests he was not as sanguine as he wished to appear. The relentless shifts at the munitions factory, the hours poring through law books, and the stress of the disbarment were taking their toll.

Apparently, even Cole was shocked by the benchers' decision. In his own lengthy letter to the *Sierra Leone Weekly News*, he began by saying that "it was with the profoundest sorrow that I learnt of the Disbar

Order ... it was not my intention and never has been that Mr. Merriman should have suffered to such an alarming extent."[70] But his professed regret did not lessen his willingness to further discredit Merriman. Although Cole distorted the timeline and alluded to cautioning letters that may never have existed, the overall letter offered a cogent and at times brilliant account of their dispute. With a folksy appeal and commonsense approach, he observed that "instead of taking three or more weeks now to examine a 500 years' defence, and other Herculean labours of attacking the giants, he could easily have refunded my money and so saved the whole situation." He ended with a dazzling display of mockery: "If we accept Mr. Merriman's verdict," Cole wrote, "then the Benchers of Lincoln's Inn are wrong. The Master of the Rolls is wrong; two or three other Judges of the Supreme Court are wrong ... the Government as well as the Chief Justice of Sierra Leone is wrong, in short forty men exclusive of several more are wrong, only Mr. Augustus Merriman is right. Such is the fallibility of human nature. How extraordinary!"[71] Cole's sharp words added yet another barb to Merriman's crown of thorns. In the end, Cole would have the last word. After the events that were to follow, Merriman would never write to the *Sierra Leone Weekly News* again.

Despite his public displays of confidence, Merriman was growing increasingly more distressed by the benchers' silence. They had yet to answer his letter from late January. Beset with anxiety, he wrote again in the middle of February, this time appealing to their compassion. "I am suffering serious and much damage as a result of the disbar," he pleaded.[72] They responded only to reassert his dishonesty in his relationship with Cole and offered no hope that he would ever be reinstated.

His only recourse now was to appeal to the most powerful legal figures in the nation. He could apply to the Lord Chancellor and other High Court judges to act as visitors to the Inns of Court and hear his case. That his situation was worthy of the attention of the leading men of the bench echoed the Mansfield decision: the black man's plight would be heard by the highest authorities in the land. With an undaunted faith in the British legal system, he was sure he would find justice at last.

In late July 1916, the quaint courtyards of the Middle Temple, with their blooming hydrangeas, shady trees, and bubbling fountains, seemed very close to their monastic origins. Wandering through Fig Tree Court and Elm Court, past the cloisters and the famous medieval church, Augustus Merriman felt he had entered a very old world that knew nothing of the city at war beyond its walls. Along the King's Bench Walk, he was arrested by the sight of an unexpected figure: a life-size statue of an African kneeling on a short pedestal with a large sundial balanced on his head. It was dated 1731, long before slavery had been abolished in the British empire. Naked except for a loincloth of leaves, this was the African of the European imagination—a creature of the body, not of the mind. Still, Merriman may have mused, he looked strong enough to carry the weight of time until the world changed and he could lay his burden down.

As for himself, he felt unspeakably weary. Weary of the war, of the long nights of munitions work, of streets filled with men and women in khaki; weary of the other weary faces around him, of the paint chipping from neglected store fronts, of Hyde Park filled with military huts instead of flower beds; weary of the terrible rumble of military trains dragging their cargo of battered men into Waterloo Station; so very weary of the hours on the tram slogging back and forth from the Arsenal to the British Museum Library, from the Library to home, of preparing hour after hour for this day; weary of being unable to sleep; weary of dread, anticipation, fear; so very weary of weariness itself.[73]

He sank down on a stone bench. His hearing would begin at 4:15.[74] By the time he started his night shift that evening, he would know whether or not he had been restored to the bar. Although he could feel his strength drain from his limbs, he refused to let his hope fail. It had all dragged on so long. He had submitted his appeal in early April. After three long months the hearing date was finally set for July 24.[75] And yet, so many terrible things had happened in the intervening months. Now all single men and childless widowers between the ages of eighteen and forty-one could be called up for duty under the Military Service Act. Only those seen as unfit or in special categories were exempted: clergy, priests, ministers, and, as the notices had put it, "visitors from the dominions."[76] Lord Kitchener, the great Secretary of State for War whose mighty mustache and steely eyes had been calling men to voluntary service for two years, had sunk to his death at the bottom of the ocean on a secret mission to Russia. That day, people all over London had rushed the news-stands in disbelief, halting traffic in places. The sudden death of the man who represented unwavering resolve to win the war left the nation in shock. At the Arsenal, it had not been difficult to read the signs that something big was coming. Weeks before the fighting on the Somme had begun, the "big push" was on: twelve- or fourteen-hour shifts seven days a week; men working for thirty-six hours every weekend, only stopping for meals and tea.[77] The newspapers couldn't say so, but rumors flew about disasters at the Front. When names of casualties from the Somme began appearing in *The Times*, they required columns upon columns to list the dead, missing, and wounded. No one had ever seen anything like it. It was a catastrophe.

And now, after a month of cold summer days, Merriman sat on a bench in a courtyard at Middle Temple waiting to join the judges in Parliament Chamber where he would defend his integrity. He glanced at a fistful of notes. For weeks he had been rehearsing what he would say. First, he would discredit the procedure the committee had used— he would question their handling of evidence, their faulty cross-examinations, their disregard for rules of law and ignorance about business practices.[78] He would challenge the policy of allowing a tribunal of three to determine a man's professional fate. Then he would move to the issue relating to his reasonable expectation of paying Cole. There he felt confident he could make his case. He would assure the judges that he could prove his honesty by providing testimony from scores of people throughout Britain and Africa who had worked with him. He would turn their attention to his record of honesty and accountability as a civil servant and advocate. He would pull no punches. The judges had to understand that the order against him was not the work of justice. The benchers, he would say, "acted with disregard and nonchalance" toward him. He would reveal the disbarment for the travesty it was. "After a mock trial in less than twenty minutes," he would tell them, "his twenty years' labours were brought to naught, his reputation defamed, and his prospects blasted."[79]

Heaving himself from his bench, he took one last look across the Inn's luxurious gardens and then entered the Great Hall. He made his way down the long corridor toward the Parliament Chamber, past engravings of famous lawyers, the shields and swords and armors of ancient battles, past prints of the Inn's idyllic grounds. At the door of the chamber room stood a pedestal adorned with an ancient burial stone, a relic from Britain's Roman past.[80] Britons, too, had once been colonized, had been people ruled by a mighty empire far from their own shores. The thought gave him hope as he pushed open the heavy doors to the room and entered.

The only surviving description of the hearing is a brief report for Lincoln's Inn from the solicitor representing the benchers. He notes that the Lord Chief Justice and six other judges heard the appeal. "Mr. Merriman," he wrote, "was heard at length on all points raised in the statement lodged by him." He goes on to explain that "the appeal was dismissed without calling on counsel for the Inn."[81] Unmoved by Merriman's claims, the judges didn't even need to hear the lawyer for the benchers.[82]

There was no further recourse. The leading men of the bench, the highest magistrates in the land, had sided with the benchers and upheld this harsh sentence against him. Only a few years before, he had assured his readers in *Britons through Negro Spectacles* that "the Negro is sure to get not only mercy, but justice" in Britain. But when his own time had come to be judged, he had received neither.

Earlier that afternoon, as he looked at the statue of the "blackamoor" sundial, had Merriman known there was a famous story about it?[83] Lamenting "the legal atmosphere the African had to breathe," a legal wit had written a little lyric and attached it to the statue:

In vain, poor sable son of woe,
    Thou seek'st the tender tear;
From thee in vain with pangs they flow,
For mercy dwells not here.

From cannibals thou fled'st in vain,
    Lawyers less quarter give;
The first won't eat you till you're slain,
    The last will do't alive.[84]

Merriman had made a foolish mistake in his dealings with Cole, but his punishment went beyond losing his legal career—it meant years wasted, character defiled, reputation destroyed. British law may have abolished slavery, but it could not end the prejudices of men.

Merriman had come to London to rise above his circumstances, to prove that he had greatness within, but instead of laurels he had reaped disgrace. A man who cared very much what people thought of him, he could not return to Sierra Leone. Having aspired to such heights only to fall so low, he feared the only thing waiting for him in Freetown would be mockery and derision. How would his countrymen treat a person who had been held out by the distinguished benchers of Lincoln's Inn as a man of questionable character?

The disbarment shattered one of the fundamental precepts of his life: the belief that British justice would ultimately prevail. He knew, of course, the brutalities of colonial rule—the discrimination, the contempt, the violence. But, like many other Krios, he had believed one could work within the system to address grievances, right wrongs, change the balance of power. He had been proud to be British, proud to be from one of the nation's oldest colonies, proud of the lilting tune of his British birth name: Augustus Boyle Chamberlayne Merriman-Labor. The disbarment shattered his faith in British law and imploded his British identity. The very signature he had so extravagantly flourished now seemed tarnished with betrayal.

Forsaken by the nation on which he had pinned every hope, he now realized he would never be accepted as truly British. Perhaps for the first time, he wholly embraced his African identity. He cast off his given name and replaced it with one that carried no hint of England. He would no longer be Augustus Merriman. From now on he would be Ohlohr Maigi.

"Ohlohr" was a common Krio name, perhaps from Yoruba roots.[85] It came from the intimate language of the Krio people, spoken among family and friends, a name that rejected the language of colonial power. Why he chose Maigi is harder to reckon, but he may have chosen it as a way to connect himself to powerful Christian imagery of black royalty.[86] In the familiar nativity story of the gospel of St. Matthew, visitors from the East called "magi" worship the infant Jesus and present him with gifts. For many centuries in Christian art, one of the three (popularly called "Kings") was portrayed as a black man. By adopting the name Maigi—a possible variation of magi—he associated himself with a vision of a regal Africa intimately connected to the Christian story. His new name repudiated the colonial representation of Africans as a downtrodden, uncivilized, savage race, and replaced it with a noble vision loaded with biblical significance. "Maigi" suggests a vision of Africa not as a heart of darkness, but as the source of the first Christian worshipers, a continent of spiritual insight and indigenous wisdom.

After the humiliation of the disbarment, Maigi retreated from public view. He no longer wrote letters to the Sierra Leonean newspapers, advertised his educational services, or announced forthcoming publications, yet his daily life remained largely unchanged. For the duration of the war, he worked at the Arsenal and lived in South London.[87] Although the British Museum had been closed to the public in March 1916 "in the interests of economy," the Reading Room remained open and Maigi renewed his reader's ticket and continued his research.[88] Despite his expulsion from Lincoln's Inn, he was not ostracized from his social circle. Black people who were "ready to champion the cause of this ill-used race of ours," such as O'Kagoo Logemoh, a Liberian entrepreneur, recognized Maigi as a fellow traveler and asked to meet him.[89] Although Africans were reluctant to criticize authorities openly during wartime for fear of being considered disloyal, many of Maigi's friends must have seen his treatment by the benchers as yet another example of systemic injustice that could be challenged once the war was over.

As the fighting dragged on, the chances that Maigi would be able to publish any books grew increasingly remote. A paper shortage hit the country, limiting availability, driving up costs, and even forcing the penny morning papers to increase their price to twopence by early 1917.[90] Despite the shortage, Maigi did not abandon his publishing dream or give up on Literature Limited. Ironically, the disbarment gave him the freedom to become one of Literature Limited's directors and legally control his own company. The other director was his number one supporter: his mother, Gillian Merriman-Wilson. It must have seemed to him that it was just a matter of time before he could bring his ideas out in print, achieve the recognition he had so long sought, and ultimately restore his good name. Yet the prospect of the war ending any time soon now appeared distant.

On his way to the British Museum Reading Room after an all-night shift, Maigi saw how the war continued to alter the face of the metropolis. Boards and sandbags protected important buildings, statues, and old stained glass. The shimmering lake of St. James's Park had been emptied and housed temporary Admiralty and War Office buildings. Now that petrol was restricted, the roar of omnibuses and motor cars had given way once again to the clip-clop of horses' hooves. Because driving was considered unpatriotic, few privately owned motor cars were on the street. Amazingly, hansom cabs and even growlers had returned to service. The organ grinders and street singers Maigi had found so irritating in peacetime had vanished.[91] Nor did one see the sight so common before the war: men in immaculate frock coats and "twelve-inch chimney pot" hats buying flowers for their velvet-clad ladies. The order of the day was a uniform or a shabby pair of trousers and a soft hat—anything to show you were doing "your bit" to win the war.[92] All around the city, people had built makeshift shrines in memory of their loved ones: wooden panels decorated with crosses and the names of the neighborhood dead, below a little shelf for a jar of daisies.

At the end of September 1916, a midnight Zeppelin raid shattered homes and businesses in Maigi's South London neighborhood. The raider dropped flares to light its path along the tramway as it passed along Streatham Common and Brixton Road into Kennington, releasing bombs along its route. After the attack, people held flashlights and lanterns against the moonless night as men searched through the rubble of bricks and mortar for survivors. Twenty-two of Maigi's neighbors died; many more were injured. Shattered glass littered the pavement, shrapnel pitted walls, and what was formerly a children's playground in Kennington Park—just three blocks from Maigi's lodgings—was now a crater of dirt and grass. Where bombs had torn away walls, people's demolished lives were there for all to see: "wall-paper hanging in tatters, pictures awry, stairs ending in mid-air, furniture broken and covered with thick dust of lath and plaster."[93]

A week later, the roar of anti-aircraft guns brought Arsenal workers out into the frozen night to catch a glimpse of a monster Zeppelin caught in a net of searchlights. The cannonade roared as the giant slipped in and out of a bank of clouds. All at once, one of the munitions workers observed, the thing "seemed to burst from the centre into a great crimson red flare shot with gold and jagged blackness all round; then down, down increasing in size and in the multiplicity of flaming light until the whole heavens seemed ablaze."[94] People all over London watched the beast plummet. "A gigantic pyramid of flames," journalist Michael MacDonagh wrote, "red and orange, like a ruined star falling slowly to earth."[95] Suddenly, Maigi and his co-workers heard a strange sound rising up. Standing on the frosty mud, looking into the night sky, they heard an immense chorus of cheers. "All the millions in and around London had looked on breathless at the struggle," one munitions worker recalled, "and their pent-up feelings were now having vent."[96] MacDonagh described it as a "hoarse shout of mingled execration, triumph and joy; a swelling shout that appeared to be rising from all parts of the metropolis, ever increasing in force and intensity."[97] After two years of war, four marauders had been shot down in one month. Many who witnessed the burning carcass falling out of the sky felt an unfamiliar emotion. Victory.

The feeling did not last. At the end of November a new terror arrived. In the middle of the day, a high-flying airplane dropped six bombs around Eaton Square, Brompton Road, Victoria Station, and Belgravia, reaching as far as Harrods department store.[98] To be attacked from the air while one was going about one's daily affairs seemed unimaginable before the war; now it was merely another of the terrors this awful conflict had wreaked.

On a dark winter's night, January 19, 1917, Maigi was probably just beginning his shift at the Arsenal when suddenly the sky lit up as if it had instantly become day. On the opposite side of the river, flames and plumes of smoke poured upward in hues of orange and violet. "A huge fountain of flame, crowned by a myriad of sparks, shot up to a great height," reported the *West Ham and South Essex Mail*, "and this awe-inspiring spectacle was immediately followed by a sharp crack and roar and a general vibration that made everything tremble."[99] The explosion—which was heard more than fifty miles away in Cambridge—hurled a fireball over the Arsenal. This was not an air raid, but a terrible accident at the Silvertown TNT factory less than three miles away where the volatile explosive caught fire and exploded. The eruption spewed molten metal into the air, destroying homes, buildings, docks, and warehouses. Even though the Arsenal was unharmed, the disaster was a munition worker's worst nightmare, a vivid reminder of the imminent danger of the job. It was a grim beginning to what was to be a grim year—food prices so high they exceeded the increases in wages, relentless submarine attacks sending hundreds of ships to the bottom of the ocean each month, desperate battles, high causalities, limited information, and frequent air raids causing fear and anxiety.

In 1917, London became the land of queues. If Maigi's landlady wanted to purchase meat or a block of margarine, she would have to stand in long lines, often for hours at a time, knowing she might come away empty-handed. The only bread she could offer was chewy government stuff—a heavy brown loaf full of husk. Nor could she keep his room warm. Coal was in short supply. She and her neighbors in South London mobbed coal merchants and carried away as much as they could get using whatever was at hand: perambulators, go-carts, boxes, baskets, or boxes.[100] By the end of 1917, there was no longer sugar for tea—sometimes there wasn't even tea—no butter or margarine, little milk or bacon. Even rice and raisins were hard to come by.[101] Working long hours, travelling daily on a tedious and crowded commute, fearing air raids, missing regular food, mourning the dead, and enduring an usually cold winter had become Maigi's new normal.

A bud of hope bloomed in the spring of 1917 when the United States entered the war. In April, perhaps Maigi joined thousands of other Londoners on a warm sunny day in Whitehall to celebrate "America Day." The Lord Mayor in his ruby gown and ermine cape paraded through central London with other red-gowned dignitaries, the American Ambassador, and the King in his wartime khaki. Old Glory and the Union Jack fluttered side by side above Buckingham Palace, the Houses of Parliament, the War Office, and other government buildings. Parents tucked little penny American flags into their buttonholes and children waved large Old Glories as the procession passed. Yet, Maigi's excitement about the Americans joining the war was measured. The thought of thousands of them surging into London must have reminded him of his experience as a lodger in a Bloomsbury hotel when a group of Americans had refused to have a meal as long as he was in the room. Although his protest had ended the matter, the thought of thousands of American soldiers bringing their segregationist expectations to London must have been added to the daily strain of the war.

Hoping to create such hardship that the British people would lose the will to continue fighting, the Germans renewed their program of unrestricted submarine warfare in 1917, torpedoing hundreds of ships each month and sending vast supplies of meat, wheat, sugar, and other essentials to the bottom of the ocean. By the end of the war, sixty of Elder Dempster's West African fleet would be sunk by enemy action— including ships Maigi had travelled on himself.[102] In the spring of 1917, the Germans torpedoed the *Abosso* carrying 127 passengers and 3,500 tons of produce from West Africa to Liverpool. On board was a young man very much like Maigi: his name was Kobina Sekyi. Because they traveled in similar circles and shared similar views, if Maigi didn't know Sekyi personally, he almost certainly knew of him.

Sekyi was a Gold Coast writer and law student who had first come to England in 1910 to study at the University of London. He had arrived, like Maigi, an enthusiastic anglophile, but had left Britain disillusioned. Nonetheless, he had decided to return to study law at Inner Temple in 1917 and was aboard the *Abosso* when a German submarine fired a single torpedo through the engine room as the ship steamed along the coast of Ireland. Sekyi described the attack in the pages of *West Africa*. The strike, he wrote, had come "like a bolt from the blue."[103] He was trapped in his cabin until a white steward "hearing of his attempts to get out, came to his rescue by helping force open the jammed door." Once in the lifeboat, Sekyi was horrified at being parted from his friends.

> Then comes the pang of parting. You see all the other boats still on the side of the ship, which is slowly overturning. You say 'Are we leaving all these people behind?' You are told that your boat must get out of the reach of the suction that must soon be drawing all that are near enough to be thus sucked. The ship is no doubt doomed, but there is no reason why those in your boat should not attempt to save themselves. You acquiesce in the inevitable."[104]

In the end, sixty-five people died including, Sekyi wrote, all of his countrymen. He was the only native Gold Coaster to survive.

In the pages of *West Africa*, Sekyi reported a wartime tragedy. But he revealed a much more sinister version of events to his African friends. As he was climbing into the lifeboat that terrible night, he told them, a European man had yelled at him demanding that he get out. No black man should be saved, the man insisted, while white people were drowning. The event changed Sekyi's thinking about the relationship between black and white, Africa and Britain forever.[105]

While there is some dispute whether Sekyi's story of the white man trying to eject him from the lifeboat was factually true, it expressed a profound emotional reality that would have resonated with Maigi and other Africans living in Britain. The white man flinging the black man from the lifeboat into the icy sea offered a powerfully symbolic image for their experiences of hostility, cruelty, and injustice.

10

THE WEARINESS, THE FEVER, THE FRET

In the middle of August 1918, H.M.S. *Mantua* was only two days into its familiar route from the Royal Navy base in Devonport, England, to Sierra Leone when influenza broke out on board. By the time the vessel arrived in Freetown on August 15, more than two hundred of its crew were sick.[1] The *Mantua*'s captain sent a private note to Sierra Leone Governor Richard Wilkinson indicating that he would be unable to attend his Honor that evening at Government House owing to illness on board. It happened that Wilkinson was entertaining a substantial naval party, including a Brazilian admiral, a British rear admiral, and several captains. When he mentioned the influenza aboard the *Mantua* to his guests, they offered "the most positive assurances that no communication whatsoever was being permitted between the *Mantua* and the shore."[2] Convinced all was being handled appropriately, Wilkinson thought no more of it. The following day Freetown colliers sailed out to the *Mantua* and, as usual, loaded coal into its hold. Ten days later, five hundred of the six hundred men working in the Freetown coal yard were too sick to come to work.[3] The "Spanish flu" had arrived in Africa.

Influenza had swept the globe earlier in the year, but as it was generally mild it had caused little concern. But at the end of summer, a mutation transformed the mundane virus into a lethal disease, and the massive transport of people around the world in service of the European war spread it rapidly. In late August 1918, the flu epidemic erupted simultaneously in three places: Boston, Massachusetts; Brest, France; and Freetown, Sierra Leone.

The disease cut its deadly swathe through Freetown, the *Sierra Leone Weekly News* reported, beginning "from the Government Wharf straight on to Kissy Road, Fourah Bay Road and Foulah Town."[4] Hundreds of people who had become suddenly ill swarmed to the Colonial Hospital. They had no idea how to deal with the distressing symptoms—high fever, bleeding from the nose and ears, excruciating headaches focused behind the eyes, nausea, vomiting, pain in the back and limbs, and delirium. Some were so ill they collapsed in the streets. One person described waiting for hours with three hundred other sick people at the Colonial Hospital. Another recalled that he was admitted, but didn't see a doctor for four days because many of the medical staff were desperately sick themselves.[5]

Business in Freetown ground to a halt. Shops were closed, train service suspended, churches emptied, the main thoroughfares deserted. The death rate soared: hundreds died each week. The dead came, the *Sierra Leone Weekly News* reported, "from all classes and conditions—white and black; Agents of European Firms and Native clerks of Government offices, and mercantile establishments; unmarried young men and women as well as married."[6] The disease carried away the vulnerable—infants and the elderly—but was especially dangerous for those in the prime of life.

As with every household in Freetown, members of Maigi's family were fatally struck. Eleven-year-old Hannah Labor, his cousin or perhaps half-sister, was dead by the end of August. Sawetta Labor, just seven months old, died before the close of September. Ribbons of newspaper columns announcing the "Deaths for the Week" illustrated the sweeping grip of the deadly illness: Woodley Metzger, Patton-Street, 2 years 8 months; Elkanah Rhodes, Fourah Bay Road, 24 years; Mary Jones, Sackville-Street, 37; Thomas Wilson, John-Street, 60; Unknown Timni, Colonial Hospital, 30; James Cosine (European) S.S. *Aleppo*, 35; son of Matilda Taylor, Smythe-Street, 1 month.[7]

At first, it seemed incredible that such a virulent disease could be influenza. People suspected it was some strange new fever introduced into the country by foreigners.[8] With so many people sick and the virus spreading quickly, the government closed schools, established temporary dispensaries around town, and disseminated information for preventing and treating the symptoms. For prevention, they recommended gargling with an antiseptic available through the Sanitary Department. Once a person became ill, they advised a "sharp purge" (a laxative) followed by bed rest. All expectoration was to go into a "receptacle containing antiseptic." The sick were told to stay at home "until all signs of cough, sore throat, and fever have disappeared."[9] Eager to maintain the superiority of Western medicine in the face of this emergency and unwilling to admit that control of the virus was beyond their scope, the colony's medical staff made a point of dispensing "medicines," some of it nothing more than colored water.[10] As the disease ravaged the population, Sierra Leoneans concluded that the colonial medical staff were not able "to cope with tough situations." They blamed the government for not having done enough to protect them from the plague.

The virus exposed the limitations of Western medicine. Gargling with antiseptic did nothing to prevent illness. The dispenser's "medicine," not surprisingly, failed to relieve its symptoms. Desperate for relief, people turned to local remedies. Newspapers ran letters giving advice on how to brew bush tea, perform deep-breathing exercises, and make pepper and camphor tonics. In the face of this mysterious enemy, indigenous knowledge appeared superior to Western medicine. The *Sierra Leone Weekly News* observed that "a large number of the people who have died have been those who had the doctors' treatment for influenza, while the majority of the saved ones have drugged themselves on native herbs and used pepper freely as a drink."[11] The sad truth was explained by "An English Contemporary" in the *Colonial and Provincial Reporter*: "there is really very little to be done, beyond looking after the general health." Wholesome food, exercise, good ventilation, covering the nose and mouth with a handkerchief when sneezing or coughing was the best advice anyone could offer.[12]

Although the majority of people would recover from the flu, it brought sudden, painful death to many, especially young adults between the ages of fifteen and thirty-five. The decline of a European man employed by one of the mercantile firms provides a startling illustration of how quickly the disease could progress. He went to work on August 26, but became ill and went home. Within a day he had a high temperature, was vomiting a dark substance, and had difficulty breathing. Thirty-six hours after becoming sick, he was dead.[13] For the space of three weeks, "bells were tolled incessantly from all the steeples of all the Churches," reported the *Sierra Leone Guardian*, "giving notice of the departed ones who were, as it were, hurried out of life."[14]

Of the twenty-four thousand people who lived in Freetown, twenty thousand were afflicted. Entire households were stricken. Those who were the least ill would try to nurse those who could not care for themselves. Sometimes two, three, or even four people would die in one household within twenty-four hours. People who could barely function had to clean up the blood, vomit, and feces of the living and at the same time deal with the quickly putrefying corpses of the dead. There were not enough gravediggers to keep up with the demand, and coffins piled up in the cemetery. The Reverend F.H. Johnson and a group of men took matters into their own hands. Praying and singing hymns, they dug long trenches to accept the rows of caskets. "For the first time in the history of epidemics in our land," wrote the *Sierra Leone Weekly News*, "more than one trench has been dug wherein have been laid together to sleep the final sleep, men and women, poor and rich, literate and illiterate."[15]

At the end of September, the government issued a communiqué to the local papers in an attempt to quash rumors of its incompetence in dealing with the epidemic. In the missive, E. Evelyn, the Acting Colonial Secretary, censured the African community for not volunteering to tend the sick at the temporary hospital for the poor in the New Model School. The accusation added unforgivable insult to terrible suffering and underscored the dysfunction of the colonial system. The Labor family was among the outraged. To make such a complaint against them, wrote Maigi's half-brother W. Coulson Labor, "betrays either a woeful ignorance of or else a callous indifference to the real condition of the people." He went on to observe that "the Europeans are the lords of the land. They have servants to see after their domestic arrangements, which is not the case with 99 per cent of our people. They were not burdened with family responsibilities, or sick relatives and dependants to attend."[16]

The incapacitating influenza continued to ravage Maigi's family. "We regret to announce," his uncle wrote in the September 20 issue of the *Sierra Leone Guardian*, "that owing to the Influenza Epidemic, no issue of this paper was made on the 6th and the 13th inst., as the whole staff were down with the fever."[17] Nevertheless, by the middle of September, the terrible scourge was abating, businesses had reopened, and people were back on the streets.[18] One thousand people had died—more than four percent of the population—but the worst seemed to be over.[19] The world, it appeared, could return to normal.

By late October 1918, the deadly strain of the flu had invaded London. "Influenza is spreading to an alarming extent," reported the *Daily Mirror.* "The virulent disease is seizing victims wholesale and the doctors in London are unable to cope with the stream of patients."[20] People who seemed perfectly well one moment, it reported, would be seriously ill an hour later. As it spread, crowds lined up outside hospitals, doctors' offices, and pharmacies that didn't have enough staff to serve them. It seriously disrupted the bustling city. Hundreds of policemen and firemen were too ill to work. So many drivers were down with the flu that buses, trams, and trains were placed on limited schedules. Places of business struggled on with skeleton crews. Because more than a thousand operators were sick, the Postmaster General asked Londoners to limit phone calls.[21] Even milk and bread were in short supply, according to the *Daily Express.* In some places, the paper declared, one needed a doctor's certificate to get a pint of milk.[22]

As in Freetown, doctors recommended bed rest, gargling morning and evening with an antiseptic mixture, and getting as much fresh air as possible. As panic rose with the death rate, medical officers assured people that "prompt and proper treatment would avert fatal developments."[23] When conventional medical treatment didn't work, desperate Londoners also sought out alternative remedies. The list of products that claimed to prevent or cure influenza was mind-boggling. Alleged remedies included aspirin, opium, quinine, cinnamon, ammonia, camphor, creosote, saltwater, beef tea, cocoa, snuff, and alcohol.[24] "One must smoke, say some," the *Daily Mirror* reported, "others, however, say 'Smoking is no use.'"[25] With no clear explanation why the disease was so virulent, one West End doctor laid the blame on women's fashions. "Thousands of women victims of the epidemic owe their serious illness," he claimed, "to the wearing of low-necked thin blouses."[26]

According to one sardonic columnist, some people saw contracting the flu as a badge of honor. "We know that nothing can make you feel more virtuous than to appear at the office, at your war work, in tubes, omnibuses, and public places 'believing' that you 'have a touch of the 'flu,'" wrote W.M. for the *Daily Mirror*. These "patients, victims, and culprits," he claimed, were quite proud of it. "Everywhere they talk so of the 'flu and of their pride in spreading it about." The only thing to be done with them, he mockingly concluded, was punishment "with penal servitude, or bed."[27]

As in Freetown, undertakers were overwhelmed with the bodies and could not keep up with the demand for coffins or graves. One survivor remembered attending his father's funeral in a church overflowing with mourners, and coffins stacked "one on top of the other" at the altar.[28] According to the British Undertakers' Association, during the period from late October to early November 1918 the death rate was higher than it had been for nearly a hundred years. For the first time since Britain had begun keeping records, the number of deaths exceeded the number of births.[29]

The morning papers on November 11, 1918, had reported that the Armistice was not yet settled, so Maigi must have been alarmed when firecrackers began exploding from police stations and fire stations at 11:00 a.m. Perhaps, like memoirist Hallie Miles, he mistook explosions for a daytime air raid. It wasn't until he heard the sound of the bugles and saw Boy Scouts furiously pedaling their bicycles through the streets signaling the "All Clear" that he realized what had happened. Everywhere people rushed out of buildings waving flags and shouting for joy.[30] Later he learned the Armistice had been signed at 5:00 that morning, and all hostilities had ceased at the eleventh hour of the eleventh day of the eleventh month. The war was over.

It is easy to imagine Maigi among the crowds of people pouring into central London and gathering in Whitehall, the Strand, Trafalgar Square, and Piccadilly. Everywhere he heard shrieking whistles, squealing trumpets, blaring motor car horns, banging tea trays, and wild, continuous cheering.[31] "Never ... has London resounded with such shouts of exultation," the *Daily Mirror* reported.[32] Maigi probably saw people clambering onto the tops of motor cars, taxicabs, and even omnibuses where they waved flags and shouted. Church bells that had been silent for years began to ring out, shopkeepers closed their stores, students surged out of their schools, and people who had never met before hugged one another and kissed openly on the streets. Perhaps he even caught sight of the "sexual affairs between perfect strangers" which "took place promiscuously in the parks, shop entrances, and alley-ways," according to poet and veteran Robert Graves.[33] The loud, heavy boom of Big Ben echoed across the city. "Isn't it glorious?" people said smiling and laughing.[34]

Newspaper bills—long banned because of the paper shortage—reappeared with the exalted news: "Fighting has ceased on all Fronts." Suddenly, there were thousands of pieces of paper fluttering down around him. Looking up, Maigi caught sight of women clerks throwing now obsolete war forms out of office windows.[35] As he reeled through the crowds, perhaps he saw a colonel sitting on top of a motor car banging a dinner gong, or a parson with a Union Jack stuck in his silk hat leading his parishioners in song, or stockbrokers in their frock coats marching four abreast while they jangled tea kettles filled with stones.[36] The rain that came in the afternoon dampened clothes but not spirits. That night when people tore shades from the street lamps, and the porticoes in front of music halls and cinemas blazed once more, Maigi must have thought with his fellow Londoners, "Light, light! Let there be light!"[37]

Three days after the Armistice, the flu struck one last fatal blow to the Labor family. On the evening of November 14, the Great Scourge took Maigi's father, Joshua William Labor. He was sixty-seven years old.

On November 15, the body was carried in a polished oak casket from Labor's house in Pyne Street to Holy Trinity Church where the Archdeacon of Sierra Leone conducted the funeral service. Afterward, the choir in their vestments sang hymns as they walked with the mourners to the Kissy Road Cemetery where the body was interred. The church was full of the many children from Labor's three marriages as well as other relatives.[38] It probably took weeks for the news to reach Maigi in London. How he took the end of this long-strained relationship we can only guess. Sadness perhaps, and maybe even anger, mixed with an elemental grief at the loss of the man he was never able to please.

There was one final wave of influenza in Britain in February. By the time it had passed, the disease had infected more than 500 million people and killed some 50 million worldwide, although some epidemiologists believe as many as 100 million may have died.[39] In London alone, it took the lives of some 23,000 people.[40]

Luck, it seemed, was on Maigi's side. The flu had killed millions, but he had survived. Now the dreadful war was over, and he had made it through without being blown up or maimed in an air raid or industrial accident. The 886,000 British men killed in the war had not been so lucky. Nor had the thousands of men who had lost limbs or sight or had had their minds ravaged by "shell shock." To honor their sacrifice, the British public paid tribute to these men and preserved their memories in private and public rituals, shrines, monuments, and gravestones.

Recognition of the sacrifice made by Africans in the war was more problematic. More than two million Africans served European forces in the Great War—several thousand as soldiers, but the vast majority as carriers in various African campaigns, hauling wounded men or sixty-pound packs across rugged terrain.[41] At least 200,000 carriers died—perhaps many more.[42] The actual number—now impossible to calculate—was shocking. The number of "native victims," observed one delegate to the Versailles Peace Conference, "may be too long to give to the world and Africa."[43] It was an attitude shared by the Governor of Tanganyika Territory in East Africa, who remarked that he "did not care to contemplate the statistics of the native African lives lost" and preferred the "vast Carrier Corps Cemeteries ... should be allowed to revert to nature as speedily as possible."[44] As another colonial official observed, "the conduct of the campaign only stopped short of a scandal because the people who suffered most were the carriers—and after all, who cares about native carriers."[45]

The Imperial War Graves Commission supervised the commemoration of war dead and went to great lengths to identify British men who had died in Africa and memorialize them with individual graves. Digging through mass graves in Africa, commission employees searched for false teeth and other dental fixtures in order to identify British remains and rebury them in separate cemeteries. Although the commission worked on the principle that "in death, all, from General to Private, of whatever race or creed, should receive equal honor under a memorial," that equality was not always recognized. In some places, the commission erected separate memorials for African soldiers and laborers killed and did not list the names of the dead.[46] This practice did not sit well with some local officers. Throughout Africa, surviving officers established public subscriptions and pressured colonial governments to erect memorials for the African dead that included the name of each man lost. The Commanding Officer of the Sierra Leone Regiment, for example, demanded monuments in Freetown honoring the Sierra Leone men who had died in service. Included in the memorial were not only soldiers, but carriers who had given their lives as well. But for many, individual graves were not maintained by the country that had demanded from them the supreme sacrifice.

As Londoners pulled the collars of their winter coats tighter against sleet and late snow during the unsettled spring of 1919, Maigi's luck ran out. First a bad cough took hold of him, then he found himself waking at night in a fevered sweat. One morning, he saw it: the fatal drop of blood staining his pillowcase.

He undoubtedly recognized the symptoms. The privations of war— food shortages, overcrowded military camps and munitions factories, as well as a housing shortfall—created conditions that had revived the tuberculosis epidemic.

Although the course of the disease was unpredictable—it could linger or kill rapidly—its social effect was unmistakable: sufferers were frequently humiliated, ostracized, and blamed for their illness. To carry a sputum bottle was to mark oneself as a pariah. Even those on the front lines of prevention sometimes blamed the victims. The well-known anti-tuberculosis campaigner Robert Philip wrote that people had to be made to understand that "the disease is maintained through ignorance and folly, and that its removal lies completely in their hands."[47] H. de Carle Woodcock, another board member of the National Association for the Prevention of Consumption, called it a "coarse, common disease, bred in foul breath, in dirt, in squalor." He went on to say that it "attacks failures. It attacks the depressed, the alcoholic, the lunatic of all degrees."[48] People didn't want to work with consumptives, and employers didn't want to hire them. Sufferers often concealed their medical history, as did many who had been treated and given a clean bill of health. In 1906, when residents near Lambeth Infirmary complained that consumptive patients might be spreading the infection by looking out of the window, the guardians moved the ward.[49] Patients dealing with the physical stress of the disease would often find themselves estranged from their communities, shunned even by family and friends.[50] One patient described the experience as two kinds of suffering: one was "the distressful horror of the disease itself. The other is the mental agony born of the knowledge that when I emerge from the fight … I am taboo to my fellowmen."[51]

Perhaps like tens of thousands of sufferers, Maigi went in search of miracle cures. Charles Henry Stevens became rich on the declaration that his tonic "Sacco"—*Stevens African Consumption Cure, Original*—could conquer tuberculosis. His miracle formula, he claimed, was "80 grams of Umckaloabo root," a South African herbal remedy used for cough and congestion.[52] Another exploiter of desperation, Dr. Derk P. Yonkerman, declared "Consumption Can be Cured" in the pages of newspapers worldwide. His advertisements in England asserted that his patent drug, Tuberculozyne, "was the only known remedy" for the disease.[53] When the American Medical Association analyzed the tonic, it discovered that its ingredients varied: sometimes it was a bromide mixed with glycerin and cinnamon, other times glycerin, almond oil, and burnt sugar.[54] The estimated cost of the ingredients was about two and a half pence for which Yonkerman charged over £2. Investigation of "Doctor" Yonkerman's qualifications revealed that his training was in veterinary medicine.[55]

In April 1919, Maigi's Sierra Leonean friend John Eldred Taylor published a notice in the *African Telegraph* that Augustus Merriman "alias Ohlohr Maiji" was "suffering from a severe chill" and had entered a nursing home.[56] The benign notice masked the seriousness of Maigi's condition. Searching for a cure, he may have gone to a nursing home or to one of the many tuberculosis sanatoria in Britain. Before the age of antibiotics, fresh air and sunlight were considered the first line of treatment, and sanatoria specialized in the widely advocated "open-air" regime. Patients essentially lived outdoors. Such places would have made Maigi bundle up in sweaters, overcoats, wool caps and gloves and spend his days in an outdoor shelter designed to provide maximum exposure to air and sunshine. Heating was considered not only unnecessary, but detrimental. In her memoirs, Mary Hewin writes about going to see her sister in one of these wide-open shelters, which she describes as "a little wooden hut, 'bout the size of a garden shed. There was no door, no glass in the windows; the wind and rain blowed through."[57] During the cold, wet April of 1919, only hot-water bottles hugged to his chest and steamer rugs covering his legs would have kept Maigi warm.[58]

He also might have received a range of other treatments, including rubdowns with coarse towels, massages, hydrotherapy, deep-breathing exercises, and injections or inhalations of germicides—sulphides or iodine—as part of his recovery plan.[59] To counter the often severe weight loss of this wasting disease, his doctors would have prescribed a diet heavy in dairy products. For breakfast, he would get a cup of cocoa, a pint of milk, and two eggs; at lunch, a creamy soup, beef juice, ice cream, gelatin, and two more eggs; dinner would be junket (a soft cheesy custard), another pint of milk, some gruel, a tablespoon of olive oil, and two more eggs. For a bedtime snack, he would consume yet another glass of milk and one more egg.[60] If he had a fever, he was confined to bed. Most afternoons, he and his fellow sufferers were allowed to read, but not to talk. Stacked on the tables of their little 'cow sheds' were cards, puzzles, Bibles, popular magazines, and assorted bestsellers of the day such as Zane Grey's *The U.P. Trail* or Mary Roberts Rinehart's *The Amazing Interlude*. Who knows how many patients hung their hopes on movie star Douglas Fairbanks's promise in his chart-topping self-help book *Laugh and Live* that "it is possible to stand with one foot on the inevitable 'banana peel' of life with both eyes peering into the Great Beyond, and still be happy, comfortable, and serene—if we will even so much as smile."[61]

In an effort to keep the sick from focusing solely on illness, the medical staff at the sanatoria often discouraged "conversation between patients about their disease."[62] Dr. W.M. Crofton, a pathologist from University College Dublin, noted the importance of a positive outlook. The more hopeful the patient, he observed, the "better chance of complete and rapid recovery."[63] If so, then Maigi, who had always shown remarkable resilience, had a better chance than most. Though battered by prejudice, poverty, and failure, he had always overcome his defeats by pursuing new intellectual and creative opportunities. But the violent summer of 1919 threatened to devastate his reservoir of hope.

That summer white working-class veterans from Liverpool, Cardiff, and other seaport cities returned home from the war to discover that

England was not a "land fit for heroes" as Lloyd George had promised, but rather a country suffering from a severe post-war slump. Along with more than two and a half million others who had been discharged from military service, they found widespread unemployment, an extreme housing shortage, and men of color doing the jobs they thought of as theirs.[64] Feeling they had "done their bit" for the country, they took their anger out on Africans, Arabs, and Southeast Asians who had been heavily recruited to shipping, munitions, and chemical industries during the war. Afraid they would reduce their earning power, white seamen refused to work with black laborers, and their unions raised a color bar which prohibited the hiring of non-whites, even if they were British subjects. A black seaman from British Guiana complained to the Colonial Office. "We are badly treated by the British People," William P. Samuels wrote. "Foreigners of all nationality get preference" as long as they were white.[65]

While black seamen who had lost their jobs and black soldiers who had been demobilized in Britain slept outside and sold their clothing to pay for food, the Ministry of Labour's Employment Department sent instructions to labor exchange managers explaining that these men were "eligible for out-of-work donation, but they have apparently not realised this, and it is not considered desirable to take any further steps to acquaint them of the position."[66]

As Maigi's health deteriorated, white mobs two to ten thousand strong roamed the streets of Liverpool, Inspector Hugh Burgess reported to the Colonial Office, "savagely attacking, beating, and stabbing every negro they could find."[67] In South Wales, violence broke out when a black man allegedly put his arm around a white woman. Violent white gangs plundered black-owned hostels and hotels; they broke windows of private homes, smashed doors, hauled furniture and bedding into the streets, and set fire to it. In fifteen years of living in Britain, Maigi had never seen this kind of racial violence. In the seaport cities and even in the East End of London, black men were being attacked, even dragged out of their homes and beaten. Three West Africans were stabbed in Liverpool; West Indians were bludgeoned with stones in Cardiff; and men with black skin were attacked in the London boroughs of Stepney and Limehouse. Their homes, belongings, and businesses looted and destroyed, some of them sought refuge in police stations, social clubs, schools, and fire stations. Others barricaded themselves in their neighborhoods and fought back.

Although later trials would prove otherwise, many newspapers claimed that the riots had been perpetrated by black people. The *Liverpool Courier* approvingly reported that "the howl of the mob dies away on a delighted note when the word goes about that 'another bloomin' nigger has been laid out.'"[68] Accusing the "black scoundrels" of instigating the riots, the *Courier* went on to explain that "one of the chief reasons of popular anger behind the present disturbances lies in the fact that the average negro is nearer the animal than is the average white man ... The white man ... regards [the black man] as part child, part animal, and part savage."[69] A particularly volatile component of white rage fixated on the idea of inter-racial relationships. In a letter to *The Times*, Sir Ralph Williams, a former colonial administrator, declared that "intimate association between black or coloured men and white women is a thing of horror." He argued that it would be natural for white men living in Cardiff and Liverpool to "resort to violence."[70] The mood of the country could not be clearer: black men had been useful during the war as laborers, soldiers, and sailors. Perhaps a few of them had risked life and limb, but they were fundamentally untrustworthy and maybe even dangerous. They were no longer welcome in the mother country.

On Friday, June 13, in Cardiff, "a sad little procession of black seamen with kit-bags on their backs and sticks in their hands, escorted by police and followed by jeering crowds," surrendered their homes and left the city.[71] *The Times* that day took the opportunity to belittle the empire's black subjects, many of whom had contributed to the war effort. "The negro," it scornfully observed, "is almost pathetically loyal to the British empire and he is always proud to proclaim himself a Briton."[72] The next afternoon, Maigi's friends at the *African Telegraph*, who had been closely watching the events and reporting on the white-initiated violence, organized a protest in Hyde Park asking: "Has the African Any Friends?"[73]

Felix Hercules, editor of the *African Telegraph* and leader of the Society of Peoples of African Origin, articulated the powerful feelings of anxiety and alienation which were tormenting Maigi and others of African descent. "It is upon his head," Hercules wrote, "that the vials of the world's prejudice have been poured." He went on to say that any refinement a black man acquires "is regarded as a mere veneer. If he be gentlemanly—and even an African can be a gentleman—he is regarded with suspicion, with mistrust, or as a curious freak. Whatever his social standing, he is regarded as an outcast."[74] The dignity, equality, and justice for Africans that Maigi had spent his life pursuing seemed nowhere to be found. Three years earlier, he had appealed without success to the highest court in the land to acknowledge the racial bias of the Lincoln's Inn barristers who had ended his legal career. Now the British government appeared to be doing nothing when black people were attacked in the street. "We have had quite enough of these stories of racial riots in the East End of London," wrote the *African Telegraph*. "When will the Home Secretary and police use their powers?"[75] As one black Glaswegian asked, "Is this treatment … compatible with the British teaching of justice and equity?"[76] As he lay dying, Maigi must have felt the world utterly bereft of the truths on which he had based his life.

Maigi was taken to the Lambeth Infirmary on a warm Friday, June 13, probably because he had run out of money for care in a private hospital.[77] That day, fifteen people came through the cheerful white door of the receiving ward. They held jobs common to the laboring classes who wound up in Poor Law hospitals: rag sorter, needle worker, lamp cleaner, sandwich man, tram driver, collar maker, sponge cleaner, sign writer, tea blender, cork cutter, flannel weaver, brush maker, road sweeper, housekeeper, and bottle washer.[78] Maigi alone identified himself as an elite professional. Sitting at the receiving desk, clutching a bloodied handkerchief, he told the admitting nurse that he was a barrister. He had earned the title at enormous personal cost and refused to let the legal establishment strip it from him. Perhaps he thought it would afford him some dignity in this place of last resort.

Warm June air flooded the bright upstairs room of the tuberculosis ward when he arrived. A long table covered with ceramic pots of leafy green plants ran along the center of the room with rows of beds on either side. A few tired-looking men sat in straight-backed wooden chairs, but most of the twenty patients lay in bed. Nurses offered the men sips of hot lemon water against fits of coughing and tucked them under red wool blankets.[79] More than half of those admitted to the

Lambeth ward would not leave alive. Only a drowsy numbness induced by morphine or opiate sedatives muted the cacophony of dying.

During the few warm days of June, Maigi may have sat in a chair by one of the large windows. From there he could hear church bells and watch the breeze dance the leaves of the plane trees. When the weather turned cool and unsettled again, the fireplace crackled with burning coal. His condition worsened. As the doses of pain-deadening opiates increased, the sounds of the fire popping, the bells ringing, the hems of the nurses' uniforms brushing against the floor, and children's laughter floating up from the street below might have begun to intertwine with memories of rain pounding against a corrugated iron roof, palm leaves whipping in the wind, the feel of red earth under the feet, and the scent of bananas and guavas and pineapples in woven baskets. In the whirl of pain and painkiller, memory and dream, he might have heard his mother's voice, seen his grandfather's face, or felt the clap of his uncle's familiar hand on his shoulder. But there was no family at his bedside. Ashamed that he had failed to achieve the promise of his early years, that he was suffering from a disease of the destitute, that he had been unable to change the plight of his people, that he had dishonored his family, he concealed his condition.[80]

On Monday, July 14, as French troops marched past the Arc de Triomphe in a celebration of Bastille Day and the end of the war, the man who had been christened Augustus Boyle Chamberlayne Merriman-Labor died in the tuberculosis ward of a workhouse infirmary at 2:40 p.m. He was just forty-one years old.

Someone in the ward made sure his African name accompanied him to his grave. On the hospital death register, just above the entry for "Augustus Merriman," the words "properly Ohlohr Maigi" have been penciled in.[81] The registrar accepted the addition and wrote the death certificate for "Ohlohr Maigi otherwise Augustus Merriman," but did not acknowledge his legal or literary career. For posterity, his occupation was listed merely as "munitions worker."[82]

No family was present to make funeral arrangements. Instead, a middle-aged Brixton woman named Mary Hillier collected his body and arranged for his burial. Hillier and her husband James had been Maigi's landlords on Knatchbull Road, Brixton, in 1913. James Hillier had been one of the first investors in Literature Limited.[83]

Why Mary Hillier claimed his body and where she laid him to his final rest are still mysteries.

It took several weeks for the devastating news to reach his family in Freetown. A month after Maigi's death, on August 15, an obituary appeared in his uncle's newspaper, the *Sierra Leone Guardian*. The notice refers to him by his birth name: Augustus B.C. Merriman-Labor and faithfully reports his successful schooling, civil service career in Freetown, and his call to the bar. The writer, probably his uncle Joseph Labor, strikes a note of sadness when he describes one of Maigi's rare visits, explaining that "he was advised to return home altogether and practice in Sierra Leone, yet unfortunately, he could not be prevailed upon to be with his people." If he had only come home, Joe Labor seems to lament, perhaps he would still be alive. "He dabbled his head a little in Journalism," Labor continued, writing for various African and British newspapers, publishing a few brochures and the *Handbook of Sierra Leone*. There is no mention of *Britons through Negro Spectacles*. Perhaps his uncle, a devout Christian and a part-time newspaperman himself, could not take seriously the irreverent book that may have contributed to the ruin of his favorite nephew.

There is also no mention of his disbarment, perhaps because his family saw it not merely as an embarrassment but as a serious miscarriage of justice. Nor does the obituary mention tuberculosis. It simply reports that "during the war Mr. Labor was seconded for service in one of the munition factories and there he caught the germs of the disease which ended fatally."[84]

The obituary makes clear that Maigi was deeply loved and that his loss would be acutely mourned. Although he never married nor had a family of his own, he had friends who would not forget his kindness and generosity. "He was a great help to many of his young friends," his uncle observed, "who will greatly miss him." Remembering the nephew he had loved, his uncle summed up his most essential quality for those who mourned him. "He was a young man of indomitable spirit."[85]

The end of Maigi's life took place during a half-decade of unimaginable tragedy. Between 1914 and 1919, the Great War and the Spanish flu killed some 57 million people. The equivalent of almost the entire U.K. population today was wiped out in just five years.

Writing his story has made me think about history—the way it consumes individual stories into its grand narratives, leaving most lives invisible. Maigi understood the importance of one's story being heard, especially if one is not of the majority. It was only through books and articles and Afro-focused businesses, he believed that the merits of West African people could become known.[86] He wanted to write to include West Africans in the larger chronicle of British and world history.

By conventional standards, Ohlohr Maigi was a failure. He never achieved the commercial success he sought, nor conquered the injustices of the colonial world. But he bequeathed a remarkable legacy nonetheless: a fistful of articles and pamphlets and the singular *Britons through Negro Spectacles*. Because of the words he left behind, we possess an intimate portrait of Edwardian London through African eyes, a richer view of the past.

The story of his life is another gift. Through it, we learn about Africans at the heart of empire in the early twentieth century, a reminder that people of color have long contributed to British life and culture. We are also reminded that courage, wit, and resilience do not always reward us with the fulfillment of our desires. Time, with its caprices and injustices, always has its way. But if Maigi's life exposes this exacting truth, it also reminds us that our dreams provide a sense of purpose. Undaunted by failure and prejudice, Ohlohr Maigi stands as a hero for anyone who has ever aspired despite lack of recognition or reward. He is the patron saint of the resilient spirit.

Our bodies fail us—they grow ill, they grow tired, they die. But written words live on. In the pages of *Britons through Negro Spectacles* the thirty-two-year-old Merriman-Labor—clever, irreverent, jovial—still makes us laugh. His work reminds us that forgotten voices have important things to teach us.

NOTES

PROLOGUE: FREETOWN, SIERRA LEONE, CIRCA 1881

1. The scene is based on the story in the first chapter of *Britons through Negro Spectacles*.
2. Merriman-Labor, *Britons*, 9–10.
3. Merriman-Labor, *Britons*, 11.
4. Merriman-Labor, *Britons*, 13.
5. Merriman-Labor, *Britons*, 13.
6. Merriman-Labor, *Britons*, 14.
7. *Nigerian Chronicle*, December 3, 1909, 7.
8. *Anglo-African and Gold Coast Globe*, April 9, 1904, 328.
9. J.R. Spurgeon, "The Africans Abroad," *Sierra Leone Weekly News*, October 5, 1901, 5.
10. Merriman-Labor, *Britons through Negro Spectacles*, preface.

INTRODUCTION: LAMBETH WORKHOUSE INFIRMARY, SOUTH LONDON, 1919

1. Almost 11,000 of them were being treated at Poor Law infirmaries. "A Tuberculosis Service: Experts' Scheme for Prevention and Treatment," *Justice of the Peace and Local Government Review* 83, no. 8 (1919), 91.
2. For his travels throughout the United Kingdom, see "Through the United Kingdom: My Wanderings and Impressions" series, November 1905 to July 1906 in the *Sierra Leone Weekly News*. (Note: Chapter V, dealing with Ireland no longer survives.) Also see "Whitsuntide with the French in Paris" in the *Sierra Leone Weekly News*, August–October 1906.
3. Sukhdev Sandhu, *London Calling: How Black and Asian Writers Imagined a City* (London: HarperCollins, 2003), xvii. Joseph Conrad, *Heart of*

Darkness, Norton Critical Edition, 4th edn (New York: Norton and Company, 2006), 50.

4. Virginia Woolf, "Sunday 17 May, 1925," *Diary of Virginia Woolf*, vol. 3: 1925–1930, ed. Anne Olivier Bell (New York and London: Harcourt Brace Jovanovich, 1980), 23.

5. A.B.C. Merriman-Labor, *A Series of Lectures on the Negro Race* (Manchester, England: John Heywood, 1900), 30.

6. Eldred Jones, "Turning Back the Pages," *Bulletin of the Association of African Literature in English* 2 (1965).

7. A.B.C. Merriman-Labor, "Building Castles in the Air," *Gambia Intelligencer*, June 1895. Mentioned in *Alexander's Magazine*, August 15, 1907, 201–203 and in *Britons through Negro Spectacles*, flyleaf.

8. Merriman-Labor, *Britons through Negro Spectacles, or, A Negro on Britons with a Description of London* (London: Imperial and Foreign Company, 1909), preface.

9. Merriman-Labor, *Britons*, flyleaf.

10. "Africa: Written Literature," by Herbert L. Shore. *The Encyclopaedia Americana*, vol. 1 (New York: Americana Corporation, 1977), 274.

11. A.B.C. Merriman-Labor, *Handbook of Sierra Leone for 1901 and 1901* (Manchester: John Heywood, 1901), 13.

12. Daniel Domingues da Silva, David Eltis, Philip Misevich, and Olatunji Ojo, "The Diaspora of Africans Liberated from Slave Ships in the Nineteenth Century," *Journal of African History* 55, no. 3 (2014), 347.

13. It is difficult to know the number of black people living in London at the time. See David Olusoga, *Black and British: A Forgotten History* (London: Macmillan, 2016), chapter 3.

14. Olusoga, *Black and British*, 161.

15. Christopher Fyfe, *A History of Sierra Leone* (Oxford: Oxford University Press, 1962), 14.

16. Isaac Land and Andrew M. Schocket, "New Approaches to the Founding of the Sierra Leone Colony, 1786–1808," *Journal of Colonialism and Colonial History* 9, no. 3 (2008), https://muse.jhu.edu/ (accessed January 22, 2018).

17. John Peterson, *Province of Freedom: A History of Sierra Leone* (London: Faber and Faber, 1969), 17.

18. Fyfe, *History*, 15; James W. St. G. Walker, *The Black Loyalists: The Search for the Promised Land in Nova Scotia and Sierra Leone 1783–1780* (New York: Africana Publishing, 1976), 97.

19. Land and Schocket, "New Approaches to the Founding of the Sierra Leone Colony."

20. Olusoga, *Black and British*, 175.

21. Olusoga, *Black and British*, 185.

22. Land and Schocket, "New Approaches to the Founding of the Sierra Leone Colony."
23. Walker, *The Black Loyalists*, 127.
24. James Sidbury, "'African' Settlers in the Founding of Freetown," in *Slavery, Abolition and the Transition to Colonialism in Sierra Leone*, edited by Paul E. Lovejoy and Suzanne Schwarz (Trenton: Africa World Press, 2015), 28.
25. Land and Schocket, "New Approaches to the Founding of the Sierra Leone Colony."
26. Land and Schocket, "New Approaches to the Founding of the Sierra Leone Colony."
27. Deirdre Coleman, ed., *Maiden Voyages and Infant Colonies: Two Women's Travel Narratives of the 1790s* (London: Leicester University Press, 1999), 25–26.
28. Walker, *The Black Loyalists*, 127.
29. Coleman, *Maiden Voyages and Infant Colonies*, 102.
30. Fyfe, *History*, 59.
31. Walker, *The Black Loyalists*, 194.
32. Walker, *The Black Loyalists*, 154.
33. Land and Schocket, "New Approaches to the Founding of the Sierra Leone Colony."
34. Land and Schocket, "New Approaches to the Founding of the Sierra Leone Colony."
35. Walker, *The Black Loyalists*, 250–251.
36. Peterson, *Province of Freedom*, 36.
37. Walker, *The Black Loyalists*, 257.
38. Land and Schocket, "New Approaches to the Founding of the Sierra Leone Colony."
39. Interview with Merriman-Labor, *Manchester Evening Chronicle*, March 13, 1907. The interview says "great-great-grandparents," almost certainly a mistake. In another newspapers article (*Sierra Leone Weekly News*, October 29, 1906, 2) and a pamphlet (*Funeral Oration Delivered over the Grave of the Late Father Merriman*, 1901), Merriman-Labor refers to the Liberated African as the father of John Merriman and his own great-grandfather.
40. Despite Britain's efforts, 2.8 million people would be shipped to enslavement in the nineteenth century. Domingues da Silva, Eltis, Misevich, and Ojo, "The Diaspora of Africans Liberated from Slave Ships in the Nineteenth Century," 348.
41. Quoted in Olusoga, *Black and British*, 304.
42. Quoted in R. Anderson, "The Diaspora of Sierra Leone's Liberated Africans: Enlistment, Forced Migration, and "Liberation" at Freetown, 1808–1863," *African Economic History* 41 (2013), 106.

43. Suzanne Schwarz, "Reconstructing the Life Histories of Liberated Africans: Sierra Leone in the Early Nineteenth Century," *History in Africa* 39 (2012), 180–181.

44. Schwarz, "Restructuring the Life Histories of Liberated Africans," 182, 191.

45. Domingues da Silva, Eltis, Misevich, and Ojo, "The Diaspora of Africans Liberated from Slave Ships in the Nineteenth Century," 353. They estimate that perhaps 26,000 liberated Africans opted to leave the colony. See also Paul E. Lovejoy and Suzanne Schwarz, "Sierra Leone in the Eighteenth and Nineteenth Centuries," in *Slavery, Abolition and the Transition to Colonialism in Sierra Leone*, 21.

46. Maeve Ryan, "'A Moral Millstone'? British Humanitarian Governance and the Policy of Liberated African Apprenticeship, 1808–1848," *Slavery and Abolition* 37, no. 2 (2016), 402.

47. Anderson, "The Diaspora of Sierra Leone's Liberated Africans," 107.

48. Anderson explains that new company of African recruits was formed in 1810.

49. I am especially grateful to Dr. Richard Anderson for a lengthy email (December 21, 2017) helping me think through the ways a Liberated African might have fought against Napoleon.

50. "Africa: Southern Division: Sierra Leone," *Report upon the Commercial Relations of the United States with Foreign Countries for the Years 1880–1881* (Washington: Government Printing Office: 1883), 377.

51. David Northrup, "Becoming African: Identity Formation among Liberated Slaves in Nineteenth-Century Sierra Leone.," *Slavery and Abolition*, 27, no. 1 (April 2006), 6–12; Anderson, "The Diaspora of Sierra Leone's Liberated Africans," 111.

52. Contemporary accounts and earlier historical accounts refer to these people as "Creoles." However, that has changed over time. As Sierra Leonean historian Akintola Wyse wrote in 1991, "The fusion of the Nova Scotians, Maroons and Liberated Africans between 1850 and 1870 created the society which Porter calls 'Creoledom.' We prefer to call it 'Kriodom' and the people 'Krio.'" *The Krio of Sierra Leone: An Interpretive History* (Washington, D.C.: Howard University Press, 1991), 6. As Christopher Fyfe explains, "The spelling 'Krio' we owe to Thomas Decker, a journalist and author, later in government service and politics who championed the language and published Shakespeare translations in it. Though he began with 'Creo' by 1948 it had become 'Krio.'" See "Akintola Wyse: Creator of the Krio Myth," in *New Perspectives on the Sierra Leone Krio* (New York: Peter Lang, 2006), 26.

53. Leo Spitzer, *The Creoles of Sierra Leone: Responses to Colonialism, 1870–1945* (Madison: University of Wisconsin Press, 1974), 41.

54. Leslie Probyn, "Sierra Leone and the Natives of West Africa," *Journal of the Royal African Society* 6, no. 23 (1907), 254.

55. Herodotus, "Intellectual Degeneracy in West Africa. What's the Cause," *Sierra Leone Weekly News*, November 23, 1907, 4.

56. Elmet, "Our Elementary Educationists," *Sierra Leone Weekly News*, August 6, 1892, 3.

57. Merriman-Labor, "The Late Father Merriman," *Sierra Leone Weekly News*, February 24, 1900, 6.

58. *Alexander's Magazine*, August 15, 1907, 201.

59. Father Merriman influenced so many lives in Freetown that a collection was taken up to erect a memorial to his life. A tablet was ordered from England carved with a dove and featuring "a medallion on which a bust of the deceased was struck." The inscription read, "To John Merriman, a distinguished disciplinarian and teacher of Hastings fame. Died 10th February 1900. Age 70." It was broken into pieces while being shipped from Manchester and was never replaced.

60. No documents survive explaining his middle names "Boyle" and "Chamberlayne." It is possible that Boyle was in honor of Syble Boyle, a Liberated African, who became enormously wealthy and served on the Legislative Council. (He took on the name "Syble" after H.M.S. *Sybille*—the ship that delivered him from slavery—and Boyle, the name of his first master according to Fyfe, *History*, 333.) Chamberlayne may perhaps be for the Acting Governor of Sierra Leone, Colonel William John Chamberlayne of the 3rd West India Regiment. Perhaps it was in admiration for Chamberlayne's efforts during his brief tenure to establish a mission for the Society for the Propagation of the Gospel on the Îles de Los, just off the coast of Guinea. A.H. Barrow, *Fifty Years in Western Africa* (London: Society for Promoting Christian Knowledge, 1900), 90–91.

61. Merriman-Labor, *Britons*, dedication.

62. "Death of Mr. J.W. Labor," *Sierra Leone Weekly News*, November 16, 1918, 15.

63. "Death of Mr. J.W. Labor," *Sierra Leone Weekly News*, November 16, 1918, 15.

64. Merriman-Labor, *Sierra Leone Handbook 1901–1902*, 179.

65. "Some Jottings by J.," *Sierra Leone Weekly News*, August 13, 1898, 5; "General News: City Chats," *Sierra Leone Weekly News*, August 20, 1898, 9.

66. The obituary for J.W. Labor in his brother's newspaper, the *Sierra Leone Guardian*, only reports three of his children: Merriman-Labor, W. Coulson Labor, editor of the *Aurora*, and Dalton Labor "of the Wilberforce Physio-Pharmacy, Opobo." It is unclear if the three marriages listed include the marriage to Merriman-Labor's mother.

67. Spitzer, *The Creoles of Sierra Leone*, 50.
68. Christopher Fyfe, "1787–1887–1978: Reflections on a Sierra Leone Bicentenary," *Africa: Journal of the International African Institute* 57, no. 4 (1987), 414.
69. *Sierra Leone Times*, January 2, 1904. Quoted in Spitzer, *Creoles of Sierra Leone*, 61.
70. Alfred Burdon Ellis, *West African Sketches* (London: Samuel Tinsley, 1881), 149–150.
71. Ellis, *West African Sketches*, 152.
72. Akintola J. G. Wyse, "The Dissolution of Freetown City Council in 1926: A Negative Example of Political Apprenticeship in Colonial Sierra Leone," *Africa: Journal of the International African Institute* 57, no. 4 (1987), 425.
73. Ellis, *West African Sketches*, 160.
74. Ellis, *West African Sketches*, 153.
75. An Africanised Englishman Twenty Years in British West Africa [A.B.C. Merriman-Labor], *The Last Military Expedition in Sierra Leone or, British Soldiers and West African Native Warrior* (Manchester: John Heywood, 1898).
76. Merriman-Labor, "The Last Military Expedition in Sierra Leone," 8, 9; National Archives, Kew, CO/267/438. Telegram of 10 May 1898, Governor to Secretary of State, quoted in La Ray Denzer and Michael Crowder, "Bai Bureh and the Sierra Leone Hut Tax War of 1898," in *Protest and Power in Black Africa*, edited by Robert I. Rotberg and Ali A. Mazrui (Oxford: Oxford University Press, 1970), 169–212.
77. Merriman-Labor, *The Last Military Expedition in Sierra Leone*, 14.
78. Merriman-Labor, *The Last Military Expedition in Sierra Leone*, 15.
79. Merriman-Labor, *The Last Military Expedition in Sierra Leone*, 24,
80. Merriman-Labor, "*The Last Military Expedition in Sierra Leone*, 40.
81. *Lagos Weekly Record*, January 21, 1899, 5.
82. U.K. Military Campaign Medal and Rolls, 1793–1949. National Archives, Kew, WO/100/92.
83. Merriman-Labor, *The Last Military Expedition in Sierra Leone*, 39.
84. Merriman-Labor thanks Blyden in his preface to *A Series of Lectures on the Negro Race*, saying, "My sincere thanks are also due for his fatherly counsel to be diligent and persevering, to that literary lion the learned Professor Blyden." The pamphlet is dedicated to Sir Samuel Lewis.
85. The African General Agency and Its Founder," *Alexander's Magazine*, 202.
86. Spitzer, *Creoles of Sierra Leone*, 122.
87. Advertisement. *Sierra Leone Weekly News*, February 23, 1901, 10. When Lewis died in 1903, Merriman-Labor wrote a long, admiring remembrance of him for the *Sierra Leone Weekly News*, July 25, 1903, 2.

88. *Manchester Guardian*, July 7, 1900, 10. *The Times*, July 7, 1900, 12. Quoted in David Killingray, "Harold Arundel Moody" (unpublished MS), chapter 2, 21.
89. "Our Coloured Fellow-Citizen: Mr. S. Williams," *Review of Reviews*, March 1905, 251.
90. "Our Coloured Fellow-Citizen: Mr. S Williams," *Review of Reviews*, March 1905, 251.
91. *Manchester Guardian*, July 24, 1900, 8. Quoted in Killingray, "Harold Arundel Moody," 22.
92. *Daily News*, July 24, 1900. Quoted in Killingray, "Harold Arundel Moody," 22.
93. "The Revolt against the Paleface," *Review of Reviews*, July–December 1900, 131.
94. "The Problems before Liberia," *Sierra Leone Weekly News*, February 24, 1906, 9.
95. W.E.B. Du Bois. "To the Nations of the World," in *W.E.B. Du Bois: A Reader*, edited by David Levering Lewis (New York: Henry Holt and Company, 1995), 639.
96. "General News: Mr. Merriman: Labor," *Sierra Leone Weekly News*, April 25, 1903, 12.
97. "Mr. Merriman-Labor's Oration," *Sierra Leone Weekly News*, March 9, 1901, 12.
98. Robert Wellesley Cole, *Kossoh Town Boy* (Cambridge: Cambridge University Press, 1960), 77.
99. Quoted in Spitzer, *Creoles of Sierra Leone*, 40.
100. Paul Thompson, *The Edwardians: The Remaking of British Society* (Chicago: Academy Chicago Publishers, 1975), 27. In *The History of Sierra Leone*, Fyfe notes that the "average life-span of the members of Balfour's cabinet … was seventy-five" (618).
101. Robert Cecil, *Life in Edwardian England* (London: B.T. Batsford, 1969), 99.
102. Simon Nowell-Smith, *Edwardian England: 1901–1914* (London: Oxford University Press, 1964), 156.
103. John Paterson, *Edwardians: London Life and Letters 1902–1914* (Chicago: Ivan R. Dee, 1996), 37; Thompson, *The Edwardians*, 33.
104. Stephen Inwood, *City of Cities: The Birth of Modern London* (London: Macmillan, 2005), 37.
105. Thomson, The Edwardians, 55.
106. Jeffery Green, Black Edwardians: Black People in Britain 1901–1914 (London: Frank Cass, 1998). Also see his website: http://www.jeffreygreen.co.uk/.
107. Pascal Blanchard, Nicolas Bancel, Gilles Boëtsch, Eric Deroo,

Sandrine Lemaire and Charles Forsdick, eds., *Human Zoos: Science and Spectacle in the Age of Empire* (Liverpool: Liverpool University Press, 2008), 378. Although exploitation remained part of the dynamic, by the 1880s, the professionalization of these performers meant that most of them had negotiated contracts detailing the terms of their employment including wages, conditions, and bonuses.

108. Ben Shephard, "Showbiz Imperialism: The Case of Peter Lobengula" in *Imperialism and Popular Culture*, edited by John M. MacKenzie (Manchester: Manchester University Press, 1986), 97.
109. Shephard, "Showbiz Imperialism," 97
110. Shephard, "Showbiz Imperialism," 97.
111. Shephard, "Showbiz Imperialism," 99.
112. Shephard, "Showbiz Imperialism," 101.
113. Shephard, "Showbiz Imperialism," 102.
114. *Galveston Daily News*, 20 August 1899, 3. For a film of the landing of the South Africans, see: http://www.colonialfilm.org.uk/node/1186.
115. *Encyclopaedia Britannica, 11th Edition*, vol. 19 (Cambridge: Cambridge University Press, 1910–1911), 345.

1. THE VOYAGE OUT

1. A.B.C. Merriman-Labor, *A Series of Lectures on the Negro Race* (Manchester: John Heywood, 1900), 31.
2. Joe Labor was especially active in the civic and spiritual life of Freetown, founder of the "Unity Club" (to supply weekly "intellectual food as might make [the members] useful citizens of the community") and the Scriptural Association (to fight the "agnostic bent of the rising generation") and in 1908 the *Sierra Leone Guardian and Foreign Mails* newspaper. His wife ran a popular bakery from her home, and the two of them hosted community events, including an "At Home," where dozens were served refreshments, played games, and were entertained with music and literary readings. Merriman-Labor was intimately involved with all of his uncle's organizations. When Joe Labor's name was reported in the paper, generally his nephew's was not far behind.
3. His entry on "Some Popular Sierra Leoneans" in his *Handbook of Sierra Leone for 1901 and 1902* lists more than sixty men, including R.B. Blaise, "a lover of English literature and an advocate of his race"; J.A. FitzJohn, the editor of the *Sierra Leone Times*, "a genial humorist" and a first-rate musician; Cornelius May, the editor of the *Sierra Leone Weekly News*, "a great believer in his race"; and J.J. Thomas, another successful business-man well known as "a reader, a humanitarian, and a pronounced con-versationalist." *Handbook of Sierra Leone for 1901 and 1902* (Manchester, England: John Heywood, 1902), 108 and113

4. See Merriman-Labor, *Handbook of Sierra Leone for 1901 and 1902* for descriptions of literary societies, etc.

5. Merriman-Labor's descendent Monte Labor told me about the quip "Vote for Labor and your labour's lost." I believe the playful allusion to Shakespeare's play refers to his success with this labor dispute.

6. Merriman-Labor, *Britons*, 144; *A Series of Lectures on the Negro Race*, 7.

7. "A Difficult Case," *Health and Strength* 6, no. 8 (1903), 294.

8. "Magical Event at the Grammar School," *Sierra Leone Weekly News*, December 26, 1896, 7.

9. Merriman-Labor, *A Series of Lectures on the Negro Race*, advertisement.

10. "A Difficult Case," 294.

11. "A Difficult Case," 294–295.

12. "A Difficult Case," 294.

13. Merriman-Labor, *Handbook of Sierra Leone for 1901 and 1902*, 179.

14. Inspired by the farewell Sierra Leonean writer William Conton got from his father on his first trip to London. Described in Conton, *The African* (London: Heinemann, 1960), 22.

15. A.B.C. Merriman-Labor "Through the United Kingdom: My Wanderings and Impressions," *Sierra Leone Weekly News*, November 25, 1905, 6.

16. Merriman-Labor, *Britons*, 23; "Through the United Kingdom: My Wanderings and Impressions, Chapter II," *Sierra Leone Weekly News*, February 12, 1905, 4.

17. Merriman-Labor, *Britons*, 22–41. William Conton is more explicit than Merriman-Labor about the shock of seeing white laborers: "The sight of white people *en masse* was itself something which required some getting used to; but the thing that took us really aback was our first sight of a white man sweeping a gutter." *The African*, 45.

18. Merriman-Labor, "Through the United Kingdom," 6.

19. Merriman-Labor, "Through the United Kingdom," 4.

20. Merriman-Labor, *Britons*, 59.

21. December 24, 1907 letter to costumers, African General Agency, Merriman-Labor file, Lincoln's Inn Archive.

22. Merriman-Labor, "Through the United Kingdom: My Wanderings and Impressions, Chapter III," *Sierra Leone Weekly News*, December 9, 1905, 7.

23. Merriman-Labor, *Britons*, 24.

24. "Mr. Merriman's Lecture: Problems of the Anglicised West African Negro," *Sierra Leone Weekly News*, May 30, 1914, 10.

25. I want to thank Dr. Victor Labor, Wakefield, England (a descendant of Merriman-Labor's), for his thoughts about Merriman-Labor's illness and also Heather Heggem, Director of Physician Assistant

Program, and her class for an interesting discussion of his medical
case.

26. Merriman-Labor, *Britons*, 69–70.
27. Merriman-Labor, *Britons*, 72–73.
28. Merriman-Labor, *Britons*, 73–74.
29. John Gibson and H.G. Chukerbutty, *How to Become a Barrister* (London:
    Cornish and Sons, 1902), 5.
30. "Becoming a Barrister," *Pitman's Phonetic Journal*, June 6, 1903, 458.
31. "From the Bar to the Bench," *The English Illustrated Magazine*, February
    1907, 454–455.
32. He was admitted on April, 25, 1904.
33. E.T. Cook, *Highways and Byways in London* (London and New York:
    Macmillan and Co., 1903), 427. "Stony-hearted stepmother" comes
    from Thomas De Quincey's *Confessions of an Opium Eater*.
34. Most West African writers of the early twentieth century were jour-
    nalists, though a few, such as Merriman-Labor, also published books.
    See *A History of Twentieth Century African Literature*, edited by Oyekan
    Owomoyela (Lincoln: University of Nebraska Press, 1993), 13.
35. Quoted in Killingray, "Harold Moody," 1.
36. Merriman-Labor "Through the United Kingdom. Chapter II,"
    December 2, 1905, 4.
37. Sir Ronald Roxburgh, ed., *The Records of the Honorable Society of Lincoln's
    Inn: The Black Books*, vol. 5 (London: Lincoln's Inn, 1968), 35.
38. Merriman-Labor, *Britons*, 140.
39. Merriman-Labor, *Britons*, 30, 31, 36, 33, 47.
40. Merriman-Labor, *Britons*, 42, 45.
41. Merriman-Labor, "Through the United Kingdom: My Wanderings and
    Impressions, Chapter II," 2.
42. A. Ponsonby, "The Camel and the Needle's Eye." Quoted in Donald
    Read, ed., *Documents from Edwardian England 1901–1915* (London:
    Harrap, 1973), 209.
43. Merriman-Labor, *Britons*, 28.
44. Merriman-Labor, *Britons*, 182.
45. Pauline Stevenson, *Edwardian Fashion* (London: Ian Allan, 1980), 23.
46. Only gentlemen wore top hats. Respectable clerks and shop owners
    donned bowlers. For everyone else it was caps. Roy Hattersley, *The
    Edwardians* (New York: St. Martin's Press, 2004), 11.
47. Cecil, *Life in Edwardian England*, 49.
48. Merriman-Labor, *Britons*, 37.
49. Merriman-Labor, "Through the United Kingdom, Chapter II,"
    December 2, 1905, 4; Jack London, *The People of the Abyss* (London:
    Macmillan and Co., 1904), 7–8.

50. Merriman-Labor, *Britons*, 39.

51. Merriman-Labor, *Britons*, 40.

52. Gregory Anderson, *Victorian Clerks* (Manchester: Manchester University Press, 1976), 52–64. The National Clerks' Association bemoaned the oversupply of workers and recommended jobseekers look for other employment Michael Heller, "Work, Income and Stability: The Late Victorian and Edwardian London Male Clerk Revisited," *Business History* 50, no. 3 (May 2008), 253–271.

53. E.M. Forster, *Howards End* (New York: Barnes and Noble, 1993), 112.

54. Arthur Beavan, *Imperial London* (London: J.M. Dent and Co., 1901), 189.

55. Marian M George, *A Little Journey to England and Wales* (Chicago: Flanagan Company, 1901), 27.

56. Merriman-Labor, *Britons*, 127–128.

57. Merriman-Labor, *Britons*, 127.

58. Merriman-Labor, *Britons*, 101

59. Merriman-Labor, *Britons*, 128.

60. Quoted in Winston James, "Black Experience in Twentieth-Century Britain," in *Black Experience and the Empire*, edited by Philip D. Morgan and Sean Hawkins (Oxford: Oxford University Press, 2006), 350.

61. Merriman-Labor, *Britons*, 130.

2. IMPRESSIONS OF A YOUNG AFRICAN IN ENGLAND

1. The African Society—part social club, part research institute—had been founded three years earlier as a memorial to the British naturalist Mary Kingsley, who had travelled to West Africa in the 1890s and written two remarkable books about her experiences. Famously celebrated as a single woman venturing alone into the African wilderness—and by "alone" it was meant with only African carriers, no European escort—she journeyed, as Cornelius May put it in the *Sierra Leone Weekly News*, "beyond the confines of civilization, penetrating into regions where no white man has ever been before." In striking contrast to the disparaging portraits of Africans in other books by European travelers, Kingsley's work appreciated African cultures and stressed the importance of understanding the African world in order to improve trade and colonial relations. Historian Angus Mitchell argues that her books "did as much to disrupt perceptions of Africa as any work of her time." It was Kingsley's wish before her untimely death at age thirty-seven to establish a society dedicated to research about Africa and its people. The African Society was known to Merriman-Labor long before he arrived in London. Its inauguration had been enthusiastically reported in the Sierra

Leone press, and his friends Sir Samuel Lewis, J.J. Thomas, and Cornelius May quickly established an auxiliary branch in Freetown. May lauded the organization. "There is no doubt that in spite of the countless books which have been published on Africa," he wrote, "there still exists in Europe deplorable ignorance of the true character and condition of the natives." May immediately began publishing a series of articles about Kingsley and the African Society in the *Sierra Leone Weekly News*. When he collected the pieces into a pamphlet, Alice Stopford Green, a friend of Kingsley's and the Africa Society's Honorary Secretary, wrote the introduction. See Angus Mitchell, "Alice Stopford Green and the Origins of the African Society," *Historical Ireland* 14, no. 4 (July–August 2006) 19.

2. He was the Archdeacon of St. George's Cathedral. Merriman-Labor called him the best preacher in Freetown. Merriman-Labor, *Handbook of Sierra Leone for 1901–1902*, 181. Also spelled M'Cauley.

3. Mitchell, "Alice Stopford Green and the Origins of the African Society," 21. At a time when the Royal Geographical Society excluded women from its membership, the African Society included both women and Africans, some of them in leadership roles. Marika Sherwood, *Origins of Pan-Africanism* (London: Routledge, 2011), 169. Guests included anti-slavery advocate Thomas Fowell Buxton, and several members of parliament. Sir Arthur Havelock, former Governor of Natal and Zululand, who had known Merriman-Labor's grandfather, was there, as well as Sir William MacGregor, the Governor of Lagos Colony (now Southern Nigeria), who opposed new colonial regulations barring Africans from senior medical posts.

4. Adam Hochschild, *King Leopold's Ghost: A Story of Greed, Terror, and Heroism in Colonial Africa* (Boston: Houghton Mifflin, 1999.)

5. "The Alake of Abeokuta: African Society's Reception," *Sierra Leone Weekly News*, July 2, 1904, 8. Reproduced from the *African World*, June 11.

6. "Universities and Schools: Scotland," *Journal of Education* 36, no. 421 (August 1, 1904), 543.

7. *Lagos Standard*, quoted in Green, *Black Edwardians*, 26; Theophilus Scholes, *Glimpses of the Ages*, vol. 2 (London: John Long, 1908), 177.

8. Alexander Shewan and John Duguid, *Meminisse Juvat: Being the Autobiography of a Class of King's College in the Sixties* (Aberdeen: Aberdeen University Press, 1905). The poem appears as an appendix written by Alexander Shewan. A lengthy introduction and even lengthier footnotes as well as an English translation accompany the 240-line poem.

9. Shewan and Duguid, *Meminisse Juvat*, 207–208.

10. By 1901, 77 percent of British people were urbanites. By 1911, a full

80 percent lived in cities. Derek Fraser, "The Edwardian City," in *Edwardian England*, edited by Donald Read (New Brunswick: Rutgers University Press, 1982), 56.

11. Geoffrey Keynes, ed., *Letters of Rupert Brooke* (London: Faber and Faber, 1968), 164, quoted in Paterson, *Edwardians*, 11.
12. Paterson, *Edwardians*, 11–31.
13. Quoted in Paterson, *Edwardians*, 14
14. Merriman-Labor, "The Natives of Sierra Leone," *West Africa*, July 16, 1904, 59.
15. Merriman-Labor, "The Natives of Sierra Leone," 59. He was taking a page from Edward Blyden, who had long preached the importance of an authentic African identity untainted by Europe.
16. Merriman-Labor, "The Natives of Sierra Leone," 59. In the 1880s, some Sierra Leoneans gave up their British clothes and even British names for a period. Christopher Fyfe describes the Dress Reform Society and the Africanized names in *A History of Sierra Leone*, 468.
17. Merriman-Labor, *Britons*, 76.
18. Merriman-Labor's companions are rarely named in surviving records, but later events demonstrate that John Roberts was a close friend who likely accompanied Merriman-Labor on outings and adventures.
19. Merriman-Labor, *Britons*, 214.
20. Merriman-Labor, *Britons*, 215.
21. Merriman-Labor, *Britons*, 215.
22. Only ten minutes away was the Hippodrome, where the stage converted into a 100,000-gallon tank allowing "a bevy of bathers" to plunge and dance in a "miniature lake." Arthur H. Beavan, *Imperial London* (London: J.M. Dent and New York: G.P. Dutton, 1901), 472.
23. Merriman-Labor, *Britons*, 217–218.
24. Merriman-Labor *Britons*, 218
25. National Archives, Kew, CO 368, 1904, 10 May 1904, Entry 16673. All that remains of this correspondence is an entry in the Colonial Correspondence Register noting the request (May 10, 1904) and the response (June 16). The letters have been "destroyed under statute" by the archive.
26. Merriman-Labor, *Britons*, 176–177.
27. David Killingray, email to author, July 3, 2015.
28. Merriman-Labor, *Britons*, 146.
29. H.G. Wells, *Tono-Bungay* (Lincoln and London: University of Nebraska Press, 1978), 87.
30. Charlotte Brontë, *Villette* (New York: Dover, 2007), 28.
31. "Merriman-Labor, "Impressions of a Young African in England," *Sierra Leone Weekly News*, August 20, 1904, 4.

32. Merriman-Labor, "Impressions of a Young African in England," *Sierra Leone Weekly News*, August 20, 1904, 4 and October 1, 1904, 4.

33. Merriman-Labor, "Impressions of a Young African in London," *Sierra Leone Weekly News*, October 15, 1904, 5.

34. Arthur Reynolds, *English Sects: An Historical Handbook* (London: A.R. Mowbray and Co., 1921), 118.

35. Merriman-Labor "Impressions of a Young African," October 15, 1904, 4.

36. *Encyclopaedia Britannica, 11th Edition*, vol. 1, 365.

37. "Clapton Messiah's Lady Converts," *Daily Mirror*, July 2, 1904, 5.

38. *Daily Mirror*, July 2, 1904, 5.

39. *Daily Express*, July 4, 1904, 1.

40. John Kent, review of *The Sixth Trumpeter: The Story of Jezreel and His Tower*, by Philip George Rogers, *Victorian Studies* 7, no. 2 (December 1963), 217–219.

41. Merriman-Labor, "Impressions of a Young African," October 15, 1904, 5.

42. CO 267 1904, No. 28031,. Letter from Merriman-Labor, August 10, 1904.

43. http://museumvictoria.com.au/collections/items/1475175/lantern-slide-ten-little-nigger-boys-ten-little-nigger-boys-went-out-to-dine-circa-1900s.

44. "Play for Children: Mr. Bourchier's Charming Christmas Comedy at the Garrick," *Daily Mirror*, December 22, 1904, 4. "Ten Little Nigger Boys" was an adaption of an earlier poem "Ten Little Injuns" by Septimus Winner, written in 1868, a standard of blackface minstrelsy.

45. Merriman-Labor, *Britons*, 54.

46. *Sierra Leone Weekly News*, December 24, 1904, 5.

47. British Museum Library records. Merriman, Augustus Boyle Chamberlayne (formerly Merriman-Labor), A80241.

48. *A Guide to the Use of the Reading Room* (London: Trustees of the British Library, 1938), 6.

49. *A Guide to the Use of the Reading Room*, 7, 38.

50. "A West African's Tribute," *African Mail*, April, 20, 1906, 87.

51. W.C. Edmunds obituary, *The Publishers' Circular*, November 4, 1905, 519; *The Bookseller*, November 8, 1905, 1032. For Merriman-Labor's admission letter and Edmonds's reference letter, see the archives of the British Museum Library.

52. Merriman-Labor, *Britons*, 54.

53. "London Lost in Fog," *Daily Express*, December 22, 1904, front page.

54. "Shortest-Day Fog," *Daily Mirror*, December 22, 1904, 4; "In the Fog," *Daily Mirror*, December 23, 1904, 3.

55. Merriman-Labor, *Britons*, 54.

56. "In the Fog," *Daily Mirror*, December 23, 1904, 3. "Fog's Death-Toll," *Daily Mirror*, December 24, 1904, 3.

57. *British Museum: Reading Room and New Library* (London: Trustees of the British Library, 1906), 10–12. The dome was remodeled in 1907. See Ruth Hoberman, *Museum Trouble: Edwardian Fiction and the Emergence of Modernism* (Charlottesville: University of Virginia, 2011), 154.

58. They were all holders of reader's tickets between 1891 and 1914. Philip Rowland Harris. *A History of the British Museum Library: 1753–1973* (London: British Library, 1998), 773.

59. *The Library World*, 8 (June–July 1906), 239; *British Museum: Reading Room and New Library*, 18. Pneumatic tubs were not installed until 1906.

60. Adapted from Merriman-Labor, *Britons*, 118–119.

61. They may not have known it, but their mutual friend, former Bishop of Sierra Leone Sir John Taylor-Smith, would appear on stage with Torrey and Alexander on opening night.

62. Merriman-Labor, "Impressions of a Young African in England," *Sierra Leone Weekly News*, April 15, 1905, 11. Merriman-Labor reports that 20,000 attended, but some British newspapers reported 12,000.

63. "Rival Methods," *Church Times*, March 24, 1905, 375. Reprinted in *Sierra Leone Weekly News*, April 29, 1905, 7.

64. Merriman-Labor, "Impressions of a Young African in England," *Sierra Leone Weekly News*, August 19, 1905, 7.

65. "The African Agency and Its Founder," *Alexander's Magazine*, August 15, 1907, 202.

66. Inwood, *Cities of Cities*, 32.

67. Merrman-Labor, "The African Agency and Its Founder," 201.

68. Merriman-Labor, "The African Agency and Its Founder," 201–203.

69. Merriman-Labor, "The African General Agency and Its Founder," 203.

70. Merriman-Labor, *Britons*, 26–27.

71. Merriman-Labor, "Through the United Kingdom: My Wanderings and Impressions, Chapter III," *Sierra Leone Weekly News*, December 9, 1905, 7.

72. Merriman-Labor, "Through the United Kingdom, Chapter III," 7.

73. See Old Southeronians' Association Website, "Railway Collection Dogs," http://osamemories.yolasite.com/our-faithful-friends.php; and Justin Parkinson, *BBC News Magazine*, 30 July 2014, "The Dog That Changed Colour Twice," http://www.bbc.com/news/magazine-28420246.

74. J.C. Gray, "The Present Status of Cooperation in Great Britain," *The Arena*, 33 (January–June), 260.

75. Merriman-Labor, "Through the United Kingdom, Chapter III," *Sierra Leone Weekly News*, December 9, 1905, 7.

76. Merriman-Labor, *Britons*, 91, 92, 134.

77. Merriman-Labor, *Britons*, 177.

78. Merriman-Labor, *Britons*, 174.

79. An annual subscription of five shillings conferred the privilege of using the Colonial Office Refreshment Club for tea, an invitation to an annual white-tie dinner hosted by the Secretary of State for the Colonies, and a copy of the dinner speech. Membership extended to a colonial civil servant was not unusual. From the beginning the organizers resolved that "all officials shall be eligible irrespective of rank." But the cost of the annual dinner—fifteen shillings—might have been too steep for Merriman-Labor in 1905, when he was living on his savings.

80. Merriman-Labor, "Impressions of a Young African in England," *Sierra Leone Weekly News*, April 15, 1905, 11.

81. *The Publishers' Circular*, November 4, 1905, 519; Merriman-Labor, "Through the United Kingdom," December 9, 1905, 2.

82. Merriman-Labor, "Through the United Kingdom: My Wanderings and Impressions, Chapter I," *Sierra Leone Weekly News*, November 25, 1905, 6.

83. Merriman-Labor, *Britons*, 175–176.

84. Merriman-Labor, *Britons*, 170, 14.

3. THE AFRICAN GENERAL AGENCY

1. *Sierra Leone Weekly News*, September 3, 1904, 16. The ad ran regularly to December 31, 1904.

2. "The African General Agency and Its Founder," *Alexander's Magazine*, 202.

3. "The Terms and Notes of the African General Agency," January 1908, Merriman-Labor file, Lincoln's Inn Archives.

4. Merriman-Labor, "Impressions of a Young African," *Sierra Leone Weekly News*, September 16, 1905, 7.

5. Merriman-Labor, "Through the United Kingdom, Chapter II," *Sierra Leone Weekly News*, December 2, 1906, 4.

6. Merriman-Labor, "Impressions of a Young African," *Sierra Leone Weekly News*, September 16, 1905, 7. Merriman-Labor, "Through the United Kingdom, Chapter II," *Sierra Leone Weekly News*, December 2, 1906, 4.

7. Merriman-Labor, "Impressions of a Young African," *Sierra Leone Weekly News*, August 19, 1905, 7.

8. Merriman-Labor, "Impressions of a Young African in England," June 24, 1905, 10; *The Sphere*, June 10, 1905, 236; *Review of Reviews*, 32 (July–December 1905), 520.

9. *The Baptist World Congress, London July 11–19, 1905, Authorized Record of Proceedings*, with introduction by Rev. J.H. Shakespeare (London: Baptist Union Publication Department, 1905), vi.

10. *Sierra Leone Weekly News*, August 19, 1905, 7.

11. *Daily Mirror*, April 26, 1905, front page.

12. "Pigmies' Visit to London," *Daily Mirror*, May 6, 1905, 4.

13. *Daily Mirror*, April 26, 1905, 6.

14. *The Sphere*, June 10, 1905, 236, quoted in Green, *Black Edwardians*, 120.

15. *Beverley Guardian*, June 3, 1905, quoted in Green, *Black Edwardians*, 120.

16. "Our Captious Critic," *Illustrated Sporting and Dramatic News*, August 12, 1905, 912.

17. For more, see Jeffery P. Green, "A Revelation in Strange Humanity: Six Congo Pygmies in Britain, 1905–1907," in *Africans on Stage: Studies in Ethnological Show Business*, edited by Bernth Lindfors (Bloomington: Indiana University Press, 1999).

18. "Amusements, Concerts, etc.: Crystal Palace, Bank Holiday," *Daily Mirror*, April 18, 1905, 2; "Crystal Palace Attractions," *Daily Mirror*, April 22, 1905, 15.

19. *The Palace and Park: Its Natural History and Its Portrait Gallery* (London: Crystal Palace Library, Bradbury and Evans, 1855), 168.

20. *The Crystal Palace Sydenham, to be Sold by Auction* (London: Knight, Frank and Rudley, 1911), 19.

21. Karl Baedeker, *London and Its Environs* (Leipzig: Karl Baedeker, 1902), 409. Also see Samuel Phillips, *Guide to the Crystal Palace and Park* (London: Euston Grove Press, 2008), facsimile of the 1856 edition.

22. My descriptions come mostly from the 1885 Somali Village show at the Crystal Palace. I have extrapolated that the 1905 program was similar.

23. Merriman-Labor, "Impressions of a Young African in England," *Sierra Leone Weekly News*, September 16, 1905, 7.

24. Marika Sherwood, *Origins of Pan-Africanism: Henry Sylvester Williams, Africa and the African Diaspora* (New York: Routledge, 2011).

25. *Sierra Leone Weekly News*, April 6, 1912, 7.

26. Specifically Sierra Leone, Northern and Southern Nigeria, Lagos, Gold Coast, and the Gambia.

27. Mr. Walter Jones of Dulwich, "The African General Agency," *Sierra Leone Weekly News*, October 28, 1905, 2.

28. Merriman-Labor, "The African General Agency," *Sierra Leone Weekly News*, October 28, 1905, 2.

29. Letter from Merriman-Labor, December 24, 1907, Merriman-Labor file, Lincoln's Inn Archive. Merriman-Labor never specifies what "trade protection societies" were critical of his business. "The African General Agency," *Sierra Leone Weekly News*, October 28, 1905, 2.

30. "West African Information Bureau and General Agency," *Sierra Leone Weekly News*, September 2, 1905, 16.

31. Over the course of two weeks, he planned to see producers of straw hats in St. Albans, cotton goods in Manchester, woolens in Leeds, boots and shoes in Leicester, ironware in Birmingham, and additional companies in Nottingham, Sheffield, Glasgow, Edinburgh, Aberdeen, and Dublin.

32. Sierra Leonean newspapers didn't have the technology to publish pictures, but Merriman-Labor invited readers to drop by the newspaper office to see them.

33. Merriman-Labor, "Through the United Kingdom: My Wanderings and Impressions, Chapter III," *Sierra Leone Weekly News*, December 9, 1905, 7.

34. Merriman-Labor, Through the United Kingdom: Chapter IV," *Sierra Leone Weekly News*, December 16, 1905, 10.

35. Merriman-Labor, "Through the United Kingdom, Chapter IV," *Sierra Leone Weekly News*, December 16, 1905, 10.

36. Merriman-Labor, "Through the United Kingdom, Chapter IV," *Sierra Leone Weekly News*, December 16, 1905, 10.

37. Merriman-Labor, "Through the United Kingdom, Chapter IV," *Sierra Leone Weekly News*, December 16, 1905, 10.

38. Merriman-Labor, "Through the United Kingdom: My Wanderings and Impressions, Chapter IV," *Sierra Leone Weekly News*, December 16, 1905, 10. This was probably Said Ali: see *Daily Express*, January 14, 1905, 1.

39. Merriman-Labor, "Through the United Kingdom, Chapter IV," *Sierra Leone Weekly News*, December 16, 1905, 10.

40. Merriman-Labor, "Through the United Kingdom: My Wanderings and Impressions, Chapter VI," *Sierra Leone Weekly News*, July 14, 1906, 6.

41. He was currently studying at the United Methodist Free Church Training College. Merriman-Labor, *Handbook of Sierra Leone for 1901–1902*, 72.

42. Merriman-Labor, "Through the United Kingdom: My Wanderings and Impressions, Chapter VI," *Sierra Leone Weekly News*, July 14, 1906, 2. Note: Mr. Clay is probably George Clay with whom he lodged years later and who acted as secretary for Literature Ltd.

43. Merriman-Labor, "Through the United Kingdom: My Wanderings and Impressions, Chapter VI," *Sierra Leone Weekly News*, July 14, 1906, 6.

44. "Ethiopian Progressive Union," *Sierra Leone Weekly News*, July 22, 1905, 8.

45. *Sierra Leone Weekly News*, November 25, 1905, 9; also *The Constitution of the Ethiopian Progressive Association* (Liverpool: D. Marples, 1905). See http://credo.library.umass.edu/view/pageturn/mums312-b002-i204/#page/3/mode/1up. Merriman-Labor probably articulates his view of the Ethiopian Progressive Association in Chapter V of "Through

the United Kingdom: My Wanderings and Impressions," but I have been unable to locate this article.

46. "Ethiopian Progressive Association," *Sierra Leone Weekly News*, November 25, 1905, 9.
47. "The Constitution of the Ethiopian Progressive Association," *Sierra Leone Weekly News*, July 22, 1905, 8.
48. "Ethiopian Progressive Association," *Lagos Standard*, March 20, 1907, 7.
49. Merriman-Labor, "Whitsuntide with the French in Paris," *Sierra Leone Weekly News*, October 13, 1906, 4.
50. Merriman-Labor, "Whitsuntide with the French in Paris, Chapter IX," *Sierra Leone Weekly News*, October 13, 1906, 4.
51. Merriman-Labor, *Britons*, 48.
52. Inspired by *Britons through Negro Spectacles*, 47–49 and "Whitsuntide with the French in Paris, Chapter IX," *Sierra Leone Weekly News*, October 13, 1906, 2.
53. "The Boy," *The Outlook*, February 3, 1906, 160; "'Daily Mail' Searchlights," and "'Daily Mail' Flashlights," *Daily Express*, January 17, 1906, 4.
54. Martin Meredith, *Diamonds, Gold, and War: The British, the Boers, and the Making of South Africa* (New York: Public Affairs, 2007), 496.
55. Meredith, *Diamonds, Gold, and War*, 495.
56. Meredith, *Diamonds, Gold, and War*, 499.
57. *Izwi Labantu*, reprinted in the *Lagos Weekly Record*, April 21, 1906, 5.
58. Quoted in Shula Marks, *Reluctant Rebellion in Natal* (Oxford: Clarendon Press, 1970), 189.
59. *Parliamentary Papers, 1850–1908, Colonies and British Possessions Continued, Africa Session, 13 February 1906 to 21 December 1906*, vol. 79, 30.
60. Official communications between Lord Elgin and Sir Henry McCallum, see *Parliamentary Papers, 1850–1908, Colonies and British Possessions Continued, Africa Session, 13 February 1906 to 21 December 1906*, vol. 79, 30.
61. Two men were captured quickly, found guilty in a drumhead court martial, and executed.
62. *Parliamentary Papers, 1850–1908, Colonies and British Possessions Continued, Africa Session, 13 February 1906 to 21 December 1906*, vol. 79, 27.
63. Akilagpa Sawyerr from the Gold Coast also helped and three white supporters offered financial assistance. See David Killingray, "Significant Black South Africans in Britain before 1919: Pan-African Organisations and the Emergence of Africa's First Black Lawyers," *South African Historical Journal* 64, no. 3 (2012), 393–417.
64. "The Richmond Murders," *The Advertiser* (Adelaide), April 4, 1906, 7.
65. "Debate in the Commons," *The Advertiser* (Adelaide), April 4, 1906, 7.
66. "Execution of the Natives," *Daily Mirror*, April 3, 1906, 3.

67. "Debate in the Commons," *The Advertiser* (Adelaide), April 4, 1906, 7.
68. *Mafeking Mail* (South Africa), April 4, 1906, 4; *The Advertiser*, April 4, 1906, 7.
69. Meredith, *Diamonds, Gold, and War*, 500.
70. Gebuza, *The Peril in Natal* (London: T. Fisher Unwin, 1906), 6. This was the pseudonym of Francis Ernest Colenso, who had participated in the preparations for the Pan-African conference, a diligent campaigner for Zulu rights, and who helped Mangena draft Jellicoe's appeal to the Judicial Committee of the Privy Council. See Killingray, "Significant Black South Africans in Britain before 1912."
71. Meredith, *Diamonds, Gold, and War*, 502.
72. First published in the London journal *Argosy*, reprinted in the *Gold Coast Leader*, March 10, 1906, 5, then the *Jamaica Times*, September 8, 1906, 9. The attendees included both students and businessmen. Students who attended were Moses Taylor (Sierra Leone), Akilagpa Sawyerr (Gold Coast), Peter E. Sampson (Gold Coast), and Joseph Eminsang (Gold Coast.) Also attending, barrister John Theo Holm (Gold Coast) and businessmen Thomas Brem Wilson (Gold Coast), Albert. S. Cann (Gold Coast), and A. Kwesi Bhoma (Gold Coast.)
73. Soga may well have been the newspaper editor who condemned the African General Agency. Peter Limb, "Representing the Labouring Classes: African Workers in the African Nationalist Press 1900–1960," in *South African's Resistance Press: Alternative Voices in the Last Generation under Apartheid*, edited by Les Switzer and Mohamed Adhikari (Athens, OH: Ohio University Press, 2000), 87.
74. Meredith, *Diamonds, Gold, and War*, 507.
75. *Des Moines Daily News*, August 8, 1906, 7, quoted in Killingray, "Significant Black South Africans in Britain before 1912," 21–22.
76. "The Invasion of 1910," *Daily Mail*, April 13, 1906, 2, 6.
77. Merriman-Labor, "Whitsuntide with the French in Paris, Chapter VIII," *Sierra Leone Weekly News*, September 29, 1906, 6.
78. Merriman-Labor, "Whitsuntide with the French in Paris, Chapter VI," *Sierra Leone Weekly News*, August 11, 1906, 6.
79. Merriman-Labor, "Whitsuntide with the French in Paris, Chapter VII," *Sierra Leone Weekly News*, August 11, 1906, 6.
80. This and the following scene are inspired by Merriman-Labor's descriptions in "Whitsuntide with the French in Paris, Chapter IX," *Sierra Leone Weekly News*, October 13, 1906, 4.
81. It is possible he may have rented an office, but considering it is an address he uses again in 1915, at the height of his legal crisis, that is unlikely. See Thomas Leaming, *A Philadelphia Lawyer in the London Courts* (New York: Henry Holt, 1911), 30, for more information about this practice.

82. *Sierra Leone Weekly News*, August 11, 1906.
83. *Daily Mirror*, December 12, 1906, 5.
84. *Law Students' Journal*, February 1, 1907, 46.
85. Council of Legal Education, Questions Set for Examinations 1906–1907, 28–29.

4. BE RIGHT AND PERSIST

1. *The Mercury*, February 15, 1907, 2; *Cambridge Independent Press*, February 15, 1907, 6.
2. Merriman-Labor, *Britons*, 206, 205, 207, and 205.
3. *Daily Express*, February 11, 1907, 5.
4. Lisa Tickner, *The Spectacle of Women: Imagery of the Suffrage Campaign, 1907–1914* (Chicago: University of Chicago Press, 1988), 74–80.
5. Tickner, *The Spectacle of Women*, 75. The suffragists' colors were red and white. The suffragettes used white, green and purple.
6. Tickner, *The Spectacle of Women*, 81.
7. *Cambridge Independent Press*, February 15, 1907, 6.
8. *Cambridge Independent Press*, February 15, 1907, 6
9. *Manchester Courier and Lancashire General Advertiser*, February 11, 1907, 8.
10. *Daily Mirror*, February 11, 1907, 4.
11. Merriman-Labor, *Britons*, 211.
12. Merriman-Labor, *Britons*, 145.
13. "African General Agency," *Lagos Standard*, March 20, 1907, 7.
14. To get a sense of the range of his business, see sheet outlining his current clients, July 23, 1908, Merriman-Labor file, Lincoln's Inn Archive.
15. Christmas Eve letter, December 24, 1907, Merriman-Labor file, Lincoln's Inn Archive.
16. African General Agency," *Lagos Standard*, March 20, 1907, 7.
17. African General Agency," *Lagos Standard*, March 20, 1907, 7.
18. "African General Agency Terms and Notes," Merriman-Labor file, Lincoln's Inn Archive.
19. *Sierra Leone Weekly News*, February 26, 1910, 9.
20. Merriman-Labor, Letter February 18, 1907, Merriman-Labor file, Lincoln's Inn Archive.
21. Merriman-Labor, Letter February 18, 1907, Merriman-Labor file, Lincoln's Inn Archive.
22. A. Weatherley Marriott, Steward, February 20, 1907, Merriman-Labor file, Lincoln's Inn Archive.
23. "A Funeral Oration Delivered at Norwood Cemetery, London" in his manuscript for *My Earliest Miscellany* has been lost. I have assumed this was for John Roberts, although it might have been for William Curtis

Edmonds. His announcement of Roberts's death appears in the *Sierra Leone Weekly News*, "Mr. John Roberts in England," March, 16, 1907, 8.

24. Merriman-Labor, *Britons*, flyleaf.

25. See the Campaign and Medal Awards Rolls 1793–1949, National Archives, Kew, WO 100 92.

26. Merriman-Labor, "Report of the Secretary of the Committee for the Celebration of the Centenary of the Abolition of the Slave Trade," *Sierra Leone Weekly News*, April 13, 1907, 11.

27. Merriman-Labor, "Report of the Secretary," *Sierra Leone Weekly News*, April 13, 1907 11.

28. *The Times*, March 13, 1907, 7. His call did bring in some donations— the Carpenters' Defensive Union of Freetown, for example, gave over £2 for wreaths—but he was unable to solicit enough to hold the banquet or to publish the commemorative book.

29. Merriman-Labor, "Report of the Secretary," *Sierra Leone Weekly News*, April 13, 1907, 11.

30. Merriman-Labor, *Britons*, 151. This is a quotation from Edward Bickersteth, Jr.'s hymn, "Peace, Perfect Peace."

31. Merriman-Labor, "Report of the Secretary," *Sierra Leone Weekly News*, April 13, 1907, 11.

32. Merriman-Labor, *Britons*, 156

33. J.L. Franklin of the Great Ormond Street Homeopathic Hospital, J.E. Barnes, a civil engineer, Samuel Lewis, Jr., J. Otonba Payne, G.D. Montsioa, and E.A. Ejesa-Osora, all African students. Barnes's and Payne's names are misspelled in the *Sierra Leone Weekly News* articles.

34. Merriman-Labor, *Britons*, 156.

35. Merriman-Labor, "Report of the Secretary," *Sierra Leone Weekly News*, April 18, 1907, 11; "Grateful Africans," *Daily News* March 26, 1907, 9; "The Abolition of Slavery," *London Daily Standard*, March 26, 1907, 10.

36. "100 Years of Freedom," *Daily Mail*, March 26, 1907, 5.

37. "London Notes: The Slaves of a Century Ago," *Manchester Evening Chronicle*, March 13, 1907. The idea of a Krio calling himself a "black Englishman" was controversial in Sierra Leone. In 1894, when lawyer and bookseller A.J. Shorunkeh-Sawyerr defended the idea of Krios being black Englishman, the *Sierra Leone Weekly News* retorted that "there can be no such being as a 'Black-Englishman.'" *Sierra Leone Weekly News*, 22 April 1863. Also see Fyfe, *History*, 469.

38. *Sierra Leone Weekly News*, April 18, 1907, 8.

39. Merriman-Labor, "Report of the Secretary," *Sierra Leone Weekly News*, April 18, 1907, 8

40. It appeared in the *Lagos Standard*, *Jamaica Times*, and *Alexander's Magazine*,

an African American journal published in Boston. It was no doubt published in other publications which have been lost.

41. "The African General Agency and Its Founder," *Alexander's Magazine*, August 15, 1907, 202, 203.

42. *Jamaica Times*, September 7, 1907, 6. This is probably the booklet sent out July 1907 which Merriman-Labor refers to in his December 24, 1907 letter, Merriman-Labor file, Lincoln's Inn Archive.

43. "The Craft of the Advertiser," W. Teignmouth Shore, *Fortnightly Review*, February 1907, 307.

44. "African General Agency Terms and Notes," Merriman-Labor file, Lincoln's Inn Archive.

45. "African General Agency Terms and Notes," Merriman-Labor file, Lincoln's Inn Archive.

46. "African General Agency Terms and Notes," Merriman-Labor file, Lincoln's Inn Archive.

47. Samuel Hynes, *The Edwardian Turn of Mind* (Princeton, N.J.: Princeton University Press, 1971), 141.

48. "African General Agency," *Lagos Standard*, March 13, 1907, 7; "African General Agency Terms and Notes," Merriman-Labor file, Lincoln's Inn Archive.

49. "Antiquarian News," *The Antiquary*, 44 (January–December, 1908), 472.

50. A. St. John Adcock, "Sideshow London," in *Living London*, vol. 3 (London: Village Press, 1990), 112. First published by Cassell, under the title *Living London* in three volumes.

51. Adcock, "Sideshow London," 115–116.

52. Disbarment papers, Merriman-Labor file, Lincoln's Inn Archive. The book, apparently, was never published and no manuscript survives.

53. Merriman-Labor misspells São Tomé in the letter.

54. Letter, December 24, 1907, Merriman-Labor file, Lincoln's Inn Archive.

55. Letter, December 24, 1907, Merriman-Labor file, Lincoln's Inn Archive.

56. Merriman-Labor, "Petition to the Masters of the Bench of Lincoln's Inn to Re-open the Case," "Mr. Augustus Merriman and the Honourable Society of Lincoln's Inn: Statement on Behalf of the Society," 16. Lincoln's Inn Archive.

57. Letter, December 24, 1907, Merriman-Labor file, Lincoln's Inn Archive.

58. Letter, December 24, 1907, Merriman-Labor file, Lincoln's Inn Archive.

59. Draft letter, March 19, 1908, Merriman-Labor file, Lincoln's Inn Archive.

60. Merriman-Labor file, Lincoln's Inn Archive.
61. "Report of the Special Committee appointed to consider the case of a Student of the Society: Report of the Special Committee appointed by the Council on 31st January 1908 to look into the case of Mr. M-L a student of this Society carrying on business," Merriman-Labor File, Lincoln's Inn Archive.
62. Letter, March 20, 1908, Merriman-Labor file, Lincoln's Inn Archive.
63. "Further Report of the Special Committee appointed by the Council on the 31st January 1908 to look into the case of a Student of this Society carrying on business and re-appointed by the Council on 25th May, 1908," Merriman-Labor file, Lincoln's Inn Archive
64. Anthony Glyn, "Elinor Glyn," quoted in James Laver, *Edwardian Promenade* (Boston: Houghton Mifflin, 1958), 21.
65. In ancient times, it was said, barristers wore a money bag at the back of their gowns where clients could deposit fees without the barrister knowing the amount. M. Garsia, *A New Guide to the Bar* (London: Sweet and Maxwell, 1923), 7.
66. "African General Agency, Terms and Conditions," Merriman-Labor file, Lincoln's Inn Archive
67. "Further Report of the Special Committee appointed by the Council on 31st January 1908 and re-appointed by the Council on the 25th day of February 1908 to look into the case of Mr. M-L," Merriman-Labor file, Lincoln's Inn Archive.
68. Further Report of the Special Committee," Merriman-Labor file, Lincoln's Inn Archive.
69. Undated indenture, Merriman-Labor file, Lincoln's Inn Archive.
70. Merriman-Labor letter, April 10, 1908, Merriman-Labor file, Lincoln's Inn Archive.
71. African General Agency letterhead, Merriman-Labor file, Lincoln's Inn Archive.
72. Merriman-Labor, Letter, April 7, 1908, Merriman-Labor file, Lincoln's Inn Archive.
73. *Sierra Leone Weekly News*, May 9, 1908, 3.
74. "Report of the Special Committee," Merriman-Labor file, Lincoln's Inn Archive.
75. Topham was the author of *Principles of Company Law*, 1904. As a reader at Lincoln's Inn, it is likely that Topham might have been Merriman-Labor's instructor.
76. Merriman-Labor, Letter, April 10, 1908 and April 13, 1908, Merriman-Labor file, Lincoln's Inn Archive.
77. "Further Report of the Special Committee," Merriman-Labor file, Lincoln's Inn Archive.

78. "Further Report of the Special Committee," Merriman-Labor file, Lincoln's Inn Archive.
79. McIntyre and Capel Peters Letter, May 22, 1908; David Ferguson, Letter, May 22, 1908, Merriman-Labor file, Lincoln's Inn Archive.
80. National Archives, Kew, BT226/3686, 1913, Merriman-Labor bankruptcy proceedings.
81. "Statement intended for the Masters of the Bench of the Honorable Society of Lincoln's Inn in the Termination of the African General Agency," July 23, 1908.
82. "Further Report of the Special Committee," Merriman-Labor file, Lincoln's Inn Archive.
83. Alison Griffiths, "'To the World the World We Show': Early Travelogues as Filmed Ethnography," *Film History* 11, no. 3, Early Cinema (1999), 282–307; X. Theodore Barber, "The Roots of Travel Cinema: John L. Stoddard, E. Burton Holmes and the Nineteenth-Century Illustrated Travel Lecture," *Film History*, 5, no. 1 (March 1992), 68–84.
84. The title was not just a send-up of European books about Africa, but a conscious echo of his father's inflammatory articles about life in the Sierra Leonean village of Waterloo.
85. Merriman-Labor, Letter, July 7, 1908, Merriman-Labor file, Lincoln's Inn Archive.
86. Note from Cecil Russell to Steward, July 9, 1908, Merriman-Labor file, Lincoln's Inn Archive.
87. Email, February 6 2012, from Todd Gustavson, Curator, Technology Collection, George Eastman House: "This is the first I've heard of the telescopigraph, but assume it would be a magic lantern projector; most of the companies had rather impressive sounding names for them such as Balopticon, Delineascope, or Kodioticon. I looked through a number of catalogs from various English manufactures, but did not come across the telescopigraph. The closest I found was a projector with a telescoping front from the 1907 Wrench Illustrated Catalogue."
88. In a notice in the *African Mail* on July 8, 1908, Merriman-Labor noticed that he intended to call on "Freetown, Sherbro, Accra, Cape Coast, Lagos, Liberia, Calabar, Gambia, Warri, Bonny, Opobo, and elsewhere for the purpose of delivering lectures on the following subjects: 'The Commercial and Political Outlook of West Africa', 'The Places of Religion and Education in Modern Existence', 'Five Years with the White Man: What I Saw'." *African Mail*, July 17, 1908, 404.

5. FIVE YEARS WITH THE WHITE MAN: WHAT I SAW

1. The lectures and slides came in a package from the Reliance company

along with the book *Readings in Prose and Verse: with Supplementary Lecture Book Containing Lectures and Readings for the Magic Lantern* (London: Theobald and Co., n.d.). Merriman-Labor chose *The Life of Christ, Modern London, Life in the Soudan*, as well as the tragic French love story of *Paul and Virginia*. "To Elevate, to Amuse," *Sierra Leone Weekly News*, May 2, 1896, 9.

2. The photographer is only described a "clever photographer"—but is surely Merriman-Labor's uncle, J.C. Merriman.

3. "An Imposition on the Public," *Sierra Leone Times*, April 11, 1896, 3.

4. "To Elevate, to Amuse," *Sierra Leone Times*, April 4, 1894, 3; "To Elevate, to Amuse," *Sierra Leone Weekly News*, May 2, 1896, 9.

5. "Mr. Merriman-Labor's Arrival," *Sierra Leone Guardian and Foreign Mails*, August 14, 1908, 2.

6. J.R. King, Superintendent of the United Brethren of Christ Mission, *Sierra Leone Weekly News*, June 13, 1908, 12.

7. *Sierra Leone Weekly News*, August 1, 1908, 9. This interview inspired the following scene. The dialogue is largely taken from the reported conversation.

8. "Mr. Merriman-Labor," *Sierra Leone Weekly News*, August 22, 1908, 9.

9. "Proposed Visit of Mr. Merriman-Labor," *Sierra Leone Weekly News*, July 25, 1908, 7.

10. "Mr. Merriman-Labor Thanking Gambia," *Sierra Leone Weekly News*, September 19, 1908, 7.

11. He was in the Gold Coast on November 10 and 11, then Lagos on the 24th. "Mr. Merriman-Labor's Lecture," *Sierra Leone Guardian*, November 27, 1908, 5.

12. "Mr. Merriman-Labor Thanking Gambia," *Sierra Leone Weekly News*, September 29, 1908, 7.

13. Constance Larymore, *A Resident Wife in Nigeria* (London: Routledge, 1908), 5.

14. Larymore, *A Resident Wife in Nigeria*, 5.

15. John Downie Falconer, *On Horseback through Nigeria; or, Life and Travel in the Central Sudan* (London: T. Fisher Unwin, 1911), 38–39.

16. Falconer, *On Horseback through Nigeria*, 39.

17. Larymore in *A Resident Wife in Nigeria*, 5–6.

18. George Douglas Hazzledine, *The White Man in Nigeria* (London: Edward Arnold, 1904), 36.

19. Larymore, *A Resident Wife in Nigeria*, 7.

20. Falconer, *On Horseback through Nigeria*, 39.

21. *The Art of Projection and Complete Magic Lantern Manual, by "An Expert"* (London: E.A. Beckett, 1893). Edward Justus Parker, *The Lantern: Being a Treatise on the Magic Lantern and Stereopticon* ([New York, Salvation Army, 1901]).

22. Also Herbert Ward's *Five Years with the Congo Cannibals* (1891); Lionel Decle's *Three Years in Savage Africa* (1898); Agnes McAllister's *A Lone Woman in Africa: Six Years on the Kroo Coast* (1896); and Charles John Andersson's *Four Years in Africa* (1885?).
23. Merriman-Labor, *Britons*, 120–121.
24. Merriman-Labor, *Britons*, 28.
25. Merriman-Labor, *Britons*, 17–18.
26. Merriman-Labor, *Britons*, 25.
27. This scene is drawn from John Downie Falconer, *On Horseback through Nigeria*, 40.
28. Falconer, *On Horseback through Nigeria*, 40.
29. Falconer, *On Horseback through Nigeria*, 40.
30. Falconer, *On Horseback through Nigeria*, 40.
31. Merriman-Labor, *Britons*, 150.
32. Merriman-Labor, *Britons*, 138.
33. Falconer, *On Horseback through Nigeria*, 40.
34. This is the route Larymore describes when she travels from Lokoja to Zungeru, *A Resident Wife in Nigeria*, 64–65.
35. Larymore, *A Resident Wife in Nigeria*, 65.
36. In September 1903, the *Sierra Leone Weekly News* announced her new position, but misidentified both the place and her position, stating that she would serve as the "Assistant Lady Superintendent of the Slave Home at Lokoja." *Sierra Leone Weekly News*, September 5, 1903, 10. The *Protectorate of Northern Nigeria Blue Book* lists her as "Matron" and explains that the Home includes "two large dormitories, divided into various rooms for inmates of different age and sex; a laundry, store, Native Matrons' house, dispensary, hospital and an office for the Lady Superintendent." *Protectorate of Northern Nigeria*, *Blue Book for the Year 1903* (Protectorate of Northern Nigeria, Government Printer.
37. See G.O. Olusanya, "The Freed Slaves' Homes: An Unknown Aspect of Northern Nigerian Social History," *Journal of the Historical Society of Nigeria* 3, no. 3 (December 1966).
38. Olusanya, "The Freed Slaves' Homes," 524.
39. *Protectorate of Northern Nigeria*, *Blue Book for the Year 1903*.
40. Olusanya, "The Freed Slaves' Homes," 529.
41. Olusanya, "Freed Slaves' Homes," 530.
42. Olusayna, "Freed Slaves' Homes," 531.
43. Olusayna, "Freed Slaves' Homes," 531.
44. "Mr. Merriman-Labor," *Sierra Leone Guardian*, January 15, 1909, 3.
45. Merriman-Labor, *Britons*, dedication.
46. Merriman-Labor, *Britons*, preface.
47. "Mr. Merriman-Labor," *Sierra Leone Guardian*, 15 January, 1909, 3.

48. "Mr. Merriman-Labor," *Sierra Leone Guardian*, 15 January, 1909, 3. Merriman-Labor, *Britons*, flyleaf advertisement for *A Tour in Negroland*, He says he took a 15,000-mile tour through West, South-west, and Central Africa. His name appears on no passenger lists for steamers returning from West Africa to London. As he was back in London by the end of February, it is likely he did not make it to Palestine.

6. HOME TRUTHS

1. See "Report of the Special Committee," especially letters, February 27, 1909, March 1, 1909, March 25, 1909, April 1, 1909, and April 2, 1909, Merriman-Labor file, Lincoln's Inn Archive.
2. "The Inns of Court," *Chambers's Journal of Popular Literature* (London: W. and R., Chambers, 1879), 539.
3. Henry Leach, "Wig and Gown in London," *Living London*, vol. 2, 84.
4. Merriman-Labor, *Britons*, 141.
5. "Mr. Merriman-Labor," *Sierra Leone Weekly News*, May 22, 1909, 9.
6. "Calls to the Bar," *The Times*, May 6, 1909, 4.
7. "Mr. Merriman-Labor," *Sierra Leone Weekly News*, May 22, 1909, 9. Email, November 15, 2010, to author from Mrs. F. Bellis, Lincoln's Inn Archive Librarian regarding the Certificate of Admission; "18 April 1909," Notes on meeting with Merriman-Labor, Lincoln's Inn Archive.
8. "Mr. Merriman-Labor," *Sierra Leone Weekly News*, May 22, 1909, 9.
9. "Editorial Notes," *Gold Coast Leader*, June 16, 1909, 1.
10. "Mr. Merriman-Labor," *Sierra Leone Weekly News*, May 22, 1909, 9.
11. Merriman-Labor, *Britons*, preface.
12. Merriman-Labor, *Britons*, preface.
13. Merriman-Labor, Britons, preface.
14. "Under Which Flags," *Daily Express*, February 8, 1909, 1.
15. *Daily Mail*, February 25, 1908.
16. Arthur Marder, *From the Dreadnought to Scapa Flow: Volume I: The Road to War 1904–1914* (Annapolis: Naval Institute Press, 1961), 167.
17. Merriman-Labor, *Britons*, 106–107.
18. Merriman-Labor, *Britons*, 107.
19. Meredith, *Diamonds, Gold, and War*, 513.
20. Meredith, *Diamonds, Gold, and War*, 514.
21. "South African Act of Union," *Dundee Courier*, July 5, 1909, 5.
22. Meredith, *Diamonds, Gold, and War*, 517
23. Merriman-Labor, *Britons*, 160.
24. Merriman-Labor, *Britons*, 160.
25. Merriman-Labor, *Britons*, 161.
26. "South Africa Bill Passes," *Daily Express*, August 20, 1909, 1.

27. "South Africa Bill Passes," *Daily Express*, August 20, 1909, 1.

28. Merriman-Labor, *Britons*, 164.

29. Adam Lorimer [pseudonym for William Lorimer Watson], *The Author's Progress: or, The Literary Book of the Road* (London: Blackwood and Sons, 1906), 37.

30. Samuel Hynes, *The Edwardian Turn of Mind* (Princeton, N.J.: Princeton University Press, 1968), 296–297.

31. Lorimer, *The Author's Progress*, 34

32. Merriman-Labor had become friends with A.W. Leslie, a prosperous African American man living and working in London, "a well-known dealer in motor tyres and scrap rubber." *Motor Car Journal* 10 (September 19, 1908), 636. Also see an ad for A.W. Leslie "Waste Rubber, Gutta-Percha, Ebonite, etc.," in *Rubber Trade Directory* (New York: Office of the India Rubber World, 1908), 170.

33. "Our Position Re: Mr. Labor's 'Britons,'" *Nigerian Chronicle*, June 3, 1910, 10.

34. African American missionary William Henry Sheppard—sometimes called the Black Livingstone—had describes his experiences in Africa. He gave a lecture at the Hampton Institute on November 14, 1893, about his work and travels in the Congo. A copy of the address was printed in *Southern Workman* as "Into the Heart of Africa," December 1893, 182–187.

35. Merriman-Labor, *Britons*, advertisement.

36. Merriman-Labor, *Britons*, advertisement.

37. Merriman-Labor, *Britons*, advertisement.

38. "First Glance," *The Observer* (London), August 22, 1909, 4

39. "Other New Publications," *The Outlook*, August 28, 1909, 280.

40. "Books of the Week," *Manchester Courier*, September 3, 1909, 9.

41. "As Others See Us," *Dundee Courier*, September 4, 1909. The thoughtfulness of the provincial reviews squares with Adam Lorimer's observation that those from outside London tended to be more "thorough and well considered" than London reviews. He attributes this to the fact that they were done by amateurs who took the work quite seriously, not the jaded metropolitan reviewers.

42. "Through Negro Spectacles," quoted in the *Jamaica Times*, October 23, 1909, 13.

43. "Trespass to Reality," *Law Journal*, September 11, 1909, 546.

44. "Britons through Negro Spectacles," *Sierra Leone Weekly News*, July 10, 1909, 10; *Sierra Leone Weekly News*, June 19, 1909, 11.

45. "Britons through Negro Spectacles," *Sierra Leone Weekly News*, September 18, 1909, 4

46. "Britons through Negro Spectacles," *Sierra Leone Weekly News*, September 18, 1909, 4.

47. *Sierra Leone Weekly News*, November 13, 1909, 5. A final review appeared in the *Nigerian Chronicle* in December 1909. The reviewer suggested changing the title to the tedious "Life and Scenes in Britain" and recommended the synopsis should be moved to the front of the book. Other than these banal suggestions, the reviewer commended the book's "unbiased and unprejudiced tones" in its portrait of the British and recommended it for "stay at homes" "who will know a Negro's view of the Briton as it brings to their doors the fruits of years of experience and observation." *Nigerian Chronicle*, December 3, 1909, 7.
48. Merriman-Labor, *Britons*, 88.
49. Merriman-Labor, *Britons*, 88.
50. Merriman-Labor, *Britons*, 108.
51. Merriman-Labor, *Britons*, 113.
52. Merriman-Labor, *Britons*, 182.
53. Merriman-Labor, *Britons*, 183.
54. Merriman-Labor, *Britons*, 184.
55. Merriman-Labor, *Britons*, 187–188.
56. Merriman-Labor, *Britons*, 190.
57. Merriman-Labor, *Britons*, 237.
58. Merriman-Labor, *Britons*, 237–238.
59. Merriman-Labor, *Britons*, 220.
60. Merriman-Labor, *Britons*, 221.
61. Merriman-Labor, *Britons*, 221.
62. J. Forbes Munro, "Monopolists and Speculators: British Investment in West African Rubber, 1905–1914," *Journal of African History* 22, no. 2 (1981), 272.
63. National Archives, Kew, BT226/3686, 1913, Merriman-Labor bankruptcy proceedings. He reported that the *Financial Outlook* agreed to pay him £10 an article and £20 a report.
64. National Archives of South Africa, Secretary for Native Affairs (SNA) 447, Letter from Peregrino to William Windham, Secretary for Native Affairs in the Transvaal, October, 14, 1909.
65. "Mr. Merriman's Lecture," *Sierra Leone Weekly News*, May 30, 1914, 10.
66. "Mr. Merriman-Labor," *Sierra Leone Weekly News*, March 19, 1910, 8; "Britons through Negro Spectacles," *Sierra Leone Weekly News*, April 30, 1910, 10.
67. "The King," *Daily Express*, May 6, 1910, 1.
68. "Through 'The Mirror': Outside Buckingham Palace," *Daily Mirror*, May 7, 1910, 6.
69. The unsigned "London Letter" column in the *Sierra Leone Weekly News* was a regular feature long before Merriman-Labor arrived in London.

However, the reports covering the King's illness and death possess a sense of humor I have so often found in Merriman-Labor's work. It is quite possible he submitted them. I am assuming that Merriman-Labor was the author of the reports on the King's death and its aftermath.

70. "London Letter," *Sierra Leone Weekly News*, May 28, 1910, 7.
71. "London Letter," *Sierra Leone Weekly News*, May 28, 1910, 7.
72. "London Letter," *Sierra Leone Weekly News*, May 28, 1910, 7.
73. "Le Roi est Mort," *Sierra Leone Weekly News*, May 14, 1910, 10.
74. "The Funeral of the King," *Sierra Leone Weekly News*, May 14, 1910, 11.
75. "The Procurators of the King," *Sierra Leone Weekly News*, May 21, 1910, 8.
76. This "London Letter" was not signed, but the humor is very much in keeping with Merriman-Labor's other writing, making it likely he was the author. "London Letter," *Sierra Leone Weekly News*, June 18, 1910, 7.
77. "London Letter," *Sierra Leone Weekly News*, June 18, 1910, 7.
78. "Last Journey through London," *Daily Mirror*, May 21, 1910, 7.
79. "King Edward's Funeral," *Daily Express*, May 21, 1910, 1.
80. "London Letter," *Sierra Leone Weekly News*, June 18, 1910, 7.
81. "London Letter," *Sierra Leone Weekly News*, June 18, 1910, 7.
82. Munro, "Monopolists and Speculators," 277
83. Munro, "Monopolists and Speculators," 271–272. West African wild rubber peaked between 1906 and 1910. Monro goes on to say, "While the distinction between a 'paper' and a 'genuine' company is seldom easily made, the evidence suggests that virtually all of the remaining fifteen wild rubber concerns floated in 1909–10, and possibly even one or two of the plantation companies, were vehicles for financial manipulation in the City rather than for the transfer of capital to Africa. Many were simply fraudulent; all were speculative in the extreme. With their 2s shares they were designed for the 'Penny Bazaar', that section of the rubber shares market which enabled Britain's lower middle classes to join in what had become the national pastime of gambling in rubber shares. Such was the pitch of demand for rubber shares between September 1909 and May 1910 that a second market developed in Mincing Lane, the centre of produce brokerage, while in the Stock Exchange itself there arose some of the wildest mania scenes ever witnessed … it is scarcely surprising that shares of fringe companies, ranging from the wildly optimistic to the outright bogus, should have been dumped upon gullible small investors."
84. National Archives, Kew, BT226/3686, 1913, Merriman-Labor bankruptcy papers.

85. Lorimer, *The Author's Progress*.

86. "Our Position Re. Mr. Labor's 'Britons," *Nigerian Chronicle*, December 3, 1909, 4. Chris Johnson reports he had sold £3 6s worth of books up to 31 May 1910, or 11 copies at 6 shillings. He also pointed out that six shillings was the daily wage for many middle-class workers.

87. "The John Merriman Lectures," *Sierra Leone Weekly News*, August 27, 1910, 1.

7. ON CAREY STREET

1. Quoted in Neil Evans and Ivor Wynne Jones, "Wales and Africa: William Hughes and the Congo Institute," in *A Tolerant Nation? Revisiting Ethnic Diversity in a Devolved Wales*, edited by Charlotte Williams, Neil Evans, and Paul O'Leary (Cardiff: University of Wales Press, 2015), 118.

2. H. Chadwick, *Journal of the Royal African Society* 3, no. 9 (October 1903), 104–106.

3. Merriman-Labor, *A Series of Lectures on the Negro Race*, back flyleaf.

4. Quoted in Christopher Draper and John Lawson-Reay, *Scandal at Congo House: William Hughes and the African Institute, Colwyn Bay: 1856–1924* (Penrhyn Bay: Carreg Gwalch, 2012), 229.

5. Draper and Lawson-Reay, *Scandal at Congo House*, 216–217.

6. Draper and Lawson-Reay, *Scandal at Congo House*, 213–214.

7. Merriman-Labor, *Britons*, 130–132. Arthur Adventurer doesn't appear to be based on any particular individual.

8. Merriman-Labor, *Britons*, 132–134.

9. Merriman-Labor, *Britons*, 135.

10. Thomas Farrow, *The Money-Lender Unmasked* (London, The Roxburghe Press, 1895), 3, 10, 3, 6, 4.

11. "London Money Lenders," *The English Illustrated Magazine*, January 1907, 386.

12. *Truth*, February 2, 1905, 264.

13. *Truth*, February 2, 1905, 264; April 18, 1906, 928; February 9, 1905, 348.

14. National Archives, Kew, BT226/3686, 1913, Merriman-Labor bankruptcy papers.

15. Letter, May 2, 1913, National Archives, Kew, BT226/3686, 1913, Merriman-Labor bankruptcy papers. "Until 1911 I was called Merriman-Labor. My father's name was Joshua William Labor—I ceased to use the name Labor in 1911 but did not change it by Deed Poll, but gave notice to my creditors, Inns of Court, & friends."

16. *African World and Cape Cairo-Express*, July, 8, 1911, 508.

17. *Sierra Leone Guardian and Foreign Mails*, August 30, 1912, 10.

18. Susan Pennybacker, "The Universal Races Congress, London, Political Culture, and Imperial Dissent, 1900–1939," *Radical History Review* 2005, no. 92 (Spring 2005), 103–117.

19. Advertisement for "Papers on Inter-Racial Problems," *The Crisis*, January 1912, 94.

20. Helen Tilley, "Racial Science, Geopolitics, and Empires: Paradoxes of Power," *Isis* 105, no. 4 (December 2014), 774.

21. "London Letter," *Sierra Leone Weekly News*, August 5, 1911, 9.

22. "London Letter," *Sierra Leone Weekly News*, August 19, 1911, 8. Merriman-Labor's old friend and mentor Edward Blyden was a supporter, but was seriously ill and unable to come.

23. Sierra Leoneans John Eldred Taylor and T.J. Thompson participated. They were both friends with Merriman-Labor, making it even more surprising to find his name absent on the list of attendees. The publication was the 548-page *Papers on Inter-Racial Problems Communicated to the Universal Races Congress, held at the University of London, July 26–29, 1911*

24. "Books and Writers," *Church Times*, July 14, 1911, 56. Review of *Half a Man: The Status of the Negro in New York* by Mary White Ovington, introduced by Dr. Franz Boas of Columbia University.

25. Dr. Frances Hoggan, "The Negro Problem in Relation to White Women," in *Papers on Interracial Problems Communicated to the First Universal Races Congress Held at the University of London, July 26–29, 1911*, edited by Gustav Spiller (London: P.S. King and Son, and Boston: World's Peace Foundation, 1911), 364.

26. "London Letter," *Sierra Leone Weekly News*, August 19, 1911, 8. The correspondent confuses the title of Du Bois's speech. Harry H. Johnstone gave the "World Politics of the Negro" paper. Du Bois gave the paper "The Negro Race in the United State of America."

27. Elliott M. Rudwick, "W.E.B. Du Bois and the Universal Races Congress of 1911," *Phylon Quarterly* 20, no. 4 (1959), 375.

28. Quoted in Ulysses G. Weatherly, "The First Universal Races Congress," *American Journal of Sociology* 17, no. 3 (November 1911), 327.

29. Rudwick, "W.E.B. Du Bois and the Universal Races Congress of 1911," 371.

30. Read, *Documents from Edwardian England 1901–1915*, 48.

31. National Archives, Kew, BT226/3686, 1913, Merriman-Labor bankruptcy papers.

32. National Archives, Kew, BT226/3686, 1913, Merriman-Labor bankruptcy papers. He only owed the principal, not interest, suggesting he may have been paying the exorbitant interest all along. The note to

Rev. John Harris, June 28, 1912, gives only "Birkbeck Bank Chambers" as his address with no office number, suggesting he no longer rented an office there, but probably paid a small sum to receive letters.

33. Anti-Slavery Papers, Rhodes House, MSS Brit. Emp. S22, G 431, Bodleian Library of Commonwealth and African Studies at Rhodes House, Letter to J.H. Harris from A.B. Merriman, June 28, 1912.

34. This would be the Conference with Africans, a joint program of the Antislavery and Aborigines' Protection Society as well as the African Society held on April 18, 1913 at the Westminster Palace Hotel.

35. *Daily Express*, April 18, 1912, 1.

36. *Daily Express*, April 16, 1912, 7.

37. "Titanic's Wireless Signal Brings Vessels to Scene," *Daily Mirror*, April 16, 1912, 2.

38. "How the Titanic Met Her Fate," *Daily Express*, April 17, 1912, 1.

39. "London Letter," *Sierra Leone Weekly News*, May 11, 1912, 8

40. "The S.S. Titanic," *Sierra Leone Guardian and Foreign Mails*, May 24, 1912, 7.

41. "Selling Like Hot Loaves," *Sierra Leone Weekly News*, November 16, 1912, 4.

42. Philip Mauro, *The Titanic Catastrophe and Its Lessons* (London: Morgan and Scott, 1912). Described in D. Brian Anderson, *The Titanic in Print and on Screen* (Jefferson, N.C.: McFarland and Co., 2005), 37.

43. http://www.icyousee.org/titanic.html.

44. "Titanic's Lost Crew," *Daily Express*, April 18, 1912, 5.

45. "Titanic's Lost Crew," *Daily Express*, April 18, 1912, 5.

46. "Anti-Slavery and Aborigines Protection Society," *Sierra Leone Weekly News*, November 23, 1912.

47. National Archives, Kew, BT226/3686, 1913, Merriman-Labor bankruptcy papers.

48. Draper and Lawson-Reay, *Scandal at Congo House*, 236.

49. Special Correspondent, "A Baptist Mission Scandal—1: How Natives are Prepared for the Ministry," *John Bull*, December 16, 1911, 858; "A Baptist Mission Scandal—II: A Black Scoundrel's Record—Rich Ladies and 'Converted' Negroes," *John Bull*, December 23, 1911, 904.

50. Draper and Lawson-Reay, *Scandal at Congo House*, 172.

51. Draper and Lawson-Reay, *Scandal at Congo House*, 238.

52. Draper and Lawson-Reay, *Scandal at Congo House*, 273.

53. Evans and Jones, "Wales and Africa," 120.

54. "'John Bull' and the African Institute," *Derby Daily Telegraph*, June 14, 1912, 4.

55. A.J.A Morris, "Bottomley, Horatio William (1860–1933), journalist and swindler, *Oxford Dictionary of National Biography*, http://www.oxforddnb.com/view/article/31981.

56. "Death of M. Labor," *Sierra Leone Guardian and Foreign Mails*, August 30, 1912, 10.

57. "Death of M. Labor," *Sierra Leone Guardian and Foreign Mails*, August 30, 1912, 10.

58. Quoted in Jeffery Green, *Samuel Taylor-Coleridge: A Musical Life* (London: Pickering and Chatto, 2011), 205.

59. Thanks to Jeff Green for the observation that Coleridge-Taylor's father could have known Merriman-Labor's mother in the Gambia. They both lived in Bathurst in the 1890s.

60. Green, *Samuel Taylor-Coleridge*, 208.

61. Green, *Samuel Taylor Coleridge*, 210.

62. "Forward," *African Times and Orient Review*, July 1912, 1. Ali's origins have been disputed; he claimed to be the son of an Egyptian army officer and a Sudanese woman.

63. "Forward," *African Times and Orient Review*, July 1912, 1.

64. "In the Land of the Pharaohs," *Sierra Leone Weekly News*, March 25, 1911, 8.

65. I. Duffield, "The Business Activities of Duse Mohamed Ali," *Journal of the Historical Society of Nigeria* (June 4, 1969), 571. From the summer of 1912 to winter 1913, the *African Times and Orient Review* was a monthly. For a short period in 1914—March to August—it came out weekly. But its publication was suspended for two years when it was "banned in India and the British African colonies." It was once again published as a monthly from early 1917 to the fall of 1918. The Marcus Garvey and Universal Negro Improvement Association Papers Project, A Research Project of the James S. Coleman African Studies Center, African Series Sample Documents, vol. VIII: October 1913—June 1921, UCLA African Studies Center, http://www.international.ucla.edu/asc/mgpp/sample08.

66. "To Parents and Guardians," "Our Lecture Department," *African Times and Orient Review*, July 1913, 29; "Suitable Hotels and Apartments," August 1913, 58.

67. Ali appears in Merriman's letter to John Harris listing prominent Africans in London and their addresses. Merriman's trip to Sierra Leone in 1914 is announced in the *African Times and Orient Review*, "Augustus Merriman," April 14, 1914, 84.

68. National Archives, Kew, BT226/3686, 1913, Merriman-Labor bankruptcy papers.

69. National Archives, Kew, BT226/3686, 1913, Merriman-Labor bankruptcy papers.

70. "University and Law Academy," *Sierra Leone Weekly News*, January 18, 1913, 15.

71. "Tradesman! Merchant!," *Sierra Leone Weekly News*, January 18, 1913, 18.

72. National Archives, Kew, BT226/3686, 1913, Merriman-Labor bankruptcy papers.

73. National Archives, Kew, BT226/3686, 1913, Merriman-Labor bankruptcy papers.

74. "Women Smash London Windows," *New York Times*, November 22, 1911, 2.

75. "Conference with Africans." *Journal of the Royal African Society* 12, no. 48 (July 1913), 425.

76. "Conference with Africans in London," *Anti-Slavery Reporter and Aborigines' Friend* 3, no. 2 (July 1913), 51.

77. "Conference with Africans in London," *Anti-Slavery Reporter and Aborigines' Friend*, 53, 57.

78. "Conference with Africans in London," *The Anti-Slavery Reporter and Aborigines' Friend*, 57.

79. "Conference with Africans in London," *Anti-Slavery Reporter and Aborigines' Friend*, 57.

80. "Conference with Africans," *Journal of the African Society*, 428.

81. "Conference with Africans in London," *Anti-Slavery Reporter and Aborigines' Friend*, 59.

82. "Conference with Africans," *Journal of the African Society*, 430.

83. "Conference with Africans in London," *The Anti-Slavery Reporter and Aborigines' Friend*, 60.

84. Conference with Africans in London," *Anti-Slavery Reporter and Aborigines' Friend*, 57; "Conference with Africans," *Journal of the African Society*, 429.

85. A euphemism for going bankrupt.

86. National Archives, Kew, BT226/3686, 1913, Merriman-Labor bankruptcy papers. A look at his bankruptcy papers shows that he had paid off at least a portion of nearly all the debts he owed.

87. National Archives, Kew, BT226/3686, 1913, Merriman-Labor bankruptcy papers.

88. "Death of Dr. E. James Hayford, MD, MRCS, LRCP, Barrister-at Law: In the Land of Strangers, Another National Loss," *Gold Coast Nation*, August 21, 1913, 3.

89. "Dr. E. James Hayford, MD, MRCS, LRCP, &c, &c, &c, Barrister-at Law: Death and Burial," *Gold Coast Nation*, September 4, 1913, 2.

90. "Death of Dr. E. James Hayford, MD, MRCS, LRCP, Barrister-at Law: In the Land of Strangers, Another National Loss," *Gold Coast Nation*, August 21, 1913, 4.

91. "Dr. E. James Hayford ... Death and Burial," *Gold Coast Nation*, September 4, 1913, 2.

92. "The Gambia: An Interview," *Sierra Leone Guardian and Foreign Mails*, October 24, 1913, 14.
93. "BURMESE WHO HAS BEEN NOMINATED," *Daily Mirror*, November 4, 1913, 1.
94. "Black Mayor of Battersea," *Daily Express*, November 11, 1913, 1. The second black mayor in Britain, Archer was the first black mayor of a London borough. The first black mayor was Allen Glaser Minns, a Bahamian doctor elected in Thetford, Norfolk, during 1904.
95. "'Black Mayor of Battersea," *Daily Express*, November 11, 1913, 1
96. "A Colored Mayor in London," *The Crisis*, January 1914, 120.
97. "'Black Mayor of Battersea," *Daily Express*, November 11, 1913, 1.
98. "'Black Mayor of Battersea," *Daily Express*, November 11, 1913, 1
99. "'Black Mayor of Battersea," *Daily Express*, November 11, 1913, 1
100. "Mr. Augustus Merriman," *Sierra Leone Guardian and Foreign Mails*, May 22, 1914, 9.
101. Fyfe, *History of Sierra Leone*, 527–528.

8. DULCE ET DECORUM EST

1. "Mr. Augustus Merriman," *Sierra Leone Guardian*, May 22, 1914, 9.
2. "Mr. Merriman's Lectures," *Sierra Leone Guardian*, My 29, 1914, 9
3. "Mr. Merriman's Lecture," *Sierra Leone Weekly News*, May 30, 1914, 10.
4. "Mr. Merriman's Lecture," *Sierra Leone Weekly News*, May 30, 1914, 10.
5. "Mr. Merriman's Lecture," *Sierra Leone Weekly News*, May 30, 1914, 10; National Archives, Kew, BT226/3686, 1913, Merriman-Labor bankruptcy papers. The number probably comes from adding the £125 settlement to payments he had earned for writing reports.
6. "Mr. Merriman's Lecture," *Colonial and Provincial Reporters*, June 13, 1914, 10.
7. "Mr. Merriman's Lecture," *Colonial and Provincial Reporters*, June 13, 1914, 10.
8. "Disbar of Augustus Merriman: Petition to the Masters of the Bench of Lincoln's Inn to Re-open the Case," Merriman-Labor file, Lincoln's Inn Archive.
9. The assassination story was reported in both Mozambique and South Africa on June 30.
10. Catriona Pennell, *A Kingdom United: Popular Responses to the Outbreak of the First World War in Britain and Ireland* (Cambridge: Cambridge University Press, 2014), 30.
11. Pennell, *A Kingdom United*, 30.
12. Michael MacDonagh, *In London during the Great War: The Diary of a Journalist* (London: Eyre and Spottiswoode, 1935), 8.

13. MacDonagh, *In London during the Great War*, 9.

14. Margot Asquith, *The Autobiography of Margot Asquith* (London: Weidenfeld and Nicholson, 1995), 294.

15. MacDonagh, *In London during the Great War*, 10.

16. T. Wilson, *The Myriad Faces of War: Britain and the Great War, 1914–1918* (London: Faber and Faber, 2010), 155.

17. Wilson, *Myriad Faces of War*, 11.

18. Quoted in Pennell, *A Kingdom United*, 158.

19. Adrian Gregory, *The Last Great War: British Society and the First World War* (Cambridge: Cambridge University Press, 2008), 75.

20. MacDonagh, *London in the Great War*, 25.

21. Gregory, *The Last Great War*, 74.

22. Gregory, *The Last Great War*, 279.

23. "Britain's Ebony Troops," *African Telegraph and Gold Coast Mirror*, November 14, 1914, 7.

24. Quoted in Richard Smith, "Nationalism, Pan-Africanism and Jamaican memory," in *Race, Empire and the First World War*, edited by Santanu Das (Cambridge: Cambridge University Press, 2011), 268.

25. "Is a Black Army Desirable?" *Lagos Weekly Record*, December 16, 1916, 4.

26. "The European War," *Colonial and Provincial Reporter*, August 8, 1914, 6.

27. "Britain's Ebony Troops," *Telegraph*, November 14, 1914, 7.

28. David Killingray, "African Voices from Two World Wars, *Historical Research* 74, no 186 (November 2001), 432.

29. "The Employment of Black Troops," *Birmingham Daily Post*, June 3, 1915, 6.

30. David Killingray, "Black Colonial Soldiers in the British Army during the First and Second World Wars," unpublished lecture, 6.

31. Killingray, "Black Colonial Soldiers," 7.

32. "Britain's Ebony Troops," *Telegraph*, November 14, 1914, 7.

33. Quoted in David Killingray, "The Idea of a British Imperial African Army," *Journal of African History* 20, no. 3 (1979), 425.

34. Christian Koller, "The Recruitment of Colonial Troops in Africa and Asia and Their Deployment in Europe during the First World War, *Immigrants and Minorities* 26, no. 1–2 (March/July 2008), 113–114. Churchill may have intended to use black troops to reduce the number of whites killed.

35. Killingray, "The Idea of a British Imperial African Army," 423

36. Killingray, "The Idea of a British Imperial African Army," 425.

37. Killingray, "The Idea of a British Imperial African Army," 425.

38. Quoted in Koller, "The Recruitment of Colonial Troops," 126.

39. Koller, "The Recruitment of Colonial Troops," 120
40. Koller, "The Recruitment of Colonial Troops," 119.
41. Koller, "The Recruitment of Colonial Troops," 119.
42. According to Koller, there is "much confusion over casualty rate of African troops" and "the cannon fodder thesis can be neither entirely verified nor falsified by interpreting statistic." However, he does argue that the work of John Harris Lunn suggests that the idea of Africans used as cannon fodder was real.
43. Koller, "The Recruitment of Colonial Troops," 120.
44. Koller, "The Recruitment of Colonial Troops," 120.
45. M.L. Sanders "Wellington House and British Propaganda during the First World War," *Historical Journal* 18, no. 1 (March 1975), 119.
46. Peter Buitenhuis, *The Great War of Words: Literature as Propaganda 1914–18 and After* (London: B.T. Batsford, 1989), xvi.
47. Buitenhuis, *The Great War of Words*, xvii.
48. "The Creation of Difficulties by Ourselves for Ourselves," *Sierra Leone Weekly News*, August 8, 1914, 16.
49. Pennell, *A Kingdom United*, 105–106.
50. Pennell, *A Kingdom United*, 100–101.
51. MacDonagh, *London in the Great War*, 15.
52. MacDonagh, *London in the Great War*, 19.
53. Merriman-Labor, *Britons*, 157.
54. Alan Simpson explains that there were a small number of searchlights in London at the start of the war, and in September 1914 Winston Churchill had ordered more. During the first Zeppelin raid on London, May 31—June 1, he says "the air defences of London had grown to include twelve acetylene gas-powered searchlights manned initially by 120 special constables." *Air Raids on South West Essex in the Great War: Looking for Zeppelins at Leyton* (Barnsley: Pen and Sword Aviation, 2015).
55. "At a meeting of the Special Committee appointed to consider a complaint against a Barrister of this Honourable Society there held on the 12th Day of November 1915," Disbarment papers, Merriman-Labor File, Lincoln's Inn Archive.
56. National Archives, Kew, BT 31/22608/138481, Board of Trade Dissolved Companies file: Literature Limited.
57. National Archives, Kew, BT 31/22608/138481, Board of Trade Dissolved Companies file: Literature Limited. Clay is only "Mr. Clay" when Merriman-Labor meets him in 1905, but I speculate he was George Clay.
58. National Archives, Kew, BT 31/22608/138481, Board of Trade Dissolved Companies file: Literature Limited.

59. P.E. Dewey, "Military Recruiting and the British Labour Force during the First World War" *Historical Journal* 27, no. 1 (1984), 199.

60. MacDonagh, *In London during the Great War*, 47–48.

61. http://collections.vam.ac.uk/item/O74621/daddy-what-did-you-do-poster-lumley-savile/.

62. John McDermott "'A Needless Sacrifice': British Businessmen and Business as Usual in the First World War," *Albion: A Quarterly Journal Concerned with British Studies* 21, no. 2 (summer 1989), 273. A Chamber of Commerce was the professional organization for importers and exporters.

63. "Disbar of Augustus Merriman, Petition to the Masters of the Bench of Lincoln's Inn to Re-open the Case," Disbarment papers, Merriman-Labor File, Lincoln's Inn.

64. Letter, Cole to Merriman, January 21, 1915, "Mr. Augustus Merriman and the Honourable Society of Lincoln's Inn: Statement on Behalf of the Society," 9–10, Disbarment, Merriman-Labor File, Lincoln's Inn Archive.

65. Letter, Merriman to Cole, February 16, 1915, "Mr. Augustus Merriman and the Honourable Society of Lincoln's Inn: Statement on Behalf of the Society," Disbarment papers, Merriman-Labor File, Lincoln's Inn Archive, 10.

66. Letter, Cole to Merriman, March 3, 1915. Mr. Augustus Merriman and the Honourable Society of Lincoln's Inn: Statement on Behalf of the Society," Disbarment papers, Merriman-Labor File, Lincoln's Inn Archive, 10–11.

67. "At a meeting of the Special Committee appointed to consider a complaint against a Barrister of this Honourable Society there held on the 12th Day of November 1915," Disbarment papers, Merriman-Labor File, Lincoln's Inn Archive.

68. "Disbar of Augustus Merriman: Petition to the Masters of the Bench of Lincoln's Inn to Re-open the Case," and "Mr. Augustus Merriman and the Honourable Society of Lincoln's Inn: Statement on Behalf of the Society," 17, Disbarment papers, Merriman-Labor File, Lincoln's Inn Archive.

69. "Disbar of Augustus Merriman: Petition to the Masters of the Bench of Lincoln's Inn to Re-open the Case," and "Mr. Augustus Merriman and the Honourable Society of Lincoln's Inn: Statement on Behalf of the Society," Disbarment papers, Merriman-Labor File, Lincoln's Inn Archive, 27.

70. Only 38 students kept terms in 1916. P.V. Baker, ed., *The Records of the Honorable Society of Lincoln's Inn: The Black Books*, vol. 6 (Oxford and Northampton: Honourable Society of Lincoln's Inn: 2001), 101–102.

71. Arthur Marwick, *The Deluge: British Society and the First World War* (New York: Norton and Company, 1965), 245.
72. "Elder Dempster suffered the loss of a total of 42 ships during the period covering the First World War (4th August 1914 to 11th November 1918), and 30 of these ships were lost as a direct result of enemy action." See http://www.rakaia.co.uk/downloads/elder-dempster-summary.pdf.
73. Marwick, *The Deluge*, 125.
74. Marwick, *The Deluge*, 127.

9. MERCY DWELLS NOT HERE

1. Description of Beresford Square and the hiring process at the Arsenal inspired by A.K. Foxwell, *Munition Lasses: Six Months as Principal Overlooker in Danger Buildings* (London: Hodder and Stoughton, 1917) and Peggy Hamilton, *Three Years or the Duration* (London: Peter Owen Publishers, 1978).
2. Jay Winter and Jean-Louis Robert, *Capital Cities at War: Paris, London, Berlin 1914–1919* (Cambridge: Cambridge University Press, 1997), 270.
3. Killingray, "Black Colonial Soldiers in the British Army," 6.
4. "On the Sick List," *The African Telegraph*, April 1919, 172.
5. Merriman's employment records at the Arsenal were destroyed a hundred years after his date of birth. See *The Work of the RE in the European War, 1914–1919, Supply of Engineer Stores and Equipment* (Chatham: W and J Mackay, Ltd., 1921), especially chapter 4, "Inspection Division."
6. Hamilton, *Three Years*, 30.
7. Hamilton, *Three Years*, 30.
8. Hamilton *Three Years*, 31.
9. See Foxwell, *Munition Lasses*.
10. "Juvenile Employment in Great Britain," *Monthly Review of the U.S. Bureau of Labor Statistics* 3, no. 6 (December 1916), 93.
11. Frederick A. Edwards, "The Air Raids on London," *Quarterly Review*, no. 469 (October 1921), 270–271.
12. Wilson, *Myriad Faces of War*, 157.
13. "Augustus Merriman and the Honourable Society of Lincoln's Inn. Statement on Behalf of the Society," Disbarment papers, Merriman-Labor file, Lincoln's Inn Archive, 11, 13.
14. "Augustus Merriman and the Honourable Society of Lincoln's Inn: Statement on Behalf of the Society," Disbarment papers, Merriman-Labor file, Lincoln's Inn Archive, 13, 14.
15. "Disbar of Augustus Merriman: Petition to the Masters of the Bench

of Lincoln's Inn to Re-open the case. Disbarment papers, Merriman-Labor file, Lincoln's Inn Archive.

16. "Augustus Merriman and the Honourable Society of Lincoln's Inn: Statement on Behalf of the Society," Disbarment papers, Merriman-Labor file, Lincoln's Inn Archive, 14, 15.

17. "Mr. Merriman's Letter," *Sierra Leone Weekly News*, February 5, 1916, 7.

18. Letter, Curzon Brothers to J.C Cole, 24 September 1915, Disbarment papers, Merriman-Labor file, Lincoln's Inn Archive.

19. R.J.O. Adams and Philip P. Poirier, *The Conscription Controversy in Great Britain, 1900–1918* (Columbus, OH: Ohio State University Press, 1987), 98.

20. "The records of individuals, which were collected in 1915 to form the National Register, do not survive. The Register itself was never centralised; information was collected by local registration authorities on forms filled in by each individual. The majority of these forms remained with the local registration authorities as long as the National Register Act remained in force (1915–1919). A few records of individuals were transferred to the General Register Office during this period. In 1919, however, provision was made for the destruction of all these records, whether they were held centrally or locally, by a schedule dated 19 December 1919, under the terms of the Public Records Act, 1877." See http://webarchive.nationalarchives.gov.uk/+/http://yourarchives.nationalarchives.gov.uk/index.php?title=National_Register.

21. Marwick, *The Deluge*, 79–80.

22. Hamilton, *Three Years*, 72.

23. Merriman-Labor, *Britons*, 158.

24. Marwick, *The Deluge*, 164.

25. "The German Army dispersed chlorine gas over Allied lines at Ypres on 22 April 1915,".*New York Tribune*, April 27, 1915; WWI Document Archive, 1915 Documents, http://wwi.lib.byu.edu/index.php/The Use of_Poison_Gas.

26. "The German Army dispersed chlorine gas," *New York Tribune*, April 27, 1915.

27. http://www.firstworldwar.com/diaries/firstgasattack.htm; Anthony R. Hossack, in *Everyman at War*, edited by C.B. Purdom (London: J.M. Dent, 1930).

28. Marwick, *The Deluge*, 136; Wilson, *Myriad Faces of War*, 157.

29. This letter no longer survives, but I surmise that this is how Merriman first heard of the benchers' decision to evaluate the complaint.

30. "Mr. Merriman's Books in Preparation," *Sierra Leone Guardian*, October

3, 1915. 13. He invented the word "monetic"—probably drawn from the word "monetize"—to stress the difficulty of converting an asset (say, a book manuscript) into cash during wartime.

31. "War and the Book Trade," *Review of Reviews* 51, no. 302 (February 1915), 156–157; "Reading in War Time," *The Bookman* 48, no. 287 (1915), 126–127.

32. Notes for "A Meeting of the Special Committee appointed to consider a complaint against a Barrister of this Hon. Society—there held the 8th day of November 1915," Disbarment papers, Merriman-Labor file, Lincoln's Inn Archive.

33. Beaumont's *Times* obituary quoted at http://www.saxonlodge.net/getperson.php?personID=I1164&tree=Tatham.

34. William Robert Sheldon, 1911 Census, ancestry.co.uk.

35. *Lincoln's Inn Black Books*, vol. 6, 85; Edwards, "Air Raids on London," 274.

36. Edwards, "Air Raids on London," 274.

37. "At a Meeting of the Special Committee appointed to consider a complaint against a Barrister of this Honourable Society there held the 22nd day of October 1915," Disbarment papers, Merriman-Labor file, Lincoln's Inn Archives.

38. "At a Meeting of the Special Committee appointed to consider a complaint against a Barrister of this Honourable Society there held the 22nd day of October 1915," Disbarment papers, Merriman-Labor file, Lincoln's Inn Archives.

39. "Mr. Merriman's Letter," *Sierra Leone Weekly News*, February 2, 1916, 7.

40. A private limited company did not sell shares to outside investors, nor were such companies part of the Stock Exchange. They did not need to "disclose details of business in ways expected of companies whose shareholders included a wider public." R.H. Helmholz and John H. Baker, eds., *The Oxford History of the Laws of England*, vol. 12 (Oxford: Oxford University Press, 2010), 667.

41. "Mr. Merriman's Letter," *Sierra Leone Weekly News*, February 2, 1916, 7.

42. "At a Meeting of the Special Committee appointed to consider a complaint against a Barrister of this Honourable Society there held the 22nd day of October 1915," Disbarment papers, Merriman-Labor file, Lincoln's Inn Archive, 20, 21.

43. Letter from Steward of Lincoln's Inn (Thomas Weatherley Marriott) to Curzon Brothers, October 25, 1915, Disbarment papers, Merriman-Labor file, Lincoln's Inn Archive.

44. "Mr. Augustus Merriman and the Honourable Society of Lincoln's Inn: Statement on Behalf of the Society," Disbarment papers, Merriman-Labor file, Lincoln's Inn Archive, 20, 21.

45. W. Wesley Pue quoted in *Oxford History of the Laws of England, 1820–1914*, vol. 12 (Oxford: Oxford University Press, 2010), 1097.

46. Email from Patrick Polden to author, May 20, 1914. My thanks to Professor Patrick Polden for this insight.

47. "Barred by Colour," *African Times and Orient Review*, May 1913, 334. Reprinted from the *Manchester Evening Chronicle*.

48. Professor Polden points out that there was no need for any official rules preventing colonials from practicing in Britain. "The 'gatekeepers—chamber clerks and solicitors—would have been hostile." Email correspondence, May 20, 1914.

49. "Barred by Colour," *African Times and Orient Review*, May 1913, 334.

50. Henry Hesketh Bell, "His Highness Prince Kwakoo," *The Idler*, December 1886, 687.

51. Henry Hesketh Bell, "His Highness Prince Kwakoo," *The Idler*, December 1886, 687, 689.

52. Paul Trent [pseudonym for Edward Platt], *A Wife by Purchase* (London: John Milne, 1909). David Killingray points out that Carl Reindorf (1834–1917) was an evangelical pastor who worked for the Basel Mission in the Gold Coast and was alive at the time Trent published his novel.

53. Trent, *A Wife by Purchase*, 34. Also see Grant Allen [pseudonym for J. Arbuthnot Wilson] *Strange Stories* (London: Chatto and Windus, 1884), 2: When "Ethel Berry's soul" is "stirred to its inmost depths" by the story of a "real African negro ... taken from a slaver on the Gold coast when he was a child, and brought to England to be educated," who got a degree from Oxford and became a vicar, her uncle, an "old coaster", assures her that "I've been a good bit on the Coast in my time" and "a nigger's a nigger whatever you do with him. The Ethiopian cannot change his skin, the Scripture says, nor the leopard his spots, and a nigger he'll be to the end of his days; you mark my words, Emily."

54. "Mr. Augustus Merriman and the Honourable Society of Lincoln's Inn: Statement on Behalf of the Society," Disbarment papers, Merriman-Labor file, Lincoln's Inn Archive, 4.

55. "Mr. Augustus Merriman and the Honourable Society of Lincoln's Inn: Statement on Behalf of the Society," Disbarment papers, Merriman-Labor file, Lincoln's Inn Archive, 5.

56. Leaming, *A Philadelphia Lawyer*, x, 68.

57. Email from Patrick Polden to author, May 20, 2014.

58. Merriman-Labor, *Britons*, 137; Fyfe, *History of Sierra Leone*, 616.

59. Loyal to the colonial government, Coker and his friends "suspended all appeals for redress until after the war, because they did not wish

to be thought guilty of embarrassing the Government during the increasingly anxious stages of the European conflict." Once the war was over, there was "no restoration to position, no payment of salary, nothing for the lapsed pension, nothing whatever for legal fees (over £500)," only £100 award. John Harris, "The 'New Attitude' of the African," *Fortnightly*, December 1920, 957–958. Harris was the secretary of the Anti-Slavery and Aborigines' Protection Society from 1910.

60. Merriman-Labor, *Britons*, 138

61. Letter to Steward of Lincoln's Inn, November 30, 1915, Disbarment papers, Merriman-Labor file, Lincoln's Inn Archive.

62. "The Benchers of Lincoln's Inn and Mr. Merriman," *Sierra Leone Weekly News*, January 1, 1916, 12.

63. "Disbar of Augustus Merriman: Petition to the Masters of the Bench of Lincoln's Inn to Re-open the case," Disbarment papers, Merriman-Labor file, Lincoln's Inn Archive.

64. "Augustus Merriman and the Honourable Society of Lincoln's Inn: Statement on Behalf of the Society," Disbarment papers, Merriman-Labor file, Lincoln's Inn Archive, 22.

65. "Mr. Merriman's Letter," *Sierra Leone Weekly News*, February 5, 1916, 7.

66. "Augustus Merriman and the Honourable Society of Lincoln's Inn: Statement on Behalf of the Society," Disbarment papers, Merriman-Labor file, Lincoln's Inn Archive, 22.

67. "Mr. Merriman's Letter," *Sierra Leone Weekly News*, February 5, 1916, 7.

68. Email to author, May 20, 1914.

69. "Mr. Merriman's Letter," *Sierra Leone Weekly News*, February 5, 1916, 7.

70. "Concerning Mr. Merriman's Letter," *Sierra Leone Weekly News*, February 12, 1916, 10.

71. "Concerning Mr. Merriman's Letter," *Sierra Leone Weekly News*, February 12, 1916, 10.

72. "Augustus Merriman and the Honourable Society of Lincoln's Inn: Statement on Behalf of the Society," Disbarment papers, Merriman-Labor file, Lincoln's Inn Archive, 23.

73. The young writer Virginia Woolf had written in 1916 that the sounds of guns in France sounded like "the beating of gigantic carpets by gigantic women" in "Heard on the Downs: The Generation of Myth," *The Times*, August 15, 1916.

74. Claud Schuster [secretary to the Lord Chancellor] to Justice Lawrence, Letter, July 3, 1916, Disbarment papers, Merriman-Labor file, Lincoln's Inn Archive.

75. MacDonagh, *London in the Great War*, 109.

76. Imperial War Museum: http://www.iwm.org.uk/collections/item/object/28449.

77. Hamilton, *Three Years*, 72.

78. "Re the Disbar of Augustus Merriman by the Benchers of Lincolns Inn to the Right Honourable the Lord High Chancellor of Great Britain, et al.," April 7, 1916, Disbarment papers, Merriman-Labor file, Lincoln's Inn Archive.

79. "Re the Disbar of Augustus Merriman by the Benchers of Lincoln's Inn to the Right Honourable the Lord High Chancellor of Great Britain, et al.," April 7, 1916, Disbarment papers, Merriman-Labor file, Lincoln's Inn Archive.

80. Hugh H.L. Bellot, *Inner and Middle Temple: Legal, Literary, and Historic Associations* (London: Methuen and Co., 1902), 285.

81. *Lincoln's Inn Black Books*, vol. 5, 99.

82. Patrick Polden notes that this would not have been extraordinary.

83. W.R. Lethaby, *Leadwork Old and Ornamental and for the Most Part English* (London: Macmillan and Co., 1893), 99.

84. The poem had been printed several times in the eighteenth and nineteenth century. See, for example, "Poetical Essays," *Scots Magazine* 8 (December 1746), 575.

85. Email from Professor McSamuel "Mac" Dixon-Fyle to author, June 11, 2014: "'Ohlohr,' variously spelled, is a popular Krio name, I believe from the Yoruba roots. I have known several folks called 'Ollor' over the years, in both Freetown and Lagos."

86. Alternatively spelled "Maiji" in "On the Sick List," *African Telegraph*, April 1916, 172.

87. "On the Sick List," *African Telegraph*, April 1916, 172. Merriman, it records, had been working as an inspector at Woolwich for the duration of the war.

88. Merriman-Labor renewed his reader's ticket under the name Merriman-Labor, March 7, 1916.

89. Transcript of letter from S.O. Logemoh to Dusé Mohamed Ali, UCLA African Studies Center, http://web.international.ucla.edu/africa/mgpp/sample08. In February 1917, in a letter to Dusé Mohamed Ali, Liberian entrepreneur S. O'Kagoo Logemoh asked to be put into contact with "lawyer Merriman." Fellow Sierra Leonean John Eldred Taylor announces his illness in 1918. At his death in 1919, he was still friends with the Hillier family. In the obituary published by the *Sierra Leone Guardian*, his uncle mentions the many young people to whom he was a "get help" who would miss him.

90. MacDonagh, *In London during the Great War*, 180.

91. Merriman-Labor, *Britons*, 42.

92. Merriman-Labor, *Britons*, 45; MacDonagh, *In London during the Great War*, 119.

93. MacDonagh, *In London during the Great War*, 131.
94. Foxwell, *Munition Lasses*, 127.
95. MacDonagh, *In London during the Great War*, 136.
96. Foxwell, *Munition Lasses*, 127.
97. MacDonagh, *In London during the Great War*, 136.
98. MacDonagh, *In London during the Great War*, 150.
99. See http://greatwarlondon.wordpress.com/2012/01/19/the-silvertown-explosion/.
100. Wilson, *Myriad Faces of War*, 512.
101. Marwick, *The Deluge*, 194.
102. See http://www.rakaia.co.uk/downloads/elder-dempster-summary.pdf.
103. Quoted in "Editorial Notes," *Gold Coast Leader*, August 25, 1917, 4.
104. Quoted in "Editorial Notes," *Gold Coast Leader*, August 25, 1917, 4. Earlier that year, in February, 600 men from the South African Native Labour Corps had been drowned when the S.S. *Mendi* was rammed and sunk. "The white parliament stood in silent respect, the only time Africans were so remembered." Killingray, "African Voices from Two World Wars," 435.
105. *West Africa*. July 14,1917, 409.

10. THE WEARINESS, THE FEVER, THE FRET

1. Sheldon F. Dudley, "The Biology of Epidemic Influenza, Illustrated by Naval Experience," *Proceedings of the Royal Society of Medicine* (War Section) 14, no. 37 (1920–21), 45
2. Governor Wilkinson's report, National Archives, Kew, CO 267/587, Influenza Epidemic, Sierra Leone Report 53257, 3.
3. Governor Wilkinson's report, National Archives, Kew, CO 267/587, Influenza Epidemic, Sierra Leone Report 53257, 5.
4. "The Health of Freetown," *Sierra Leone Weekly News*, August 31, 1918, 11.
5. "Medical Department and the Influenza Epidemic," *Colonial and Provincial Reporter*, September 28, 1918, 5; W.F. Campbell, Medical Officer Report, National Archives, Kew, CO 267/587, Influenza Epidemic, Sierra Leone Report 53257, 4.
6. "The Health of Freetown, no. 2," *Sierra Leone Weekly News*, September 7, 1918, 8.
7. "Deaths for the Week," *Sierra Leone Weekly News*, September 14, 1918, 12.
8. "The Health of Freetown," *Sierra Leone Weekly News*, August 31, 1918, 11.
9. "Notice on Account of the Epidemic of Influenza," *Sierra Leone Weekly News*, August 31, 1918, 8.
10. Sandra M. Tomkins, "Colonial Administration in British Africa during

the Influenza Epidemic of 1918–1919," *Canadian Journal of African Studies* 28, no. 1 (1994), 74.

11. "The Prevailing Epidemic and Some of Its Lessons," *Sierra Leone Weekly News*, September 14, 1918, 8.

12. "Concerning the Influenza Epidemic," *Colonial and Provincial Reporters*, September 14, 1918, 5.

13. W.F. Campbell, Medical Officer Report, National Archives, Kew, CO 267/587, Influenza Epidemic, Sierra Leone Report 53257, 2.

14. "The Health of the Colony," *Sierra Leone Guardian*, September 20, 1918, 4. Some people who had come to Freetown for work fled back to the Protectorate to escape the pestilence. Boat owners doubled their prices and overfilled their crafts with people desperate to leave. In one instance, reported by the *Sierra Leone Weekly News*, "a strong gust of wind upset the canoe and all hands on board lost their lives." *Sierra Leone Weekly News*, September 14, 1918.

15. "The Prevailing Epidemic and Some of Its Lessons," *Sierra Leone Weekly News*, September 14, 1918, 8.

16. "The Colonial Secretary's Communique," *Sierra Leone Weekly News*, October 5, 1918, 11. The author of the letter, "The Creole Boy," was W. Coulson Labor, Merriman-Labor's half-brother.

17. "Notice to Our Advertisers and Subscribers," *Sierra Leone Guardian*, September 20, 1918, 4.

18. "The Epidemic of Influenza in Sierra Leone, III," *Colonial and Provincial Reporters*, September 28, 1918, 9.

19. Tomkins, "Colonial Administration in British Africa," 68.

20. "'Flu' Grips Town and Country," *Daily Mirror*, October 23, 1918, 2.

21. "Flu Fright," *Daily Express*, October 28, 1918, 1.

22. "Go to Bed and Stay There," *Daily Express*, October 23, 1918, 3.

23. "Flu Fright," *Daily Express*, October 28, 1918, 1.

24. Niall Johnson, *Britain and the 1918–1919 Influenza Pandemic* (New York: Routledge, 2006), 165.

25. "What to Do with our Influenza Heroes," *Daily Mirror*, October 24, 1918, 6.

26. "More Doctors to Fight influenza," *Daily Mirror*, October 30, 1918, 2.

27. "What to Do with Influenza Heroes," *Daily Mirror*, October 24, 1918, 6.

28. March Honigsbaum, *Living with Enza: The Forgotten Story of Britain and the Great Flu Pandemic of 1918* (London: Macmillan, 2009), 132

29. Andrea Tanner, "The Spanish Lady Comes to London: The Influenza Pandemic 1918–1919," *London Journal* 27 no. 2 (October 2002), 54.

30. Hallie Eustace Miles, *Untold Tales of War-Time London: A Personal Diary* (London: Cecil Palmer, 1930), 158–159.

31. MacDonagh, *In London during the Great War*, 329.

32. "How Joyful Londoners Kept Armistice Day in the Streets," *Daily Mirror*, November 12, 1918, 2.

33. Robert Graves and Allan Hodge, *The Long Week-End: A Social History of Great Britain, 1918–1939* (New York: Norton, 1963), 17.

34. Miles, *Untold Tales of War-Time London*, 159.

35. MacDonagh, *In London during the Great War*, 330.

36. MacDonagh, *In London during the Great War*, 333.

37. MacDonagh, *In London during the Great War*, 336.

38. "Death of J.W. Labor," *Sierra Leone Guardian*, November 22, 1918, 6.

39. The exact number of dead is unknown.

40. Tanner, "The Spanish Lady Comes to London," 54.

41. Adam Hochschild, *To End All Wars: A Story of Loyalty and Rebellion: 1914– 1918* (New York: Houghton Mifflin Harcourt, 2011), 349; Santanu Das, "Introduction," in *Race, Empire and First World War Writing*, edited by Santanu Das (Cambridge: Cambridge University Press, 2011), 4.

42. Hochschild lists 400,000 (page 349), Barrett 200,000 (page 303). Michéle Barrett, "Death and the Afterlife: Britain's Colonies and Dominions," in Das, *Race, Empire and the First World War Writing*.

43. Edward Paice, *Tip and Run: The Untold Tragedy of the Great War in Africa* (London: Weidenfeld and Nicholson, 2007), 393.

44. Barrett, "Death and Afterlife," 303.

45. Paice, *Tip and Run*, 393.

46. Ruth Ginio and Suryakanthie Chetty, "Commemoration, Cult of the Fallen (Africa)," *International Encyclopedia of the First World War*, http://encyclopedia.1914–1918-online.net/article/commemoration_cult_of_the_fallen_africa, 5.

47. Linda Bryder, *Below the Magic Mountain: A Social History of Tuberculosis in Twentieth-Century Britain* (Oxford: Oxford University Press, 1988), 19.

48. Bryder, *Below the Magic Mountain*, 20

49. *Medical Press and Circular* 133, no. 6 (August 8, 1906), 141.

50. Bryder, *Below the Magic Mountain*, 5.

51. Bryder, *Below the Magic Mountain*, 224.

52. American Medical Association, *Nostrums and Quackery: articles on the nostrum evil: quackery and allied matters affecting the Public Health; reprinted, with or without modifications, from the Journal of the American Medical Association* (Chicago: Press of American Medical Association, 1921), 47–49. Only after law suits and notices from the British Medical Association did Stevens remove to America to peddle his nostrum. Eventually chased out of Chicago, by 1919 he was marketing his tonic to tubercular Canadian veterans of the Great War.

53. American Medical Association, *Nostrums and Quackery: articles on the nostrum evil and quackery reprinted from the Journal of the American Medical*

Association, 2nd edn (Chicago: Press of American Medical Association, 1912) 176.

54. AMA, *Nostrums and Quackery* (1912), 181.

55. AMA, *Nostrums and Quackery* (1912), 177.

56. "On the Sick List," *African Telegraph*, April 1919, 172.

57. Bryder, *Below the Magic Mountain*, 53.

58. Ellen N. La Motte, *Tuberculosis Nurse: Her Function and Her Qualifications. A Handbook for Practical Workers in the Tuberculosis Campaign* (New York and London: G.P. Putnam's, 1915), 212.

59. W.M. Crofton, *Pulmonary Tuberculosis: Its Diagnosis, Prevention, and Treatment* (London: J. and A. Churchill, 1917), 71–91.

60. Lawrason Brown, *Rules for Recovery from Pulmonary Tuberculosis: A Layman's Handbook of Treatments* (New York: Lea and Febiger, 1919), 47.

61. Douglas Fairbanks, *Laugh and Live* (New York: Britton, 1917), 5.

62. Richard Sucre, "The Great White Plague: The Culture of Death and the Tuberculosis Sanatorium," http://www.faculty.virginia.edu/blueridgesanatorium/death.htm.

63. Crofton, *Pulmonary Tuberculosis*, 91.

64. Jacqueline Jenkinson, *Black 1919: Riots, Racism and Resistance in Imperial Britain* (Liverpool: Liverpool University Press, 2009), 93.

65. Peter Fryer, *Staying Power: The History of Black People in Britain* (London: Pluto Press, 1985), 298.

66. *African Telegraph*, April 1919, 184.

67. Fryer, *Staying*, 301. Jacqueline Jenkinson in *Black 1919* argues that "it is important to place these riots within the wider wave of rioting and social protest across Britain during and in the months immediately after the First World War." She mentions the many anti-German riots during the war as well as anti-Jewish rioting in 1917. Former servicemen also rioted in protest at the "treatment of returning soldiers and their dependents."

68. Fryer, *Staying Power*, 302.

69. Fryer, *Staying Power*, 302.

70. *The Times*, 14 June 1919, quoted in Fryer, *Staying Power*, 311.

71. Fryer, *Staying Power*, 307–308.

72. Quoted in Jenkinson, *Black 1919*, 4.

73. "Has the African Any Friends," *African Telegraph*, May–June 1919, 227.

74. "The African S.O.S.," *African Telegraph*, December 1918, 66.

75. "A Disgrace to England," *African Telegraph*, April 1919, 170.

76. Jenkinson, *Black 1919*, 8.

77. London Metropolitan Archives, HO1/L/B10/9: Register of Deaths in the Lambeth Infirmary. Unfortunately, records that might have told us more about Maigi were destroyed in a flood, including the Creed

Register for 1916–1920, Burial Books 1918–1920, and Casebooks 1916–1920.

78. London Metropolitan Archives, HO1/L/B10/9: Register of Deaths in the Lambeth Infirmary.

79. Brown, *Rules for Recovery from Pulmonary Tuberculosis*, 121.

80. His obituary in the *Sierra Leone Guardian* appeared a month later, suggesting they had not been kept informed of his situation.

81. London Metropolitan Archives, HO1/L/B10/9: Register of Deaths in the Lambeth Infirmary.

82. Death Certificate for Ohlohr Maigi otherwise Augustus Merriman, July 15, 1919, no. 221, General Register Office, England.

83. National Archives, Kew, BT 31/22608/138481, Board of Trade Dissolved Companies file: Literature Limited.

84. "The Death of Mr. Augustus Merriman-Labor," *Sierra Leone Guardian*, August 15, 1919, 7.

85. "The Death of Mr. Augustus Merriman-Labor," *Sierra Leone Guardian*, August 15, 1919, 7.

86. "Dear Sir—I am Writing for All the Assistance You Can Give Because I Believe in the Potency of the Press," *Gold Coast Leader*, August 12, 1905, 4.

SELECTED BIBLIOGRAPHY

Adi, Hakim. *West Africans in Britain 1900–1960: Nationalism, Pan-Africanism and Communism*. London: Lawrence and Wishart, 1998.

————. "Bandele Omoniyi: A Neglected Nigerian Nationalist," *African Affairs* 90, no. 361 (October 1991): 581–605.

Alldridge, T. J. *A Transformed Colony: Sierra Leone as It Was, and as It Is, Its Progress, Peoples, Native Customs and Undeveloped Wealth*. Philadelphia: J.B. Lippincott Co., 1910.

Anderson, Gregory. *Victorian Clerks*. Manchester: Manchester University Press, 1976.

Anderson, Richard. "The Diaspora of Sierra Leone's Liberated Africans: Enlistment, Forced Migration, and "Liberation" at Freetown, 1808–1863," *African Economic History* 41 (2013): 101–138.

The Art of Projection and Complete Magic Lantern Manual. London: E.A. Beckett, 1893.

Baedeker, Karl. *London and Its Environs: Handbook for Travellers with 10 Maps and 19 Plans, Sixteenth Revised Edition*. Leipzig: Karl Baedeker Publisher, 1911.

Baku, Daniel Kofi. "An Intellectual in Nationalist Politics: The Contribution of Kobina Sekyi to the Evolution of Ghanaian National Consciousness" (D.Phil., University of Sussex, 1987).

Barber, X. Theodore. "The Roots of Travel Cinema: John L. Stoddard, E. Burton Holmes and the Nineteenth-Century Illustrated Travel Lecture." *Film History* 5, no. 1 (March 1993), 68–84.

Barry, John M. *The Great Influenza: The Epic Story of the Deadliest Plague in History*. London: Penguin, 2010.

Beavan, Arthur H. *Imperial London*. London: J.M. Dent and Co., 1901.

Blanchard, Pascal, Nicolas Bancel, Gilles Boëtsch, Eric Deroo, Sandrine Lemaire, and Charles Forsdick, eds. *Human Zoos: Science and Spectacle in the Age of Empire*. Liverpool: Liverpool University Press, 2008.

SELECTED BIBLIOGRAPHY

Booth, Charles. *Life and Labour of the People in London: First Series*. London: Macmillan, 1904.

Bradbury, Malcolm. "Under the Dome," reprinted in *Liar's Landscape: Collected Writing from a Storyteller's Life*. London: Picador, 2006.

Bressey, Caroline. "The Black Presence in England and Wales after the Abolition Act, 1807–1930." *Parliamentary History* 26, Supplement (2007): 224–237.

Brown, Lawrason, M.D. *Rules for Recover from Pulmonary Tuberculosis: A Layman's Handbook of Treatment*. Philadelphia and New York: Lea and Febiger, 1919.

Bryder, Linda. *Below the Magic Mountain: A Social History of Tuberculosis in Twentieth-Century Britain*. Oxford: Clarendon Press, 1988.

Burroughs, Robert and Richard Huzzey, eds. *The Suppression of the Atlantic Slave Trade: British Policies, Practices and Representations of Naval Coercion*. Manchester: Manchester University Press, 2015.

Camplin, Jamie. *The Rise of the Plutocrats: Wealth and Power in Edwardian England*. London: Constable, 1978.

Carver, Richard. "The Streets of London," *The Idler: An Illustrated Monthly Magazine* 32, no. 66 (March 1908): 645–653.

Cecil, Robert. *Life in Edwardian England*. London: B.T. Batsford, 1969.

Cole, Robert Wellesley, *Kossoh Town Boy*. Cambridge: Cambridge University Press, 1960.

Cook, E.T. *Highways and Byways in London*. London and New York: Macmillan and Co., 1903.

Das, Santanu. *Race, Empire and First World War Writing*. Cambridge: Cambridge University Press, 2014.

Dixon-Fyle, Mac and Gibril Cole, eds. *New Perspectives on the Sierra Leone Krio*. New York: Peter Lange, 2006.

Domingues da Silva, Daniel, D. Eltis, P. Misevich, and O. Ojo. "The Diaspora of Africans Liberated from Slave Ships in the Nineteenth Century," *Journal of African History* 55 (2015): 147–169.

Draper, Christopher and John Lawson-Reay. *Scandal at Congo House: William Hughes and the African Institute, Colwyn Bay*. Llanrwst, Wales: Gwasg Carreg Gwalch, 2012.

Duffield, Ian, "Duse Mohamed Ali: His Purpose and His Public." In *The Commonwealth Writer Overseas: Themes of Exile and Expatriation*, edited by Alastair Niven, 151–173. Brussels: Librairie Marcel Didier, 1976.

Edwards, Frederick A. "The Air Raids on London," *Quarterly Review* 236, no. 469 (October 1921): 270–291.

Farrow, Thomas. *The Money-Lender Unmasked*. London: The Roxburghe Press, 1895.

Foxwell, A.K. *Munition Lasses: Six Months as Principal Overlooker in Danger Buildings*. London: Hodder and Stoughton, 1917.

SELECTED BIBLIOGRAPHY

Francis, C. "London Money Lenders," *The English Illustrated Magazine* 46 (January 1907): 386–389.

"From the Bar to the Bench," *The English Illustrated Magazine* 47 (February 1907): 454–455.

Fryer, Peter. *Staying Power: The History of Black People in Britain*. London and Sydney: Pluto Press, 1985.

Fyfe, Christopher. *A History of Sierra Leone*. London: Oxford University Press, 1962.

Fyfe, Christopher and David Killingray. "A Memorable Gathering of Sierra Leoneans in London, 1919," *African Affairs* 88, no. 350 (January 1989): 41–46.

Garsia, Marston. *A New Guide to the Bar, Containing the Most Recent Regulations and Specimen Examination Papers*, 5th edn. London: Sweet and Maxwell, 1923.

Geiss, Immanuel. *The Pan-African Movement*. Trans. Ann Keep. London: Methuen and Co., 1974.

Gibson, John and H.G. Chukerbutty. *How to Become a Barrister*, 2nd edn. London: Cornish and Sons, 1902.

Gikandi, Simon. "The Fantasy of the Library," *PMLA* 128, no. 1 (2013): 9–19.

Grayzel, Susan R. *At Home and under Fire: Air Raids and Culture in Britain from the Great War to the Blitz*. Cambridge: Cambridge University Press, 2012.

Green, Jeffrey. *Black Edwardians: Black People in Britain 1901–1914*. London: Frank Cass, 1998.

———. "A Revelation in Strange Humanity: Six Congo Pygmies in Britain, 1905–1907." In *Africans on Stage: Studies in Ethnological Show Business*, edited by Bernth Lindfors, 156–187. Bloomington and Indianapolis: Indiana University Press, 1999.

Gregory, Adrian. *The Last Great War: British Society and the First World War*. Cambridge: Cambridge University Press, 2008.

Griffiths, Alison. "'To the World the World We Show': Early Travelogues as Filmed Ethnography," *Film History* 11, no. 3, *Early Cinema* (1999): 282–307.

Hamilton, Peggy. *Three Years or the Duration*. London: Peter Owen Publishers, 1978.

Helmreich, Anne. "On the Opening of the Crystal Palace at Sydenham, 1854," *BRANCH: Britain, Representation and Nineteenth Century History*, Dino Franco Felluga, ed., *Extension of Romanticism and Victorianism on the Net*. http://www.branchcollective.org/?ps_articles=anne-helmreich-on-the-oppening-of-the-crystal-palace-at-sydenham-1854.

Hoffman. *Modern Magic: A Practical Treatise on the Art of Conjuring*. London and New York: George Routledge and Sons, 1877.

Hopkins, Albert A. *The Scientific American Handbook of Travel: With Hints for the*

Ocean Voyage, for European Tours and a Practical Guide to London and Paris. New York: Munn and Co., 1910.

Hynes, Samuel. *The Edwardian Turn of Mind*. Princeton, N.J.: Princeton University Press, 1968.

Inwood, Stephen. *City of Cities: The Birth of Modern London*. London: Macmillan, 2005.

James, Winston. "Black Experience in Twentieth-Century Britain." In *Black Experience and the Empire*, edited by Philip D. Morgan and Sean Hawkins, 347–386. Oxford: Oxford University Press, 2006.

Jenkinson, Jacqueline. "The 1919 Riots." In *Racial Violence in Britain in the Nineteenth and Twentieth Centuries*, edited by Panikos Panayi, 93–111. London: Leicester University Press, 1996.

Killingray, David, ed. *Africans in Britain*. Portland: F. Cass, 1994.

———. "African Voices from Two World Wars," *Historical Research* 74, no. 186 (November 2001): 425–443.

———. "The Idea of a British Imperial African Army," *Journal of African History* 20, no. 3 (1979): 421–436.

———. "A New 'Imperial Disease': The Influenza Pandemic of 1918–19 and Its Impact on the British Empire," *Caribbean Quarterly* 49, no. 4, Colonialism and Health in the Tropics (December 2003): 30–49.

———. "Rights, Land, and Labour: Black British Critics of South African Policies before 1949," *Journal of Southern African Studies* 35, no. 2 (June 2009): 375–398.

———. "Significant Black South Africans in Britain before 1912: Pan-African Organisations and the Emergence of South Africa's First Black Lawyers," *South African Historical Journal* 64 (2012): 393–417.

Kirk-Greene, A.H.M. *The Corona Club, 1900–1990: An Introductory History*. London: A.H.M. Kirk-Greene, 1990.

Koller, Christian. "The Recruitment of Colonial Troops in Africa and Asia and Their Deployment in Europe during the First World War," *Immigrants and Minorities* 26, no. 1/2 (March/July, 2008): 111–133.

Kreutzinger, Helga. *The Picture of Krio Life: Freetown 1900–1920*. Vienna: University Institute for Anthropology, 1968.

Leaming, Thomas. *A Philadelphia Lawyer in the London Courts*. New York: Henry Holt, 1911.

Lorimer, Adam [pseudonym for William Lorimer Watson]. *The Author's Progress: or, The Literary Book of the Road*. London: Blackwood and Sons, 1906.

Lovejoy, Paul E. and Suzanne Schwarz. *Slavery, Abolition and the Transition to Colonialism in Sierra Leone*. Trenton, N.J.: Africa World Press, 2015

MacDonagh, Michael. *In London during the Great War: The Diary of a Journalist*. London: Eyre and Spottiswoode, 1935.

MacKenzie, John M. *Imperialism and Popular Culture*. Manchester: Manchester University Press, 1986.

Marwick, Arthur. *The Deluge: British Society and the First World War*. New York: Norton, 1965.

Merriman-Labor, A.B.C. *Britons through Negro Spectacles, or, A Negro on Britons with a Description of London (Illustrated)*. London: The Imperial and Foreign Company, 1909.

————. *Funeral Oration Delivered over the Grave of the Late Father John Merriman at the Kissy Road Cemetery in Freetown, Sierra Leone, on the evening of Sunday, the 18th of February 1900, by his grandson, Mr. Merriman-Labor*. Freetown: A.B.C. Merriman-Labor, 1901

————. *Handbook of Sierra Leone for 1901 and 1902, being a Treasury of Information relating to the Colonial and Municipal Governments, Trade and Commerce, Religion and Education, Army and Navy, and every conceivable matter of interest connected with the Colony and its Protectorate*. London: John Heywood, 1902.

————. *Handbook of Sierra Leone for 1904 and 1905, being a Treasury of Information relating to the Colonial and Municipal Governments, Trade and Commerce, Religion and Education, Army and Navy, and every conceivable matter of interest connected with the Colony and its Protectorate*. London: John Heywood, [1904?].

————. *The Last Military Expedition in Sierra Leone, or British Soldiers and West African Native Warriors*. London: John Heywood, 1898.

————. *The Negro Race, Delivered during Eastertide, 1897, in the Baptist Chapel, at Rawdon Street, in Freetown, Sierra Leone*. London: John Heywood, [1900?].

————. *The Story of the African Slave Trade in a Nutshell: Being the Substance of a Paper read before the Greensfield Club, at the Club Room, Wellington Street, in Freetown, Sierra Leone, on the evening of Friday, the 14th of September, 1900*. Manchester: John Heywood, 1901.

Miles, Hallie Eustace. *Untold Tales of War-Time London: A Personal Diary*. London: Cecil Palmer, 1930,

Morens, David M. "At the Deathbed of Consumptive Art," *Emerging Infectious Diseases* 8, no. 11 (2002): 1353–1358.

Newell, Stephanie. "Local Cosmopolitans in Colonial West Africa." *The Journal of Commonwealth Literature* 46 (2011): 103–117.

Northrup, David. "Becoming African: Identity Formation among Liberated Slaves in Nineteenth-Century Sierra Leone," *Slavery and Abolition* 27 no. 1 (April 2006): 1–21.

Oguamanam, Chidi and W. Wesley Pue. "Lawyers' Professionalism, Colonialism, State Formation and National Life in Nigeria, 1900–1960: 'The Fighting Brigade of the People.'" Allard Research Commons. http://commons.allard.ubc.ca/cgi/viewcontent.cgi?article=1271&context=fac_pubs.

Olusanya, G.O. "The Freed Slaves' Homes: An Unknown Aspect of Northern

Nigerian Social History," *Journal of the Historical Society of Nigeria* 3, no. 3 (December 1966): 523–538.

Olusoga, David. *Black and British: A Forgotten History*. London: Macmillan, 2016.

Parker, Edward Justus. *The Lantern: Being a Treatise on the Magic Lantern and Stereopticon*. New York: R. Caygill, 1901.

Peterson, John. *Province of Freedom: A History of Sierra Leone 1878–1870*. London: Faber and Faber, 1969.

Piggott, J.R. *Palace of the People: The Crystal Palace at Sydenham 1854–1936*. London: Hurst and Company, 2004.

Phillips, Samuel. *Guide to the Crystal Palace and Park. Facsimile Edition of the 1856 Official Guide*. London: Euston Grove Press, 2010.

Read, Donald. *Documents from Edwardian England 1901–1915*. London: Harrap and Co., 1973.

Reeves, Mrs. Pember. *Round about a Pound a Week*, 2nd edn. London: G. Bell and Sons, 1914.

Sandhu, Sukhdev. *London Calling: How Black and Asian Writers Imagined a City*. London: HarperCollins, 2003.

Schneer, Jonathan. *London 1900: The Imperial Metropolis*. New Haven and London: Yale University Press, 1999.

Scholes, Theophilus E. Samuel. *Glimpses of the Ages: or the 'Superior' and 'Interior' Races So-called, Discussed in the Light of Science and History*. London: John Long, 1908.

Schwarz, Suzanne, "Reconstructing the Life Histories of Liberated Africans: Sierra Leone in the Early Nineteenth Century," *History in Africa* 39 (2012): 175–207.

Sherwood, Marika. *Origins of Pan-Africanism: Henry Sylvester Williams, Africa, and the African Diaspora*. New York: Routledge, 2011.

Shewan, Alexander and John Duguid. *Meminisse Juvat: Being the Autobiography of a Class of King's College in the Sixties*. Aberdeen: Aberdeen University Press, 1905.

Sims, George R. *Edwardian London*, vols. 1–4. London: Village Press, 1990.

Spitzer, Leo. *The Creoles of Sierra Leone: Responses to Colonialism, 1870–1945*. Madison: University of Wisconsin Press, 1974.

———. "Assimilation and Identity in Comparative Perspective: André Rebouças, Cornelius May, Stefan Zweig, and the Predicament of Marginality," *Biography* 3, no. 1 (Winter 1980): 28–64.

Tanner, Andrea. "The Spanish Lady Comes to London: The Influenza Pandemic 1918–1919," *London Journal* 27 no. 2 (October 2002): 51–76.

Thom, Deborah. "Women at the Woolwich Arsenal 1915–1919," *Oral History* 6, no. 2 (Autumn 1978): 58–73.

Thompson, Paul. *The Edwardians: The Remaking of British Society*. Chicago: Academy Chicago Publishers, 1975.

SELECTED BIBLIOGRAPHY

Timbers, Ken and Royal Arsenal Woolwich Historical Society. *The Royal Arsenal, Woolwich*. London: Royal Arsenal Woolwich Historical Society, 2011.

"Training of Barristers." *The English Illustrated Magazine* (July 1912): 330–333.

van Wingerden, Sophia A. *The Women's Suffrage Movement in Britain, 1866–1929*. New York: St. Martin's Press, 1999.

Walker, James W. St. G. *The Black Loyalists: The Search for a Promised Land in Nova Scotia and Sierra Leone 1783–1870*. New York: Africana Publishing Company, 1976.

Washington, B.T. with Robert E. Park. *The Man Farthest Down. A Record of Observation and Study in Europe*. Garden City, New York: Doubleday, Page, and Co., 1912.

Williams Charlotte, Neil Evans, and Paul O'Leary, eds. *A Tolerant Nation? Revisiting Ethnic Diversity in a Devolved Wales*. Cardiff: University of Wales Press, 2015.

Winter, Jay and Jean-Louis Robert. *Capital Cities at War: Paris, London, Berlin 1914–1919*. Cambridge: Cambridge University Press, 1997.

The Work of the Royal Engineers in the European War, 1914–19: Supply of Engineer Stores and Equipment. Chatham: W. and J. MacKay and Co., n.d.

Wyse, Akintola. *The Krio of Sierra Leone: An Interpretive History*. Washington, D.C.: Howard University Press, 1991.

———. "The Dissolution of Freetown City Council in 1926: A Negative Example of Political Apprenticeship in Colonial Sierra Leone," *Africa* 57, no. 4, Sierra Leone, 1787–1987 (1987): 422–438.

INDEX

Abbensetts, C.E.M. 165
Abeokuta, Alake of 51–3
Aberdeen, University of 52–3
Abode of Love 59
Aborigines' Protection Society 28
Abosso 220
Academy, The 138
Adcock, A. St. John 107
African General Agency and
  Information Bureau 71–2,
  78–86, 94–5, 99–101, 105–8,
  122, 158, 162, 163, 185, 202;
  closure after dispute with
  Lincoln's Inn 108–13, 131, 166,
  200
African Institute 147, 149–5,
  158–60
African Methodist Episcopal
  Seminary 140
African Society 103, 164
*African Telegraph and Gold Coast
  Mirror* 179, 180, 232, 235–6
African Times and Orient Review
  161–2, 165
African troops in First World War
  179–82, 199–200, 230–31
African World and Cape-Cairo Express
  78, 153

Agapemonites 58–9
air raids 195–6, 200, 201–2, 217
Alexander's Magazine 107
Anglican church 15, 18, 43, 58,
  64–5
Anti-Slavery and Aborigines'
  Protection Society 164
Anti-Slavery Society 102, 103
Anversville 37–40
Archer, John 168, 169
Armistice 228–9
Ashurst, Ernest Sydney 186
Asquith, Herbert 178
Assumpçai, Padeyemo 165
Athenaeum, The 138
auctions in London 106
auctions in Sierra Leone 71
Austria-Hungary 176–7

Bai Bureh 20–21
Baines, J.E. 103
Bank of England 66
Baptist World Congress 74
Barrie, James M. 182–3
Bathurst 36, 123
Battersea 168, 169
Beaumont, Edward 201
Bechuanaland 103

INDEX

INDEX

INDEX

INDEX

24, 25, 37, 45, 59, 74, 77, 78, 85, 89, 94, 95, 100, 101, 104, 121, 123, 132, 139–41, 143, 144, 147, 149, 154, 157, 158, 162, 163, 190, 208, 210–11, 224, 225, 226

Sierra Leone 6–22, 25, 31–8, 119–23, 125, 162, 167, 169, 173–6, 180, 183, 189, 223–7

Silvertown munitions explosion 218

Simpson, Arthur 79

Singh, Saint Nahal 153–4

slavery and slave trade 6–9, 11–14, 22, 207; slave trade abolition 13, 102–4

Smeathman, Henry 7

Smyth, John Albert 181

Smyth-Pigott, J.H. 58–9

Society of Authors 25

Society of Peoples of African Origin 235

Soga, Allan K. 89

Somalis exhibition 75–8

Somme, Battle of the 213

South Africa 27, 66, 78, 86–9, 90, 104, 107, 130, 132, 134–6, 137, 143, 150

South African Spectator 107, 143

South Western Star and Battersea and Wandsworth Advertiser 168

Speakers' Corner 57

Spectator, The 138

St. Albans 80–81

St. Barnabas Church 74

St. Lucia Guardian 107

St. Pancras 79

stage shows of Africans 27–8, 74–8

Stead, W.T. 23

Stevens, Charles Henry 232

Stowe, Harriet Beecher 103

suffragists 97–8, 138–9, 163–4

Swyers, David 162, 166

Tanganyika 230

taxation 20, 86–9

Taylor, John Eldred 161, 179, 232

Temne 9–10

"Ten Little Nigger Boys" 60–61

Thames 40–41, 185

The Times 132, 138, 139, 155, 213, 235

theatre 55–6, 60–61

Thomas, James Jonathan 73–4

Thompson, Maximilian "Max" 169

Thompson, Thomas John 23, 175–6, 180

Titanic 157–8

Tooting 90

Topham, Alfred Frank 111

Torrey and Alexander 64

Tour in Negroland, A 138, 146

Tower Hill 19

Tower of Jezreel 58, 59

Transvaal 134, 143

Travelogues 113–14

Trent, Paul 205–6

Truth 153

tuberculosis 231–3, 236–7

Tull, Walter 181

Uncle Tom's Cabin 103, 159

United African Association 88–9

Universal Races Congress 153–5

USA 8, 105, 141, 219, 224

Vigilance Society of New York 141

Wales 149–51, 236

War Propaganda Bureau 182

Ward, Herbert 126

Warwick, Lady 109

Washington, Booker T. 65

Waterloo (Sierra Leone) 18

INDEX